Writing the Poetic Soul of Philosophy

Other books of Interest from St. Augustine's Press

Michael Davis, *The Poetry of Philosophy: On Aristotle's* Poetics

Michael Davis, *Wonderlust: Ruminations on Liberal Education*

Seth Benardete, *Achilles and Hector: The Homeric Hero*

Seth Benardete, *The Archaeology of the Soul:
Platonic Readings of Ancient Poetry and Philosophy*

Seth Benardete, *Herodotean Inquiries*

Seth Benardete, *Sacred Transgressions: A Reading of Sophocles'* Antigone

Ronna Burger and Patrick Goodin (editors),
The Eccentric Core: The Thought of Seth Benardete

Ronna Burger, *The* Phaedo: *A Platonic Labyrinth*

René Girard, *A Theater of Envy: William Shakespeare*

Alexandre Kojève, *The Concept, Time, and Discourse*

Nalin Ranasinghe (editor), *Logos and Eros: Essays Honoring Stanley Rosen*

Nalin Ranasinghe, *Socrates in the Underworld*

Stanley Rosen, *Essays in Philosophy: Ancient*

Stanley Rosen, *Essays in Philosophy: Modern*

Stanley Rosen, *G. W. F. Hegel: An Introduction to the Science of Wisdom*

Stanley Rosen, *The Language of Love: An Interpretation of Plato's* Phaedrus

Stanley Rosen, *Nihilism: A Philosophical Essay*

Stanley Rosen, *Plato's* Sophist: *The Drama of Original and Image*

Rémi Brague, *The Anchors in the Heavens*

Rémi Brague, *Eccentric Culture: A Theory of Western Civilization*

Peter Kreeft, *A Socratic Introduction to Plato's* Republic

Peter Kreeft, *Socrates' Children: The 100 Greatest Philosophers*

Writing the Poetic Soul of Philosophy

Essays in Honor of Michael Davis

Edited by Denise Schaeffer

ST. AUGUSTINE'S PRESS
South Bend, Indiana

Library of Congress Control Number: 2019955162

St. Augustine's Press
www.staugustine.net

Table of Contents

Editor's Acknowledgements

I would like to thank all of the authors of these essays for their wonderful contributions, with special thanks to Ronna Burger, Mary Nichols and Michael Zuckert for their advice throughout the process of bringing this volume into the world. I would also like to thank Claudia van der Heuvel for her meticulous copyediting of the original manuscript, as well as Jacob Marcus and Charles Planck for their assistance with proof reading. Finally, I would like to thank Bruce Fingerhut and Benjamin Fingerhut at St. Augustine's Press for their unwavering support of this project.

Introduction

Denise Schaeffer

I begin this introduction by making note of an observation that Michael Davis offers about introductions in general in his first book, *Ancient Tragedy and the Origins of Modern Science*:

> If a good book is like an animal, its parts fitting together with the same necessity as the parts of a living body, an introduction would seem to be at best superfluous and, at worst, like an autopsy performed in order to prove that the patient is alive.[1]

This analogy of the book to the living body, which draws explicitly upon Aristotle's *De Anima* and also calls to mind Plato's *Phaedrus*, raises the question of what it would mean for a book to be "alive," or to have something akin to a soul. How can a piece of writing capture the activity of thinking, in its dynamism and contingency, rather than serving as a collection of thoughts-as-artifacts? What can we learn about the activity of thinking, and about the human soul, by reflecting on this fundamental question about *writing*? I think it is fair to say that these concerns, in various forms and in different registers, have preoccupied Michael Davis throughout his distinguished career, and to this day.

Another of Davis's books, *The Autobiography of Philosophy*, opens with some observations about the transformation of "philosophy" from a fundamental human activity to a specialized body of knowledge, an academic discipline. The word can refer to a product or to a way of life. Philosophy

---

1   Michael Davis, *Ancient Tragedy and the Origins of Modern Science* (Carbondale, IL: Southern Illinois University Press, 1988), 1.

in this latter sense "never wanders far from the verb to philosophize. But we perennially run the risk of losing the verb in the noun, the body of philosophy being the most visible manifestation of its soul."[2]

More recently, in *The Soul of the Greeks*, Davis explores several human experiences that bring the soul's activity, which is generally hidden from view, to light—such as becoming angry, seeking justice, engaging in ritual, thinking, and falling in love—and then proceeds to show why it is the case that the most essential qualities of these experiences elude our attempts to theorize them. The nature of soul does not admit of being spelled out directly, Davis maintains, and any attempt to do so is likely to render the soul static—draining it of its vitality precisely in our attempt to know it. This does not mean that *no* account of soul is possible, only that an account that strives to do justice to soul as a living entity will consist not of a discursive theory of soul but rather of a "repeated unfolding of the problem of the unity of soul."[3] This problem, and the questions that surround it, can be found in one form or another throughout the works of history, philosophy, and poetry that Davis analyzes, all of which explore, in different contexts, the human desire for completion and why that completion inevitably eludes us.

It is this attentiveness to the "soul" of philosophic thinking and writing that characterizes the distinctive voice of Michael's own writing. In his essay included in this volume, Paul Stern observes of *The Soul of the Greeks* that, rather than proceeding in chronological order, "[its] argument unfolds like a plot, each chapter developing a point on which its successor depends." Michael's books are not a straightforward presentation of the fruits of his thinking, but rather an invitation to join him in the activity of thinking. As such, they seek to preserve the dynamic quality of that thinking—to keep thinking *alive* on the page—an aspiration nevertheless accompanied by an acute awareness of the ultimate impossibility of doing so.

Michael's distinctive author-voice is recognizable to his readers, colleagues, and especially his students. The experience of being in the seminar

2   Michael Davis, *The Autobiography of Philosophy: Rousseau's* The Reveries of the Solitary Walker (Lanham, MD: Rowman & Littlefield, 1999), 1.

3   Michael Davis, *The Soul of the Greeks* (Chicago: The University of Chicago Press, 2011), 22.

room or lecture hall with Michael is the experience of being drawn into his experience of thinking, which then becomes a shared experience that enriches all involved. His profound impact on his students is evident in this volume, as is his impact on professional colleagues at colleges and universities around the country. All of the contributors to this volume have been privileged to engage in dialogue with Michael Davis, whether in the classroom, in face-to-face conversation, or through his published work and lectures. All have cherished these ongoing conversations about life's greatest and most puzzling questions, and about some of the greatest and most puzzling works of philosophy and literature. And it is out of that cherishing that this volume came to be.

The diversity of works and issues explored in these essays testifies to the broad scope and influence of Michael's work. Part I opens with two essays that take *The Soul of the Greeks* as a point of departure for thinking about the nature of soul through the lens of tragedy. Paul Stern provides an overview of that book's argument with a view to exploring various ways in which indeterminacy and ambiguity contribute to the possibility of a non-tragic existence, while Jonathan Badger builds on the contrast Davis draws between Achilles and Socrates to illuminate the fragile connection between the tragic and the ethical. These are followed by two essays that look at how the lens of tragic poetry illuminates the human desire for unity. Lisa Vetter reads Euripides' *Trojan Women* as an exploration of the impulse to express "that which cannot be said." Vetter shows that, in a democratic spirit, Euripides "gives voice to those who are not typically heard and acknowledges the polyphonic nature of their contributions." Next, Kenneth DeLuca traces the veiled references to the tragic figure of Oedipus in Plato's *Republic*, deploying these references to shed light on the differences between Adeimantus and Glaucon, as well as the role that poetic imagery plays in the differing educations appropriate to their respective souls. Finally, turning from the ancients to Nietzsche, Paul Kirkland explores what it would mean to understand will to power as the animating principle of soul. Leading us through an examination of several of Nietzsche's images and "sublime metaphors" of soul, Kirkland shows that the art of tragedy remains the model for unifying opposition without destroying multiplicity.

Part II is made up of four essays that explore the human longing for perfect knowledge and completion—and the obstacles to the fulfilment of that longing—in relation to the divine. Ronna Burger explores the relationship between chance and divine providence that emerges in the biblical Book of Esther, and the implications for understanding human agency. Robert Berman's penetrating dissection of *Phenomenology of Spirit* demonstrates that Hegel's response to the problem of philosophy's attempt to arrive at the truth of reality as a whole is ultimately more Socratic than Kantian. By distinguishing between Absolute Knowing and knowledge of the absolute, and disentangling human wisdom from metaphysics, Hegelian phenomenology shares the Socratic understanding of a form of genuinely *human* knowing that "directs its philosophical eros toward a non-metaphysical wisdom."

Next, Ann Ward shows how poetry mediates between philosophy and faith in Kierkegaard's *Philosophical Fragments*, a work in which "Christianity unfolds as a poetic account of the philosophic condition of the awareness of the unknown as a missing part of the self." The tension between the eternal and the historical, which looms so large for Kierkegaard, is also a theme in Shakespeare's *Antony and Cleopatra*, in which, Mary Nichols argues, the characters' "immortal longings" confront human limits. In Nichols' interpretation, Shakespeare does not only dramatize these limits, emphasizing that which is kept "in reserve" from human attempts to grasp it, but also portrays how limited, *partial* knowledge and freedom makes it possible for human beings to love.

In Part III the essays address the distinctive challenges of the political sphere and philosophy's relation to it. The role of poetry in negotiating this tension remains part of the discussion, as all three essays consider the poeticized origins of a variety of "foundings." Scott Hemmenway considers the philosophical significance of the mythic discourse one so often finds in accounts of political origins, focusing on the myth of the flood in Plato's *Laws*. Michael Zuckert's essay on Shakespeare's *A Midsummer Night's Dream* emphasizes the similarities between love and political life, insofar as both exhibit a tendency toward tyrannical longings. At the same time, Zuckert argues, the play suggests that the experience of love also offers resources against such tyrannical impulses. Shakespeare thus offers an instructive corrective to Machiavelli's understanding of political foundings. Lee Ward continues the focus on Shakespeare, looking at how the figure of the philosopher-king is satirized in *Love's Labour's Lost*. Ward argues that the play reveals the incoherence and hypocrisy at the heart of the characters' attempt to found an unerotic, purely contemplative community, and defends the superiority of poetry over this vision of the philosophic life.

While the relationship between philosophy and poetry is a percolating theme throughout this volume, the essays in Part IV focus directly on philosophy's aestheticizing tendencies, beginning with Richard Velkley's essay on the philosopher's "art" in Kant's *Critique of Judgment*. Velkley explores the kinship between "the art of philosophic architectonic" and fine art, which are linked in revealing "nature's eternal self-concealment." Turning back to Plato, Gwenda-lin Grewal analyzes the *Euthydemus*, illuminating both the kinship between philosophy and sophistry as well as the crucial distinction between them—a distinction in which the tendency of genuine thinking to "poeticize" is of vital importance. This is followed by Catherine Zuckert's essay which poses the question of whether Plato is best understood as a poet, a philosopher, both or neither. Focusing on Socrates' arguments on behalf of poetry at the end of Book X of the *Republic*, and using the Myth of Er as an illustrative example, Zuckert argues that the Platonic dialogues are themselves exemplary of the kind of comprehensive poetry Socrates defends as superior to the Homeric epics. "In sum, Plato was a distinctive kind of poet or imitator, because he was a distinctive kind of philosopher."

If Plato appears so frequently throughout these essays, it is perhaps because, as Michael Davis puts it, in the figure of Socrates, Plato offers an example of "the living soul at work" as well as an example of the philosophic life for emulation. Davis brings these two points together in a question he poses at the end of *The Soul of the Greeks*: "Why do men need living models in order to learn?"[4] This question about the necessity of emulation lies at the heart of the final two essays in this volume, which look at two examples of modern authors who appropriate Plato's example with a mixture of admiration and ambivalence. Abraham Anderson compares Shaftesbury and Plato on "how to write," and Denise Schaeffer considers Rousseau's semi-faithful imitation of Plato in "On Theatrical Imitation." In both essays, the question of how one might capture the "living" quality of Plato's writing—whether in theoretical understanding or in deed—without rendering it

4   Davis, *The Soul of the Greeks*, 220.

formulaic and inert, returns us to our initial question of how one might adequately "write" the vitality of the human soul at work, especially as it is engaged in the activity of thinking. As Michael Davis reminds us, this question, in its various forms, can only be answered as a "repeated unfolding" of the problem. The "unfoldings" offered by the essays in this volume have been gathered together in the spirit of that insight.

Part I –
Philosophy, Poetry and the Tragedy of Soul

Poetry and Philosophy in *The Soul of the Greeks*
Paul Stern

In *The Soul of the Greeks* Michael Davis explores the meaning of the soul through a collection of "thinkers" that includes Homer, Herodotus, Euripides, Plato, and Aristotle.[1] His examination of these ancient authors aims not only to provide a better understanding of the soul but to address defects in the contemporary intellectual situation. More specifically, he shows how the Greek understanding of soul, which highlights the soul's enduring tensions, can point us toward a possible remedy for those defects. The notion that poetry is the appropriate medium for the philosophic inquiry into the soul plays a particularly important role in bringing this ancient understanding to bear on the contemporary situation.

The order in which Davis examines his authors suggests how important this relationship between poetry and philosophy is to him. Instead of proceeding chronologically, the book's introduction, entitled "The Soul of Achilles," reflects on Homer and Aristotle, The Poet and The Philosopher (1–17). It invites the reader to re-examine the relationship between poetry and philosophy. Davis points to the result of that re-examination by his use of the term "thinkers" to refer to both poets and philosophers (6). He also points to that result when, prior to the text proper, he places a poet's "Ode to Plato." The overall arc of the book affirms these indications of the harmony between poetry and philosophy as it takes the reader from the soul of Homer's epic hero, Achilles, to Plato's poetic depiction of the soul of Socrates. Philosophy, to avoid becoming "politicized," is properly understood through a consideration of the philosopher's soul (4). And whether

1   Michael Davis, *The Soul of the Greeks: An Inquiry* (Chicago: University of Chicago Press, 2011). All parenthetical citations in this chapter refer to this volume.

it belongs to the epic hero or the philosopher, the soul is best explicated through poetry.

Davis's gloss on the title of his intensely self-reflective book begins to explain the connection between the significance of poetic form and the proper understanding of soul. The "soul" of *The Soul of the Greeks* refers both to how the Greeks understood soul and to how soul became manifest among the Greeks (7). The ambiguity reflects Davis's view that the soul comprises both a structure and an activity. The former lends itself to determinate understanding; the latter, as the activity of reflection that makes determinate understanding available, evades such determination. As Davis relates throughout the book, it is insofar as the soul is a "what" and a "how" that its wholeness is elusive, its being a problem. With its self-conscious use of language, its self-aware deployment of images, poetry reflects the mediacy of our knowing that results from this imperfect integration of soul and whole. It is less liable than other modes of expression to treat the soul as something fixed, determinate, and wholly intelligible. Poetry thus responds to what Davis takes to be the great danger to our intellectual health—namely, that we will neglect the soul's problematic character, reify it, and attempt to understand it as we would any other being. The danger posed by this perennial danger is now particularly acute.

Why think the reification of soul is the greatest danger in current intellectual life? Is such dogmatism the most serious intellectual threat? The book does conclude with Plato who, Davis writes elsewhere, is the "cure" for "an overly dogmatic age."[2] Perhaps this take on the problem arises from concerns related to the latest efforts of modern science to understand cognition through a determinate account of the brain. But clearly Davis also has in mind the equally prevalent, deeply skeptical theoretical view that dissolves the soul or self into a fluctuating intersection of ever-shifting vectors of force. How does the re-examination of the distinction between poetry and philosophy respond to these divergent theoretical orientations? We need to know more about the character of this problem, its cause, and recommended remedy. To begin, I need to say a few words about the book's form.

---

2   Michael Davis, *The Poetry of Philosophy: On Aristotle's "Poetics"* (South Bend, IN: St. Augustine's Press); reprint of *Aristotle's "Poetics": The Poetry of Philosophy* (Lanham, MD: Rowman and Littlefield, 1992), 160.

The book's argument unfolds like a plot, each chapter developing a point on which its successor depends. A phrase in the opening poem, "we find ourselves," helps explain why it's arranged in this way. The phrase suggests that we are always already immersed in soul-shaping practices, already distant from self-understanding, before we realize the need for and possibility of such understanding. But the proper experiences can make us aware of this possibility and need. These lessons must be experiential, *ad hominem*, because the obstacles to such understanding are overcome only by each individual: each finds, or fails to find, him or herself. This observation suggests another reason for the aptness of poetry for the inquiry into the soul. With its use of images and artfully arranged sounds, poetry addresses the senses and through them the passions. It thus involves the reader not simply in a generalizing argument but in an individual experience—an experience that can open the door to self-understanding. The crucial moment of self-discovery is precisely when we realize we must find ourselves, when we learn that and why the soul's character is hidden. The need for this discovery means that we must work through a course of progressive misunderstandings or partial views. Davis's book charts this course. It arranges the necessary misunderstandings in the proper order.

As we've seen in its disruption of chronological order, the book conveys meaning by the way in which it unfolds. There are lessons that can only be appreciated having seen other, more immediately attractive, alternatives come up short. There are lessons that must be experienced to be credible, so at odds are they with the initial impetus of our most powerful longings. Most prominent of these is the book's culminating recommendation of a "non-tragic" way of life as most choice-worthy. Such a life must emerge out of a previous orientation on tragedy, which is itself a step beyond its predecessor. But were it not for the experience afforded by the book, we might well dismiss out of hand the notion that a life fascinated by the mundane, by error and ambiguity, is the most humanly satisfying. In what follows I will attempt to chart the book's movement that leads to this end to see how it addresses the questions posed above.

Davis notes that among the authors he considers, only Aristotle takes the soul as his direct theme, apparently treating it as any other being available for study (19). Had Davis treated his authors in chronological order, we might regard Aristotle's approach as a culmination, exemplifying how philosophy, freed from its immature poetic trappings, ought to treat the soul. Instead, he links Aristotle with Homer and exhibits the surprisingly poetic character of *De Anima*. The Poet discovers soul as a problem; the Philosopher's poetizing treats it as such. In *De Anima* Aristotle poetizes by his self-conscious use of the possibilities of language, making the manner of his presentation convey meaning, even using the sounds of words to this end. The music of *De Anima* acknowledges the necessity of poetry.

The opening section of Davis's treatment of Aristotle also clarifies why the reluctance to recognize the soul's indeterminacy is such a problem and what the source of this reluctance might be. That indeterminacy, as indicated above, is rooted in the soul's power to apprehend form: the power that enables objects to be apprehended as such cannot itself be an object. To deny the soul's indeterminacy is to misunderstand ourselves, and thus miss the proper object of our greatest longing. This observation brings home the human significance of understanding the relationship between poetry and philosophy. To think they are in inexorable tension is to think an unproblematic account of nature, including human nature, is available. It is to believe that philosophy can achieve certainties, about the whole and humanity, whose expression can dispense with the needlessly obscure manner of poetry. But this means there's a link between the need for poetry and the unavailability of these certainties. And this unavailability begins to explain why we would be so reluctant to appreciate this indeterminacy, even when such appreciation is crucial to attaining our true good.

Davis considers this reluctance, expressed in Homer's Achilles and Plato's Alcibiades, a permanent feature of the human soul.[3] Its home is the *thumos* that moves us to impose our will on the world out of a sense of incompleteness. Responding to this powerful inclination, we want the control that can help secure what's most our own: self, family, and community. Certitude promises such control. Whatever eludes it—which the soul understood as a problem most emphatically does—thwarts this desire.

But why think this reluctance is particularly entrenched in our age? It

---

3   But it is not so expressed by Plato himself. One way to understand our intellectual problem is in terms of the conflict between Plato and Platonism, and the related issue of how to read a Platonic dialogue. See Davis, *Soul of the Greeks*, 3–4.

could be argued that modern science and its technological achievements have responded to this impetus with unprecedented comprehensiveness, making it seem possible to banish all uncertainty. But Davis does not make this argument. The only intellectual source Davis mentions between the ancients and us is Christianity. Is it Christianity that first mires us in "'a cave beneath a cave,'" blocking access to the experiences that might correct our self-misunderstanding (2)? This view might hold that because Christianity first expresses this idea of the good in a comprehensive account of all things, it provides a *theoretical* basis for the good of closure, of certainty, that prepares the modern understanding. It persuades those with a theoretical inclination, those who might otherwise have resisted the impetus of *thumos*, that theory does not demand such resistance.[4]

Whether or not these speculations touch on Davis's view on this issue, the first section of the book does aim to lift us back up into the cave, to enable us to see why the soul's good requires the inquiry that begins with a consideration of political life. The first step in doing so is to see more clearly why the character of the soul is elusive and its good is therefore the most compelling question.

Davis's reflections on the source of this elusiveness or indeterminacy implicate poetry still more deeply in the inquiry into the soul. His discussion of *De Anima* shows that, beyond its being an apt vehicle for the expression of uncertainty and ambiguity, poetry reflects the character of thinking itself. This point emerges from the central importance of the imagination in our cognition, to which we now turn.

Our cognition is dependent on the image, available to us in and through the imagination. As a representation, the image, whether picture or word, both is and is not the thing. It's detached from the object, severed from the real. Cognition is not simply a record of what is; there is a mediacy in our knowing that contributes to the distinction between seeming and being. As Davis points out, we are most aware of the consequent distinction

---

4   Given the theme I am pursuing, I should mention that this orientation on certainty fits in with the animus against poetry expressed by theologians such as Aquinas. See, for example, St. Thomas Aquinas, *Summa Theologica Volume I*, trans. Fathers of the English Dominican Province (Allen, Texas: Christian Classics, 1981), vol. I, 6 (Ia.q.1, a.9).

between the object and the act of cognition when conscious of error (34–35). At those moments, we're not sure *we* get *it*. We become aware of our selves as such and of the self's contribution to cognition. This detachment enables the manipulation, the reconstruction of reality. It makes us aware that what we have access to is, in some sense, a product, something not perfectly reflective of what's real that can therefore be otherwise than we take it to be. Imagination conveys the awareness of the partiality of our understanding as it brings to mind that which is absent. It thus also links thinking and desire. Out of awareness of this partiality, this lack, thinking constructs less partial, more explanatory unities. These wholes would make sense of these parts, put them in a broader context, show them as parts and thus account for them. All thinking has this constructive, poetic character. The activity of the poet, especially one who is self-aware, makes this character explicit.

Recognizing the poetic character of all thinking raises the question, what, if anything, guides this construction? In his move from *De Anima* to the *Nicomachean Ethics*, Davis points toward an answer. Instead of taking up the *Nicomachean Ethics* after his discussion of *De Anima*, Davis might have proceeded from *De Anima*'s seemingly direct consideration of soul to the *Metaphysics* and its exploration of the principles of the whole to which the soul is open. Both movements are plausible. Both express aspects of the soul: its receptivity to the whole and with what endures, on the one hand, and its being as a self, a particular subject concerned for its own good, on the other. These aspects contend in the soul, as they do throughout the book: in Herodotus' Egyptians versus his Scythians; Euripides' *Helen* versus his *Iphigenia Among the Taurians;* and Plato's *Cleitophon* versus his *Hipparchus*. But the move to the *Ethics* indicates which takes precedence in the soul's economy. Because the soul's nature is problematic, its good is a question. The movement back into the cave is an image of the recovery of this question as a question. The primacy of the question of good is crucial in guiding our thinking.

By making imagination central to cognition, Davis argues, Aristotle gives priority to the "I," the self, that particular perspective made possible by the detachedness imagination affords us. Given that priority, we pursue the true for the sake of the good. We want to know what is worth pursuing, and what we should avoid. We want to know what is truly good. The act of constructing more comprehensive unities is undertaken with a view to one's good. The issue of wholeness comes to sight as a moral question, motivated by the concern for "what is most important to us" (55). The detachedness made possible by the imagination enables one to ask, do my particular actions have any meaning? Do they contribute to some overarching unity that defines my life as something more than a series of disconnected moments? The soul's capacities, its self-awareness properly understood, leads inexorably to good as a question. The suggestion seems to be that what properly guides thinking as poetic-constructive is awareness of this character. That is, we ought to think with the problem of soul and the consequent questionability of good always in mind.

Davis's subsequent treatment of Herodotus substantiates this suggestion. His turn to Herodotus' inquiry into comparative culture is explained by the primacy of the question of the good. The path through Aristotle has done its work: we have ascended to the cave. The political community or the culture answers this question of our good comprehensively before we begin to think about it. If we are to think through this question we must do so through a consideration of these answers, these necessary misunderstandings.

Herodotus' poetic inquiry into comparative cultures relies on "exemplary stories" (157 n33). It aims to articulate where *phusis* exceeds the boundaries of *nomos*. Davis notes that the move through *nomos* to *phusis* may seem odd to us because we share the Persians' view that "'*nomos* is king of all,'" that culture is comprehensive, wholly determinative of the human (88). Culture should not be judged by nature because nature's inadequacy as a guide prompts the development of culture in the first place. On this view, nature places us in tragic circumstances that are redeemed only by our own constructions or by supra-natural assistance. The move to nature only makes sense if Herodotus' cultural comparison points to an alternative view of nature, one that could provide guidance for humans, a "non-tragic" nature. We are brought a step closer to this view by seeing that a culture is an answer to a question posed by our nature—as it must be if every culture is an attempted, if inadequate, understanding of soul. As shown by Herodotus' relative judgment of the Greeks compared with the Egyptians and Scythians, nature guides human affairs if only by posing this question, determining the soul as problematic.

Herodotus employs the tool of contradiction to question cultures, especially the contradiction between what's said and what's done. Cultures inevitably give rise to this contradiction because no culture, no unitary set of principles, can fully express the tensions within the soul. For example, satisfaction of the longing for permanence expressed by Egyptian culture would deny our capacity for agency; Scythian satisfaction of the longing for complete freedom would deny its natural restraints. In preserving both longings, Greek culture is most human because most reflective of our problematic nature. Moreover, appreciating the ambiguous guidance of nature it sees the need to deliberate how to live, and by its own efforts, that is, by the political art, to actualize the results of those deliberations. Because Greek culture is "most human" in the foregoing sense, it is genuinely political (100–101). The problem of soul, with its consequent detachedness, makes art in general and the political art in particular possible and necessary. Hence Davis connects the political character of the Greeks to their being "genuinely poetic," acutely aware of the problematic character of soul that makes poetry possible and necessary (101).

Yet, as depicted in Socrates' trial and execution, even with its openness to poetry, Greek culture cannot fully resolve all the tensions that call for poetry. Athens could not fully abide Socrates' reflections on his culture, especially insofar as they displayed its contradictions without resolving them, making questionable precisely what culture is supposed to resolve. Even being Greek is not enough because "We are none of us simply 'Greek'" (104). The issue of the most humanly satisfying culture must give way to the issue of the most humanly satisfying way of life for an individual.

But if culture's inadequacy follows from its inability to reconcile fully the tensions of the human soul, it is not clear how we can expect greater success on the individual plane. Awareness of the questionability of good may properly guide our thinking, but can such awareness provide for a fulfilled life? In light of the reasons underlying our persistent need for poetry, can any life be satisfying by nature? With this question, Herodotus' inquiry into culture brings us to tragic poetry. Before considering Davis's treatment of Euripides, I should note that his path to Plato does not pass through Aristophanes' comedies. Perhaps because he understands Socrates' life as non-tragic and Plato's work as "deeply funny," Davis thinks the distinctiveness of Socrates' life appears more vividly against the background of tragedy (191).

Davis examines two of Euripides' tragedies, *Helen* and *Iphigenia among the Taurians*, that pursue the deformations of soul already seen, respectively, in Herodotus' Egyptians and his Scythians. He praises tragic poetry for preserving the tension between our conflicting desires for the permanent good, and for that good to be ours. In preserving this tension, tragic poetry secures civilization or Greekness over against barbarism because, as we have seen, to be civilized or Greek involves openness to the problematic, to the ambiguous and diverse, as opposed to the flatness and uniformity of barbarism. This openness and diversity is achieved in reaction to the homogenizing force of a purportedly all-encompassing nature. Against the undeniable reality of the basic forces of nature, tragic poetry affirms the possibility of, and need for, the interpretive act that bespeaks our incomplete subsumption by these basic natural forces. Perhaps, then, the deepest understanding is that of the tragic poet who sees these irresolvable tensions of human life and constructs ways to make that life bearable.

But the book ends with Socrates rather than Euripides. Something about Euripides' understanding must point to the possibility of Socrates. The depth of Euripides' understanding makes the determination of just what this might be all the more challenging, as is appropriate for this penultimate stage in the plot.

At first it seems that the very power of tragic poetry is its defect. Tragic poetry aims to preserve the distinction between the reality of basic nature and our interpretation of its significance. The tragic poet recognizes that if the distinction between significance and reality is lost, if all becomes a matter of interpretation, obscuring the bearing of reality, the very question of significance is also lost (130–32, 136–37). That question only arises in relation to reality, when we encounter it as wonderful or perplexing. But the power of tragic poetry's images does threaten to obscure this underlying reality. Thus the rituals that Euripides portrays in the plays that address the rift between significance and reality seem ultimately aimed at healing it. To this extent they still respond to the impetus, evident in Homer's Achilles, to achieve the wholeness toward which our deepest longing seems to direct us. And when, inevitably, this desire cannot be satisfied, the rift cannot be healed, human life is judged tragic.

But Euripides *knows* the rift cannot be healed, he knows "that their complete togetherness is never simply possible" (137). Moreover, his goal is to preserve the tension between reality and significance. He must think it is beneficial. Speaking of *Iphigenia among the Taurians*, Davis calls it "self-consciously imperfect" (137). In seeing the good of this tension, Euripides himself does not succumb to the Achillean yearning for imposed wholeness. But this means there is a distinction between Euripides' own understanding and any of the possibilities portrayed in his work. The possibility expressed in Euripides' own life stands outside his poetry. Is this tragic poetry's deepest flaw? Is it the failure to appreciate fully the human possibility expressed in the self-aware poet's own activity?

As Davis suggests in his treatment of Plato's *Phaedrus*, to know "the nature of this self-conscious imperfection" is to know the soul as erotic (198). Knowing the soul as erotic, as aware of its own imperfection, would be to understand why we strive after perfection or wholeness and why this goal is a mistake. We cannot help but think that rifts ought to be healed, what's partial made whole, the imperfect perfected; insofar as it seeks ever more comprehensive unities, the very act of thinking inclines us in this direction. The knowledge that such wholeness is "never simply possible" only comes, if it does, after numerous failed attempts that presume this very possibility. Yet, to repeat, such knowledge is based on a clear view of the soul's nature, its character as erotic. And this clarity offers the prospect, explored fully in the Platonic dialogues, that such impossibility need not mean human life is tragic. A humanly satisfying life may nevertheless be available. It offers the prospect that we can know what's truly good for us as enduringly erotic, unlike either beasts or gods.

Euripides' absence from his own poetry points to the final turn in a plot that begins with the surprising harmony of poetry and philosophy. We now see that this harmony involves a hierarchy. Euripides' own activity, based as it is on his own insight into the nature of human imperfection, determines that philosophy ultimately guides poetry. Davis writes that "the nature of this self-conscious imperfection is the issue that underlies all Platonic dialogues," which are, of course, eminently poetic (137).

This priority does not mean then that philosophy dispenses with poetry. Precisely because of the necessarily imperfect character of our nature, the exact character of our good is an object of perpetual inquiry. It requires an ongoing way of life, best conveyed as such through the kind of depiction made possible by poetry. In addition, because it is a way of life, the obstacles to the non-tragic, philosophic life are not simply intellectual. Because they respond to our greatest longings, we do not easily relinquish the misunderstandings that block the path to this life. It's not enough simply to have the mistake explained. There must also be a response to the passions that guard these misunderstandings. And these passions are formidable; very few pursue the Socratic life. With its capacity to address the passions, poetry is indispensable in this regard: the Platonic dialogue does not only "[teach] through speeches"; it "[seduces] us with the person of Socrates" (140). Most importantly, the philosopher's self-aware use of poetry keeps before us the rationale for this continual inquiry of the Socratic life.

Plato's poetry depicts this man, Socrates, engaged in conversation with a range of other characters. Through these conversations he encourages his interlocutors, and Plato's readers, to reflect on their actions. Frequently, these reflections bring to light a contradiction between their actions and their beliefs, a contradiction made available through the poetic depiction of individuals. In this tension we see the soul's imperfectly reconcilable capacities for activity and awareness. That tension is captured in the self-knowledge that is the object of Socrates' quest.

With their "second sailings" and repeated calls to "return to the beginning," the dialogues show how we progress through fruitful misunderstandings. As Davis explains in his examination of the *Republic*'s story of Gyges, political life expresses the most dominant misunderstanding. Politics responds to the soul's longing for completeness, creating a whole if one cannot be discovered. Animating political life is the tyrannical urge to re-make the world if it refuses to provide what we want. The best that we can do within the political realm is to emulate the Greeks who pointed out the incompleteness of the political from within that realm (152–53, 158). Although, Davis writes, these efforts of the Greeks only serve to retard the tendency of the political "to become unjust out of justice," it would seem that the philosopher who best understands the object of his inquiry would want to encourage them (158). Davis's treatment of the dialogues, *Cleitophon* and *Hipparchus*, provides an alternative to the desire for perfect and unattainable justice that animates the move to tyranny.

As he does so often in the dialogues, Socrates shows his interlocutor, Cleitophon, that the fulfillment of his deepest desire would in fact annihilate its object. Specifically, Cleitophon's demand for an objective, perfect account of justice requires a rejection of subjectivity that would undermine the notion of justice. If perfect justice were perfectly intelligible it would be "mechanical"; it would not therefore include the internal struggle to *be* just that characterizes our experience of it (167). In this case, justice would not even arise as a question. The desire for such justice presumes the inwardness, the subjectivity that makes justice intelligible as something we care about and struggle to achieve. But this inwardness, insofar as it makes us opaque to others and to ourselves, precludes the perfect sharing required by perfect justice. Again, what enables justice to arise as a question makes it irrevocably imperfect.

This characteristically Socratic move makes a more general point. If Cleitophon were to reflect more deeply on his own desire and its pre-conditions, he would see more clearly the good that is truly available to him. Equipped with this self-knowledge, he might understand the role of indeterminacy in connection with what he wants. Rather than seeking to eradicate it, he might appreciate its worth, a step on the road to the non-tragic life.

While the *Cleitophon* thus addresses the "Egyptian" inclination, the *Hipparchus* addresses the "Scythian" problem. Davis's interpretation shows that the soul is in an important sense the source of worth insofar as the good is always good for some individual. As such, it depends on particularities that make things appear of different worth to different people, and even differently to the same person at different times. But it is of the utmost importance to see that recognition of the soul's activity in this regard does not mean that whatever any soul deems worthy is so. To acknowledge the subject's role in understanding need not entail the collapse of all understanding into the particular will and perspective of each. To ask questions, to inquire, would make no sense if we were the sole source of worth. In that case, we could simply deem something worthy and be done. Likewise, inquiry would be unnecessary if we already know our good completely. We investigate because we don't yet know the object's true worth, which is not wholly dependent on our say-so.

The premise of every view that makes inquiry unnecessary is that we know ourselves through and through. Socrates knows this is not so. The heart of Socrates' wisdom, his knowledge of ignorance, is his understanding of the limit on subjectivity that arises out of awareness of the importance of subjectivity. Being subjective, I do not fully know my intention, hence my good. I need to be open to things I may not think on first appearance are good. Socratic open-mindedness opposes the predominant misunderstanding of soul expressed ultimately in the tyrannical life. Socrates knows that his attention does not alone grant worth to things, but rather recognizes the worth latent within them (184–85, 191). The source of this worth consists in what they contribute to our understanding of the world. And such understanding can be good for someone because it lets each see what's really possible to attain, that is, what's truly good. To want to know all, to question comprehensively, is to be open to the possibility of good in everything (191). The former makes possible a non-tragic life because it sees vast worth in those aspects of our existence—impermanence, indeterminacy, falsehood, tyranny itself—whose persistence leads many to judge human life as tragic.

But if the Socratic path of true open-mindedness is so essential to the true good, why do so few follow it? Davis blames "excessive" or "Puritanical moralism" (181, 227). He leaves it to us to connect "excessive moralism" to the tragic life that stands as the alternative to Socrates. That connection is not immediately apparent; the exemplars of the tragic inclination, Achilles and Alcibiades, are not remembered for their moralism. Perhaps Davis's discussion of the gods in this context points to the link. It does make clear that he's not in the business of invigorating the distinction between reason and revelation. This discussion also brings the connection between poetry and philosophy into view.

Throughout the book, Davis indicates that the gods express the problematic desire to have the good permanently for oneself (e.g., 114 and n13). The implications of selfhood conflict with the prerequisites of permanence, and the gods as immortal yet distinct beings embody the conflict. Davis maintains that we create the gods and seek to emulate them out of that same misunderstanding of soul that animates politics and, ultimately, tyranny. More specifically, we initially engage in theopoiesis prompted by perplexity in our self-understanding, but ultimately the gods are created to exert control over an all too often mysterious world, the mystery extending to our own nature (218–20). Through moralism, our self-imposed adherence to proper practices, we can believe we control those beings endowed with the power to exert the control that we lack.

In his "natural history of religion," Davis distinguishes Socrates by his refusal to engage in such god-creation (220, 218). Poetry requires the guidance of philosophy so that it does not succumb to the political understanding of soul and the concomitant effort to make the world provide what we believe to be our good. Socrates' refusal makes possible the true open-mindedness that refuses to decide without inquiry what might be truly good for us. That open-mindedness is the alternative to "excessive moralism."

As we have seen, Davis thinks the obstacle to true open-mindedness is particularly formidable in our time. Unlike those living in other ages, we require preliminary inquiries even to see the central issue. While some trace this situation to the modern philosophers' adoption of political ends, Davis seems to point to Christianity as the ultimate source. Unlike the worship of the Olympians, Christianity leaves us in "a cave beneath the cave" because, despite its overtly a- or anti-political stance, it expresses the tragic, political view of the soul in an unprecedentedly comprehensive manner. But even if this is the case, it can hardly be that Christianity remains the problem. Rather, the problem persists in the contemporary theoretical orientations on certitude that are its heirs. I think that Davis includes among these not only the scientists who examine the soul as if it were a being like all others, but the theorists who deny it any enduring structure; Plato's is the proper response because these are but two variants of the same dogmatism. One reason for the heightened danger is that although the two most prevalent theoretical possibilities regard themselves as alternatives, they in fact share a premise that considers philosophic inquiry either unnecessary or impossible. But if this is true, why think that reflection on the ancient intra-Greek alternative, the soul of Achilles versus the soul of Socrates, is the best response to this danger? How does this reflection constitute the heart of Davis's case for true open-mindedness? Let me suggest a response based on my understanding of the book.

To begin, it is helpful to follow Davis's lead and note the form of these essential alternatives. Both are characterized in terms of fictional figures' souls. There is an important continuity between the poet's work and the philosopher's. While thinkers such as Nietzsche and Strauss attempt to prompt open-mindedness by reanimating dormant conflicts, Davis thinks it more effective to reconcile one "ancient quarrel." Deeper than the quarrel between poetry and philosophy is their common root in the enduring natural tensions of the soul, grasped philosophically and best expressed through poetry. Appreciation of this common root can address the twin threats to open-mindedness. One is met by seeing the philosophic need for poetry, the other by seeing the poet's reliance on philosophy.

The soul is best expressed poetically insofar as its being is a problem. As Davis notes in his discussion of the importance of the middle voice in the *Euthyphro*, the soul alters itself in the course of its distinctive activity (206). Any effort to determine its character alters that character. To neglect this self-relational activity in the name of certainty must result in distortion. But poetry's self-conscious reflection on form highlights exactly the power that makes soul resist such determinative understanding. Its philosophic use can thus give pause to the self-forgetting rationalist who regards the soul as an object like any other, available for thoroughgoing understanding and manipulation.

But the use of poetry to oppose the claims of reason goes too far if it entails a denial of the nature that makes poetry possible. This is self-forgetting of a different sort. Thinkers such as Heidegger who reject the claimed certitude of "rationalism" in this manner pay insufficient heed to the implications of the endurance of the soul's tensions. Persisting at least as long as the conflicting inclinations of Herodotus' Egyptians and Scythians, their endurance provides evidence that these conflicting inclinations may be elements of human nature. In foregoing the possibility that philosophy may grasp nature in all its problematic character, these thinkers endorse the perceived conflict between poetry and philosophy that presumes philosophy's orientation on certitude. That endorsement effaces the distinction between wisdom and philosophy. It thus fails to secure the ongoing intellectual activity and openness at which they aimed. But by eliciting the common root of poetry and philosophy in the natural tensions of the soul, Davis speaks directly to these thinkers. He shows, specifically, how genuinely "to *secure* our incompletion" (226, emphasis in original) Or, in the words of another philosophic poet, he preserves the soul's opportunity to "[taste] that food which, by satisfying, makes one thirst for it."[5]

5   Dante, Purgatorio, XXXI, 127–29. *The "Divine Comedy" of Dante Alighieri, Volume 2,* "Purgatorio" trans. Robert M. Durling (Oxford: Oxford University Press, 2003), 537.

The non-tragic, Socratic life depends upon the embrace of the indeterminate, the ambiguous and uncertain, as worthy of our attention because conducive to our good. It requires us to see that the best response to our self-conscious partiality is not to insist on a necessarily false wholeness. That only results in our inability to explain or preserve the things we care most about because that care itself becomes inexplicable. Instead, this life asks us to acknowledge that "the imperfect is our paradise."[6]

As between the twin threats to open-mindedness, it seems that Davis's "poetic" approach might find greater purchase with the opponents of "rationalism" than with its adherents. Perhaps he hopes to reach the latter group through the former; if scientists will heed any theorists, it would be those who are most up-to-date. In any case, if I am not mistaken, Davis would acknowledge that relatively few will see the good of overcoming the formidable obstacles to open-mindedness. That number would be fewer still had Michael Davis not written his extraordinary book.

6   Wallace Stevens, "The Poems of Our Climate," in *The Collected Poems of Wallace Stevens* (New York: Vintage, 1990), 193–94.

The Tragedy of Soul
Jonathan N. Badger

The aim of unifying soul with world, whether by transforming the world into the image of soul or by resolving soul into a fixed being like other beings, is an aim that is unwittingly hostile to soul. Michael Davis highlights a Platonic contrast to assist in making this problem clear. The contrast is between Achilles and Alcibiades on the one hand and Socrates on the other. The former two Davis characterizes as tragic. Achilles and Alcibiades presume that they are known to themselves, and they wish for this fixed and known self to persist, to survive the effects of time. The problem is that what they each understand their self to be cannot be soul. They become transfixed by a still image of self, projected through particularity. In the case of Achilles this still image is *self as lover of the fallen Patroclus*. In the case of Alcibiades it is a resplendent image of himself he mistakes for the soul of Socrates. In both cases the aim is the preservation of self through glory and fame. It is a love of self, seeking to preserve self, but based upon a misunderstanding of self. Davis identifies this as *tragic*. He says that Socrates, on the other hand, is *nontragic* in that he maintains a continuous openness to new visions of self that are available through a parade of beloveds, none of whom he fixates upon. Socrates does not make the mistake of believing he knows himself, and so does not "kill" his soul by freezing it within a reified idealization of another, which is the great hazard for erotic souls (226–28).[1]

Davis offers a profound account of the relationship between Alcibiades and Socrates in the *Symposium*. This essay will not explore this account,

1   Michael Davis, *The Soul of the Greeks* (Chicago: University of Chicago Press, 2011), 226–28; all other references to this work will be parenthetical page numbers in the text.

which includes a wonderful treatment of the nature of *eros* and the beautiful, but will instead take it as a point of departure and focus on what we mean when we speak of Socrates and Socratic philosophy as being "nontragic." Further, I would like to suggest taking Davis's soaring analysis of Achilles a step further in the same direction Davis begins, arriving at a somewhat different bearing with respect to the tragic.

The linchpin here is in what we actually mean by the term "tragic." A popular assumption is that the tragic implies lamentation and despair. Certainly the rejection of tragic poets in the Republic suggests that this is correct. Socrates proscribes poetry that, among other things, depicts maudlin heroes moaning about death. Achilles crying over the death of Patroclus is mentioned in particular here. We notice, however, that many notable plays we call tragedies do not end in ruin and tears. Aeschylus's *Oresteia*, Sophocles' *Ajax, Philoctetes*, and *Oedipus at Colonus*, and Euripides' *Helen* and *Iphigeneia among the Taurians*—all these plays end without tears and with tensions seemingly resolved. The *Ajax*, for example, portrays the disgrace and suicide of the hero Ajax, but while the play is certainly somber, its conclusion leads the audience beyond ruin and despair. Odysseus succeeds in bridging the two opposing perspectives that constitute the primary drama of the second half of the play, and he apparently resolves or at least contains the tension between them. Similarly, the other plays mentioned above all have endings that do not appear to be calamities, but rather resolutions.

I take it as uncontroversial that all these plays are tragic. What then does it mean to call them tragic? There are of course many answers to this question. I would like to offer one that is very compelling to me and then to appropriate a portion of one of Davis's key insights in *The Soul of the Greeks* to advance this conception of the tragic. I don't think I'm doing too much violence in the process, although I end up applying the term tragic to Plato's characters in a somewhat different way.

What makes a play tragic is that it presents fundamental features of soul that are as mutually contradictory as they are necessary. This contradiction is marked by a tension within which we must abide. To seek escape from this tension by establishing ourselves on one side of the antinomy results in the ruin and sorrow depicted in some tragic plays (the *Antigone*, for example). Other plays, such as the ones mentioned above, illuminate and explore this psychic dynamic without resorting to calamity, and some even seem to present what seems to be a stable poise within the tension.

Davis's description of the doubleness of soul gives us a version of this necessary contradiction. Soul is always at odds with itself (7). It requires the simultaneous reality of both motion and rest. The soul must be in motion to be alive, and a crucial aspect of its vitality is its striving outward toward the transcendent, by way of the beautiful. The aim of this striving, however, is a unification with a formal stillness where soul as self is permanent, eternal—self-same and fixed—the opposite of motion and change. In terms of perceiving, thinking, and understanding, soul seems to be compelled to see itself and things in the world as fixed and stable, but it also craves meaning, which requires that things point beyond themselves, that beings be in service of other, less vivid beings, which soul in turn strives to make more vivid. Soul constantly undermines itself. This compulsion toward a goal, which, if reached, would constitute self-annihilation is what I am calling tragic.

These contradictory drives must exist together for soul to be, but this being-together requires some kind of constraint; it is always in danger of dissolution. The constraint is a self-conscious self-rootedness, which, as Davis observes, is the condition for authentic ethical and political life. To be sure, this stressful arrangement is elusive to peoples or individuals who are gripped by one side or the other of the tension that makes soul possible. Creon is such a character, as is Antigone. These are half-souls, as it were. They come to ruin, and tragedy can make its point by exhibiting this ruin, but this does not mean that tragedy is synonymous with ruin. Tragedy can also exhibit its insight through the Odysseus of Sophocles' *Ajax*—Odysseus holds together the two psychic impulses that dominate that play, and he thereby paves the way for political life.

Strictly speaking, this language of "two sides" of the soul and even "half-souls" is not meaningful. A husband and a wife are not each half a marriage. Marriage is the relation. It does not have being in the same sense that the two people do. Soul seems to be like this. Its two "halves" are separable only in speech. They are together as the convex and the concave. They manifest as a tension between opposing commitments or opposing ways of seeing. We strive for fixity and permanence in the face of dissolution in time, but we also move. Not only are we in motion, but we go into motion precisely in our pursuit of the goal of fixity. The peculiar tension that this constitutes is the essence of soul. Soul consists precisely in the tension between two contradictory impulses. Insofar as they are contradictory yet necessary, the soul is tragic. This sounds strange because given our common vernacular it may seem as though we are saying that soul is doomed, that tears and despair are our lot. But as we have just seen, the tragic need not imply this. The tragic nature of soul *does* mean that it is vulnerable to collapsing into the in-humanity of a Creon or an Antigone, but this need not be the fate of soul. Health consists in abiding within the tragic tension without striving to fix the soul into ordinary being. We associate this kind of health with Socrates, and perhaps this is connected to what we hear him say at the end of the *Symposium*—that the writer of tragedy could also be a writer of comedy. A good tragedian can make us laugh.

At this point I want to turn to Davis's treatment of Herodotus' *History*,[2] which is extremely helpful for thinking about tragedy as it manifests culturally, which in turn helps us think through the meaning of tragedy for soul and self-understanding. How does tragedy fit into an account of the phenomenology of soul expressed in cultural terms?

In books 1 through 4 of the *History*, Herodotus enunciates a set of persistent chrateristics within a typology of culture. One of these is the human soul's longing for permanence. This is characteristic of Egypt, and as an example Davis points to the Egyptian belief that Egypt is defined by the Nile. An ancient and seemingly permanent geological formation circumscribes and discloses the essence of the Egyptian. Yet the Nile proves to be unfathomable—its source cannot be plumbed, and therefore what it means to be Egyptian remains unknown (82). Another of the manifestations of this character is in the Egyptian conception of history. Egyptians see themselves as mere effects of a monolithic and divine past. They deny that individuals are also causes (82–83). The mistake of the Egyptians is that they take the first things historically to be the first things in all other senses. Not understanding that first things are hidden, they mistake history for philosophy.

Further, the Egyptians maintain a rigid and radical separation between the human and the divine. The private realm, including the human body

2   *The Soul of the Greeks*, chs. 4 and 5.

itself, is considered shameful. There are no heroes, for the divine and human do not mix. The divine is stable, fixed and inhuman—the Egyptians suffer from an excessive reverence. Egyptian religion is the pursuit of what is most stable. Corpses are mummified to render the human into something permanent and fixed and therefore worthy. The living body is unworthy. Davis associates these Egyptian traits and practices with a sort of conventional Platonism. Ideal forms are the proper objects of reverence (88).

Herodotus presents the Scythians as an opposing form of culture to the Egyptians. The Scythians see only surfaces and live within poetry. They are always "new"—they are a nomadic people and so the ancestral and the geographic are not present for them. They think and act in symbols and signs. Snow, for example, looks like feathers, and so they call snow "feathers." Theirs is a literal poetry; things are their images. Images do not point beyond themselves, and in this way causality becomes tautology (96). Their world is an altogether poetic world, which is therefore blind to the presence of poetry. This obscures incompleteness and cultivates a false sense of wholeness. Unable to see the difference between image and thing, the Scythians believe they are always in the presence of ultimate reality. In their commitment to the surfaces of things, they elevate superficiality to wisdom. Their world of self-contained meaning ostensibly is the source of their cherished freedom, but Herodotus indicates their brand of freedom—freedom from all constraints—is finally a form of slavery.

Davis observes in this case of the Scythians that seeing must be double. "Everything that is evokes something other than itself . . . To be means to be ambiguous." To remove the evocative power of ambiguity results in blindness, and this blindness results in slavery for the Scythians. By denying the fixed and the permanent—that which would be a constraint on radical freedom—they lose any kind of cultural rootedness and cease to *be*. Freedom for the Scythians means being unduplicitous—being nothing else. This means *being nothing* (99).

Through Davis's view of Herodotus' Scythians we see a remarkable and perhaps familiar cultural possibility. The literal interpretation of poetry undermines the crucial capacity of poetry to disclose meaning, and hence excludes meaning from living. Further, identifying as the Scythians do with the putative freedom of unambiguous vision is slavish and self-annihilating.

The longing for permanence as exhibited in Herodotus' idealized Egyptians is opposed to the Scythians' commitment to motion. While the Egyptians are radically historical, effectively presuming Being to be just another being at the beginning of a long historical sequence, the Scythians are purely poetic, seeing no distinction between significance and things. The Scythians live in a world of purely poetic images, and are hence blind to the presence of poetry, while the Egyptians reduce all meaning to things, and see ancient monuments and mummified corpses as the most real elements of their civilization, owing to their position in history. These two principles of soul, made visible through Herodotus' poetic purification of cultures, are opposite. They can be held together, however, just as two north poles of magnets can be held together. The tension between them is exquisite and vivid, and is born of diametric opposition.

If we combine this Herodotean cultural opposition with what I said just now about tragedy, we might call the Egyptians and the Scythians non-tragic in that they do not possess the tragic perspective. They have each succumbed to one extreme of the tragic polarity, and they lack the awareness that their impulses are one-sided, with the consequence that they are unstable: they fall into either diffuse unrest or ossified tyranny. Following Davis's reading of Herodotus's highly idealized Egyptians and Scythians, we can say that the Egyptians aspire to resolve human life into fixity and rest, and the Scythians seek to keep it in free flux. Herodotus's idealized Greeks, by contrast, hold together both sides of the psychic antinomy, and live within the tension. As a result Greek culture is *fully human* and therefore capable of authentic political life. The Greeks are fully alive. They have *soul* in the richest sense through the holding-together of the opposing tendencies of soul. This holding-together is the achievement of their characteristic poetry, namely tragic poetry. The Greeks cultivate and exhibit a tragic view, and thereby attain a fuller and richer view of themselves in the world. As Davis writes, they are "genuinely poetic," or better, "imperfectly poetic" (101). This version of poetics is *tragic poetry*, which as Davis points out is "the necessary means for preventing the decay of this double sense of the world into a uniformity and flatness that is the limited case of which various barbarisms are approximations" (103). Extending Davis's formulation, we may say that while the Egyptians are a historical culture and the Scythians a purely poetic culture, the Greeks are a *tragically* poetic culture.

Being tragic implies that they make themselves into an object and that they see double. They are capable of self-awareness and of poetically sustained meanings. They see themselves and things in the world as simultaneously real *and* pointing beyond themselves. This doubleness of vision that Davis identifies, and which I am perhaps a bit more emphatically associating with the tragic perspective, is the necessary condition for self-conscious political life.

Now, ideally we might like to say that it is really *true* that the Greeks achieve this fullness of soul and life—that the tragic view disclosed in the poetry of the Greeks is the highest and most fully human perspective. But this does not seem to be correct. The self-conscious instability of tragic poetry is the psychic mode that allows for both continuity and motion, and this is unique to the Greeks. This finally and necessarily fails, however, and in fact "we are none of us simply Greek" (104). Tragic poetry successfully frames the problem of soul, and it aims for a solution. It fails, however, to achieve this solution.

We see in Euripides' *Helen*, for example, that identity would require a recognizability of soul despite the fact that every individual changes through time. This recognizability as well as the corresponding recognizing turns out to be divine. But Davis shows in his reading of the *Helen* that the very articulation of the problem calls into question the coherence of the divine. This is one example of the failure of tragedy. Similarly, in *Iphigeneia among the Taurians* we come to see that ritual civilizes the barbaric, but in so doing it always blinds us to our barbaric origins, thus draining ritual of its meaning. Reality is replaced by symbol. On the surface at least, Greeks differ from barbarians in the capacity to be aware of the primacy of significance over reality, but Euripides merely achieves giving the Greeks a new single vision—significance without reality. This makes one wonder if the Greeks do not finally reduce to just another species of Scythian. The resolution of the *Iphigeneia* points to the vanishing of the sacred. Greekness undermines itself. It represents a unification of soul which in effect is a kind of blindness. Davis believes that Euripides is aware of this problem and that he attempts a rekindling of wonder through tragedy, which is a ritual for rebarbarizing hollow ritual. Tragedy aims at a renewed experience of the coincidence of reality and significance. This coincidence is never fully possible, however, and therefore tragedy is a failure. Davis's argument is that tragedy is in fact attempting to achieve this coincidence but that it misses the mark, with the result that the Greeks are left in a condition of empty significance.

But what exactly are we judging when we say that tragedy fails? If we confine ourselves to Herodotus' rarified images of culture, *viz.*, the Egyptians, the Scythians, and the Greeks, and then evaluate the degree to which these Greeks abide within the doubleness of vision Davis describes, then, to the extent we attribute Greek political and ethical life to tragic poetry, it looks like tragedy is pretty successful. If, on the other hand, we are judging particular tragic plays according to whether or not they dispense a serviceable civic or personal teaching that initiates us into the highest life, in which we become shimmering, indeterminate objects for ourselves, always at work, always in motion, avoiding both stasis and chaos, then tragedy could rightly be judged to fail. Though it still seems to achieve quite a lot, if it doesn't give us Socratic philosophy then we rightly observe that it does not give us the crown jewel. Still, in the phenomenology of soul, would it not be correct to say that the tragic view is a necessary condition for philosophy? The soul of Socrates is the solution to the fundamental problematic of soul, but this is an answer to a question posed only by tragedy. Only after soul is an object for itself, and subsequently elusive as an object, do we confront the questions that animate Socrates.

In Davis's words, Socrates is an example of a "living soul at work," and in this he is nontragic (221). He is an object for himself, though an indeterminate object. He maintains a radical openness to the other, which is identified with self-love. He maintains poise between motion and rest. So, if what we mean by the term "tragic" is a collapse into stasis or chaos, into tyranny or unrest, or into any characterization we might choose to describe the antinomes that give rise to the calamities of tragic drama, then it is certainly true that Socrates is nontragic. If, on the other hand, by "tragic" we mean *possessed of the insight into the problem of soul as such*, then might it be apt to describe Plato as a tragedian who makes us laugh? If we adopt Nietzsche's language of a tragic insight or Hegel's view of tragedy as rights in opposition, then we see the tragic poets as offering a full vision of soul that is more complete than that of their heroic characters. Neither Antigone nor Creon possesses the tragic view, but Sophocles does. Odysseus understands the tragic, while Ajax, Philoctetes, Agamemnon, and Menelaus do not have the tragic insight.[3] In the same way, Plato gives us a Socrates who perceives the antinomes of soul and dwells within the tension of their contradiction.

It is with this conception of tragedy in mind that we turn to the question of Achilles. Is Achilles tragic, and what do we mean by this? How does this help us understand soul? Davis says at the beginning of his chapter on Achilles that in the *Iliad* soul is shown striving for perfection; in this it is tragic (6).

I'll briefly summarize Davis's characterization of Achilles, and then offer a response to his interpretation. Achilles seeks immortality. In the beginning of the poem, this is an immortality of an Achilles in name or symbol—a divine emblem for something like a force of nature or cosmic principle (15). Achilles' name and his armor are signs of his being, and their effects in the world are automatic, not soulful. This is a nominal or symbolic immortality that Achilles is initially committed to. It abstracts from any particularity of the living Achilles. Only his name and his glory will live on. Immortality seems incompatible with soul, and hence the gods themselves are called into question through Achilles' striving (14). After the death of Patroclus, however, Achilles embraces a different aim, namely, the immortalizing of his particularity. His striving now is for the perfect affirmation of his grief for a fallen companion. Lacking a definitive category of relationship, Achilles' love of Patroclus is radically particular. When Patroclus dies Achilles is moved by the idea of particularity. It is this lost love—this lost particularity of relation—that Achilles seeks to render permanent and fixed in books 16–24. He seeks to "idealize the defective" (16). This "perfecting of humanity" as Achilles pursues it, however, can only be an aspiration to combine the fixity of divine or cosmic principle with the incoherent idea of loving the dead. This, says Davis, is the tragedy of heroic honor. If we wish to be gods, the sadness of death is without limit.

So we have two kinds of immortality: (1) force of nature or cosmic principle, and (2) idealizing the defective or the perfecting of humanity. The first is an imitation of gods. Davis's gods are not soulful; they are principles or forces. This kind of immortality does not leave room for

---

3   Jonathan N. Badger, *Sophocles and the Politics of Tragedy* (New York: Routledge, 2012), ch. 1.

personality or particularity. One lives forever only in name or as an emblem of oneself. This status is gained by exhibiting mechanical activity in life. Achilles' armor (his original armor) is a sign or symbol that affects victory in battle mechanically. Men fight and die before the armor, which is only the superficial *appearance* of the great Achilles. It is only a shell without content that is immortal. The substance of this immortality is fame and glory as opposed to soulful personhood. The second kind of immortality— the idealizing of the defective or the perfecting of humanity—is closer to what a soul would want for itself. This is a personal deathlessness, a perpetuation of one's idiosyncratic situatedness in the world. We see a striving for this on the part of Sophocles' Ajax, who wishes to overcome the alterations of time and remain eternally an enemy to Odysseus. This idea is present in Homer's presentation of Ajax's shade in Hades in the *Odyssey*. There Ajax forgoes the opportunity to speak with the living because it would mean softening his disposition towards Odysseus; he will remain an enemy forever. This is an affirmation of a particular relationship or set of relations for all time. It is the preservation of hate, love, and grief. These are the passions and relations that constitute the human and it is this that is "perfected" and rendered undying. Thus Homer gives us two conceptions of Achilles: Achilles as force of nature and Achilles as a unique instantiation of love and grief. In Davis's reading Achilles starts out aiming at the first type and then changes his goal to the second.

I would like to explore this idea of Achilles as a force of nature. Davis holds that in his initial aspiration to immortality, in which he is striving for godlike status through glory, Achilles' power is non-soulful, like the force of a cosmic principle, which is what gods are prior to being particularized through personality. This automatic or mechanical prowess is imaged by Achilles' armor, which is an emblem for the power of Achilles. The armor does the work, in a sense. Patroclus can put on the armor and just show up in battle, and until Apollo shakes the armor loose, events transpire as though Achilles himself is really there. This is an image of immortality as contentless principle. Glory that lives on eternally does so without soul. Its presence in the world is impersonal and independent of any particular self. Achilles in his first sailing thus aspires to take on an existence without self.

We begin to see something strange. The rage of Achilles, which would appear at first to be pure *thumos*, outrage at having his sacrifice of a long life for the sake of immortal glory spoiled by dishonor at the hands of Agamemnon, is essentially a rage over the loss of a self-less immortality. There is something perplexing about a thumotic display of selflessness.

We should note that this aspiration is imaged in Achilles' success in battle as a force of nature, *prior* to the death of Patroclus. It therefore seems quite striking that Homer depicts Achilles soon *after* the death of Patroclus almost explicitly as a force of nature. He enters the battle like a shooting star. He assaults the Trojan warriors like a whirlwind and like a blazing forest fire laying waste (20.490). The most astonishing image is his battle with the river Skamandros in book 21. Achilles gluts the river with so many bodies that the river rises up and attacks him. Various gods enter the fray, which culminates in a full-on battle of elements. Hephaestus sends fire to burn Achilles' victims, scorch the land and boil the river, which is forced to retreat back into its bed.

Davis's language about Achilles as a force of nature immediately brings these passages to mind. Now, this naturalistic imagery occurs after Achilles would have moved into the second phase of his wrath, into his project of "idealizing the defective" in Davis's terms. And indeed, the episode with the Skamandros includes the moment in which we see Achilles pulling twelve living Trojan youths from the river, binding them, and sending them back to the ships to be sacrificed at Patroclus' funeral. This is an early example of Achilles making what he hates visible to himself, of turning things undeserving of hatred into objects of his hatred. This is how Davis describes Achilles' treatment of Hector's corpse, which in his analysis is emblematic of the final version of Achilles' wrath. So this encounter with the river is quite illustrative in that it nicely combines conspicuous elements of *both* versions of Achilles' striving. This suggests that if we are to speak of two versions of immortality, then we should notice that the second version includes the first, or that the original project of becoming divine has now been expanded to include the "perfecting of humanity." The episode with the Skamandros is an indication that the project of raising personhood to the level of godlike existence is so problematic, indeed so horrific in aspect, that it is disruptive of nature itself. Nature is disrupted by the attempt to combine a force of nature with particularity and personality.

That Achilles *is* such a combination at this point in the poem is indicated by the details surrounding Homer's account of Achilles' new armor. Insofar as Achilles' armor is a symbol or sign for the power of Achilles, and insofar as *that power* channeled through *this sign* has the character of a force of nature, as opposed to the dynamism of soul, then we should read with particular interest Homer's description of the construction of the *new* armor Hephaestus forges as a replacement for the old armor that Hector took from the corpse of Patroclus. This new armor indicates the inauguration of Achilles' new ambition of idealizing the defective and perfecting humanity.

In book 18 Thetis goes to the glorious house of Hephaestus to request the new armor. When she enters the house we see Hephaestus working on a set of twenty tripods that he is fashioning with golden wheels, which will give the tripods self-motion. They will be able to initiate their own motion to go into the assembly of the gods and then return on their own initiative to Hephaestus' house (18.375). A few lines later we see golden machines with the form of young women moving about the house. Homer tells us that they work in support of their master, and that they have intelligence (*nous*) in their hearts (*phresin*), that they possess the ability to speak, and that "they have learned how to do things from the gods"(*theōn apo erga isain*, 18.420). These android girls are receptive to gods. They know *erga* from them. They have *learned* from them.

Hephaestus greets Thetis by acknowledging that it was she who saved his soul (*thumos*) from suffering pain when she intervened on his behalf when Hera tried to hide him away on account of his being lame. Thus we see that Hephaestus is a god capable of spiritual suffering in addition to his physical malady. Hephaestus and Thetis here seem conspicuous. In the Homeric world of powerful and capricious gods, they exhibit private suffering, brokenness, and compassion. It is from this region of the divine that Achilles receives the emblem of his second striving. The symbol for the affirmation of fixed and permanent personality is the product of crippled and compassionate divinity.

The armor that Hephaestus makes for Achilles is certainly intricate and elaborate, but what is so interesting in this context is that the images upon it would seem to be animated; they are alive with motion. The narratives on the shield are too complex to be a simple set of still images; they are motion pictures. We are led to imagine holographic dramas upon hammered metal. In one of the scenes on the shield, Homer tells us there is a youth playing a lyre charmingly and singing beautifully while others step in time to his song (18.570). The charm, beauty, and rhythm of music cannot be displayed in a still image. At the very least, the images would need to involve many panels for each scene in order to convey the dramatic complexity of the action. Even this would suggest that the armor is meant to convey motion and life, in contrast to the soulless face of horror that we see on Agamemnon's shield in book 11.

At the beginning of book 19 the new armor is delivered. It is apparently terrifying. The Myrmidons cannot even look at it directly. As Achilles himself studies it, his eyes glitter like sun flare, and anger comes hard upon him (19.10–20). If the old shield was an emblem of a cosmic principle that set events in motion soullessly, the new shield is a cosmos unto itself, working alive with particularity, desire, strife, joy, and grief. It is made by a soulful, imperfect god who works at animating machines, at infusing artificial beings with self-motion, intelligence, and learning. Hephaestus presides over the ambition to connect necessity to agency, to combine fixed mechanical nature with intelligence and particularity. As Achilles enters the battle with his new living armor—like a whirlwind and a blazing forest fire, disrupting the natural world as he goes—he is a test case for a force of nature with a life of its own.

Where does Achilles end up? What is the fate of this test case? Davis presents Achilles as finally tragic. Leaving aside the narrow and perhaps idiosyncratic use of the term I have argued for, I still have a question about the sense in which Achilles is tragic. *The Soul of the Greeks* explores and clarifies the idea that while soul is necessarily indeterminate, it is still something we *can* come to know ethically and politically. Greeks can be distinguished from barbarians in their relative success in making themselves objects for themselves even as they avoid freezing themselves into automatic non-souls by failing to sense the limits of politics. They are to some degree capable of holding together duty and self-interest, honor and expedience, or in other words, of holding together the beautiful and the good. This is of course never perfectly achieved, even by Herodotus' Greeks. But Davis reminds us of Themistocles, who exemplifies a characteristically Greek capacity to hold together duty and self-interest in a fashion that we can call soulful. He further points out that Herodotus' Greeks are the paradigmatic political people, which means that they are the paradigm of the human simply.

So what do we see when we compare Achilles to this paradigm? What exactly is the tragedy of Achilles? Is it that he fails to combine the dual principles that are necessary for soul, starting out as some version of Egyptian and only succeeding in moving over to the other extreme, becoming something like a Scythian? Or is he like Herodotus' Greeks, who rise to the level of the human, but who still ultimately fail to bring the beautiful and the good into full coincidence? Is this particular failure what we in fact mean by "tragic"?

I would at least want to argue that Achilles demonstrates a modest achievement by the end of the poem. In book 24, in his encounter with Priam he is moved by a kind of sameness with Priam. As they look upon each other in amazement, Achilles sees double. He sees his enemy, the king of the Trojans, but he also sees his own father and weeps for him, and this sorrow gives way to sorrow over Patroclus. At the same time Priam is also weeping for Hector. The two men, who are not only military enemies but also deeply personal enemies, are unified in their grief. Achilles experiences a moment of existence that is both radically particular and beyond particularity. In the immediate sequel we see him taking steps to work with himself toward a conscious goal. He wishes to honor Priam and return Hector's corpse, but he understands enough of himself to know what might spoil this aim. He gently tells Priam to be still lest he stir Achilles' *thumos*, causing Achilles to return to a hostile stance and make himself guilty before the god. He then tells the servant girls to wash the body of Hector in order to make it less horrible for Priam. The reason Achilles gives is that if Priam sees the corpse in its present condition it might move him to anger, and if this happens Achilles knows that he (Achilles) would lose control and kill Priam, which again would make him guilty before the god.

Achilles has thus made himself into an object for himself. This takes him outside himself and outside of time. He sees multiple possible futures, and he takes steps to exert control over himself and thereby realize the future that is consistent with the god. I wish to suggest that in this moment, in his seeing double and his being-an-object-for-himself, Achilles has acquired the soulful basis for ethical life. Perhaps he is tragic, but it seems important to acknowledge this achievement and its place within the tragic.

We might go further and say that it is precisely in becoming tragic that Achilles becomes fully human. The self-redemptive nature of soul is essentially tragic. In becoming tragic Achilles achieves the unstable equilibrium of psychic wholeness, in which "he" is neither fixed nor impersonal, neither a principle nor simply particular. Achilles, like soul in its essence, becomes double, and strains against himself. By becoming tragic he becomes ethical, just as the Greeks become political.

A version of this paper was delivered to the American Philosophical Association Central Division Meeting, Chicago, Illinois, February 17, 2012.

The *Logos* of Grief and the Shadow of War in Euripides' *Trojan Women*

Lisa Pace Vetter

The attempt to say that which cannot be said is the epitome of tragedy. Grief, loss, pain, and death cannot be captured, it seems, in mere words, and any attempt to do so will ultimately fail. That tragedy draws on a number of dramatic devices to express that which eludes mere words, compounds the futility. And yet the allure of tragedy seems to be in its very failure, as playwrights nevertheless work to express the inexpressible in powerful messages that continue to resonate with audiences who themselves struggle to explain its appeal. We are all familiar with the effects tragedy has on us as members of an audience. The grief and pain of the characters remind us of our own grief and pain. The effect is intensified as the tragedian draws from a variety of dramatic techniques to convey his messages on multiple levels. At the end, we feel a sense of hopelessness and resignation because the cycle of tragedy never seems to end. Although we may feel kinship with those who have suffered, perhaps thousands of years ago, we also may experience some relief as we realize that we will never experience exactly the same pain and grief as the characters portrayed before us. What are we to make of these experiences?

Euripides' *Trojan Women (Troades)* provides an excellent opportunity to gain some insight into the paradoxes of the tragedy of saying the unsayable. Set in the aftermath of the Trojan War, the play focuses on the effects of the conflict among the most silent and silenced of ancient Greek society: women on the losing side of battle, slaves, children, and the dead. The drumbeat of war drowns out speech, reason, argumentation, and persuasion, as perceived danger becomes imminent. War takes on a life of its own, freedom becomes necessity, and the often unspeakable effects of conflict are widely felt well after the fighting has ceased.

Of all the extant works by the triumvirate of ancient Greek playwrights, Euripides' *Trojan Women* enjoys wide popularity among contemporary audiences, second perhaps only to Sophocles' *Antigone*. The allure of its anti-war message to societies that seek to heal their own war wounds is unmistakable. Indeed, the play has been adapted to the Russian Revolution, the Holocaust, the nuclear bombings of Hiroshima, the Algerian war, the Vietnam war, the 1984 Lebanese war, the Balkan war, the Iraq war, the civil wars in Sierra Leone and Liberia, and, most recently, the conflict in Syria. To drive home the contemporary relevance of the *Trojan Women*, actual refugees from war-torn countries have recently been cast in leading roles, and antiwar activists from Jean-Paul Sartre to Vanessa Redgrave and others have been frequently involved in adapting and staging the work.

Although the play has broad popular appeal, it occupies a less prominent position in scholarly circles when compared with other works. A quick glance at *Troades* suggests some reasons for the relative neglect. The play is emotionally wrenching in its portrayal of postwar devastation, but it contains little dramatic action to tantalize academics and scholars. The pivotal event, the defeat and destruction of Troy, has already occurred.[1] The characters are effectively suspended in time and space between the ruins of Troy and the Achaean ships awaiting departure.[2] Although the specific fates of the characters unfold as the play progresses, there is no mystery about their future: it will be utterly miserable. The plethora of speeches and dialogues that fill the void of inaction heap grief upon grief on its hapless

1   Others have noted structural oddities in the play. "The beginning and the ending of this play show that the structure of the action has been inverted . . . . [T]he ending includes none of the features usually found in the epilogue, while the prologue includes a number of features usually found only in the ending. [S]ince the play begins with an ending and ends without one, it also frustrates the audience's desire for a goal. This novel inversion of the action gives *The Trojan Women* its startling power"; Francis M. Dunn, "Beginning at the End in Euripides' 'Trojan Women,'" *Rheinisches Museum fur Philologie* 136 (1993): 22–35, at 24.

2   "The inversion of beginning and ending accompanies a more general inversion in the action of the play. Rather than a sequence of events leading to some conclusion *The Trojan Women* portrays a situation in which movement is impossible: the play begins and ends with the destruction of Troy and the departure of all survivors"; Dunn, "Begining at the End," 32.

audience, which is left without a single source of hope as the play draws to a close.[3] It is not for nothing that Aristotle offers a backhanded compliment to Euripides by declaring that he "appears of all the poets the most tragic" precisely because he is the most consistently depressing: "most of [his plays] end in ill fortune" (*Poetics* 1453a24–26, 29–30).

This is not to say that scholars have ignored the *Trojan Women*. Their attention has been a mixed blessing, however, as interpretations often risk oversimplifying the complex nature of the play. Euripides has been placed in a variety of contradictory pigeonholes, as "patriot, anti-war poet, feminist, misogynist, oligarch, sophist, anti-sophist or grocer's son."[4] Some revel in his Dionysian nihilism; others express "interpretative dismay" at the "hopeless hodgepodge of aesthetic mistakes," inconsistencies, and anachronisms in his works.[5] Efforts to

---

3   As Gilbert Murray declared, "The whole drama, one may almost say, is a study of sorrow, a study too intense to admit the distraction of plot interest"; quoted in Mary C. Stieber, *Euripides and the Language of Craft*, *Mnemosyne Supplements*, *Monographs on Greek and Roman Language and Literature* (Leiden; Boston: Brill, 2011), 1 n1.

4   N. T. Croally, *Euripidean Polemic: the Trojan Women and the Function of Tragedy*, *Cambridge Classical Studies* (Cambridge and New York: Cambridge University Press, 1994), 94.

5   Daniel Mendelsohn, *Gender and the City in Euripides' Political Plays* (Oxford and New York: Oxford University Press, 2002), 12, 7. Mendelsohn provides a detailed and insightful overview of feminist interpretations of Euripides' plays and offers an alternative that better accommodates the complexity with which the playwright approaches the "gender politics" of Athens. "For if we accept that the feminine represented those elements of diversity and otherness that posed problems for the unitary ideology of the *polis*," as feminist interpreters contend, "it is possible to see in these alternating repressions and expressions of female action, in the women's attempts at heroism and their subsequent feminizing effects on the plays' central male figures, not merely the enactment of patriarchal fantasy or nightmare—i.e., the representation of one extreme by the other—but dramatizations of ideological negotiations, of the tensions and ambiguities between those extremes. In political terms, the characters' experience of 'altered states' with respect to gender is an enactment of the ongoing process of alteration and negotiation among constituent parts of the state itself." As a result, "the deployment of scenes of feminine transgression thus emphasizes the way in which masculine civic identity is enhanced through interaction with the feminine" (*Gender and the City*, 48).

connect the *Troades* historically with the Athenian conquest of Melos and its expedition to Sicily have been relatively common, but the notion that Euripides' sole intention is to criticize the Peloponnesian War in particular or the Athenian government generally has been undermined by the sheer variety of lessons interpreters have gleaned from his works.

Fortunately, not all examinations of Euripides' tragedies have led to tragic consequences. Although Euripides is still seen as an Athenian ideologue, the concept of ideology itself has been reconsidered. Ideology is still *"the authoritative self-definition of the Athenian citizen,"* but it is no longer seen as a single point of view defined by a (patriarchal or imperialist) elite and imposed on the masses, and it is produced in civic discourse that draws from a wide variety of sources.[6] In addition to the particular ideas expressed through tragedies and other dramatic texts, political speeches, oratory, inscriptions from the Athenian assembly, or Athenian art, an essential part of Athenian ideology is "self-examination," specifically the exploration of "a series of interdependent and mutually reinforcing polarities, which the audience employed in its self-definition," the most important of which is self/other but also includes Greek/barbarian, free/slave, man/god, and man/woman.[7] "Though sponsored by the polis to be performed on a great civic occasion," tragedy serves a crucial didactic function in Athenian society by encouraging audiences to question and begin to shape their identities: "tragedy questions as well as affirms ideology."[8] Others have expanded on the intellectual sophistication of Euripides' work generally. Although his work fosters a kind of "tragic *aporia*" by which it "compels a thoughtful recipient to acknowledge difficulty and uncertainty, to perceive the fragility of cherished structures and values, and to accept the insufficiency of man, whether in isolation or in a social and political group," the audience is not wholly at a loss. For Euripides is perhaps also the greatest instructor in "the need to know one's limits, to gain the wisdom that comes from accepting doubt, uncertainty and ignorance," themes that have "strong resonance in the Greek philosophical and intellectual tradition, with its

6   Croally, *Euripidean Polemic*, 44, emphasis in original.
7   Ibid., 262, 12.
8   Ibid., 45.

critique of, and struggle to get beyond appearances, sense perception, and received conventions."[9]

These examinations dovetail nicely with Michael Davis's work on Greek tragedy, which will be used as an interpretive frame for my study (thereby adding a touch of *Fest* to this admittedly meager *Schrift*). By examining the various *logoi* in the *Troades*—classified here as "Doublespeak," "Rhetorical Speech," and "Ambiguous or Futile Speech"—I hope to show that the didactic nature of the play arises not simply from an examination of the prevailing ideology of ancient Athens understood narrowly. Nor does the play leave audiences with only a vague appreciation of complexity or some undefined insights into human nature. Instead, the polyphonic nature of the *Troades*, which arises from the utter disorder of war, creates a complex dynamic between the characters and the audience, a multilayered process of identification and distance that is constantly shifting. In other words, Euripides' play shows not only what Davis describes as "the double way in which human beings see first objects and then themselves in the world—as at once real and pointing beyond themselves, as other than themselves"—a worldview that would include polarities such as those that comprise Athenian ideology properly understood. But this way of thinking also provides "the necessary means for preventing the decay of this double sense of the world into a uniformity and flatness" by encouraging "the self-consciousness of this instability" through the use of tragedy.[10] The emergence of the various *logoi* surpasses simple "double ways" or dichotomies such as speech v. silence because there is never really any silence in the play, but rather multiple expressions through multiple paths, some direct, others far less so. Other dichotomies such as self/other, public/private, male/female, reason/emotion are destabilized in a similar way by pointing beyond themselves in an awareness of instability.

The "tragic *aporia*" that is the self-consciousness of instability and, with it, an awareness of tragic imperfection, is emblematic of the ancient Greek understanding of the soul (as opposed to the barbarian view) as Davis sees

9   Donald J. Mastronarde, *The Art of Euripides: Dramatic Technique and Social Context* (Cambridge and New York: Cambridge University Press, 2010), 311.

10   Michael Davis, *The Soul of the Greeks: An Inquiry* (Chicago: University of Chicago Press, 2011), 103.

it. Equally important, the wisdom that comes from doubt, uncertainty, and ignorance is also "the issue that underlies all Platonic dialogues," which are themselves philosophy "in its nontragic form."[11] The tragic and the philosophic become politically relevant, and hence become instructive as political philosophy, because the same self-consciousness of the Greek soul is necessary for justice which, at least for Plato (and Aristotle), is itself characterized by an awareness of the tension between the unchanging and permanent order of nature, on the one hand, and the particular and hence imperfect manifestations of that order through the *nomoi*.[12] The saying of that which is not or cannot be said through the philosophic tragedy of Euripides' play in turn creates a longing for order, peace, and freedom from necessity that is shared among all of those involved, whether on stage or in the audience. Through his peculiar craft Euripides invokes a longing in the human soul that surpasses strict dichotomies or ideologies and provides crucial orientation toward justice and humanity in a complex polyphonic world.

The central importance of speech broadly understood is reinforced at the end of the play, as Hecuba reflects:

> Yet, had not some god turned our world upside down
> and buried our towers in the earth, we would have been *ciphers*.
> We would never have been the subject of song;
> We would never have provided an *argument*
> For the Muse of mortal poets yet to be born. (*Tr.* 1243–45, emphasis added)[13]

Without the multiple voices of tragedy speaking to us, we would take for granted the pleasures of peace. In so doing we would become a bit less human, with a diminished soul and sense of self—we would become ciphers. Although the longing for order by no means guarantees its

11   Ibid., 137.
12   Ibid., 157.
13   Unless otherwise noted, passages from the *Troades* refer to Euripides, *The Trojan Women*, trans. Diskin Clay (Newburyport, MA: Focus Classical Library, 2005).

realization, it nevertheless provides vital orientation to human beings as they try to navigate a profoundly disorienting and fragile world. By speaking in various songs and arguments, perhaps Euripides' *Troades* reveals itself to be democratic in its purest sense.

Doublespeak

A frequently studied form of speech in the *Troades* in particular and Greek tragedy in general is what are referred to as "double structures," "structures of opposition" or "polarities." Consistent with the notion that the upheaval of war displaces any conception of order, Euripides through his characters draws parallels between related yet different concepts in an effort, I believe, to disorient the audience and simultaneously create a desire for normalcy. As soon as the audience is pulled in one direction, however, it is reminded of the opposite course. The effect is that Euripides constantly reminds his audience that tragedy and grief, especially in the extreme situation of war, mirror an alternative realm of normalcy, peace, stability, and even happiness that is longed for by all human beings. And yet this longing is constantly interrupted by the reminder that tragedy and grief are never far in the background, that the human condition is precarious.

A striking example of this polarity is the character of Hecuba herself. The deposed queen, wife of slain Priam, mother to several children, will live out her days as a slave to Odysseus, the "abominable trickster" whom she blames for the fatal ruse that destroyed her city. To compound the tragedy of her fate, whereas other women were deliberately chosen by particular officers, Hecuba was elected randomly by lot to live with Odysseus (*Tr.* 282, 277–78). Not only will Hecuba be dishonored as a queen, wife, and mother. She will not even be treated in a manner appropriate for any elderly woman, royal or no: "In my old age I am dragged from my home as a slave," Hecuba laments, "I am a trophy from the sack of Troy" (*Tr.* 140–41).

Hecuba introduces herself in the play through various *logoi* —rolling on the ground, muttering to herself, issuing inarticulate cries—and finally asks: "Why should I remain silent? Why should I speak out?" The variety of expression cannot fully convey the depth of her grief, however, so she describes the actual physical agony she feels: "This body, contorted by the weight of some heavy god. I lie stretched out on my back on this hard bed. I feel the pain of my head my temples, my breast" (*Tr.* 112–16). Her status is reminiscent of death, as she describes herself as "the counterfeit of a corpse, the cold statue of a dead woman" (*Tr.* 193–94). A normal human being is either alive or dead, yet Hecuba is denied even this privilege. Instead, she is merely a image of an image, "a facsimile of a facsimile."[14]

Hecuba draws an explicit dichotomy between her past life and future destiny when she addresses the leader of the chorus: "First, now: It is my pleasure to sing of our blessings, for by their *contrast* I will impart a more tragic strain to our disasters" (*Tr.* 471–73, emphasis added). Whereas "I was born to royalty and destined to it," she explains, she finds herself in a state in which "my masters will assign me tasks that are not at all fitting for a woman of my age, to hold keys . . . to grind meal and sleep with my back on a hard floor and ache" (*Tr.* 491–92). Hecuba's fate hearkens back to a bygone age in which Troy lived in peace, marriages occurred, children were born, families thrived, gods were properly honored, and citizens treated one another with dignity. And yet this dramatic order is clearly tenuous, as the audience is constantly reminded of the tragedy that inexorably unfolds before them. The contrast between past and present is further emphasized by the Chorus, who recount the story of the Fall of Troy in agonizing detail. Mistaking the wooden horse for a gift from Athens, men and women alike rejoiced at its arrival. Yet the women's songs of joy were drowned out by a "blood-curdling shout" as warriors poured out of the horse and began to mercilessly slaughter the Trojans.

Hecuba is not the only character to undergo drastic reversal. Her daughter Kassandra offers an extended contrast between marriage and death, joy and grief, love and revenge, wisdom and madness. The herald Talthybius foreshadows the confusion when he mistakes Kassandra's sacred torch, a sign of marriage, for an instrument of death, asking, "What are the women of Troy doing? . . . . Do they want to commit suicide by immolating themselves?" (*Tr.* 298, 300). Shouts and dances of joy and grief intermingle in Kassandra's frenzy. Although the dismayed chorus concludes that Kassandra is "possessed by a god" and asks the fallen queen to restrain her,

14   Stieber, *Euripides and the Language of Craft*, 123.

Hecuba's reaction reminds the audience that she is still the caring mother of a beautiful young daughter: "Give me the torch. You are not holding it straight, but dart about like a maenad possessed." She then gently admonishes the girl: "Child, your misfortunes have not taught you any restraint. You have not changed" (*Tr.* 348–50). But Kassandra is oblivious to Hecuba's tenderness and quickly transforms from jubilant bride to fierce avenger. Although she will be "married" to Agamemnon as his concubine, effectively rendered his servant/slave, Kassandra will be "a bride more disastrous than Helen," which is certainly saying something. She will "kill him and make him pay for the destruction of my brothers and father" (*Tr.* 357–60). Further reinforcing Kassandra's metamorphosis from bride to warrior are her repeated threats that she will "sack" the house of Agamemnon to avenge her family (*Tr.* 359-60, 364, 461).[15] And yet, Kassandra's mad rantings and incongruous swagger are balanced with some of the most sober observations in the play.[16] Her comment, "Anyone with any sense should avoid war," is surely a statement with which the audience would sympathize as the multiple tragedies of conflict unfold in agonizing, almost predictable, sequence. War is hell indeed.

Hecuba's pain is compounded further by her daughter's delusions and the recurring mirror image of the domestic happiness of marriage and political peace of just rule. Yet Euripides is not finished here. There are other pitiful voices to be heard. To the miserable fates of the royal family Euripides adds the most tragic of all, that of Astyanax. Instead of living a "blessed life," the child has only "seen these blessings . . . but never actually experienced any of them" because his life is prematurely and brutally cut short by victorious warriors who nevertheless fear a helpless child (*Tr.* 1169–

15   Cited in ibid., 84.

16   Although her prominence in various commentaries is often overshadowed by Hecuba, Kassandra plays a unique role in the tragedy. "What is common in both the Trojans' (the vanquished's) and the Greeks' (the victors') attitude is the total ignorance of the divine plan to destroy the Greeks and thus gratify the Trojans. The only person to cause a breach in this ignorance is Cassandra. . . . No character on the human level, as we have seen, is aware of the divine plan, while nobody believes Cassandra, who is herself the conveyor of divine knowledge." Thalia Papadopoulou, "Cassandra's Radiant Vigour and the Ironic Optimism of Euripides' 'Troades,'" *Mnemosyne* 53 (2000):513–27, at 515.

73).[17] Holding the dead boy in her arms, Hecuba speaks for him and declares: "I will not conceal the brutality!" (*Tr.* 1177). She draws excruciating contrasts between past and present:

> Your mother would often comb this hair and press it to her lips.
> Now your head is shattered and gore grins out from it
>
> . . . .
>
> Little hands, you bear the sweet likeness of your father's hands.
> Now you lie before me limp and disjointed.
> Sweet lips! Once you had brave words for me.
> Your voice is gone. You deceived me
>
> . . . .
>
> It is not you who are burying me, but I you, who are younger
> than I, you a battered corpse
>
> . . . .
>
> I remember those greetings and your sweet embrace.
> I remember all my care for you, your deep slumber. All is gone.

Lest anyone forget the horror of the young boy's death, Hecuba vows to place the epigraph, "THE ARGIVES ONCE KILLED THIS CHILD IN FEAR OF HIM," on his grave-stone (*Tr.* 1175–91). But it is impossible to convey the hideousness of his death in mere words, engraved in stone or otherwise. The epigraph will remind others of the horrific event that took place, but they will never actually relive or experience the killing itself or its immediate aftermath. The outrage of slaughtering an innocent child, whether future king or no, cannot help but resonate deeply with any audience that reflects on its own children and families.[18] The murder is the

---

17 The horror of the child's death is compounded by additional ironies: "He is buried in a shield which could not protect him; he was murdered by being thrown from walls built to protect him; this child's end marks the end of whatever that shield and those walls stood for too. . . . Somehow this child represents all the children of Troy, and therefore the city's future is laid to rest with him." M. Dyson, and K. H. Lee, "The Funeral of Astyanax in Euripides' Troades," *The Journal of Hellenic Studies* 120 (2000): 17–33, at 26–27.

18 "The original democratic audience would have been likely to find Hecuba's attitudes unsympathetic" because even she admits that Astyanax will even-

logical conclusion of the total defeat of Troy, and yet an audience would surely recoil at this particular application of "reason."

As if to heighten the horror of Astyanax's impending death, Euripides introduces the (in)famous choral ode to Ganymede as the doomed young boy is led away and the sun paradoxically begins to rise over the city. Like Astyanax, Ganymede is a native son of Troy. Both were at the mercy of divine powers. Whereas Ganymede was raised up by Zeus to serve as his cupbearer, Astyanax was thrown down from the city walls to his death. Ganymede "step[s] daintily" among the gods and performs his "noble service" while "the city of [his] birth is ablaze." In effect, he fiddles as his city burns. The Chorus observes:

> Gone now are the fresh pools where you once bathed
> And the running courses of the gymnasia.
> But you, Ganymede, now thrive beside
> The throne of Zeus.
> Peace and light and the calm of the sea radiate from your young face.

And yet, down "below Greek spears have destroyed the land of Priam" (*Tr.* 834–40). Whereas the "calm of the sea" radiates from Ganymede's face, the "cliffs at the sea's edge cry out the shrill cry of a sea bird that has lost her young" (*Tr.* 826–29). Lest any of these parallels escape our notice, Euripides' chorus describes the cliffs that, like the walls of Troy, cry out with the lamentations of Hecuba and Andromache, and which "echo, along the shore, the lament for a marriage lost" for Kassandra, for "children lost" by these women, and "for old mothers" such as Hecuba (*Tr.* 826–33). The only thing differentiating the two boys and status of Troy is the specific kind of interference that is arbitrarily and unpredictably chosen by the gods.

tually become a political threat to the Greeks, and they "would have felt some sympathy with the Greek leaders as they tried to operate in impossible circumstances," having been forced to kill a child. "One's heart breaks but one's head nods sagely. Such are the grim realities of war." James Morwood, "Hecuba and the Democrats: Political Polarities in Euripides' Play," *Greece & Rome* 61 (2014): 194–203, at 201; doi: 10.1017/S0017383514000060. Nevertheless, the "agonies" of the war victims still "tear at the heartstrings," 202.

Euripides does not limit himself to dichotomous parallels and contrasts. One of the most remarkable examples of polyphonic speech in the *Troades* is the multifaceted use of the Greek term *pergamon*, and the frequent evocation of architectural concepts. In generic terms, *pergamon* denotes a city's actual walls and other protective structures. Metaphorically and allegorically, *pergamon* is the sign and symbol of the integrity and strength of a city and even its rulers: "*Purgon* and its cognates are often applied to the *idea* of a city and what makes a city a civilized place for humans to dwell, which would include walls and towers."[19] The crumbled walls of Troy are repeatedly invoked throughout the play to express the visually and orally inexpressible, namely, the city's utter destruction. The same fortifications that were meant to protect its citizens were used as a weapon to mangle the helpless body of Astyanax. As the structures were destroyed, the men of Troy, the protectors of the city, were slaughtered. The absence or invisibility of any men in the *Troades*—save the weak and inarticulate herald— is a stark reminder of the city's ruin.[20] The violation of the city's walls, combined with the absence of men, is also evocative of the sexual violation of vulnerable women. It is clear that "as the most conspicuous visual sign of Troy's onetime power, the doomed walls serve as a kind of psychic structure which iterates and corroborates the escalating desperation of the city's surviving women."[21]

To further reinforce Troy's own identity in terms of its walls, the term functions in the play as a proper noun for the city itself. "The city of Troy, as an entity, mostly a sacked one, is referred to or alluded to some fifty-six times" in the *Troades*, and its circuit walls are mentioned over twenty times.[22] The repeated references to walls were surely not lost on the audience in Athens, itself a walled city, which began contemplating the Sicilian expedition when the play was first performed.[23] Themistocles' fateful

---

19 Stieber, *Euripides and the Language of Craft*, 104, emphasis in original.

20 Ibid., 21.

21 Ibid., 3.

22 Ibid., 12.

23 For Stieber, "the topographical landscape of Troy functions as a *dramatis persona* in *Trojan Women*" (Ibid., 3). The references to the city are not simply metaphors or personifications, nor are they theatrical devices to provide a backdrop where there was none.

decision to abandon the walled city of Athens and take to its ships helped secure an Athenian victory, but there is no guarantee that the success can be repeated.

Although the importance of intact protective walls cannot be overstated, it is possible to have too much of a good thing. To be "towered up" (*epurgosas*) is to possess overconfidence and hubristic arrogance. In the Ganymede ode, Eros "towered up Troy at the time" by encouraging Zeus to become obsessed with the young Trojan, thereby providing the city with a false sense of divine entitlement that was so clearly denied them (*Tr.* 843–44).[24] Hecuba also alludes to the tendency of the divinities to betray the trust of human beings: "I see the handiwork of the gods, how the same things they tower up from nothing they destroy when they give the appearance of [too much] power" (*Tr.* 612–13).[25]

The references to walls and related architectural terms take on additional meanings throughout the play. Hecuba attempts to convey the extent of her suffering by comparing herself with the shattered structures of her own city. Using the term for the architrace or cornice of a building, Hecuba laments that the culmination (*urigkos*) of her fate is to be enslaved to Odysseus.[26] She then asks the chorus: "Guide those feet which once were so delicate in Troy but are now the feet of a slave, so that I might fall headlong toward the padded earth that shall, with its stony crown, be my resting place, and perish at last, rent to shreds by my tears" (*Tr.* 506–09; Stieber's translation). The term for "stony crown," *kredemnon*, connotes a woman's headdress or veil as well as the "crown" of a city, namely, its battlements. With this double meaning, Euripides suggests that Hecuba, like a violated woman robbed of her chaste veil, wants to die on the spot and somehow melt into the soil of her native city through her tears. Equally important, the reference foreshadows the shredding of Astyanax's body as he is thrown from the city walls.[27]

Even Hecuba's opening remarks, which are widely interpreted as comparing the rolling and tossing of her own suffering body with the rocking

24 Ibid., 107–08.
25 Ibid., 109.
26 Ibid., 49.
27 Ibid., 78–82.

of a ship at sea, also allude to the walls of Troy. For Hecuba, the term *toichos/teichos* refers not just to the "alternate sides" of her body, to which she wants "to twist and turn and to shift the weight of my back and spine" as she mourns her fate (*Tr.* 116–19, Stieber's translation). Commentators have assumed that Hecuba is simply drawing from the nautical imagery contained within the same passage (*Tr.* 102–04, 125, and 137; and the references to the Achaean ships in the choral parados). However, it is equally plausible that Hecuba is again invoking the destroyed walls of her city, to which she specifically refers at the beginning of her first speech (*Tr.* 98–99).[28]

The parallels and polarities drawn between the material world of Troy and its physical structures, on the one hand, and the inner world of the grieving victims of war, on the other, reflect the fact that the true extent of tragedy cannot be fully captured by either realm alone or both realms joined together. When all is said and done, the ruins of Troy cannot be fully represented in the mind's eye through speech, nor can the rubble truly represent the inner turmoil of Hecuba or any other character in the play. Even if the ruins could actually be seen or very closely approximated somehow (as digital special effects purport to do these days), the extent of the disaster could never be fully appreciated. Perhaps it is for this reason (and not simply because of cultural desensitization) that observers of the attacks on September 11, 2001 would claim that the falling towers "looked like a movie"—regardless of whether it was shown on a screen, experienced in person, or later contemplated in a museum. Nor can the psychic pain of the Trojan women be adequately conveyed through their lamentations, award-winning actors notwithstanding.

This realization, however, does not necessarily lead to an exercise in futility. The back and forth between the material and spiritual world that

28   Stieber explains: "Given the prominence of architecture in word and image in this play, the allusion to the walls of the city would have been difficult to miss in Hecuba's wish. The audience has been primed to keep the walls in mind since the very first words of the prologue. We have seen that walls and the like are sometimes used metaphorically to refer to humans. There can be no mistaking that Hecuba's degraded status mimics that of her city's fortification walls. She, the wife of a king, mother of princes and, above all, the mother of Hector, is justified in considering herself a bulwark of the city that has been obscenely breached"; ibid., 87.

is achieved in Euripides' tragedy allows us to realize their respective importance as well as their limitations. His work points to something beyond itself and its limitation by instilling a longing for integrity that is an essential part of the human condition and political life.

Rhetorical Speech

Another form of *logos* that appears prominently in the *Troades* is what commentators often refer to as "sophistical" speech.[29] Sophistry's tendency toward manipulation and deception contributes to the negative connotation it enjoys today, yet the speeches discussed here are not intentionally deceptive or manipulative per se. Therefore, the more neutral term "rhetorical" seems more appropriate.[30] What really distinguishes these rhetorical speeches from others is their conspicuously formal structure and the paradoxical juxtaposition between the structural "logic" of the speeches, on the one hand, and the utter "illogic" of the messages they actually convey. They inspire the same sort of longing for order, peace, and happiness as do the "double-speak" of paradoxical speeches, but in a different way.

The interchange between Poseidon and Athena that opens the play is jarring in its inhumanity. Poseidon gazes down at the utterly destroyed city of Troy and describes the scene in grim clinical detail. In spite of the pity he feels for his city, Poseidon did nothing to aid or comfort the very people who worshipped and sacrificed themselves to him. Why? Because he lost a wager to the female gods Athena and Hera and he was affronted by the desecration of the shrines that were dedicated to him, as if to ignore the fact that it was the Argives, not the Trojans, who despoiled the sites. It does not take much to distract him from the spectacle before him, for as soon as Athena approaches, Poseidon agrees to help her wreak vengeance on the Greeks even before hearing the details of her plan. The rhetorical nature of the interchange is reinforced by the "moderate attitude" Athena observes in her interlocutor, who agrees to listen because "conversation with kin is a

---

29 Croally, *Euripidean Polemic*, 221–27.

30 Although historicist interpreters have found connections between Euripides' sophistical speeches and the works of Gorgias and Protagoras, they are not sufficiently strong to justify the use of the term.

powerful drug over the mind" (*Tr.* 50–52). The cold-bloodedness and fickle nature of these gods contrasts profoundly with the human spectacle of suffering below. In the absence of divine guidance, human beings are left to their own devices. The spectacle creates a longing for order and peace that must be created by human beings who are abandoned by the gods.

Kassandra's subsequent rational "demonstration" before her mother and the chorus of women contrasts sharply with her divinely inspired madness. The paradox is compounded by her equally paradoxical hypothesis, namely, that Troy is "more fortunate than are the Achaeans" in spite of the fact that the former has been utterly defeated and destroyed by the latter (*Tr.* 366). For her, "life in Greece *mirrors* life in Troy" (*Tr.* 379, emphasis added). That the Greeks risked everything for a conniving woman betrays their very weakness. On Kassandra's reasoning, although they "won" the battle, the Greeks would lose the war. Whereas the Greek dead were denied proper burial by their families in their homeland, Troy maintained its honor by fighting a primarily defensive war and, most important, its dead were mourned by their families in their native city. The desecration of the Trojan shrines further undermines the heroic nature of the savagely victorious Greeks and inspires sympathy for the defeated. By observing the profound disjunction between the surface "logic" of Kassandra's "arguments," on the one hand, and the underlying paradox or "illogic" of the message, on the other, the audience reflects on the very nature of victory and defeat, whose meanings are reversed in the "fog" of war. The audience longs for greater harmony between logical structure and rational meaning by observing the effects of their very separation.

Perhaps the best known rhetorical interchange in the *Trojan Women* is between Helen and Hecuba. In a mock trial, Helen emerges beautifully dressed from Menelaus' tent and stands before the utterly ruined Trojan women and their smoldering city. Faced with the prospect of death soon after she departs from Troy, Helen desires to "reply" to Menelaus by "anticipating the charges" that he will "lodge" against her (*Tr.* 916). Hecuba asks Menelaus to allow Helen to speak so that the women can have "the chance to refute her" and ensure that "she will never be acquitted" (*Tr.* 906–10). Helen's speech is a tour de force of denial. First, she blames Hecuba for giving birth to Paris, which set the convoluted story in motion. Second, she blames the gods for using her as a pawn and reward for a wager.

Third, she did not try to escape because she was mad, thereby pleading temporary insanity. Fourth, when she did try to escape, she was discovered. Fifth, she was forced to marry and lived in servitude, not in victory. A walking cliché, Helen declares, in effect, don't hate me because I'm beautiful. She explains: "I was destroyed by my beauty, and I am blamed for acts for which I deserve a victor's crown placed upon my head" (*Tr.* 936). Incensed, the chorus pleads with Hecuba: "Your majesty, come defend your children and your country. Demolish this woman's specious arguments. She is a bad woman who speaks well, and this alarms me" (*Tr.* 966–67). Hecuba responds with a "demonstration" of her own that addresses each of the shameless woman's arguments in turn. The most devastating refutation is Hecuba's insistence that "any decent woman would have killed herself in her longing for her former husband" (*Tr.* 1014). Hecuba concludes by laying down a "law for other women: The wife who betrays her husband dies!" (*Tr.* 1033–34). The contrast between the legalistic tone of the interchange and the illogic of the defense cannot be sharper to the incredulous audience, which surely wishes that the gulf between style and substance could somehow be bridged.

Another paradoxical rhetorical "argument" is offered by Andromache, who hypothesizes that "it is better to be dead than to live a life of distress" (*Tr.* 636–37). Her rationale is simple: "The dead are done with suffering and feel absolutely no pain; but the person who has experienced good fortune and falls into ill fortune is distraught at the thought of lost happiness" (*Tr.* 638–40). That Andromache would consider herself less fortunate than her sister-in-law Polyxena, who was slaughtered at the grave of Achilles *and* whose body was left unburied, is unsettling. Andromache's coldness is reinforced by her blunt declaration to Helen that "Polyxena is dead. . . . Slaughtered, a victim at the grave of Achilles, an offering to a lifeless corpse" (*Tr.* 622–23). Andromache's callousness is even more jarring considering her firsthand knowledge of Polyxena's hideous fate, for she had approached the body closely enough to place a shroud on the girl. Even the herald Talthybios could not bring himself to tell Hecuba the truth.

Andromache's subsequent explanation of her pitiful fate mirror's Helen's pseudo-justification. What should have been a blessing for each woman—in Helen's case, her beauty, and for Andromache, her virtue and unimpeachable reputation—is transformed into a curse. The "rumor" of her honor, she explains, "reached the Achaean camp and destroyed me. When it came to the distribution of the women set apart, the son of Achilles chose me as his wife. I will live as a slave in the house of murderers" (*Tr.* 655–60).

Rational, logical speech is a vital component of the order sought by human beings. Although style and substance of speech will never align perfectly, it is important to strive toward greater compatibility so that communication and persuasion are even possible. Without reliable speech, a peaceful and orderly community will never come to fruition.

Ambiguous and Futile Speech

There are many examples in the *Trojan Women* of *logoi* whose imperfections point to the need for greater harmony between style and substance in forging rational connections between human beings. I will briefly mention some of them. In the play there is an abundance of "futile speech" as characters rail at the gods and lament their absence and neglect. Other types of futile speech include the innumerable explanations of the causes of the Trojan War. The sheer abundance of the "origins of evils" confounds the very purpose of these accounts, namely, to explain clearly and persuasively why the war began. The characters seem utterly disoriented by the dizzying array of these justifications, and the audience is not far behind.

Helen proves herself to be a truly "Teflon" character as Hecuba fruitlessly tries to place complete responsibility for the war on her lovely, delicate shoulders.[31] In spite of Hecuba's claims to the contrary, Helen is a lover, not a fighter. It is true that "she will make [men] captive with desire" and

---

31 The futility of the exchange in determining the cause of the suffering has been noted by others as well. "Of course it is ridiculous for Helen to place the primary responsibility on Hecuba, but is it much more ridiculous than Hecuba doing the same to Helen? How many of all those involved in the Trojan war are free from guilt of some sort? The strength behind Helen's position is that behind the whole catastrophe as we see it spread out in front of us, there is seen to be a whole network of causes and responsibilities, of which no one— Hecuba, Priam, Menelaus, Paris, Helen, Aphrodite—can be wholly absolved"; Adrian Poole, "Total Disaster: Euripides' the Trojan Women," *Arion* 3 (1976): 257–87, at 274.

"turns men's eyes," but Helen leaves the literal overturning of cities and the burning of men's homes to her male fans (*Tr.* 890–95). Everything in the city (and one of its smallest citizens) may be in torn to shreds, but Helen's beautiful garments will never be "in ruins" (*Tr.* 1025).[32]

Futility reemerges in a poignant scene toward the end of the play as Hecuba and the chorus of women are directed to the ships. Before they depart, the women kneel to the ground and beat the earth in a vain attempt to "speak" to their dead husbands, seeking help from below to no avail.

Additional examples of futile speech include interchanges in which the speakers talk past one another or fail to communicate clearly, again pointing to the human need to connect and attempt to form orderly communities. Talthybios is a truly imperfect herald, as even the mad Kassandra observes. Although the job of heralds is to convey messages between communicants, Talthybios' first attempt fails.[33] Alluding to Polyxena's death by telling Hecuba that her daughter is "blessed," "happy," settled in "her lot in life" and "free of trouble," Hecuba fails to comprehend the truth. It is up to Andromache to deliver the news in a blunt, straightforward fashion that would befit any self-respecting herald but is surely ill-suited for a daughter-in-law. Talthybios compensates for his earlier "failing," however, when he declares to Andromache "the evil truth," namely, that the Greeks "mean to kill your son" (*Tr.* 718). Yet the herald's "success" conveys the most awful of messages to a mother about her beloved child. Finally, Talthybios bargains with Andromache by promising to arrange burial for Astyanax only

32 Stieber offers a nuanced explanation of this notoriously oblique reference in *Euripides and the Language of Craft*, 82–84.

33 The herald's role has been characterized more charitably by other interpreters. "Talthybius communicates orders for actions that will occur in the future rather than narrating actions that have already transpired. These orders constitute the narrative catalysts in the plot, which is thereby revealed bit by bit, and sustain the structure of the drama"; James Sullivan, "The Agency of the Herald Talthybius in Euripides' Trojan Women." *Mnemosyne* 60 (2007): 472–77, at 474; doi: 10.1163/156852507X215472. And, at a strictly logical level, "although Talthybius has no part in the decision-making process that results in the assignment of the Trojan women . . . [o]nstage, however, he is the very agent of their fates," 475.

if she agrees to relinquish her son and leave quietly (*Tr.* 726–39). Again, the sense in which this communication is "successful" is profoundly unsettling, given the tragic subject matter.

The inability to communicate through grief emerges as a theme when Andromache appears with Astyanax at her side and speaks with Hecuba. Their fragmented interchange of disjointed, choppy phrases fails to address the concerns of either woman. Andromache temporarily deludes herself into believing that Hector is still alive and will come to rescue her (*Tr.* 588–91). Whereas Hecuba sees their doomed fate as the unstoppable "work of the gods," "force," and "necessity," Andromache characterizes it in terms of "laws of change" (*Tr.* 611–15).

These passages and others reflect a larger phenomenon of "futile speech" at work in the play. It has been observed that the entire *Troades* is comprised of a series of lamentations of various kinds: Poseidon laments for his city; Hecuba laments her fate; the chorus matches Hecuba's lamentations with its own; Kassandra's madness is expressed in the meter of lament; and so on. The larger purpose of lamentation is "to mend the fabric which has been torn by loss, and to reconcile those close to the dead to their loss," and this is precisely what happens at the end of the play: "Talthybios and Hekabe share the chores: Talthybios has washed the body [of Astyanax], the soldiers dig the grave. The women gather flowers, Hekabe speaks the lament. The women mourn in response, the soldiers carry the body to the grave. Together they bury Troy's last remnant, and together prepare to sail to homes which they think they will share."[34] The formal structure of the *Trojan Women* also follows the basic structure of a lament as a whole, for the play can be seen in terms of "the antiphony between two kinds of groups—solo and group, and kin and nonkin."[35] Although it is the case that a kind of reconciliation has been achieved at the end of the play, it is equally true that the ability of lamentation—whether solo or group, kin or nonkin—to fully capture the horrors of war and death is fundamentally limited. What appears to be a kind of closure is also a disturbing reminder that there are things that must ultimately remain unsaid.

---

34 Ann Suter, "Lament in Euripides' Trojan Women," *Mnemosyne* 56 2003: 1–28, at 12.
35 Ibid., 13.

Conclusion

Aristophanes' *Frogs* offers some useful guidance in navigating the polyphonic world of Euripides' tragedy, though on a much lighter note. The comic play-wright portrays the tragedian as a favorite of Dionysus who is also admired by populist Athenians for addressing "the things of everyday life" and for giving voice to a variety of people, masters and slaves, women young and old, and children, in true "democratic" spirit (*Frogs* 945–50).[36] With "the intro-duction of subtle rules and squared-off words," Euripides has taught all walks of life to "think, to see, to understand, to love to twist, to connive, to suspect the worst, [and] to overthink all things" (*Frogs* 956-58). On his view, Euripides has supplied Athenians with the tools they need to maintain a critical watch on the city and its elite—including himself. He accepted the responsibility of "introducing familiar things, that we use, that we live with, by which I would be brought to the test; for these, the knowledgeable ones, would cross-examine my craft" (*Frogs* 959–61; Stieber's translation). Not only has the tragic playwright equipped Athenians with the tools to keep an eye on the city. He has also prepared his fellow citizens to examine themselves and their own affairs: "I instructed these folks here, putting logic in my art and scrutiny, so now they notice everything and know through and through, most especially how to run a household better than before, and they inquire, 'How's this doing? Where's this? Who took that?'" (*Frogs* 971–79). In this regard, Euripi-des is the poet who should be admired "for cleverness, and giving good advice, since we improve the people in the cities" (*Frogs* 1010).

And yet, in spite of Dionysus' nostalgic affection for Euripides, and the various gifts he has provided to his fellow citizens, the tragedian loses a dra-matic contest to determine which poet would be best able to save the corrupt city from itself. The victor, Aeschylus, represents the halcyon days of Athens when manly courage ruled the day, warfare dominated political life, and the perceived need for action took precedence over debate, deliberation, and

---

36 Aristophanes. 1907. *Aristophanes Comoediae*. Volume 2. Edited by F. W. Hall and W. M. Geldart. Oxford: Clarendon Press. http://www.per-seus.tufts.edu/hopper/text?doc=urn:cts:greekLit:tlg0019.tlg009 (accessed 10 July 2015). The down-to-earth character of Euripides' work is further rein-forced by Aristotle's observation that the playwright was the first to use "the language of everyday" (*Rhetoric* 1404b28–30).

especially dissent. So it is not surprising that from the perspective of Aeschylus and his tradition-bound sympathizers, Euripides appears to be a sophist not unlike Socrates whose subversive wordplay and challenges to authority threaten to undermine the city and corrupt its citizens.

Lest we strip the comic play of its humor and interpret it literally by assuming that Aristophanes, in an apparent rush of patriotic conservatism, has rejected Euripides in favor of his old-fashioned compatriot and urges us to do the same, we should note that the judge of the competition, Dionysus, is a most unreliable authority. Of all the gods to call upon to save Athens at the nadir of the Peloponnesian war, Dionysus would not be at the top of the list—especially as he is presented by Aristophanes. The Dionysus of the *Frogs* has no fixed identity on which to base sound judgment: his ludicrous disguise as the tough, masculine Heracles fails to hide his effeminacy, and the masquerade is worn only when it is to his advantage, either to enjoy the reputation of the resilient hero he does not deserve, or to avoid the brunt of the abuse he does deserve. The god of wine, song, and theater abandons his nostalgia for Euripides only after the fear of Zeus is put into him by the chorus of frogs and has his affection for the tragedian quite literally beaten out of him.

If we were to accept Euripides' advice, which Dionysus rejects, namely, "if we now are suffering under the present circumstances, why wouldn't we be saved by doing the opposite?" we should vacate the god's verdict for the curmudgeonly playwright and his ilk (*Frogs* 1448–49). In this retrial, Euripides would maintain an important didactic role in Athenian life. His lessons would still hold true, but in less obvious ways. Aristophanes replaces the initial longing for Euripides with a nostalgia for Aeschylus and the days of yore, only to reinstate the longing for Euripidean wisdom at the end, as if to highlight its importance through its absence. "Viewed from this perspective, the comedy would seem to entrust a great interpretational responsibility to its spectators, who are left to think through for themselves vital questions about their polis and its best interests—and it would thus empower them," and it is "this empowerment" which is perhaps "the ultimate goal of the comedy and its many complications."[37]

---

37   Elizabeth W. Scharffenberger, "'Deinon Eribremetas': The Sound and Sense of Aeschylus in Aristophanes' 'Frogs'," *Classical World* 100 (2007): 229–49, at 249.

Looking at Aristophanes' portrayal of Euripides through the lens of our examination, we see a number of parallels. The references to the everyday nature of Euripidean tragedy reflect the complexity with which plays such as the *Troades* portray the human condition in all its forms, humble and otherwise. The Trojan War is seen from the perspective not of the political leaders and warriors who fought the battle but rather through the personal lamentations of the victims whose everyday existence is shattered.[38] In true "democratic" spirit, Euripides gives voice to those who are not typically heard and acknowledges the polyphonic nature of their contributions. In the *Troades* Euripides performs an act of creative destruction. The disorienting process of identification and distancing among characters and audience develops the ability to reflect on one's own condition and on human affairs generally. Euripides encourages us to contemplate ourselves and others, to become aware of our imperfections, and to develop an appreciation for the fundamental instability of human affairs—all essential requirements for justice. The pull of this profound longing for direction, for order, for peace, and for freedom from absolute necessity, is itself compelling and tenuous, powerful and elusive, edifying and mystifying. Like Plato, Euripides has provided us with profound insight into the Greek soul and places us on the path of political philosophy: *Pathe mathein*.

---

38 Stieber hypothesizes that the "everyday" and "familiar" nature of Euripides' work arises from his frequent use of terminology from the material world, including architecture, art, and various crafts; Stieber, *Euripides and the Language of Craft*, xvii–xviii, 431–33.

The Oedipal Complexity of Plato's *Republic*
Kenneth DeLuca

Plato's *Republic* is about the relationship between and the confluence of knowledge and power or philosophy and politics. It both illuminates and exemplifies political philosophy. It facilitates understanding of political philosophy while drafting the reader into its own political-philosophy building project. It is what it is about. Since the *Republic* is an act of, in addition to being a reflection on, political philosophy, and politics is about taking responsibility or putting things in their place, in the *Republic* nothing is left alone. Couches and meat are not just elements of a more pleasant life, but are root causes of imperialism and of the necessity of a strict merit-based class system;[1] direct discourse is not just a device for making a story seem more vivid, but a vehicle of moral corruption;[2] music and gymnastic are not just forms of entertainment, but essential elements of education.[3] The *Republic* is artificial through and through. In the *Republic* things are vested with significance that the things themselves cannot bear and that were inconceivable at their inception. What is true of the subject matter of the *Republic* is also true of the *Republic*, for what starts out as a sightseeing trip and pilgrimage ends up supplying—after being reworked by Socrates—the material for the most profound meditation on politics of all time.[4] What gets the *Republic* started generates a result so far removed from its point of origin as to make its origin point impossible to know except through what

---

1   372c3–376d3. Platonis, *Rempublicam*, ed. S. R. Slings (New York: Oxford University Press, 2003). All translations are my own.
2   392c7–398b5.
3   376e1–e3.
4   327a1–4. Socrates and Glaucon are at the Peireus to pray to the goddess and to see a novel religious rite.

comes to light at the end. Putting things together seems to necessitate violence against that without which putting things together would have been impossible. This is made evident in ways big and small, at the very beginning and also at the end.

> Having prayed and looked we went off toward town. Then observing us from afar, Polemarchos, the son of Cephalos, on our way back to town commanded his slave to run and tell us to wait. And from behind me the boy grabbing my cloak said, "Polemarchos orders you to wait." And I turned around and asked where he himself was. "There," he said, "coming towards us from behind, just wait." "Certainly we shall wait," Glaucon said. And later by a little Polemarchos came . . . (327b1–c1)

In a sense, this episode kicks off the *Republic*. Socrates' account shows that Polemarchos gets things started, but the intelligibility supplied by Socrates' account of the beginning requires Socrates to impose in reflecting on it what was unknowable in the beginning. Socrates and Glaucon are heading back to town, and Polemarchos and his slave are behind them, as is indicated by Socrates' question to the slave ("And I turned around and asked . . ."). And yet in Socrates' reconstruction of the episode, Socrates establishes Polemarchos' position and what Polemarchos said to his slave before Socrates could see or hear Polemarchos. Socrates presents an account of an episode flavored with an intelligibility it could not have had at first. Socrates in his narration weaves together time-dependent steps of an event and an understanding or interpretation regarding the event that comes later and that makes the event worth narrating. The *Republic*, which supplies an account of political life as the culmination of deliberation and choice, begins not only with a command transmitted to and executed by a slave, but with a command from a man, Polemarchos, who will later defend the proposition that justice is doing good to friends and harm to enemies. And he has no account of what constitutes a friend or enemy. Friends are those wearing the same jersey, and justice demands working against those with different jerseys.[5] Socrates enables us to see here the radical break between the

5   331d4–336a8, especially 334a10–b9, 334d10–e4.

beginning and the end of the *Republic*. It begins with the hollow application of force, and yet somehow ends with an absolutely moral partnership. How is absolute moral agency possible if its beginning is the morally blind and self-serving application of force?[6]

Political life seems to require the overcoming of what exists at first, but it is what exists at first that forms us. According to Socrates' myth of Er, Er dies, sees the afterlife, that is, the whole, and then makes known that every soul chooses a life and on that choice everything rides; however, according to Er, the choice that each soul makes is based on the habituation it received while alive. In other words, in order to really choose, a soul needed to have made the right choice at first.[7] When the chorus in *Oedipus Tyrannus* asserts that Oedipus is a παράδειγμα or paradigm for human beings, the *Republic* helps us see that the chorus is more right than it knows.[8] Political life is a father-beater. Its end is to disown its beginnings. Its end is to begin again. In Greek, the word for rule, αρχη or *arche*, also means beginning. How is it possible to have rule, that is, government, and at the same time be constantly starting over? How could one word house two such seemingly conflicting meanings? Does the *polis* house the same problem? No wonder Socrates never leaves Athens.

It is perhaps not surprising, then, that a problem, which attracts the

---

6 Overcoming what exists at first is a question throughout the *Republic*, and shows up in a variety of forms. For example, in Adeimantus' city how does the city graduate from the private need that drives people to live with one another to a different kind of need, a need for one another? See 372a1–2. And how can these two sorts of need exist side by side? Would not the second kind of need corrupt the workings of the first kind? How are conflicts between the two kinds of need resolved? It does not even occur to Adeimantus to raise these questions, let alone the question of how their conversation could even take place if need were driving motivation to such an extent. Adeimantus' explanation of the world explains everything except his explanation. His explanation is yet another example, then, of the overcoming of what exists at first. See also 1.ii., of Aristotle's *Politics*; and Michael Davis, *The Politics of Philosophy* (Lanham: Roman and Littlefield, 1996), chapter 1.

7 614b1–21d3, and in particular 617e1–e5, 618b3–b4, 618b7–619b1, 619e6–620a3, 620c3–d1.

8 Sophocles, *Oidipous Turannos*, ed. Jeffrey Rusten (Bryn Mawr, PA: Bryn Mawr College, 1990), 48, lines 1193–96.

attention of a Sophocles and shows up in simple political vocabulary, would also be at the core of the *Republic*. In the *Republic* this same conflict gets dramatic representation in the form of the split between Glaucon and Adeimantus. Overcoming this split—the same as that within *arche*—is the plot of Books 2–7. Glaucon represents political life as beginning or freedom or being all you can be; Adeimantus represents political life as rule or order or everything in its place. Glaucon is courage; Adeimantus moderation. Glaucon exemplifies interestedness; Adeimantus disinterestedness. Glaucon gets involved—he makes a case for subjectivity; Adeimantus holds back—he's objective to the core. Both are built for politics, but for opposing reasons.

Politics caters to or perhaps generates Glaucon's premonition that there must be something more to life than mere living. The freedom implicit in the praise and blame of political life, the honor that the polis bestows on heroes, the standards it vaunts, seduce Glaucon into becoming an unknowing disciple of courage metaphysics. The yearning for immortality makes no sense unless it is rooted in immortality, that is, some essence beneath the surface that accounts for agency and makes it possible. Thus, two traits as fundamental to Glaucon as to political life are constantly at work in Glaucon: activism and essentialism. Throughout the *Republic* Glaucon involves himself; he refuses to sit on the sidelines. And Glaucon likes boiling things down to principle; he will not settle for surface description; he wants the thing in itself. What is the connection between these characteristics? The former seems rooted in the particular or selfishness, the latter in the universal. Is Glaucon incoherent and so too political life which Glaucon is standing in for?

Glaucon's activism shows itself almost immediately, as we see above, for after Polemarchos' slave conveys Polemarchos' order that he and Socrates wait, it is Glaucon, not Socrates, who speaks up ("Certainly we shall wait").[9] Glaucon volunteers not only himself but Socrates. And, it is Glaucon, in the very beginning of Book 2—where Socrates says of him,

> For Glaucon always happened to be most courageous towards
> all things (357a2–3)

9   327b7-8. Platonis, *Rempublicam*.

—who intervenes and brings the dialogue and the *Republic* back to life by restoring a reformed version of Thrasymachus' argument that justice is someone else's good, and he does this despite witnessing the trouble Thrasymachus had with it and the mere lip service that Thrasymachus pays the argument in the end.[10] In the very speech Glaucon makes in defense of Thrasymachus' position, Glaucon, unbeknownst to himself shows his activism. In the hypothetical example he creates in defense of injustice, at first he posits that the just man is weak, and his weakness makes him the plaything of the manly just man, but in the end Glaucon rallies to the just man's side, for he portrays him as enduring every kind of torture without abandoning justice.[11] Glaucon cannot even stay on the sidelines of his own hypothetical example.

Glaucon's activism is also at work, and is exploited by Socrates, in the transition from Adeimantus' city, or the city of necessity, to Glaucon's city, or the city of luxury. Glaucon's eruption against Adeimantus' city is orchestrated by Socrates, as is apparent in the way Socrates introduces the city:

> "Now then," I said, "a city comes to be, as I suppose, since each of us happens to be non-autarchic, and instead needs much . . . Come now," I said, "in speech from the beginning (εξ αρχης *ex arches*) let us make a city. Our need, so it seems, shall make it." (369b7–8, 369c9–10)

Need compels people to form a city in which to live and need compels those in the dialogue to form a city from which to learn. Socrates suggests that need is driving both what is going on inside the city in speech and outside it as well. No sooner does Socrates form the city than it teaches him something, namely that need rules everywhere. Although Socrates had with Adeimantus' support determined to make a city back at 369a6–b6, it is only after they "see" that it is being driven by necessity that Socrates establishes

---

10   For Thrasymachus, see 336b1–354c3, and especially, 343a1–a4, 344d1–d4, 346b11–c1, 350c12–d7, 351d6, 351e9, 352b1, 352b4–5, 354a5, 354a10–11. For another example of Glaucon's activism, see 337d6–10.

11   358e3–359c6, 360d1–d7, 360e3–361b8, 361e4–362a2.

that their own making of the city is also the product of necessity (at 369c9–10). The thought that need comes first induces Socrates to conclude that thinking is a need. But if thinking is a need in the sense experienced in the city in speech, the city in speech could not supply a vantage point to reflect on need, for the need behind their creating the city in speech would infect the content of the city in speech.

The need that Socrates finds in, or hypothesizes to be at the root of, the first city gets transformed into a founding principle, that is, that which not only comes first in time, but is first in importance. Socrates' call to found a city in speech at 369c9–10 might be expressed, "Come now . . . let us make in speech a city from principle. Our need, so it seems, shall make it." Need starts out as just what happens, but on reflection becomes a source of pride. And, making an *arche* of need results in a city where need alone rules. The thinking or agency of Socrates and Adeimantus makes thinking or agency unnecessary inside the city in speech, which must vex Glaucon who only moments ago felt the pride of being a co-founder. In any case, as Socrates and Adeimantus proceed and the city in speech takes shape, Socrates makes sure Glaucon does not lose sight of the fact that his name is still on the door:

> "Carpenters, then, and smiths, and many some such workers are becoming partners of the small city with us, making it populous." (370d5–7)
> "And so there is a need of more farmers and other workers by our city." (371a7–8)
> "And what about this in the city itself? How with one another would they exchange each of what they make? For we founded a city making a partnership also for the sake of these very things." (371b5–7)
> "Then, this need," I said, "produces in our city a race of hucksters." (371d4–5)
> "So, then, Adeimantus, has the city for us now grown such as to be complete (*telea*)?" (371e8–9)

One should mention at this point that Greek has a noun declension and verb conjugation system that applies when there is a plurality of two, and here Socrates does not use it, but instead simply uses the plural.[12] In other words, when Socrates speaks of us and ours, there is no doubt that Glaucon is included. As the city of necessity grows, as Socrates and Adeimantus increase its size or insert a new trade, while Adeimantus must derive pleasure in his role of maker, Glaucon cannot, for that which causes its growth merits no praise and makes it impossible to win honor. In this city, the end of every action is supplied by body and the means to that end by art. And, Glaucon with Socrates' help cannot help thinking of himself as one of its citizens. It is Glaucon's involvement in the city that drives him not only to argue against it, but to take umbrage at its very existence. He so loses himself in his contempt for it that he does not see the problematic character of his spirited rebellion against it. In the beginning of Book 2, where Glaucon insists that Socrates find justice to be a type one good, that is, good in and of itself apart from its consequences, Glaucon eschews convention or how things look.[13] The goodness of such an elevated good as justice, he suggests, should not be definable in ordinary coin. However, in rebelling against the first city in speech, Glaucon insists that the city in speech provide meat and furniture.[14] Holding the city of necessity in contempt because everything flows from necessity, all Glaucon can think to do is bless the non-necessary with spiritual significance.

The city in speech was merely supposed to be a bigger place with bigger

---

12 This system is aptly called the dual.

13 See 357d4–358b7. Glaucon so rejects convention or opinion or the seeming that he even—in pursuing justice as a type one good—rejects Socrates' opinion that justice is a type two good— good for itself and its consequences. Glaucon is so committed to the essential truth that despite the fact that Socrates professes justice to be a type two good, he still delegates to Socrates the job of showing justice to be a type one good. Before Socrates introduces the tripartite division of the soul, a version of it is already at work in Glaucon. He thinks being can show itself regardless of opinion. In other words, he thinks Socrates—despite Socrates' opinion that justice is good for itself and its consequences—can reveal the being of justice as good in and of itself apart from its consequences.

14 372d7–8. When Socrates asks, "How it should be?" Glaucon responds, απερ νομιζεται, or *aper nomizetai*, which could be translated, "As things are practiced."

letters, that is, a magnifying glass or vehicle of intelligibility,[15] but Glaucon cannot keep his distance. Getting at things in themselves is showing itself to be more difficult than it seems at first, perhaps because what drove Glaucon to want to know things in themselves at first is now corrupting the thinking required in order to get what he wants. What he wanted was the good unmediated by any terms by means of which to express it. He wants greatness, and true greatness stands only on its own two feet. There is no commensurability between it and other things. Here, it comes to light, with Socrates' help, that when push comes to shove all Glaucon can do is put his longing for greatness in conventional terms. Thus, Socrates shows that while Glaucon is built for politics, in not understanding what makes it interesting for him, in pursuing his ambitions, he will end up with goods even more artificial than the justice chased errantly by the just man of his early Book 2 example. Being all you can be will get replaced by shopping wherever you wish to shop. Instead of being a mad man in pursuit of a nonexistent justice, Glaucon will become a stooge of "mad men."

Although on the surface it appears that Glaucon has sold out or abandoned his idealism, Glaucon is not really interested in consumer goods, as Socrates shows:

> "Then is it necessary for us to cut off the land of neighbors . . .?" (373d7)
> "Quite necessary, Socrates," he said. (373e2)
> "Shall we go to war, then, after this, Glaucon? Or what?" "Exactly," he said. (373e3–4)

As soon as Glaucon takes over, not only is the city in speech what they are making, but it is also something in which they participate.[16] Moreover, with the institution of the guardians, Socrates both brings Glaucon into the city in speech and reforms it in order to make Glaucon feel at home. In the guardians, not only does Socrates find a place for spiritedness—the sort Glaucon just demonstrated in rebelling against Adeimantus's city, but also freedom, for the guardians violate the soul-maiming principle of one

15   368d1–368d7.
16   See also 374e7–10.

man-one art in that they must have absolute discretion. The guardians must not only have the ability to be gentle and savage, but also know when to be the one or the other. The extremes the guardians must make manifest reveal that their essence is not in either of their manifested forms. That they can be what they need to be proves they need be nothing at all. At the end of Book 3, where Socrates describes the proletarian accommodations of the guardians to which Glaucon assents, it becomes clear that while Glaucon seems to want furniture and meat, Socrates sees that what is driving Glaucon's rebellion is not material things but his longing to make manifest his superiority to all things material.[17]

The principle of Adeimantus' city that Glaucon rebels against, that necessity is the basis of justice, gets replaced in Glaucon's city by its negation, that the deprivation of need is the basis of justice. On the wings of this selfless principle, and the thumos that generates it and is generated by it, Glaucon's city, not Adeimantus', holds the potential to become global. Socrates makes clear that Glaucon's city, the city of Mr. Subjectivity, not that of Mr. Objectivity, is universalizable, for it is Glaucon who coins universals having the potential to cross borders. Glaucon's longing to act or participate inspires his essentialism, and his essentialism his longing to participate. In Book 7, after Socrates tells Glaucon that the best natures must not be permitted to remain above in the light, but must go back down into the cave, Glaucon responds:

> Shall we do them an injustice, and make them live worse, a better for them being possible? (519d8–9)

In the beginning of Book 4, in a similar situation, Adeimantus on behalf of the guardians and auxiliaries interrupts Socrates, and raises the issue of whether they are being made happy.[18] Glaucon rises up and intervenes on the basis of an abstract principle; Adeimantus on the basis of experience. Glaucon's argument is buttressed by his assessment of the philosopher-king's virtue or quality of soul. Adeimantus blames the guardians and auxiliaries for letting their idealism get the better of their common

17 See 374e1–376c8; 416d4–417b9.
18 See 419a1–420a2.

sense. Glaucon blames himself and Socrates for transgressing their own principles. Glaucon's nightmare is unused potential, which is rooted in devotion to abstract standards for they produce the worry that one is not living up to them. For Adeimantus, abstract standards are the problem.

Unlike Enlightenment rationalists who take political rights to be the product of pure reason just because they are formulated in the language of geometric corollaries, Socrates suggests that universalistic formulations are connected to the subjective. Glaucon's essentialism—his boiling virtue down to the truth itself—caused his spirited rebellion against Adeimantus' city, and his spiritedness is at work in his demand for boiled-down formulations of virtue of the sort he demonstrates in the beginning of Book 2. Political life fits Glaucon because it provides him with the justification to look down on conventional definitions of happiness, to reject them on behalf of what seems more fundamental, and in formulating a standard that both justifies his rejection and attracts others to the new ideal it articulates, Glaucon redeems himself and other citizens. Political life enables him to earn a reward by violating the law, because his violation is on behalf of a higher standard. Glaucon threatens the polis, but without him political life would degenerate into pure economics.

Socrates overcomes Glaucon's rebellion by involving him in the creation of an office and the search for those worthy of occupying it that makes the city in speech stand for something. For Glaucon, however, laying the groundwork for the realization of this goal gets in the way of the goal. If greatness comes from habituation, then greatness is in the habituation not the man. Adeimantus sees that Glaucon's reforms, which are on behalf of the soul, risk undermining the city, and in turn the soul:

> "Then being bold should we posit also in a human being, if he is going to be towards his own and the familiar a gentle one, it is necessary he be by nature philosophic and learning-loving?"
> "Let us posit," he [Glaucon] said.
> "Philosophic, then, and thumoeidetic, swift and strong for us by nature will be the gentleman going to be a guardian of the city."
> "In every which way indeed," he said.

"This man, however, would begin this way.[19] But in what way exactly shall these men be reared by us and educated? <u>And is our considering this something useful towards perceiving everything for the sake of which we are looking, in what way justice and injustice come to be in a city?</u> Let us not allow our going through a long or ponderous logos."

And the brother of Glaucon said, "very much indeed, I at least look for this consideration to be useful for this." (376c4–d5)

Socrates here appeals to Glaucon's courage, which Glaucon now also finds in the city in speech, in order to get him to accept the reforms they have made. Socrates' question at 376c9–d2, underlined above, is not neutrally phrased but expects a negative answer. The city in speech was supposed to be the most fertile instrument imaginable. It was supposed to produce an understanding of justice, which Glaucon lacked and supposedly wanted. Instead, the city in speech enables Glaucon to wipe out the past and reproduce himself. The no strings attached good-in-itself, which Glaucon demanded, in cutting off the consequences of the good also cuts away terms necessary to make it intelligible. Instead of philosophy or learning-loving standing above the virtue of the guardians, guardian-virtue puts philosophy and learning-loving in its own terms. In doing philosophy, as in being a guardian, one gives expression to one's essence. No superintendence, no habituation, no education allowed. In making a principle out of beginning, the city would never go anywhere.

Concerned that his brother is going to give Socrates a pass and forego the consideration of an education program, Adeimantus intervenes, and in typical fashion. He intervenes while at the same time standing back from his intervention. He does not say education or even that the consideration of education is useful to their inquiry, but merely that it is worth looking into. Whereas political life suits and needs Glaucon because of his activism and essentialism, political life suits and needs Adeimantus because of his objectivity and conventionality. Whereas Glaucon manifests, and through him Socrates reveals, partisanship and the funny form that political partisanship takes, Adeimantus manifests, and through him Socrates reveals, the seemingly opposite quality, that is, remaining on the outside.

19 376c8. "Begin" is *hupo* + *archo*.

Political life, as Glaucon demonstrates, collapses self-interest and self-lessness. The principle coined by and fueling the partisan's activity gives the partisan the look of the zealous defender of justice; however, the principle or justice of the partisan masks the partisan's involvement in his principle and makes it difficult to see that his principle's application causes the other to become the same. Instead of looking toward the good of the other, the partisan makes the other disappear. The city in speech was supposed to be the soul writ large, not Glaucon's soul writ large. The city in speech was supposed to provide Glaucon access to a standard by means of which to transcend himself. Instead, the city in speech becomes the vehicle of his own extension. How does political life avoid generating and applying universals whose application is effective only because they are indifferent or blind to that which they are applied? How does the polis resist becoming the tyranny it thinks it is superior to, but is perhaps worse than since the tyranny it enforces is as invisible as Gyges' ancestor with a turn of his ring? Thumos induces Glaucon to forget himself as he extends himself. Is the thumoeidetic standing in for the ring of Gyges?

In order to address this question, let us turn to a man whose very life supplies a training ground in resistance to, as well as a close-up view of, the tyrannical soul.

> After Glaucon said this, I had in mind to say something towards it, but the brother of him, Adeimantus, said, "you surely do not suppose, Socrates, concerning the logos what has been said suffices?" (362d1–d3)

Adeimantus is identified first as the brother of Glaucon, then by name. Adeimantus is both of his brother and not his brother, for he is his own man. He is not Glaucon, the man who would impose himself on the world, but it is only by knowing what his brother is, that is, being of his brother, and standing outside of himself, that he could have this view.[20] It is as if

20 This is a bit different from how Socrates introduces Adeimatus at the beginning of the *Republic*, where Socrates first gives his name, then mentions that he is the brother of Glaucon (327c1–2), and also from how Socrates introduces Adeimantus later in Book 2, where Adeimantus intervenes to prevent So-

Adeimantus grew up resisting his brother's various thumoeidetic commitments, and over the course of time developed a worldview and ethos that immunized him against this form of ambition. If, as Socrates says, Glaucon was most courageous regarding everything, being brother to such a man must have put Adeimantus in a tough spot. Take flight with his brother and forfeit himself, or stay on the sidelines and forfeit any chance at reputation except as a coward. Rather than cave in to either fear, Adeimantus makes a virtue of necessity and develops a metaphysics of moderation, which is displayed at 362d1–3 (quoted above) where Adeimantus does not mention Glaucon or suggest, à la Thrasymachus, that he is driven by the desire to prove his superiority to him. Instead, Adeimantus takes Glaucon off the hook by separating Glaucon from his action, that is, his speech. Whereas Socrates begins by closely linking Glaucon and his speech in referring to it as what "Glaucon said" and then confessing his intention to speak to it,[21] Adeimantus enables Glaucon to escape without a scratch by dismissing the agency of Glaucon and getting all eyes to focus instead on "what has been said concerning the logos." Glaucon was not able to keep his distance from his logos. Within the confines of his speech or his hypothetical example, no one notices the just man's nobility, but outside his speech Glaucon does, and in noticing it, it is as if Glaucon and the just man make eye contact, and in response the just man buffs himself up one last time for his maker. Glaucon looks to political life as a medium of self-expression, the problematic character of which shows up in the very speech he makes on political

crates' passing over how the guardians are to be reared and educated. Here, Socrates suppresses Adeimantus' name, and only refers to him as the brother of Glaucon (376d4). Since Adeimantus comes in here because he is concerned about pride or keeping the guardians in their place, it is fitting that Socrates suppresses Adeimantus' name. Needless to say, when Glaucon speaks up at the start of Book 2 and in rebellion against the city of pigs, he is introduced as just Glaucon (357a2, 372c3).

21 In referring to Glaucon's speech, Socrates does not simply use the active voice, but a genitive absolute construction. In Attic Greek, genitive absolute constructions occur in order to convey an action that is separate from the central action of the sentence. Here, even though Socrates uses the genitive absolute in order to refer to Glaucon's speaking, it is nevertheless used in an active sense as is indicated by the fact that it here takes a direct object.

life that was intended to show the inherent goodness of political life. Instead it shows the inherent goodness, and therefore the badness, of Glaucon.

Rather than pull a Glaucon on Glaucon, which will only make Glaucon more of what he is, Adeimantus sticks his finger in the chest of Socrates—"Socrates, you certainly do not suppose that what was said concerning the speech to be sufficient." Adeimantus dismisses the agency of Glaucon in his logos, but highlights the agency of Socrates in his sizing up Glaucon's logos. Whereas Glaucon goes astray by climbing inside his own speech, Adeimantus uses Socrates to get him and everyone else outside. As Adeimantus says only moments later, "For it is necessary that we go through also the opposing logoi . . . ."[22] In order to go through speeches opposite to Glaucon's it is necessary to be outside Glaucon's. Glaucon and Adeimantus both make a champion of Socrates, but with respect to opposing virtues. Glaucon sees Socrates as the champion of the boiled-down truth. No sooner does Glaucon get in the ring with Socrates than he uses him as a sounding board for his ειδη or eide, that is, forms, of the good.[23] Socrates is a vehicle for Glaucon's getting to the truth in and of itself. For Adeimantus, however, Socrates is the champion of comprehensiveness or seeing the whole, and the whole can only be seen, or so Adeimantus supposes, from the outside. As the *Republic* makes clear, Adeimantus' approach towards the truth is decidedly different from Glaucon's.

After the city of necessity has been dropped, and Glaucon and Socrates have in mind to introduce the guardians into the city of luxury, Socrates says to Glaucon, in an apparent effort to move things along:

> Then it would be our work, so it seems, if we're able, to choose who and what natures suit for the guarding of the city.

To which Glaucon responds:

> It is ours for sure. (374e7–e10)

22 362e2–3.
23 357c6.

Not only does Glaucon accept the job, or go from a maker of, to a participant in, the city, but in doing so Glaucon does not stop to consider Socrates' question regarding their ability to handle the task. For Glaucon, that the job may exceed their capabilities is merely another reason to accept it. What's the point of success if failure is ruled out in advance?[24] In a similar situation with Adeimantus, Socrates takes, and Adeimantus displays, a different manner:

> "Then, if," I said, "we should watch a city coming to be in speech, would we also see the justice of it coming to be and injustice?"
> "Perhaps," he [Adeimantus] said.
> "Then, it being generated, [is there] a hope to see more easily what we're looking for?"
> "Much more."
> "Does it seem necessary, then, to attempt to bring this about? For I don't suppose it to be a small work. Scope it out then."
> "It's been scoped," said Adeimantus. "Don't do anything else."
> (369a6–b6)

When addressing Glaucon, Socrates draws him in. Socrates suggests that Glaucon and the guardians are joined at the hip. The guardians have a

---

24 See 373d7–374a3 and Glaucon's initial demurral in response to Socrates' pointing out that the new city will need an army: "For what?" he said. "Aren't they sufficient all by themselves." Socrates' pointing out that the city will need an army deflates Glaucon, because Socrates had just pointed out the need to take land from a neighboring city and the likelihood of war, which must cause Glaucon to assume that his new city will enable him to prove himself. However, if an army is to be instituted, Glaucon might as well be back in the city of pigs, for becoming a cog in a war machine is not a ticket to the glory he had in mind. See also 374e11–12 and how Socrates responds to Glaucon's accepting the task of finding guardians: "By Zeus," I said. "It surely is no trivial business we're engaged in. But, nevertheless, cowardice is not an option, as much at least as our power would allow." Needless to say, Glaucon agrees. Socrates makes the courage now becoming necessary in the city in speech even more attractive to Glaucon by suggesting that it causes Socrates and Glaucon to make manifest their own courage.

difficult job to do on which everything rides, and so does Glaucon. When addressing Adeimantus, Socrates makes Adeimantus relish being on the outside looking in. With Adeimantus, Socrates gives stress not to doing, but to looking. He offers Adeimantus a bird's-eye view of the genesis of a city. Adeimantus does not want in, because only from the outside is one uninfected by what is incapable of being regulated from the inside, and only so long as one remains uninfected can one see what is there. Whereas with Glaucon, the other or what Glaucon is looking at is always at risk of becoming his extension; with Adeimantus, what he is looking at is at risk of becoming absolutely other, so that the understanding it yields cannot account for Adeimantus himself. With Glaucon, agency takes over; with Adeimantus, it disappears. In the passage above, the only active verbs are those having to do with looking or infinitives in which no agent of the infinitive is present.[25] Glaucon owns, whereas Adeimantus disowns, the city in speech which he and Socrates are crafting, and which Socrates goes out of his way to induce Adeimantus to accept as his:

> "It must not be accepted, according to your argument."
> "If you," he [Adeimantus] said, "wish to make it mine." (389a6–b1)

Not only does Adeimantus resist ownership of the city in speech, he also resists ownership of his own speech:

> And Adeimantus interrupting said, "How, then, Socrates, would you respond, if someone should say . . ." (419a1–2)
> And Adeimantus said, "Socrates, with respect to these things

25 One might argue that Adeimantus' use of the imperative at 369b6 is an exception, but Adeimantus' "do (ποιει or poiei) nothing else," which employs an active verb, must refer to examining the city as it comes to be, not making the city, for the context posits that the city is not made, but instead emerges on its own. Also, see Book 4, where Socrates is again addressing Adeimantus, "For sure," I said, "the regime if once well originated, rolls on in its growth just like a wheel." (424a5–6) This is part of Socrates' attempt to calm down Adeimantus who distrusts agency. He suggests to Adeimantus that virtue is in the structure, not the man, which is the opposite of Glaucon's point of view.

no one would be able to speak against you, however what they
experience every time they hear what you're now saying is such:
they believe . . ." (487b1–3)
"And now someone might say to you . . ." (487c4–5)

Adeimantus makes the leap of assuming that just because he is not Glaucon
he can be anyone. Adeimantus harnesses the particular experience of resisting one man's all-in commitments enabling him to develop a modus operandi
for resisting commitments as such; and, resisting commitments, remaining
on the outside, gives him access to everyone else's inside. In attempting to
amend his brother's speech at the beginning of Book 2, Adeimantus confesses that the goal of the speech that he is about to make is:

> . . . in order that what Glaucon seems to me to want would be
> more clear. (362e4–5)

Adeimantus has in mind not what he wants, but what Glaucon wants, which
the speech that Glaucon just made did not make sufficiently clear.
Adeimantus will make a speech whose goal is to make what Glaucon wants
more clear, which presupposes that he knows what Glaucon wants.
Adeimantus has no position of his own; he is disinterested; he is on the
outside of Glaucon's speech. And being on the outside of Glaucon's speech,
Adeimantus can see what his speech left out, in part because being on the
outside of interestedness, that is being disinterested, enables him to gauge
how Glaucon's interestedness threw him off. Interestedness causes a disjunction between what Glaucon made and what Glaucon intended in making what he made. Glaucon's interestedness, then, gets in the way of his
craving for honor, because it causes a disjunction between his intentions
and his actions, and gets in the way of his claiming the effects of those actions as his own. In fixing Glaucon's speech, Adeimantus is putting Glaucon
in a position to take credit for it. Adeimantus suggests that without him
Glaucon cannot be who he thinks he is.

In Book 8, where Socrates is providing an account of the stages of decay
of the best regime, Socrates with respect to timocracy asks, "Who, then, is
the man belonging to this regime? How generated and what sort of man is
he," which immediately induces Adeimantus to reenter the dialogue:

"I suppose he's a somewhat close approximate of Glaucon right here, at least with respect to love of victory." (549d6–9)

Adeimantus knows what makes Glaucon tick. His taking the flight of Glaucon-dissector, as it were, went hand in hand with his resisting being taken for a ride by Glaucon's ambition. Rather than succumb to the love of victory, Adeimantus instead learns to become a lover of victory over the love of victory and all self-forfeiting loves.[26] Knowing ticks immunizes him from falling prey to ticks; however never falling prey to ticks, that is, never embracing anything in particular, induces Adeimantus to treat others as mere tick-followers. Adeimantus universalizes himself through particularizing everyone else. Having been spawned by an awareness of, and categorically rejecting, his brother's tyrannizing loves, Adeimantus becomes the personification of a form of tyranny just as powerful and universalizable and exploitable by the polis as that of his brother.

Whereas Glaucon's tyranny derives from his drive to get at the truth in itself, Adeimantus' derives from his eschewing that form of truth in favor of what seems:

> Therefore, since to seem (δοκεῖν or dokein), as the wise make manifest, ravishes the truth and lords over happiness, directly towards it one must wholly turn. (365c1–3)

Just as Glaucon's activism is connected to his essentialism, so Adeimantus' objectivity is connected to the seeming or the manifest, or what we might call the conventional. On the one hand, from the vantage point of the observational heights that Adeimantus assumes, the seeming is all Adeimantus can see. On the other hand, the motive behind his seizing such ground from which to see suggests that the seeming is the only thing there is to see. How could tick-driven beings gain access to or be driven by the truth in itself? Adeimantus' judgment that this form of truth is

---

26 That Adeimantus loves this form of victory is suggested by his proud reentry into the dialogue right at the moment that Socrates asks the question about love of victory.

out of human beings' reach is perhaps what justified his abstracting from and rising above the various commitments of particular human beings in the first place. And, his rejection of this form of truth, in turn, buttresses his turn to categorizing or rule-making or what in political life takes the form of legislating. Since the truth in itself is not accessible to human beings, human beings are pure particulars, and as pure particulars, they require regulation from the outside. In order to become agents of their own advancement, they must be molded, or habituated to accept, political communities.

It is this very aspect of Adeimantus' understanding that Socrates has in mind when Socrates christens the city in speech:

> Then, is it decreed/does it seem (δοκει or dokei) necessary to attempt to bring this about?[27] (369b4)

In beginning the city in speech this way, Socrates is speaking Adeimantus' as well as conventional language, for he announces that the city in speech is the product of a seeming or what is equivalent to a seeming, that is, a legislating. Legislating does not assert that it penetrates to the internal essence or truth of that over which it legislates. What is enacted is not true, it is in fact synonymous with what seems. That when dokein is used the double-ness of its meaning is typically not seen merely supports the wisdom of the word, for not even the truth in itself of the word is seen. The truth-fulness or the belonging-together of the two meanings of dokein is not a thing seen, but rather only a seeming.

That political life takes this word and drafts it into its campaign of legitimacy reflects the wisdom coursing through political life; however, as the *Republic* makes clear, through Adeimantus, once the seeming is armed with a political mission, there is no containing it.

> "Then, right here," I said, "in music is where the guardians must build the guardian-watch-house, as it seems."

27 δοκειν or dokein not only means to seem, but also it is decreed or enacted. It is a term of Attic jurisprudence.

"At any rate," he [Adeimantus] said, "this law-breaking easily slinks in furtively."

"Yea," I said, "as partaking in a game and as doing nothing bad."

"For it doesn't," he said, "other than at any rate little by little it sets up shop quietly flowing unperceived into the temperaments and practices, and from there it migrates to greater things, the contracts towards one another, and from the contracts surely it works upon the laws and regimes with much, Socrates, licentiousness, until it reaches its end overthrowing all things with respect to the private and the public."

"Well, now," I said, "so this holds?"

"It seems to me," he said. (424c8–d5)

Adeimantus, moments ago (in Book 2) stood outside his brother; he knows, cares for, his brother, and volunteers himself for superintendence over his brother's ambition. Here, he does the same for all men. The *Iliad* corrupted Glaucon, so he holds music responsible for the corruption of the rational project of political life. Poetry stokes a desire, it plants a seed, it creates an ambition, without putting the ambition it plants under review, let alone setting up institutions for its realization or squaring these institutions with the time-tested institutions already in existence. As we have seen, Adeimantus puts great stock in seeing or oversight, and here we see that Adeimantus has a problem with music because its effects are impossible to oversee, for they operate in the soul. Both Glaucon and Adeimantus want to make the soul visible, which in effect is what the city in speech is, but for different reasons. For Glaucon it is so that he can make manifest who he is; for Adeimantus it is so that he can subject it to regulation. So swept away, here, is Adeimantus in his ambition to put to good use his oversight that he does not pause to consider how his own soul was acted upon by music, or how he is able to see that which is so good at avoiding detection let alone how it may have corrupted his vision. Music works its way up the ladder from the most particular, that is, from the furtive longings, to the most universal, that is, to the *nomoi* and *politeia*, but cannot make it all the way up to a-daimonic Adeimantus. Socrates' daimon, his private voice, keeps him in the private realm and keeps him alive. Socrates' daimon emerges from the particular, and preserves the particular, and in an irony of ironies supports a public good and a truth.[28] A-daimonic Adeimantus, on the other hand, as his name suggests, lacks such a voice, so there is no containing Adeimantus' appetite for oversight. Adeimantus' name can also mean "without fear."[29]

Socrates draws Glaucon in to the city in speech by creating the office of guardian, φυλακη or phylakei, but in drawing Glaucon in, Socrates also draws in Adeimantus, who is uncomfortable on the inside because he does not like what he sees or experiences there. By introducing the guardians, Socrates solves his Glaucon problem, but creates an Adeimantus problem. According to Adeimantus, the guardians have way too much discretion and way too little fun. The viability of the office depends on an impossible fusion of Achilles and Odysseus: the love of glory and contempt of convention of the former combined with the knack for happiness and the dexterity in the support of institutions of the latter. Adeimantus must wonder what would happen if the image the guardians are enthralled by should lose its grip or come apart at the seams, or should another come along that attracts them, for what they get is so way out of line with what they give as to cause a rebellion all by itself and certainly cannot be counted on to keep them in line. The guardians look after the city, have all the strength, and get almost nothing; the citizens get almost everything, look after only themselves, and are weak. This generates excitement in Glaucon, but anxiety in Adeimantus, for he is no guardian in Glaucon's sense of the term and has reason to worry about his prospects if things go awry. Socrates solves the Adeimantus

---

28   The truth it results in is that life is good, for his daimon enables him to draw the conclusion that should he enter public life he will surely die. In holding him back, the daimon points to the goodness of Socrates' staying alive, for Socrates and for the city, which benefits from those Socrates exhorts to tend to their souls. Plato, *Apology*, ed. Gilbert Rose (Bryn Mawr, PA: Bryn Mawr College, 1989), 30c2–32a3.

29   Δεμαινω or deimaino means "to be afraid." Adeimantus' name is, or is close to, the alpha privative of this word. Also, δειματος or deimatos is the genitive of a noun meaning fear, thus a-deimatos would mean "the lack of fear." Adeimantus' name might also mean "the seer of the unnecessary" or "the not-subject-to-the necessary seer": δει (dei) "necessity" + μαντις (mantis) "seer" or "diviner," that is, α+ δει+ μαντις or a+dei+mantis. Like moderation itself, Adeimantus' name is an alpha privative of great versatility. It suggests distance from the gods, necessity, and fear. Like moderation, Adeimantus stands out for what he lacks.

problem in two ways. First, he limits the guardians' discretion, as is evident in Socrates' account of the guardians' new responsibility, "the guardians must/it is necessary for the guardians."[30] Socrates brings back necessity. Second, Socrates gets Adeimantus back on the outside of the city in speech looking in by giving stress not to what the guardians must do, but what they must see. In Greek, what the guardians must build is a φυλακτηριον or phylakteirion, "guard station," but more literally "a guardian-observation post." The second half of the word, that is, τηριον, means "to watch" or "observe," and emphasizes the need for the guardians to surveil, which is clearly necessary given the problem that Socrates has Adeimantus thinking about. When the guardians were introduced, the problem was reconciling opposites: being a friend to insiders, but an enemy to outsiders. In order to get Adeimantus back on the outside, Socrates now introduces—in the form of music—an enemy on the inside, and since music, in addition to being the enemy within, is used to educate the guardians, Adeimantus deems it necessary to rise above poetry as well as the city in speech, for only if one is above poetry can one both judge and avoid falling prey to it. In getting Adeimantus outside the city in speech by turning poetry into the enemy, Socrates induces Adeimantus to treat the city in speech, not as a poetic instrument of intelligibility—which is what it was at first, but as a seeming, that is, a real-world phenomenon. Having discredited poetry, Adeimantus has no reason not to take the city in speech literally, which he no sooner does than exploits as he assumes the role of moral policeman of the world. On behalf of moderation, Adeimantus gets rid of the poets, but turns history into poetry pregnant with teachings uncorrupted by human hands and which objective eyes need only read.[31]

---

30 See page 81 above in this chapter, and 424d1 where Socrates tellingly uses the verbal adjective construction, οικοδομητεον τοις φυλαξιν or oikodo-meiteon tois phylaxin, "the guardians must build." Verbal adjective constructions convey necessity in such an abstract way that it is not necessary to express either the source of the necessity or its agent. It is as if the guardians are taking orders from the "facts of life." From 424a–425a, Socrates uses three verbal adjectives (424b2, 424c4, 424e7) and *dei*, "it is necessary," twice (424a1, 424c2).

31 Socrates both responds to and facilitates Adeimantus' elevation of the seeming at 424c3–4, where he derives a real world truth, through reflecting on the city

For Adeimantus, the city in speech goes from a vehicle for making universally intelligible what is right to doing what is universally right, which for Adeimantus means fixing the law, so in the same breath as Adeimantus makes an other of poetry he makes an ally of Socrates, "Socrates, it [poetry] works against the laws and regimes with much licentiousness until it reaches its end overthrowing all things public and private."[32] Right in the middle of his indictment of poetry on a charge of licentiously spreading licentiousness or causing absolute lawlessness, Adeimantus addresses Socrates—employing the vocative case—and attempts to pull Socrates outside his critique in order to enlist his help, for he needs a man whose vision is as comprehensive as the problem he aims to solve. Whereas Glaucon longs to bind with the guardians—virtue doers, Adeimantus longs to bind with Socrates—a virtue observer. The guardians are Glaucon's ticket to the ultimate in action within the ultimate city; whereas Socrates is Adeimantus' ticket to the most objective reform of the most universal problem. Though Adeimantus has his sights on the world, his indictment of poetry suggests that he is in no position to police the one or the other, for his indictment comes right out of *Oedipus the King*. Adeimantus is as much poetry's creature as any city. In putting himself above poetry, in making an other of it, Adeimantus is blind to its effects on himself. Moreover, in assuming his morals make him immune to poetry, Adeimantus almost immediately is induced by Socrates to moralize. Socrates easily induces Adeimantus to blame those who fall prey to the irresistible lie, that is, poetry, rather than the liars, the poets, for exemplifying the very quality Socrates says Adeimantus exemplifies himself. Socrates chastises Adeimantus for being harsh, χαλε-πος or chalepos, almost immediately after, and in part because, Adeimantus criticizes the poetry-duped for being χαλεπος.[33] In order to achieve

in speech, that a strange form of music puts in jeopardy the whole. Not only does Socrates set up Adeimantus' treating the city in speech as a font of practical wisdom, but he also sets up Adeimantus' elevating himself above the poets. For the truth that Socrates derives, Socrates goes out of his way to show that it originates in his taking issue with the interpretation of an excerpt from the *Odyssey*. Socrates, in fact, does not even subordinate himself to Homer for he rewords the excerpt from the Odyssey that he uses.

32   424e1–2.
33   426b3, 426e3.

objectivity, Adeimantus places himself outside what he is looking at. In order to know, Adeimantus makes what he is looking at other. Adeimantus becomes disinterested, but not completely, for he is interested in knowing. Is Adeimantus' knowledge the product of his disinterestedness, or his disinterestedness or otherness the product of his interest in knowing? In other words, does his interest in knowing turn the same into the other? As it turned out, and as we saw above, Adeimantus is just like those he thought he knew and thought were other. One also wonders whether Adeimantus' equating the knowable with the seeming or what is on the surface or what we have labeled "the real world" is in the service of that same interest. That which has a nature in and of itself might also require being looked at in accordance with that nature and resist the artifice of the legislative mind. Is Adeimantus' privileging of the real world blind to the real?

After Glaucon's speech, in the beginning of Book 2, in defense of injustice ends but before Adeimantus jumps in with his correction of Glaucon, Socrates—in a passage we touched on above[34]—confesses, "Glaucon having said these things, I had in mind to say something towards this," but after Adeimantus' Glaucon correction ends, Socrates never discloses what that something was. Socrates drops what he had in mind to say and instead agrees after being egged on by the crowd to building a city in speech.[35] Evidently, what Adeimantus says "towards this" induces Socrates to change his mind. In correcting Glaucon, Adeimantus introduces an error or perspective which must persuade Socrates that his original correction of Glaucon will come at the expense of Adeimantus. Socrates is in a pickle. One brother is a political zealot in the making, the other a scold. Showing Glaucon his moral hypocrisy will only make Adeimantus more a scold. On the other hand, showing Adeimantus the artificiality of his commitments will only make Glaucon more a zealot. As Socrates suggests, immediately after Adeimantus' speech ends, their thinking on justice has suddenly become a proving ground of justice, and most of all for Socrates because he is running the show.[36] Thinking has become a form of action, an activity worthy of praise and blame, which is to be judged for its consequences and prized for

34   See page 74 above in this chapter.
35   362d1–2.
36   See 367e5–368cd4.

what it reveals about its agent. Thinking has become political, and so Socrates assigns it the most important of political tasks, forming a polis in thought. While this polis in thought, in theory, has the potential to illuminate and benefit everyone, in practice it is meant for just Glaucon and Adeimantus. The polis in thought will enable Socrates to get the brothers to look away from, and leave unguarded, their most deeply held opinions while harnessing these opinions in the building of the city. Socrates lucked out, however, for Glaucon and Adeimantus are not just any two men. Under one roof "sons of the best" have been born, bred, and raised, who not only split excellence down the middle, but develop their respective excellences in concert.[37] Embedded in the thought behind the perspective of each is an answer to a question posed by the other. They are, as it were, two ειδη or eide, that is, "forms," of a divine genus.[38]

The working out of these two forms as the city is being built supplies the *Republic* with a structure and a plot. Every interruption by one is a sign that the other guy and his perspective have gone too far and are in need of correction. These points of contact, these dramatizations of mini-political theory wars, help us see what we perhaps had not noticed or thought about deeply enough. The collisions and reconciliations of Glaucon and Adeimantus, whose arguments are souped-up by Socrates, reflect the difficulty of housing these fundamental, and fundamentally opposed, perspectives under one political roof. Their arguments are as essential to political life as they are essentially different from one another. So argue they must, but the arguing stops in Book 7. Books 2–6 all feature an interruption or a seizing of the mic. But not Book 7. Book 6 ends with Glaucon and Book 7 ends with Glaucon, and there is no Adeimantus in between. As Socrates and Glaucon are putting the finishing touches on the city in speech, Adeimantus keeps quiet.

37 See 368a4, "Sons of Ariston," Glaucon and Adeimantus' father is meant, but αριστος or aristos means "best" in Greek.

38 After mentioning their father, the poem of Glaucon's lover— the beginning line of which Socrates quotes at 368a4—proceeds as follows, κλεινου θειον γενος ανδρος or kleinou theion genos andros, "divine offspring of a famous man." Γενος also means genus. In other words, it is as if Glaucon and Adeimantus are the two forms or ideas into which the genus of political excellence breaks down.

By the time Book 7 arrives, the fighting has ended. The debate is over. Glaucon and Adeimantus and their perspectives have been reconciled. Glaucon has what he wants, as the opening line suggests:

> "After these things, then," I said, "liken [or: make an image of] the nature of ours regarding education and lack of education to such an experience." (514a1–2)

The image of the cave is made to order. Glaucon has or thinks he has the essence or nature of truth and also ignorance. He has the truth in itself, not a vague segue between ignorance and truth. Enlightenment is a threshold-crossing event. Moreover, truth does not emerge out of ignorance. Truth dawns on you. It is not contingent on a proper upbringing or education program. The image suggests that truth has no father. There is just tolerating the pain that comes with illumination.[39] Learning is a test of manliness. Glaucon perhaps likes the image so much that he does not pause to ask how their own understanding of understanding can be trusted given the fact that they have not crossed the threshold of any cave. That he does not ask the question confirms Socrates' observation they are like those in, not out of, the cave,[40] and that the cave image of learning is problematic. If crossing the threshold is not necessary for them, why is it necessary for others?

And Adeimantus has what he wants too. The image of the cave explains ignorance as well as knowledge, and the necessary continuation of the former as well as the subordination of those with the former to those with the latter. The image of the cave is just the kind of story a polis needs to justify objectivity and rational superintendence. The image even suggests that the knowers are in need of rational superintendence, for someone will have to shepherd them through the various stages of illumination or the customization process. Knowers will need to be inculcated in certain habits.[41]

39 For example, see 515c8.
40 515a5.
41 See 516a5–b3. See also 520a6–d5, where Socrates responds to a Glaucon question similar to one Adeimantus asks at the beginning of Book 4, and provides an answer that must be music to Adeimantus' ears, for it argues for the de-

Philosopher-kings only seemingly rule. In reality, custom or what has been decreed will rule, that is, it seems will rule.

That Glaucon and Adeimantus are reconciled in the end seems to go along with the city in speech's success. The city in speech reconciles the demand of the virtuous to make manifest their virtue with the city's demand that the virtuous subordinate themselves to the law. It truly is the city of the "idea of the good" for it supplies absolute intelligibility—or the idea—as well as absolute happiness—or the good. It solves the problem of justice. The Holy Grail has been found!

But then Oedipus shows up. At first Oedipus shows up inconspicuously in a mirror where Socrates is talking about how the truth outside the cave will first be observed in shadows, and then in reflective pools of water, and from there eventually the very source of that truth will be taken in, that is, the sun and the light of the sun. To which Glaucon responds, "πως δ' ου" or pos d' ou, "certainly."[42] In order to see Oedipus here, we need to ask a question Glaucon should have just asked but does not. When the just-released cave-dwellers see images in water, won't they be thrown off by the reflection reversal effect, that is, in a mirror right looks left? Seeing causes one to mis-see, unless the seer thinks about what is seen. But how will a just-released cave-dweller know to do that? Seeing requires one to know the problematic character of sight, which neither the cave-dweller nor Glaucon nor Oedipus see.

If we take a bird's-eye view of Plato's dialogue and Sophocles' play, the fact that Oedipus shows up in Book 7 is not surprising given the similar paths the *Republic* and *Oedipus the King* take. Both works begin with an affront to justice; both works feature heroes of thought, who put their knack for the truth in the service of justice; both works presuppose harmony between truth, justice, and happiness (that is, both works presuppose that the truth is good); in both works, from within the longing for justice emerges a longing for an understanding of self that ends up splitting the truth and

---

pendence of the philosophers on habituation and ends by disclosing that the city in speech yields a practical truth that can be boiled down to this: moderation is best. That Socrates answers a Glaucon question with an Adeimantus answer reflects the level of reconciliation that has occurred.

42 See 516b4.

the good (as is suggested by the fact that in the end both Glaucon and Oedipus are kicked out of their own cities, not despite, but precisely because they have illuminated justice); in both works truth and authority come together; and both works insinuate that the political man is a tyrant. Oedipus as well as Glaucon and Adeimantus begin as useful men who want truth, and end up with a truth they can't use.

The connection between the two works is not only visible from a distance, but up close in the fine print, especially towards the end of Book 7:

> First, then, I said, it is necessary for the one undertaking it not to be a gimp in labor-loving . . . (535d1–2)
> Then, for us, I said it is necessary of all such things to take good care, since if we educate the sound of limb . . . (536b1–3)
> For instance, I said, if some fake child reared in much wealth and also in a great family and with many flatterers, and then becoming a man should hear that he is not of these reputed-to-be parents, and can't discover his parents in reality, . . . (537e9–538a3)

There is an old saying, "once maybe, twice never," and if this holds it would be foolish not to think that Socrates has in mind and is pointing us to Sophocles. Perhaps, to persuade the still skeptical reader, we might point out that amid these veiled references to Oedipus, Socrates admits to allowing, in Oedipus-like fashion, thumos to get the better of him, not because the polis is being disrespected, which sets Oedipus off, but because philosophy is being disrespected. But this is a distinction without a difference, because philosophy has become political-philosophy.[43] And, in the end both works claim to supply a "παράδειγμα" or paradeigma, that is, a paradigm. In the *Republic*, this paradigm manifests itself in the city in speech;[44] in *Oedipus the King*, in Oedipus—whom the chorus calls a paradigm for man.[45]

So, taking our cues from the *Republic* we end with a new beginning. How does the *Republic* develop or perhaps disagree with *Oedipus the King*?

43 536c1–c5.
44 540a4–540c2, especially 540a7–b1.
45 See line 1193 and context.

How would putting the works together make both more clear, and teach us something we did not already know? Sophocles thinks he has discovered the paradigmatic tragic figure in Oedipus. Does Socrates disagree? Is political life itself tragic, because it fosters virtues that culminate in their own suppression? Since Oedipus is an idiosyncrasy, he cannot truly be a paradigm. The same cannot be said of the city in speech.[46]

This paper was originally presented at the 2013 Annual Meeting of the American Political Science Association, August 29–September 1, 2013; reprinted with permission of the APSA.

---

46 One might ask, if *Oedipus the King* is so crucial to understanding the *Republic* why does the *Republic* make so little use of it, as compared with its use of Homer's *Iliad* and *Odyssey*? Why does it show up on the sly? But, does the *Republic* really use the *Iliad* and *Odyssey*, or subject these works to its own mission? The argument of *Oedipus the King* is visible in the *Republic*. Can one say the same for the arguments of the *Iliad* and *Odyssey*? The *Republic* more abuses than uses these works, but with the best of intentions.

Images of Soul in Nietzsche:
Prelude to Sublime Metaphor
Paul E. Kirkland

It may seem strange to treat images of soul in Nietzsche's thought. Nietzsche appears to reject the very notion of a soul by denying any unity or coherence to particular lives and by rejecting the sort of oppositions that would allow soul to stand distinct from other kinds of things (see, e.g., *BGE* 19, 2).[1] Debates about agent and deed and Nietzsche's naturalism have recently questioned the possibility of an account of soul in Nietzsche that cannot be reduced to a "naturalistic" one in which scientific methodology is adequate for determining explanations for morality and everything we might call soul.[2] By contrast with Leiter's naturalism, Clark's view maintains that a normative element is crucial to Nietzsche's presentation of soul in *Beyond Good and Evil*, one that enlivens the tension through which Nietzsche accounts for human life and goals.[3] As such arguments have pushed Nietzsche scholarship past a stage where it was content to speak of

---

1   I have used the following abbreviations for citations of Nietzsche's works: *BGE: Beyond Good and Evil; BT: The Birth of Tragedy; EH: Ecce Homo; GM: On the Genealogy of Morals; GS: The Gay Science; PTA: Philosophy in the Tragic Age of the Greeks; TI: Twilight of the Idols.*

2   See Robert Pippin, "Lightning and Flash: Agent and Deed (GM I:6–7)," in *Nietzsche's* On the Genealogy of Morals: *Critical Essays*, ed. Christa Davis Acampora (New York: Rowman and Littlefield, 2006), 131–46; Christa Davis Acampora, "On Sovereignty and Overhumanity: Why it Matters How we Read Nietzsche's *Genealogy* II.2," in Nietzsche's On the Genealogy of Morals, ed. Davis, 147–62.

3   Brian Leiter, *Nietzsche and Morality* (New York: Routledge, 2002); Maudemarie Clark and David Dudrick, *The Soul of Nietzsche's* Beyond Good and Evil (New York: Cambridge, 2012).

metaphors and literary analogies,[4] possibilities for an aesthetic understanding of soul in Nietzsche's thought have been neglected. This essay examines the way in which Nietzsche's view of will to power, especially as developed in Part One of *Beyond Good and Evil*, draws from ancient philosophy and enlivens images of soul that address its relationship to the whole.

Nietzsche's *Beyond Good and Evil* announces itself as a book concerning morality and it appears to open with questions of an epistemological character; yet, by the end of Part One he has declared that psychology will once again be the path to the fundamental problems (*Grundproblemen*). In a sense, the psyche is the vital subject of *Beyond Good and Evil* and especially its first Part. Indeed the question with which the main text begins, "What in us wants truth?" is already fundamentally a psychological question. It is a question about drives in "us" as much as it is about truth. It is about philosophy as a way of life and thus also about soul. As Nietzsche offers *Beyond Good and Evil* as a *Prelude (Vorspeil) to Philosophy of the Future*, it turns out that soul and the character of philosophy are intimately connected. The prelude (*Vorspeil*) treats the text as if it is a kind of musical work, one that will attune as much as it will describe, marking its attention to element of soul and its drives not wholly identified with rational understanding.

Describing the book as preliminary to something that will emerge as philosophy in the future and ending Part One with the expectation of a restoration wherein psychology "once again" becomes the path to fundamental problems introduces an odd array of time elements. On the one hand, Nietzsche rejects the past in the name of the future. On the other, he appears to welcome a return of the past. What past? When was psychology the path to fundamental problems? Was this before philosophers became prejudiced? What is the relation between the recovery of that past and the philosophy of the future? What is the relation between the prelude and the consideration of the past? He suggests four timeframes: a past when psychology had its proper place, a period of the prejudices of philosophers,

---

4   For prominent examples, see Alexander Nehamas, *Nietzsche: Life as Literature* (Cambridge: Harvard University Press, 1985); Sarah Kofman, *Nietzsche and Metaphor*, tr. Duncan Large (Stanford: Stanford University Press, 1994); Gilles Deleuze, *Nietzsche and Philosophy*, tr. Hugh Tomlinson (New York: Columbia University Press, 1983).

the present, and a time for future philosophy. Even as it becomes question-able that we should maintain the notion of a sequence, it becomes note-worthy that the first and last have the common priority of the soul. The present understood as a prelude suggests that the look to the future may be characteristic of philosophy well understood, rather than something that will emerge only at some future date.

On first glance, Nietzsche would seem to be calling for new psychology and answering the fundamental question about the nature of soul by calling it will to power. Part One of *Beyond Good and Evil*, however, tears down any assurance of any kind of unity called "soul," to which "will to power" could be attributed. To call soul will to power begs the question of the defi-nition, the boundary, of soul. The claims Nietzsche makes in Part One of *Beyond Good and Evil* about will to power as the fundamental characteristic of philosophy, life, nature, and the soul would also appear to answer the opening question of the book—What in us wants truth? Will to power wants truth. Such a statement stands in need of unpacking. The answer falls apart as it is stated. Does the will to power mean the soul wants truth for the sake of power? Does it mean that it wants power regardless of whether it has truth (occasionally deluding itself among prejudiced philoso-phers about a desire for truth)? Moreover, we still would need to ask what the entity is that wants truth. Something wants truth, it is moved by will to power, but so is everything else, and there is not a good reason to at-tribute this to any being that we can call soul. Whether Nietzsche invites us to think that some will to power wants truth or that the will to truth is an illusion of the will to power, he leads us to the conclusion that philosophy is always moved by will to power. Instead of a full explanation of the mean-ing of this claim, Nietzsche points to the question of psychology. A psy-chology of will to power does not answer the question of what it is that wants truth unless we assume some discrete and unified soul and will that is independent and free, a prejudice Nietzsche explicitly rejects (*BGE* 12).

Nietzsche introduces the will to power as the character of philosophy, asserting that philosophy is the "most spiritual will to power" (*BGE* 9). This claim raises more problems than it solves. Yes, Nietzsche says that real drive of philosophy is the will to power, but it is a will to power of a par-ticular kind, the most spiritual (*geistigste*). If all nature is moved by will to power (*BGE* 22) how can one kind be the most spiritual? How can any kind of will to power be distinct at all? Is will to power a material or spiritual force? It would appear to be both, an answer that would overcome dualism and the prejudice of opposites.[5] Soul would have to be understood in this continuum, capable of spiritual possibilities including the most spiritual as part of its range. The possibility of strictly defining soul vanishes just as it become clear that philosophy will be a needed part of getting at soul.

Before he directly addresses nature and soul, Nietzsche simply declares that *life* is will to power (*BGE* 13). Will to power names the animating drive. Life is will to power and not will to life or preservation. For life to be what it is, it needs to be animated and directed toward something other than itself. Calling life will to power is another way of saying that life reaches beyond itself and that is its fundamental character to do so. Yet, describing this reaching beyond as will to power leaves its character radically indeterminate. It reaches beyond itself but perhaps toward nothing in particular. Power in the abstract is pure potentiality, not a teleological aim.

With will to power as an indeterminate characterization of life's motion and as the fundamental nature of philosophy, Nietzsche starts to get at soul in its complexity. Will to power emerges as the common source of animation and thinking. To say that the two have a common source suggests both the possibility of and the difficulty of self-awareness. Insofar as the animating force and thinking are features of the same thing, will to power, they are not permanently sealed off from one another. Yet, as they are the same, it is not clear how there can be sufficient distance for thinking to see its own animating drive and thereby approach self-knowledge. In this distance and its difficulty, soul emerges as the problematic togetherness of its elements. As Nietzsche presents this problem in *Beyond Good and Evil*, it becomes focused on the difficulty of how it is possible to conceive philosophical life, and he sets up the problem of psychology such that it will have to preserve life and thought in something recognizable as living philosophy.

5   See Laurence Lampert, *Nietzsche's Task* (Chicago: University of Chicago Press, 2001), 57, on the relationship among the occurrences of "will to power" in accounting for philosophy, life, nature, and psychology, and their order in the first part of *Beyond Good and Evil*.

In light of the difficulty of holding philosophy and life together, Nietzsche treats the problematic way in which soul has been treated as he prepares the way for new soul concepts. In the central section of Part One, Nietzsche treats new and old soul concepts in the context of treating atomism. Nietzsche launches aphorism 12 from the theory of "materialistic atomism" and proceeds to address "soul atomism" as it has been taught by Christianity. He cites Boscovich and then demands going further to the point of making war on the "more calamitous atomism which Christianity has taught best and longest, soul atomism" (*BGE* 12). The concept of the soul as a unity is the afterlife of a doctrine that preserves the indivisibility of the soul in order to assure its eternity.

In calling for the rejection of both materialistic atomism and soul atomism, Nietzsche rejects materialism just as he rejects any enduring spiritual entity that could be called soul. It is far from obvious that a rejection of materialistic atomism would entail rejecting soul atomism as its next step. Nietzsche wages war here on the very opposition metaphysics behind both kinds of atomism. Invoking Boscovich, he instead points to energies as a replacement for a discrete soul or discrete material units.[6] The rejection of both kinds of atomism prepares the way for the new psychology, and Nietzsche offers the basis for the psychology of will to power he calls for at the end of *Beyond Good and Evil,* Part One with the images he provides here. The rejection of an indivisible and enduring soul is an effort to preserve "soul" rather than to eliminate the concept: "Between ourselves, it is not at all necessary to get rid of 'the soul' at the same time, and thus to renounce one of the most ancient and venerable hypotheses—as happens frequently to clumsy naturalists who can hardly touch on the soul without immediately losing it" (*BGE* 12). The preservation of the ancient hypothesis will go hand in hand with the preparation for the "new psychologist." It appears that past and future can fit together, and the common thing involves

6   While Leiter offers the case for understanding Nietzsche's analysis as "naturalism" in Brian Leiter, *Nietzsche on Morality* (New York: Routledge, 2014), Maudemarie Clark and David Dudrick reject Leiter's naturalism and argue that the "philosopher's soul" and its normative order of drives is the main concern of *Beyond Good and Evil*, in Clark and Dudrick, *The Soul of Nietzsche's* Beyond Good and Evil (Cambridge: Cambridge University Press, 2012), 156.

retaining "the soul," which requires preserving it as a complexity. A soul considered as having parts can neither be reduced to the naturalist's atomism nor a metaphysician's indivisible soul. Only without falling to either of these poles can we really speak of soul as anything animated at all. Both the soul as monad and the soul as material would reduce the principle of life to something non-living. In order not to get rid of the soul, it would be necessary to preserve it as animated. Only with a view to its motion can it remain alive, and, Nietzsche suggests, this requires that it be conceived as mortal and having parts.

In light of these moves, Nietzsche suggests "new versions and refinements of the soul-hypothesis," listing possibilities "'mortal soul,' and 'soul as subjective multiplicity,' and 'soul as social structure of drives and affects'" (*BGE* 12). Nietzsche's suggestions build upon one another. A mortal soul may be a complex precisely because what animates it could be separated. Such a soul could be composed of many "subjects," which of course could be further divided into parts. Understood through the notion of the will to power, it becomes necessary to consider each of the parts of the soul as moved by will to power. Will to power could then not be attributed to a soul as any kind of singularity. Rather each of the constitutive parts would have to be understood as striving for power in contest with the others. Conceiving the soul as a multiplicity of wills to power entails considering its core to be one of contest. In this light, it makes sense to use the image of a social or political structure, inviting consideration of a politics of the soul.[7] Considering the soul as a political structure entails viewing the contest at its core as the sort of contest that must find a way to establish authority rather than simply destroying the competing elements. By analogy to a political structure, the soul retains its identity through a kind of politics by which something organizes its many parts into something that operates together. The soul is metaphorically like the constitution of a regime, never completely separate from what it does and never reducible to one of its elements.

---

7   Consider Thiele's illuminating treatment of these themes in Leslie Paul Thiele, *Friedrich Nietzsche and the Politics of the Soul* (Princeton: Princeton University Press, 1990). Clark and Dudrick argue that considering the politics of the soul introduces an irreducibly normative element in Clark and Dudrick, *The Soul of Nietzsche's* Beyond Good and Evil, 27–42.

Rather than losing the soul by calling it one or reducing it to material elements, the soul's complexity requires a metaphor. The metaphor of a political structure that Nietzsche suggests does specific work. Soul as a structure of drives and affects divides it into its active and passive elements. Only insofar as it somehow contains both can it be understood as either self-aware or self-moving.[8] This metaphor of the political structure continues in Nietzsche's discussion of willing (*BGE* 19). What it means to will, he explains, is not the operation of anything that can be understood as singular or free. Rather it is the successful command or coordination of a multiplicity of drives and the metaphor is that of a "happy commonwealth" (*BGE* 19). Once willing is presented in this way it can only be understood to self-movement insofar as the thing that is moved is held together in an image. The image Nietzsche uses in this instance is that of a commonwealth, an image that multiplies the complexity as it is an image of thing made of en-souled parts. Imagining the soul as commonwealth requires the very act of imagining and we are now prepared to consider the way in which Nietzsche invites considering the will to power as an interpretation.

When he says that it is "so much the better" that his reader will call "will to power" another "interpretation," he calls attention to the need for an act of interpretation. Will to power cannot be treated as the fundamental fact; it is one way to describe a problem, an aesthetic image denoting a solution. It is even better than accepting it as a new doctrine if his readers consider it to be an interpretation because that will call attention to the need for an interpretation, the need for an image, to get at soul and the nature of the whole. Such an image is necessary because if we try to get at the whole directly, we run into the question of the place of knowing in the whole. This turns into the question of knowing how knowing is possible, and the question of nature turns into a question about the philosophic life. If philosophy is to account for itself it must address the matter of soul, which would need to be both fundamentally different enough to allow reflection on nature and similar enough to be part of the whole. Any adequate account of the whole needs to include soul, understood as what can have

8   Consider Michael P. Davis, *The Soul of the Greeks* (Chicago: University of Chicago Press, 2011), 217–18, for a discussion of soul as both active and passive and the necessarily indirect approaches to matters of soul.

knowledge and what moves. Through the problem of the soul, the character of philosophic life becomes a vital part of any knowledge of nature. Philosophic soul will need to be both different in kind from all other things and the same. Accordingly, no mere "physics" will be adequate, and psychology will involve interpretative images, and those images that present itself to itself will be both necessary and incomplete. Any portrayal of soul will stand subject to challenges regarding its interpretative status, an objection Nietzsche anticipates and welcomes because it keeps the dynamics of psychology alive.

The precedent for considering aesthetic resolutions to logical paradoxes is found in Nietzsche's early considerations on early Greek philosophy, especially Heraclitus. In his early writings on pre-Platonic[9] philosophy, Nietzsche finds an articulation of the continuity of life, nature, soul, and philosophy that provides a source for his use of the teaching of the will to power in Part One of *Beyond Good and Evil*. As Nietzsche cites Heraclitus as a possible precedent for elements of his own thought (*TI*, Reason 2; *EH*, *BT* 3), Nietzsche's treatment of Heraclitus is especially helpful for revealing his understanding of the character of philosophy and his view of his own doctrines. Nietzsche's effort to move beyond metaphysical opposition places a crucial importance on his claim that Heraclitus denies "the duality of totally diverse worlds" (*PTA* 5). Heraclitus, as an important precedent for Nietzsche, also denies metaphysical duality (*BGE* 2) while characterizing enmity and tragic tension as vital, offering an account of both plurality and unity.

The distinction between philosophy and other ways of life emerges in a distinct and initially problematic light when Nietzsche describes Heraclitus' highest power as the capacity to think intuitively in contrast to rationality governed by logical combinations (*PTA* 5). Logic is not the defining condition for the presence of philosophy because Nietzsche wants to present it, not as the achievement of a system, but as a way of life.

---

9   Nietzsche explains in his lectures that he treats pre-Platonic philosophers rather than pre-Socratic because they are distinct as "pure and unmixed types" of philosophers while the era of composite philosophers begins with Plato. Friedrich Nietzsche, *The Pre-Platonic Philosophers*, tr. Greg Whitlock (Urbana-Champagne: University of Illinois Press, 2006), 5.

Nietzsche thus excepts Heraclitus from the "will to the thinkability of all things" and draws Heraclitus in contrast to the Socrates he presents in *The Birth of Tragedy* driven by a logical urge, demonstrating that he does not define philosophy by this drive (*BT* 13). In *The Birth of Tragedy*, "logical Socratism" stands at odds with the superior aesthetic sensibility of the tragic poet, but in the case of Heraclitus he removes the logical drive from a defining role in a philosophic way of life and opens the question of what makes philosophy distinct.

Distinguishing philosophic activity from the purely rational involves the claim that genuine philosophy recognizes that there is no good reason to presume that the whole is accessible to reason. Rather than denying elements of the world in the name of a commitment to reason (see, e.g., *GS* 11; *TI, Reason* 1) or abandoning thinking, a genuine philosophy needs to include openness to what is not accessible to reason (see *GS* 110, *BT* 13). Nietzsche distinguishes Heraclitus' philosophical life not by its pure rationality or even its logical consistency, but rather something distinct about its vision of the world and the "sublime metaphor" with which he describes it. The sublime metaphor does what logical rigor cannot do, providing an image that brings together elements that cannot be logically reconciled. Nietzsche's account of Heraclitus' view of the world as play leads him to the claim that only an aesthetic man could view the world as Heraclitus describes it—as self-renewing play (*PTA* 7).

His treatment of Heraclitus invites comparison to Schiller's treatment of the play-drive (*Spieltrieb*) as the impulse toward aesthetic unity in the *Aesthetic Education*.[10] Nietzsche writes of Heraclitus:

> Only aesthetic man can look thus at the world, a man who has experienced in artists and in the birth of art objects how the struggle of the many can yet carry rules and laws inherent in itself, how the artist stands contemplatively above and at the same time actively within his work, how necessity and random play, oppositional tension and harmony, must pair to create a work of art. (*PTA* 7)

10 Friedrich Schiller, *On the Aesthetic Education of Man*, tr. Elizabeth Wilkinson and L. A. Willoughby (New York: Clarendon Press, 1982), Letter 15.

This conception of the work of art brings together a conception of inner necessity and free play. Without an externally governing purpose, a work of art may be spontaneous and original while coming to be according to an inner necessity that gives it form.

Nietzsche's claim about the position of the artist shows why his claim about aesthetic man is crucial to his interpretation of Heraclitus, for it begins to address the comprehensive problem of the possibility of any real insight: "The artist stands both contemplatively above and the same time actively within his work" (*PTA* 7). As the work of art is both the product and the fashioning, the artist is both apart from his work and within it. This togetherness of purpose and purposelessness, of spontaneity and necessity, of harmony and discord, is emblemized by playing a game, one contained by rules that give purpose to those involved in it. Only if the game (play activity) has no extrinsic purpose can it be understood to be play. If the play is understood for some purpose extrinsic to it, it can no longer be understood strictly as play. Where the activity is instead driven by some other good, one will always need an additional activity to explain what moves the action.

Conceiving of the whole as play accounts for the ultimate unity of elements that are already in logical contradiction. As art can hold together what cannot otherwise be held together in thought, the aesthetic character of Heraclitus' thinking is the key to his ability to comprehend a whole that is not limited by the bounds of the logical. If we are to understand the distinct philosophic character of Heraclitus' thinking, we will have to see in a philosophic way of life the capacity to comprehend what stands apart logically. The same thing cannot be one thing and also its opposite; it cannot be free and determined. Yet, such a pairing brings art into being. Nietzsche suggests that rather than undermining the claim, this contradiction reveals the limits of logic. Heraclitus' apprehension of this limit allows his intuitive thinking to grasp an insight born of the aesthetic sense. Nietzsche emphasizes the image of the playing child as he considers Heraclitus' use of fire as an image for the whole, describing Heraclitus' vision of the cosmos as the play of fire. Nietzsche connects the two images, fire and play, in order to give an image of the drive that explains becoming while accounting for the unity of the whole.[11] Fire operates in two different ways in Heraclitus'

11 See Heraclitus, *Fragments*, DK B50, DK 52.

presentation of the operation of the cosmos, and only because it does both of these can it account for both the oneness of the cosmos[12] and the plurality of its parts. Fire is at once the name for the whole of things[13] and one of the elements that operate in a constant flow from one to the other.[14]

In Heraclitus, fire is the fundamental element, that of which all is composed, and it is also one of the elements, from which the others spring in a continuous process of change. Heraclitus' expression of the ever-changing unity of manifold elements describes a process whereby fire becomes air and then water and earth. This same process operates in reverse in a continuous and repeating cycle. Along with depicting the whole as a continuous process of becoming, the decisive aspect of this view is that the whole is also one.[15] The process of change from one element to another is part of a larger whole and this comprehensive element is the ever-living fire.[16] Nietzsche notes the decisive move beyond Anaximander who "juxtaposed cold and warm as equal terms" with Heraclitus' decisive innovation. "If everything is fire" there is no such thing as an "absolute opposite" (*PTA* 6). Nietzsche looks to Heraclitus' accomplishment as the expression of the ultimate unity that encompasses the many transformations. All things are fire because all things can be exchanged for fire, and if they were not ultimately one with the fire, this would not be possible. Heraclitus' rejection of duality and his simultaneous vision of a comprehensive unity accompanying real transformation set his view apart.[17] Heraclitus stands as exemplar of a philosophic way of life because he is able to avoid the temptation to transform the world into something suited to dualistic thinking, metaphysical opposition, or the denial of the reality of anything not at rest. He maintains his vision of an animated whole rather than sacrificing it to a logical

12   Heraclitus, DK B50, DK B52.
13   Heraclitus, DK 50.
14   Heraclitus, DK B31. See also DK B 31, 76.
15   Heraclitus, DK B50.
16   Heraclitus, DK B30.
17   Consider the way Nietzsche presents Anaximander as bound to a view of metaphysical opposites and Parmenides as claiming that all is unity and at rest. This would leave Heraclitus as an exception who accounts for both the unity of the cosmos, participation in a common element, and the possibility of differentiation and motion. See *PTA* 9.

urge to resolve the contradiction into either duality or rest. Accordingly he avoids both what Nietzsche calls "natural errors" and what he describes as the errors of the Eleatics.[18] Rather than dividing the world to explain its motion or treating the mind as a thing that can be one with a world at rest, Heraclitus offers a vision of an animated whole.

By treating the whole as something animated, and thus like soul, he depicts it operating in tension with itself, and indeed for Heraclitus, Eris is a defining character of the whole. The self-contesting whole depicts the simultaneity of motion and rest, everlasting and eternally changing. In this way, it does not look outside itself for a principle of motion and its motion does not undermine its totality. Here, Nietzsche sees the image run into logical contradictions. Nietzsche asks:

> But does it not look as though "becoming" were but the coming to be visible of the struggle between eternal qualities? Should our talk of coming to be perhaps be derived from the peculiar weakness of human insight, whereas in the true nature of things there is not coming to be at all, but only synchronicity of many true realities— which were not born and will not die? (*PTA* 6)

The first question implies that there really are qualitatively different parts and the cosmos is constituted of many. The second question implies that plurality may be an illusion in a cosmological unity. Rather than using such problems as the basis for a refutation of Heraclitus or the beginning of a logical articulation of the problem of the one and the many, Nietzsche simply asserts: "These are un-Heraclitean loopholes and labyrinths" (*PTA* 6). At this point, Nietzsche's claim that Heraclitus is simply hostile to thinking in "logical combinations" (*PTA* 5) shows its significance. It is not that Heraclitus lacks logical rigor. Nietzsche claims that Heraclitus flies directly in the face of calculative rationality to introduce an answer not available to logic. Nietzsche describes it as follows. The many "are neither eternal substances nor fantasms of our senses" (*PTA* 5). Rather than either "rigid autocratic being" or "fleeting semblance" a third possibility unavailable to "dialectic detective work" emerges. Nietzsche does not "solve" the contradiction by suggesting a distinction

18   See *GS* 110.

between being and appearing. Instead of positing an ultimate stability that only appears as motion, a unity that only appears as multiplicity, he allows Heraclitus to say that the whole is both one and many. Nietzsche finds the answer to the problem of the one and the many in the notion of play. He describes Heraclitus' "sublime metaphor" of play as "a rarity even in the sphere of mystic incredibilities and unexpected metaphors" (*PTA* 6). Understood as fire that plays like a child, it plays innocently, purposelessly, without some external good. In this way the principle of change is inherent in the fundamental thing, for it is play.

The sublime metaphor of play allows thought of the universe as a contest of "opposing" forces without resorting to metaphysical dualism. Nietzsche writes of the impermanence of every apparent configuration, "But this by no means signifies the end of the war; the contest endures into all eternity" (*PTA* 5). Nietzsche draws from Heraclitus' claims that war (*polemos*) is the father of all and that all things come about by strife (*eris*).[19] Opposition is at the core of things that are not metaphysically opposed. Rather than viewing contest in a narrow way that sees only two opposed competitors, viewed from a broader perspective the very contest is really one thing in a constant motion of ceaseless conflict.

The place of a philosophic life in Heraclitus' vision is vital to Nietzsche's admiration for him. By beginning his treatment of Heraclitus with the lightning flash he directs attention to the life of philosophy as embodied by Heraclitus, elucidating his claim that philosophy as a way of life (*art zu Leben*) is more important than the erroneous doctrines of early Greek philosophy (*PTA* preface): "Straight out of the mystic night in which was shrouded Anaximander's problem of becoming, walked Heraclitus of Ephesus and illuminated it with a divine stroke of lightning (*Blitzschlag*)" (*PTA* 5). In Nietzsche's account, it is Heraclitus who provides the lightning strike, Heraclitus who has the insight that illuminates the whole. Accordingly, Heraclitus' life is crucial and his distinctive personality completes the account of the whole that incorporates the primordial stuff of the cosmos and the highest insight of the human mind. It reveals knowledge as part of life and part of the whole. It shows the philosopher's soul in ultimate unity with a dynamic cosmos.

19   Heraclitus, DK B53, 8

For Heraclitus, soul is a manifestation of the primordial thing, the fire. As that fire transforms into all elements, so too is a soul a transformation of water.[20] Understood in this way, the principle of animated life is one with the entire cosmos of changelessly changing things. Soul need not stand apart from the principle of physical motion in order to be what it is. From the connection between animating soul and the fundamental stuff develops the crucial step, the relation between the animating soul and the thinking soul. Heraclitus declares logos to be an aspect of soul and one capable of increase.[21] Logos is not co-equal with soul nor is it equal in all souls.[22] With this, he claims that learning is possible in a way that is less clear in the Parmenidean unity of thinking and being[23] and the paradox of learning to which it leads. Learning is possible in Heraclitus' view because all soul contains within it the capacity for thinking and the possibility of self-knowledge.[24] Logos is distinct from the primordial source of fire, yet it is not permanently distinct. Only so can Heraclitus claim it is capable of learning because it is both distinct from the object of its knowledge and fundamentally the same. Logos is fire and it is not fire. The logical contradiction here highlights the fundamental theoretical problem and offers a metaphoric response. Learning is possible as soul can become dryer. A soul that is wet stumbles along, like one who is drunk, unaware of what it is doing. The wet soul is closer to the element from which it came and to which it will return.[25] At a greater distance from water, a dry soul is wisest and noblest (*ariste*), a flash of light.[26] He can describe soul as most excellent not by some absolute measure of opposition from other things, but because it is the most distinctive manifestation of

20   Heraclitus, DK B36.
21   Heraclitus, DK B115.
22   There is considerable debate in Heraclitus scholarship on the matter of soul. See especially Charles Kahn, *The Art and Thought of Heraclitus* (Cambridge: Cambridge University Press, 1979), 126–30, 237–40; T. M. Robison, *Heraclitus, Fragments with Text and Commentary* (Buffalo: University of Toronto Press, 1989), 104–05, 15–59.
23   Heraclitus, DK B3.
24   Heraclitus, DK B113, 116.
25   Heraclitus, DK B36.
26   Heraclitus, DK B118.

the fiery whole. Logos stands out, allowing reflection on the whole, but it does not remain permanently apart.

The key to the possibility of philosophy revealed by Heraclitus is his own life. Nietzsche writes of his achievement that "No one will believe" it to be possible "except by the instruction of history that such a man did once exist" (*PTA* 8). Because his way of life, his "regal self esteem and calm conviction," allows insight into the nature of things, the example of his life is crucial to the possibility of genuine philosophy, one that does not flee into static claims or divided worlds. Insight into the nature of the whole and insight into his own soul become one, not by conceiving a static unity that divides all else into mere appearance separated from the primary unity of rest,[27] but because the thinker is a manifestation of the primordial element. *Logos* and *physis* are both fire. As an illuminating fire, the thinking soul sees the whole as a kind of self-knowledge. For this reason, Nietzsche can write, "For the world forever needs the truth, hence it needs Heraclitus, though Heraclitus does not need the world" (*PTA* 8). Describing Heraclitus as a star without atmosphere, Nietzsche declares his self-sufficiency and lack of all need from others, from anything external. On Nietzsche's telling, a philosophical way of life is the cosmos (fire) become thought (light). As all is fire even as it is also air, earth, water, soul, or logos, understanding himself as fire completes the circle. The world needs Heraclitus according to Nietzsche because the variety of metamorphoses reaches its conclusion when it becomes such a philosophical soul, a dry soul capable of seeing itself as one with the world as it is. Heraclitus' conception of becoming allows for such unity without stasis or teleology as its play simply brings about all of the manifestations of an ultimately unified world. This incorporation of knowledge into life and nature reveals for Nietzsche the example of a genuinely philosophic way of life in a way that overcomes false oppositions. By presenting these contests as driven by play, motion both purposive and not, Heraclitus accounts for motion and rest, unity and plurality, thinking and being, order and chaos, and he offers Nietzsche an example revealing the place of freedom in necessity.

When he turns to his account of Anaxagoran *nous*, Nietzsche brings back the Heraclitean vision of world at play in order to account for

27   Parmenides, DK 3; PTA 9; GS 110; TI, Reason 2.

non-teleological motion, announcing "play" as the answer to motion that starts in freedom and sets itself a goal, and the name for the purposeless purposes of an Anaxagoran whirl, and the evidence for viewing Anaxagoras' soul as that of a creative artist (*PTA* 19). Freedom can be conceived, he argues, only if it has no purpose, even if its randomly chosen purposes bind that freedom to necessity: "But absolutely free will can only be imagined as purposeless, roughly like child's play or the artist's play-drive (*Kinderspieles oder des künstlerischen Spieltriebes*)" (*PTA* 19). By suggesting that self-motion must be considered as an aesthetic phenomenon, Nietzsche closes the gap between the impulse to logic and aesthetic sensibility.

When Nietzsche accounts for nature as will to power he follows what he finds in Heraclitus:

> but he might, nevertheless, end by asserting the same about this world as you do, namely, that it has a "necessary" and "calculable" course, not because laws obtain in it, but because they are absolutely lacking, and every power draws its ultimate consequences at every moment. (*BGE* 22)

Nietzsche's counter-proposal suggests an idea of necessity that springs from spontaneity in a manner quite similar to what he attributes to Anaxagoras in *Philosophy in the Tragic Age of the Greeks*. It owes even more to what Nietzsche finds in Heraclitus as the reconciliation of freedom and necessity in the notion of play. Nietzsche's doctrine of will to power operates like the fundamental Heraclitean strife as the play of forces, resisting one another. Its necessity is not unfree because it is bound by nothing outside of itself. When Nietzsche follows this statement about a spontaneously moved world of necessity, named will to power by him, with his statement about interpretation, we see that he makes the move he attributes to Heraclitus, that move possible for only an aesthetic man. An aesthetic account of the motion of nature could see it as a kind of free play. Just where it met the limits of logical contradiction, it could find unity and multiplicity, freedom and necessity, motion and rest as ultimately identical. Conceiving the whole of nature as comprehending these tensions without making them metaphysical opposites allows for an aesthetic response. It is "so much the better" (*BGE* 22) if readers see will to power as an interpretation because it does not insist on logical finality. His claim is an interpretation, a metaphor, to be sure, but it is the sort of interpretation that shows exactly what a comprehensive metaphor requires. Through the example of Heraclitus, Nietzsche shows what counts as a *philosophic* interpretation. With such a possibility, we can view Nietzsche's teaching of the will to power in a way that gets beyond both arbitrary metaphor and metaphysical opposition. A philosophical metaphor encompasses the dilemmas of cosmology and psychology.

Will to power operates as something similar to the fundamental strife in Heraclitus. It is responsible for the particular assertion of each thing as it struggles to define itself against others. It accounts for the multiplicity of things, on the level of nature and not only morality. It does so as a unifying force that does not contain radical opposition. Nietzsche can accordingly present oppositions, enmity, and contest as fundamental while rejecting metaphysical opposition. Will to power names the assertive force of each and the fundamental name for the whole. A whole defined in such a way contains contest at its very core. By characterizing life as will to power, Nietzsche presents what animates as a version of what is fundamental to all things. As the fire of the whole transforms itself into each element and ultimately soul in Heraclitus, so too for Nietzsche is life defined by will to power. He thus offers a principle of causation that includes the material causation without being reducible to it. His psychology of will to power identifies soul as a manifestation of life: animating soul and thinking soul derive from the same source. Nietzsche's psychology of will to power identifies the commanding and obeying elements as driven by will to power (*BGE* 188); they are stronger or weaker, not different in kind. He offers the aesthetic possibility of a unity of soul by treating commanding and obeying, animating and thinking as disparate but alike, able to be coordinated by aesthetic and political efforts. Distinctive assertion and fundamental contest derive from the same source. Nietzsche's philosophical interpretation accounts for the whole and the parts and the possibility of philosophical engagement with both.

Nietzsche employs the metaphor of the commonwealth for the unity of competing drives (*BGE* 19). This image provides a metaphor for the unity of the soul that at once acknowledges the plurality of parts, presenting the unity as something brought into by structure and the analogy of political authority. What governs it identifies with the whole while the other parts find themselves in obedience. Part rules, part obeys, and in "willing" it experiences itself as unity. Nietzsche repeats his reference to "under-souls," reminding his readers that there are other parts of the commonwealth. Rather than treating each of these as a natural whole, a singular will, or unified drive, the subordinate parts of a soul are also "souls." If we follow Nietzsche's procedures, each of the under-souls that make up a body can be further divided. What makes it necessary to think in terms of governing and obedience is that such a structure describes the "relations in which the phenomenon 'life' comes to be" (*BGE* 19). Without the structure, there would not be life, nothing animated or en-souled. The elemental force, named will to power, is behind all living, but so is the structure. Without resorting to metaphysics of opposites, one would also have to treat the structure as a product of will to power. As Nietzsche treats will to power as the source of both the constituting structure and the animating motion, Nietzsche does something quite like what he claimed regarding Heraclitus—he offers a "sublime metaphor" only available to "aesthetic man" (*PTA* 7).

What Nietzsche sees as crucial is metaphor. Viewing soul requires metaphor, for talk of soul requires us to treat it simultaneously as selfsame and constituted by multiple parts. If it did not include parts, it could not be understood to move, to animate and thus not to be soul. If it were not somehow unified, its motion could not be understood to be self-motion. Soul is an image-making thing. It pulls disparate things together into an image appropriate to an aware and animated being. Its image-making allows a view of what it cannot see directly by allowing itself to be other than itself, yet separated only in an image. Such images remain partial, as they must arise from some part of the self. Yet, instead of leaving only blind spots, it can come to see its own seeing as yet another animating drive, and thereby recognize the partiality of its images. Recognizing the limits of each image, philosophical soul need not leave its images fixed. Images of soul make self-knowledge possible by showing the incompleteness of the images by which it comes to see itself. The images and awareness of their incompleteness together incorporate soul's awareness of itself into the dynamics of living.

As a view of soul requires metaphor, Nietzsche multiplies images of soul to avoid the reification of a singular image. Along with the image as a commonwealth, Nietzsche offers the image of a bow in the Preface of *Beyond Good and Evil*. The bow he envisions holds together the elements of a fight against Platonism, which he defines in this context as the dogmatist's error "the pure spirit and the good as such" (*BGE* Preface). The fight between a metaphysically separated spirit as the fundamental thing and the rejection of the same emerges as a contest between permanent structure and constant motion. A metaphor for the soul must tie these together. Animation can neither be permanence nor simple flux. Only in the tension between the two can we find something animated, something with both form and motion. Nietzsche provides images of attunement and political authority,[28] multiplying the metaphors that allow continual re-examination and re-constituting, revealing the deep connection between soul and the dynamic of living philosophy.

---

28   Cf. Plato, *Phaedo* 93a; *Republic* 369a.

Part II –
Reason, Eros and the Longing for the Whole

Chance, Providence, Prudence?:
On the Book of Esther
Ronna Burger

The unlikely is so unlikely in its meaningfulness that once it happens it seems to be by design. What couldn't have happened unless
it were "meant to be" becomes no longer only likely but necessary.
The likely and the necessary are thus unified in tragedy when tragic
reversal reveals the sequence of likelihoods leading to a conclusion
which is unlikely because it is so full of meaning.

Reversal occurs at that moment when it becomes clear that all of
what has gone before meant something other than what we thought
it to mean. . . . Reversal makes an audience reflect on the necessity
of action that at first seems unlikely. . . . Recognition introduces inference into the play so that reflection on the likelihood and necessity of the action becomes a part of the action and so has further
consequences within the play itself.

Michael Davis, *Aristotle's Poetics: The Poetry of Philosophy*[1]

The Book of Esther tells the story of a Jewish heroine who joins forces with
her bold and far-sighted guardian to orchestrate, from the royal seat of the
Persian Empire, the overthrow of a villain bent on the destruction of all
the Jews in the kingdom. This work of melodrama, with its fairy tale tone,
gives rise to questions of political, philosophical, and theological import.
Perhaps its most striking feature, as a book of the Hebrew Bible, is the
complete absence of any reference to God.[2] The intricate, tightly-woven

---

1   *Aristotle's Poetics: The Poetry of Philosophy* (Lanham, MD: Rowman & Littlefield
     Publishers, 1992), 63, 68–69.
2   In the face of this puzzle, Rabbinic commentators were inspired to find signs

plot of the work involves a seemingly miraculous reversal—or more precisely, several steps in a process of reversal—by which the wicked plan of destruction is turned against its instigator and those who were ready to carry out his plan are in the end defeated. This turnaround in the plot looks as if it is the result of a rather implausible series of coincidences.[3] But this is, after all, a book of sacred scripture. Shouldn't the appearance of chance be only a veil over the reality of divine providence at work, all the more powerful precisely because it is so hidden?[4] The narrative provides abundant grounds to raise another question: How far can the apparent coincidences driving the plot be understood as the product of deliberate human action?[5]

throughout the text of allusions to God's hand at work. Clifford Orwin refers to "proto-Rabbinic" sources—the Septuagint, *Targum Yehonatan*, an apocryphal version of Esther, and Josephus' account in *Antiquities of the Jews*—as well as the Rabbinic tradition that recognizes the problematic status of this work being included in the sacred canon. See "The Piety of Esther," *The Pious Sex: Essays on Women and Religion in the History of Political Thought*, ed. Andrea Radasanu (Lanham, MD: Lexington Books, 2010), 16 and 31 n5.

3   In an effective poetic work, Aristotle advises, "impossible likelihoods should be preferred rather than possible implausibilities," that is, even if a sequence of events could not happen in reality, it must be made to appear plausible in the fiction. See *On Poetics*, 1460a26–27, trans. Seth Benardete and Michael Davis (South Bend, IN: St. Augustine's Press, 2002), 62.

4   "The extraordinary pattern of apparent coincidences," as Jon Levenson puts it, "that characterize the narrative and make possible the deliverance of the Jews from seemingly certain extermination" might seem to require the assumption of divine involvement, despite the absence of any explicit reference to God: "a coincidence is a miracle in which God prefers to remain anonymous." See *Esther: A Commentary* (Louisville, KY: Westminster John Knox Press, 1997), 18–19. Arguing against a reading of Esther as a story that turns on coincidences and chance events explicable only by appeal to divine action, Yoram Hazony emphasizes the human initiative involved, while reflecting on a tradition of biblical texts that "sees the natural functioning of the world as itself an expression of God's actions." See *God and Politics in Esther* (Cambridge: Cambridge University Press, 2016), 192, and note 22 below.

5   The absence of God's direct involvement in the Book of Esther would then be a condition for human choice and action to become manifest. In his analysis of the *Iliad*, Seth Benardete uncovers the pattern determined by the periodic withdrawal of the gods, in contrast with their intervention, which makes it impossible to discern human merit. "Were not the providence of the gods in-

The agents involved are certainly not in full control of all the events that transpire. But the hero of the story is at work from the outset preparing for future contingencies, and once the situation demands it, he is ready to set in motion a strategic design, while the turnaround of the drama is initiated at the moment the heroine takes over that role.

The book opens with the description of the king, Achashverosh, who rules over 127 provinces of the Persian Empire from the royal court in Shushan (Susa).[6] In the third year of his reign, he holds a great feast in the castle to show off his riches—drinking and eating for 180 days!—capped by a seven-day feast for all the people of the capital. On the last day, he orders the queen, Vashti, to come and show off her beauty, wearing the royal crown (and nothing else?). She refuses.[7] The ministers worry about the precedent the first lady would set for the rest of the households in the kingdom: "This deed of the queen will come abroad unto all the women, to make their husbands contemptible in their eyes" (1:17). On the advice of his minister, the king has the queen banished from the court—we hear nothing further about her fate. At the same time, letters are sent out across the kingdom, to every people in their own language, ordering each man to rule in his own family, and to have his people's language spoken in the household. A despotic decree to guarantee male domination in the household strikes an almost comic note. The Book of Esther, in any case, clearly takes an interest from the very beginning in the condition of women, whose

constant and fitful, they would obscure completely any natural order of excellence; but as it is, they sometimes withdraw and let the heroes run themselves. Then does the world run true; then we can see the heroes for what they are." See *Achilles and Hector: The Homeric Hero* (South Bend, IN: St. Augustine's Press, 2005), 77.

6   There is some scholarly agreement that this figure is Xerxes I, whom we meet up with in Herodotus' *Inquiries* as ruler of Persia from 486–465 BCE. But among other complications, it is strange that we hear nothing of the Persian War against Greece, especially the defeat of Xerxes at Salamis in 480 BCE, which should fall in the same period as the events of the Book of Esther.

7   The king's command to Vashti is reminiscent of Herodotus' story of the tyrant Candaules, whose downfall begins when he urges his trusted bodyguard Gyges to see with his own eyes the beauty of his wife, stripped of her clothes, and her shame; *Inquiries* I. 8. Cf. Michael Davis's account in *The Soul of the Greeks* (Chicago: University of Chicago Press, 2011), 146–51.

subordinate status by convention means they must find indirect ways to maintain their rights or interests. The condition of women is parallel to the condition of the Jews in exile, a small minority in this foreign empire, and the letter at the outset to the husbands across the kingdom anticipates the letter that is to come decreeing the annihilation of this people.

The first action of the story—a manipulative minister turning the king's private frustration into a political policy—sets the stage for all the events that follow. Once the king's anger is assuaged, he regrets the loss of his wife.[8] His ministers propose a consolation: all the beautiful virgins in the kingdom should be rounded up for him to choose a replacement. The girls are to be brought to the royal court, placed under the custody of the guardian of women, and prepared—for six months with oil of myrrh and six months with other sweet ointments!—until each is brought for one night to the king. With this context in place, we are introduced to Esther, "a maiden of beautiful form and fair to look on" (2:7), an orphan being raised as if she were his own daughter by her cousin Mordecai.[9] He is identified as a certain Jew in Shushan the castle, of the tribe of Benjamin, a descendant of King Saul, among the Babylonian exiles from Jerusalem. After being introduced to the two central characters, the next thing we know, we hear of Esther being taken into the king's house (2:8); the narrative delicately skips over the detail that Mordecai must have offered up the girl he is raising like a daughter for the harem of a foreign despot, with the order, moreover, to conceal her identity as a Jewess. Esther soon manages to win the attention of the keeper of women, who "advances [her and her maidens] to the best place in the house of the women" (2:9). One might wonder, then, whether it is indeed pure chance that, when she is at last brought in to the king, Esther finds "grace and favor in his sight more than all the virgins" (2:17). In any event, the royal crown is set upon her head.

8   David Daube reports a quip from the twelfth- or thirteenth-century text, Esther Rabbah: "Ahasverus got rid of wife number 1 (Vashti) to please a counsellor (Memucan in 1:21) and of a counsellor (Haman) to please wife number 2 (Esther)." See "Esther," in *Biblical Law and Literature, Collected Works of David Daube*, Vol. 3, ed. Calum Carmichael (Berkeley, CA: The Robbins Collection), 829.

9   We hear her Hebrew name, Hadassah, only here, for a moment. The names of Mordecai and Esther have been linked to the Babylonian gods, Marduk and Ishtar.

Mordecai does not just abandon his ward: he walks every day before the court of the women's house to keep track of how Esther is faring (2:11). In an apparent digression—which will turn out to be crucial for the tale—we are told of a conspiracy against the king by two of his ministers, "and the thing became known to Mordecai" (2:22). Does he just happen to be in the right place at the right time to learn of the plot? As events develop, it becomes increasingly evident that he must have an extensive intelligence network keeping him informed. Once he reports the conspiracy to Esther, she in turn informs the king; the rumor is confirmed by an investigation, the plotters hanged, and the episode written up in the royal chronicles.

The story of the conspiracy indicates the constant threat under which the oriental despot must live. The general problem is exacerbated by the king's unwillingness or inability to exercise control, which has left a vacuum that is filled by political intrigue. One minister above all has won the king's support and seems to have become the real power behind the throne: Haman the Agagite, that is, a descendant of Agag, King of the Amalekites, a bitter enemy of the Hebrew people since the time of the Exodus from Egypt. Mordecai had been identified as a descendant of King Saul, who was ordered to kill Agag and wipe out his people, though he found himself unable or unwilling to carry out the task and the bloody deed fell to the prophet Samuel (I Samuel 13–15). Before we hear anything about the personal characters of Haman and Mordecai, their enmity is introduced with deep biblical roots. It comes to the surface in this story prompted by a royal command, requiring everyone to bow down and prostrate themselves when Haman passes through the king's gate. Mordecai refuses. This action is the starting point of the whole sequence of events that follows, placing the Jews of the Persian Empire in mortal danger. Mordecai is asked for an explanation, but no answer is reported, except

10 While emphasizing the silence about Mordecai's motivation, Levenson remarks on the parallel between his refusal to bow down to Haman and Vashti's refusal to attend the King's banquet, with the sequence of disastrous consequences that follow from each action. Levenson also calls attention to the strikingly similar description of Joseph's refusal to yield to the attempted seduction by Potiphar's wife, which seems to be a sign of the analogous pattern in the two stories. See *Esther: A Commentary*, 68.

that he is a Jew (3:4).[10] His behavior might look like a pious refusal to bow down before another human being, an acknowledgement of God as the only superior authority.[11] Yet the notion of Mordecai risking everything to act on principle—whatever that principle might be—fits uneasily with everything we discover about his character: he shows himself, as the story unfolds, to be consistently seeking, and mastering, the most clever, usually cautious means to achieve the end he pursues, in the service of his people. Not only has he done all he could to get Esther into the innermost circle of the court, but he orders her, once there, to keep her identity concealed, which would mean violating the Jewish law. And this man makes an unnecessary show of his defiance of the king's highest minister in the most ostentatious public display?! Surely he must be aware of the response he will evoke from Haman. What is his motivation for such a bold and risky action?

Haman, it goes without saying, is full of wrath. All the pleasures of his power are spoiled by this man's defiance. But he must construct for himself an enemy great enough to match the anger that drives him, and for that one individual is not sufficient. As his frustration mounts, he devises a plan and brings it to the king, expecting automatic approval. There is a certain people, he explains, dispersed through the kingdom, who do not obey the laws of the land, but their own; if the king grants him permission to destroy them, he promises ten thousand talents of silver for the royal treasury. "Do with them as it seemeth good to thee," the king grants, without raising a single question, not about the identity of this group nor the evidence for their disobedience. He looks like a puppet, with no will of his own, seemingly indifferent to the political situation. Or could he have his own interest in the annihilation of this people, with all the silver it would bring to his treasury? Does he perhaps understand the policy Machiavelli recommends?: A ruler who finds acts of cruelty

11   A Rabbinic commentary proposes that Haman wore the image of an idol on his clothing, so bowing down to him would be a matter of idol worship. In Mordecai's act of public resistance, Hazony finds a political motive—a rejection of his former path of accommodation in light of the changed situation in Persia with Haman's ascendancy—but beyond that, the refusal on principle to bow down before the idol that Haman represents. See *God and Politics in Esther*, 30–31, 40–41.

useful should make sure they are traced to the harsh nature of his minister, rather than incur hatred himself.[12]

Once word gets out of the terrible decree, Mordecai sits in the king's
gate in sackcloth and ashes, though it is forbidden to be present there in
clothes of mourning. Clearly he wants to be noticed, especially by Esther.
Indeed, as soon as she sees her guardian in his puzzling condition, she sends
out one of her chamberlains, who comes back with a report of the situation
outside the castle, not yet known to the queen. He brings Esther a copy
from Mordecai of the royal decree, along with the charge that she must beg
the king for mercy for her people. Sending back her message in response,
Esther informs or reminds her guardian that anyone who comes before the
king without being summoned can be put to death. And she has not been
called, she adds, for thirty days. Obviously the queen, who is no longer a
new wife, has no exclusive claim to the king's favors.

Mordecai's reply, which initiates the reversal of the drama, takes the
form of three points, rich in ambiguity.

> Think not with thyself that thou shalt escape in the king's house,
> more than all the Jews. For if thou altogether holdest thy peace
> at this time, then will relief and deliverance arise to the Jews
> from some other place, but thou and thy father's house will per-
> ish; And who knoweth whether thou art not come to royal estate
> for such a time as this? (4:13–14)

Mordecai reasons with Esther, first, in regard to her immediate self-interest:
in case she is thinking only of her own safety, she should realize that she will
not be able to go undetected forever and avoid the fate of her
people if they are all to be destroyed. But Mordecai also considers the contrary
possibility: if Esther betrays her people, she will be destroyed as a traitor along
with her family when the Jews are saved "from some other place." What "other

---

12 After using his cruel minister Remirro, and recognizing the hatred he had ear-
    ned, Cesare Borgia had to kill him in order "to show that if any cruelty had
    been committed, this had not come from him, but from the harsh nature of
    his minister." See *The Prince*, Ch. 7, trans. Harvey Mansfield (Chicago: Uni-
    versity of Chicago Press, 1985), 30.

place"? Mordecai leads Esther to think of divine support—at least he mentions no other hope on the horizon. But precisely for that reason, at this moment more than any other the omission of God's name is a resounding silence.[13] For Esther, in any event, there is only one outcome: whether the Jewish people are annihilated or saved, whatever the source of potential deliverance, if she does not commit herself to them, she faces the same disastrous result.

Mordecai could stop his exhortation here. Instead, he ends with a question that holds out to Esther a sense of destiny, greater than her own life: who knows what has brought her to her unique situation, in the court of the royal despot? Esther must hear him literally: whether it is pure chance, the success of her guardian's plans, or the hidden hand of God at work can, perhaps, never be known. But whatever the ultimate grounds, she alone is in a position to save her people.[14] Esther is galvanized into action. She orders Mordecai to gather all the Jews in Shushan and fast for three days, as she will with her maidens: without any explicit expression of hope for divine support, she calls for a ritual that will, presumably, strengthen the resolve of everyone involved, perhaps especially any who harbor such a hope. After this fast, Esther announces, she will go in to the king. Before Mordecai's message, she was unwilling to risk her life by entering the king's chamber unsummoned; now she declares, "If I perish, I perish." Mordecai, the account concludes, did all that Esther had commanded him (4: 17). Their roles have been reversed. Embracing a sense of her destiny, whether divinely ordained or her own construction—Esther is determined, from this point on, to take over the strategy in her own hands.

13 While recognizing that there is no literal reference here to God, Hazony finds in this passage evidence of the principle of faith at work in Mordecai, a faith that supplements and colors the confidence based on his extensive preparations and his boldness at the opportune moment for action. See *God and Politics in Esther*, 173–75.

14 Consider Seth Benardete's reflections on how a Homeric hero "comes to put on his fate" precisely through the decisive choice he makes. "Achilles believes he can either go home and die in old age or stay at Troy and be killed with great glory; Odysseus believes he can either go home or stay with Calypso and become deathless and ageless forever. What Achilles finally chooses is shown to be as inevitable and right as what Odysseus does." See *The Bow and the Lyre: A Platonic Reading of the Odyssey* (Lanham MD: Rowman & Littlefield, 1997), 2–3.

When the time has come Esther appears before the king, and he does hold out the golden scepter, indicating his acceptance: "Whatever thy request, Queen Esther, even to the half of the kingdom, it shall be given thee" (5:3). Her request is simple: "Let the king and Haman come this day into the banquet that I have prepared for him" (5:4). When they arrive for the occasion, the king offers again, "Whatever thy petition, it shall be granted thee; and whatever thy request, even to half of the kingdom, it shall be performed." He must be perplexed to hear her respond: "Let the king and Haman come to the banquet that I shall prepare for them, and I will do tomorrow as the king hath said" (5:8). Why should she delay her request? Why two banquets? Perhaps we should not forget she has not been in the chamber of the king for a month, and now offers him the opportunity of spending a first night with her before presenting her plea and hoping for a favorable response.[15] But there is something else—a miniscule variation in her repeated request: for the first night, she invited the king to a banquet she prepared "for him," the second to a banquet she will prepare "for them." What does it mean, the king must be asking himself, for the queen to prepare a banquet for *them*—for the minister on a par with himself?[16] Haman, in any case, is certainly overjoyed with his privileged status, being included in such an intimate gathering with the king and his wife. He goes home from the first banquet glad of heart—at least until the sight of Mordecai on his way home takes away all his pleasure, as he complains to his wife and friends. They offer their advice: Let a gallows be built fifty cubits high, and in the morning Haman should speak to the king about hanging Mordecai, then he can go to the evening feast undisturbed (5:14).

The lines of the plot now begin to intertwine. On the night of the first banquet, the king cannot sleep. He requests a reading of the royal

15 A suggestion of the learned and wry scholar, David Daube. See "Esther," *Biblical Law and Literature*, 827. Cf. Orwin, "The Piety of Esther," 26.

16 In fact, the king might now be even more disturbed looking back on Esther's invitation the first night, requesting the king to come with Haman to the banquet she has prepared "for him" (5:4). Which of her guests is the "him"?, Hazony asks, recognizing in the subtle but crucial detail of Esther's two invitations the mark of her strategy to arouse the king's growing suspicions about his vizier. See page 101 and the chapter, "Power Shift," in *God and Politics in Esther*.

chronicles, from which he hears about Mordecai's discovery of the plot against him (6:1–2). Surely an amazing coincidence! Or is it? There are certainly reasons for the king's sleeplessness. We know he faces potential threats to his power all the time; the possession of his queen feels no more secure to him than his throne, and just as important to him. Should he not fear his highest minister in particular? Here is a man to whom all the king's servants bow down when he passes; he issues edicts with the king's seal, barely expecting a word of approval. And now, the queen has invited this minister, not just once, but for a second night to what should have been a private gathering. In all his uneasiness, the king's thought must be drawn to the memory of the latest conspiracy against him, of which a report would be contained in the royal chronicle.

At the end of his long sleepless night, the king wishes to find out what honors have been bestowed on the man who saved his life on the occasion of that conspiracy, and he wonders whether anyone in the court might know something. Haman, of course, has just arrived, early in the morning, to propose the hanging of Mordecai. The king calls him into his bedchamber and inquires: "What shall be done unto the man whom the king delighteth to honor?" (6:6). Assuming, of course, that this refers to himself, Haman advises: such a man should be dressed in the finest attire, seated on a royal horse, led through the streets of the city, by one of the princes of the realm. "Make haste," the king replies immediately, "take the apparel and the horse, as thou hast said, do even so to Mordecai the Jew, that sitteth at the king's gate" (6:10). The reversal could not be more perfect: all the honor Haman sought for himself will be bestowed on his most bitter enemy, and he must himself carry out the servile task. Is the divine hand at work in this perfect reversal? The king, in any event, has been up all night putting two and two together: Why has this Mordecai, who was responsible for saving him, received no honor? Why, in particular, no honor at the hands of Haman, who has taken over almost all ministerial power? The king must expect Haman to misunderstand the meaning of his words: when he uses the definite description, "the man whom the king delighteth to honor," he is testing the growing suspicion he harbors of his minister by making him a victim of dramatic irony.[17]

17 It is instructive to compare the exchange between the king and his minister with Xenophon's *Hiero*, where the tyrant engages in a conversation about the

It is hard to imagine Haman concealing his response to the king's shocking disclosure of his intention; but out of fear, presumably, he manages to remain silent and waits to express himself until he returns home, despondent. His wife and friends—who the day before recommended building gallows for his enemy—now convey their sense of his impending doom: "If Mordecai, before whom thou hast begun to fall, be of the seed of the Jews, thou shalt not prevail against him, but shalt surely fall before him" (6:13). Why are they so certain of Haman's imminent downfall? Mordecai, they realize, now has the support of the ruler of the empire, indeed, perhaps they suspect that such a radical turn in palace politics must be the work of an even higher power. In any event, just as they express their dark vision, the king's chamberlains arrive to convey Haman to Esther's feast.

As the second "banquet of wine" commences, the king repeats his offer: "Whatever thy petition, Queen Esther, it shall be granted thee; and whatever thy request, even to the half of the kingdom, it shall be performed" (7:2). Esther is at last ready to present her case: "If I have found favor in thy sight, O king, and if it please the king, let my life be given me at my petition, and my people at my request; for we are sold, I and my people, to be destroyed, to be slain, and to perish" (7:2–4). "Sold to be slain"—a strange expression, but it captures perfectly Haman's plan, which must have appealed to the king, above all, with the promise of ten thousand talents of silver from the spoils. Who dares to do such a thing?, the king demands. He is focused only or above all, as he repeatedly shows, on the threat to his wife. But now he is the victim of dramatic irony; he does not realize that his words refer to himself as the one responsible for the drastic edict, the edict issued in his name, at least, sealed with his ring. Or does he in fact have some guilty recollection of how readily he approved Haman's proposal to annihilate a certain people? Of course, what he did

pleasures of the tyrannical vs. the private life with the wise poet Simonides, who has come to visit his court. As Leo Strauss demonstrates, every claim and argument in this exchange must be read in light of the distrust and fear that both the tyrant and the wise man feel for one another. See Leo Strauss, *On Tyranny*, ed. Victor Gourevitch and Michael Roth (New York: The Free Press, 1963), especially 40–43.

not know then and has just discovered is that he was condemning to death his own wife.

Esther now has all the pieces in place to reveal the author of the terrible decree, without of course suggesting any blame of the king: "An adversary and an enemy, even this wicked Haman" (7:6). Overcome with anger, the king retreats into the palace garden. Is he shocked to learn of the machinations of his highest minister? Or is he just absorbing the confirmation of suspicions that have long been building? Could he be pained at the same time by the realization of his own role in these events? Haman, now terrified, must beg for Esther's mercy. When Achashverosh re-enters, moments later, he finds his minister "fallen upon the couch whereon Esther was." Seeing before him what he takes to be a scene of seduction, the king cries out: "Will he even force the queen before me in the house?" (7:8). The king's re-entry at the very moment Haman has "fallen upon" Esther's couch certainly appears to be an extraordinary coincidence. Does the invisible hand of providence lie behind the appearance of pure chance? Or is it enough to look to Esther? Understanding perfectly well the one concern that would move the king, she has been busy all along planting the seeds of jealousy in his mind (playing Desdemona and Iago at once). The king's momentary departure from the banquet provides just the opportunity for which she has been waiting to carry her strategy to its conclusion.

The servants immediately cover Haman's face: his fate is sealed. One of the ministers—who must see where his future advantage lies—reminds the king of the gallows Haman made for Mordecai. And the king simply adds, "Hang him thereon" (7:9). Once again, the king initiates no action; he only gives voice to the idea implied by his minister. Haman hung on the gallows he built for his enemy— "poetic justice." The good man's service has been recognized and now the wicked man falls. A just order has been established, but what brought it about? Certainly not a desire to see justice done. What has moved the king is his feeling of possessiveness and insecurity, and this—the one reaction in the whole story that most belongs to the king himself—is stirred up by a misinterpretation. The critical mechanism for this turnaround, which leads to reward and punishment in accordance with just deserts, is a false belief, driven by the passion of jealousy. The plot of the Book of Esther, from this perspective, looks like a parody of a divine providential order.

With the hanging of Haman, the king's anger is soothed. He turns over "the house of Haman" to the queen, and gives the ring taken back from Haman to Mordecai, although it is now Esther who is in a position to "set Mordecai over the house of Haman" (8:1–2). Despite this development in the court, however, nothing has changed in the world outside the castle and Esther's mission to save her people remains unfulfilled. Once more she falls at the feet of the king, he holds out the golden scepter, and this time she rises to speak: "If it please the king, and if I have found favor in his sight, and the thing seem right before the king, and I be pleasing in his eyes, let it be written to reverse the letters devised by Haman . . . to destroy the Jews in all the king's provinces; for how can I endure to see the evil that shall come unto my people?" (8:5–6)? In her double prelude, Esther appeals to the king's affection for her and to the rightness of the action she calls for; but the king has little interest in this problem outside the castle walls. A decree sealed with the king's ring, he explains, cannot be revoked. He is willing, however, to do something to placate the queen: "Write ye also concerning the Jews, as it liketh you, in the king's name, and seal it with the king's ring" (8:9). Mordecai writes the letters to be sent out to 127 provinces, proclaiming the king's permission to the Jews in every city to defend themselves, on the day that had been designated for their annihilation.[18]

The reversal within the intrigues of the court is now followed by a reversal in the political world: the day that the enemies of the Jews expected to achieve a great victory is turned to their utter defeat (9:1). Of course, this fairy tale of victory covers over the harsh probability of reality. But

---

18 Mordecai's letters, sent out on swift steeds, read "that the king had granted the Jews that were in every city to gather themselves together, and to stand for their life, to destroy, and to slay, and to cause to perish, all the forces of the people and province that would assault them, their little ones and women; and to take the spoil of them for a prey, upon one day in all the provinces of King Achashverosh, namely, upon the thirteenth day of the twelfth month, which is the month of Adar" (8:11–12). His missive is the perfect reversal of the one Haman sent out originally, "to destroy, to slay, and to cause to perish, all Jews, both young and old, little children and women . . . and to take the spoil of them for a prey" (3:13). In the report of the battle, however, we hear nothing about women and children, and we are repeatedly told that no spoils were taken.

within the framework of the narrative, how is the Jews' one-day defeat of their enemies to be explained? Given the numbers, it could hardly be presented as a matter of chance on the battlefield. If the divine hand were at work anywhere, establishing the intended order, it would presumably be here, but silence prevails. Another explanation is suggested by the description of the situation of the Jews around the kingdom: "No man could withstand them; for the fear of them was fallen upon all the peoples." What has fallen upon them, more specifically, is the fear of Mordecai (9:4), who has managed to convey across the empire recognition of his standing, with the full backing of the great king. This would surely shake the confidence of his enemies, who, moreover, might imagine that this radical reversal in the standing of the Jews could have come about only with the support of a power higher than the earthly king.[19]

At the end of the day of battle, the king gives Esther a report of the news, at least in the capital, including the death of the ten sons of Haman, and he offers her one last time a request. "If it please the king," she begins, "let it be granted to the Jews that are in Shushan to do tomorrow also according unto this day's decree, and let Haman's ten sons be hanged upon the gallows" (9:13). Is Esther suddenly moved by an angry desire for vengeance? We have seen no sign of this in her character. If, instead, she is continuing to exhibit the prudence she shares with her guardian, along with dedication to her people, she would be acting on a Machiavellian insight into political necessity: they must leave behind as few as possible who were already moved by murderous hatred, which would only be intensified by the losses they have sustained.[20] In particular, the ten sons of Haman must be held up for public display as a sign of the fate of those who would destroy her people.

Mordecai, meanwhile, looks to the far future and becomes a spokesman, one might say, for the author of the book: turning the particular historical event they have lived through into an object of commemo-

---

19   If fear of the Jews has taken over, it is because, as Orwin notes, "the despotism, which had previously consigned the Jews to destruction, has now rallied to their side." "In this fantasy," he remarks, "the irresistible will of despotism comes to the rescue of the Jews in place of the irresistible will of God." See "The Piety of Esther," 28–29.

20   "The offense one does to a man," Machiavelli advises, "should be such that one does not fear revenge for it." See *The Prince*, Ch. 3, 10–11.

ration, he proclaims a festive holiday to be observed every year.[21] It is to be named "Purim," after the lot (*pur*) that Haman first consulted to determine the propitious day for the annihilation he planned (3:7). The name of the holiday introduced at the end of the tale invites us to think through again the narrative of a plot that seemed to turn on a remarkable sequence of chance occurrences. In the course of those events, no one explicitly calls upon God for deliverance in the face of the threat that looms before them, or expresses gratitude afterward; if a divine plan is at work, it remains altogether in the dark. What the biblical book dramatizes most vividly are the actions of two human beings who find themselves confronting a dangerous world, and ready to sacrifice much to prepare for it.[22] Whether products of pure chance or divine providence, events outside their control become conditions in which prudence finds its opportunity. Who knows?—as Mordecai exhorted Esther—"whether thou are not come to royal estate for such a time as this."

21 It is Mordecai who sends out letters to the Jews across the 127 provinces of the kingdom, but the account concludes by referring to "the commandment of Esther" that confirmed these matters "and it was written in the book" (9:32). Actually, the book of Esther is completed with a brief final chapter, which begins: "And the King Achashverosh laid a tribute upon the land, and upon the isles of the sea" (10:1). What looks like an afterthought is in fact, David Daube argues, an integral element in the practical message to be conveyed to future foreign powers ruling Jews in exile: the sensible way to profit from their subjects is not slaughter, but taxation. See "The Last Chapter of Esther," in *Biblical Law and Literature*. Of course, the new, or increased, burden of this tribute indicates Mordecai's very mixed success in gaining security for his people under a foreign power—on the model of Joseph's very mixed success saving his family from starvation in Egypt, while ushering in four hundred years of slavery.

22 The Book of Esther represents a world, as Hazony describes it, where God may no longer call out to man, yet "God's justice and peace" can be brought into being through actions initiated by human beings. See *God and Politics in Esther*, 179. Addressing the question of the relation between human agency and divine intervention in the Hebrew Bible more generally, Hazony proposes a notion of "emergence" that seems to go further by understanding, not only divine justice, but "God's *action* in the world" (emphasis added) as something that can be "emergent upon natural causes or human action" (193).

Self-Knowledge on Trial:
A Vest-Pocket Guide to the Argument of Hegel's
Phenomenology of Spirit

Robert Berman

Michael Davis invited me to Sarah Lawrence in March 2003 to present to students and colleagues some thoughts about Hegel that bear on matters of the soul and self-knowledge—themes central to Michael's body of work, which I have been discussing with him over the course of many years of friendship. This paper on Hegel's account of *der Weg der Seele* in his seminal work, *The Phenomenology of Spirit*, is a refined distillate of the talk given on that late winter afternoon. Its intent is to expose the nerve of Hegel's phenomenological argument. A more recent ancestor of this paper was delivered at St. John's College, Santa Fe, New Mexico, in October 2013.

Hegelian Phenomenology: A Socratic-Kantian Thought Experiment

Hegel's *Phenomenology of Spirit* of 1807[1] (*Phenomenology*) is a book preeminently about knowledge, above all self-knowledge. It conducts a thought experiment designed to probe the prospects of philosophy understood as

---

1   Throughout this essay references to Hegel's *Phenomenology of Spirit* of 1807 use the italicized abbreviation "*Phenomenology*." Citations give the page numbers both from G. W. F. Hegel, *Phenomenology of Spirit*, trans. A. V. Miller (Oxford: Oxford University Press, 1977) and the German text, G. W. F. Hegel, *Die Phänomenologie des Geistes*, in *Werke in zwanzig Bände*, ed. E. Moldenhauer and H. M. Michel (Frankfurt am Main: Suhrkamp, 1970), vol. 3. "M" designates Miller's English translation (which I have in some cases modified), and "MM" the German Moldenhauer and Michel edition. Thus, citations to these texts will appear as follows: M/MM with page numbers following a colon in each case.

the quest for a distinctive kind of knowledge having as its aim to arrive at the truth about reality as a whole. This intention Hegel shares with Kant who, a quarter-century earlier, had urged philosophers to halt their pursuit of this kind of knowledge, the rational cognition of things in themselves, which he identified as metaphysics, in order once and for all to determine whether such knowledge is even possible.[2]

---

2   Kant, *Prolegomena to Any Future Metaphysics* (Cambridge: Cambridge University Press, 2004), 5. For a recent discussion reconstructing the philosophic connection between Kant's critical project and Hegel's *Phenomenology*, see Eckhart Forster, The *Twenty-Five Years of Philosophy: A Systematic Reconstruction* (Cambridge: Harvard University Press, 2012). Houlgate classifies Hegel as a "post-Kantian metaphysician" on the grounds that Hegel "agrees with Kant that philosophy must adopt a thoroughly critical attitude to the categories of thought through which the nature of being is to be disclosed." See Stephen Houlgate, *Hegel's Phenomenology of Spirit* (London: Bloomsbury Publishing, 2013), 2–3. Kant would certainly recognize as metaphysics the kind of knowledge whose pursuit Hegel sets out to examine in the *Phenomenology*. Kant urged philosophers to suspend their commitment to metaphysics in order to decide once and for all the question of its possibility. To that end, in the *Critique of Pure Reason* he inaugurated an innovative transcendental philosophic analysis of the very nature of human cognition and knowledge. His conclusion: Although they harbor a natural metaphysical disposition, metaphysics is for humans in principle out of reach. Lacking knowledge of its congenital ignorance, human reason absurdly attempts to transcend its limits, supplying grist to radical skepticism that identifies philosophy with the achievement of this all-too-human aspiration to metaphysics. Transcendental reflection is intended to provide the needed self-knowledge, presumably non-metaphysical, of that inescapable ignorance.

In the *Phenomenology* Hegel follows a path that departs from Kant's critical philosophy. His reason for deviating from Kant is familiar but decisive: Transcendental reflection's reliance upon an account of the nature of human cognition and knowledge awakens the suspicion that the epistemological investigation is itself an instance of metaphysics. Either it dogmatically vindicates the latter, making a sham of the purported need for the called-for inquiry, or it condemns its own epistemology, which appeals to an authority it lacks, since the very legitimacy of such authority is precisely what Kant has so pointedly put into question. Hegel's own study of ancient skepticism in particular made him acutely aware of the need to steer clear of the error of self-referential inconsistency that often afflicts skeptical doubts about metaphysics, of

While heeding Kant's call, however, Hegel's way of answering it is more Socratic than Kantian. For Hegel's phenomenological inquiry is not at all an enterprise of the same kind as the knowledge project it intends to subject to scrutiny.[3] That undertaking Hegel attributes to an epistemic protagonist he calls "consciousness."[4] By that he means—to state the bare minimum most simply—a structure of opposition between a cognitive subject and its mind-independent object. Like the Socrates who examines his interlocutors' opinions rather than making any claims of his own, Hegel is at pains throughout the *Phenomenology* to maintain a bright line of demarcation between the internal perspective of consciousness, the actor or participant engaged in the quest for knowledge, and the external point of view of the

concluding from one's pretention to know the nature of human mind and knowledge that no human being can attain metaphysical knowledge. Hegel adopts his phenomenological stance to avoid this basic logical difficulty. See the Introduction to the *Phenomenology*, M: 46–49/MM: 68–72, for Hegel's considerations concerning epistemology that lead him to make his phenomenological turn. For Hegel's reception of ancient skepticism and its importance to his philosophic thought, see Michael N. Forster, *Hegel and Skepticism* (Cambridge: Harvard University Press, 1989), and more recently, Dieter H. Heidemann, *Der Begriff des Skeptizismus. Seine systematischen Formen, die pyrrhonische Skepsis und Hegels Herausforderung* (Berlin: Walter de Gruyter, 2007).

3   Hegel's phenomenological approach to Kant's urgent question is Socratic in this one decisive respect: By relying on his dialogue partner's own operative opinions, the Platonic Socrates can test the interlocutor's claim to know without having to make any such epistemic commitments of his own. Whether designated as elenchus or as maieutics, this Socratic hoisting of the interlocutor on his own petard is an exercise in immanent criticism. Hegel's phenomenological investigation of the prospects of the metaphysical quest adopts this Socratic style of criticism, albeit not in the dramatic form of dialogue. For his non-metaphysical inquiry, Hegel envisions an epistemic agent endeavoring to attain metaphysics, and affords him all the conceptual equipment he needs to embark on his project.

4   Hegel uses "natural consciousness," M: 49/MM: 72, for example, but for convenience and brevity I am shortening it to "consciousness," since, as it seems to me, in the context of the *Phenomenology* Hegel uses the two expressions as notational variants. The principal ambiguity in Hegel's use of the term is that it serves both as a proper name for the epistemic protagonist and as a kind term referring to the formal structure of opposition, the necessary condition framing the protagonist's quest.

phenomenologist, the spectator or observer. The phenomenologist describes and critically evaluates the "shapes of consciousness"[5] that represent a series of attempts by this epistemic agent to succeed in reaching its epistemic goal.[6]

The argument Hegel develops as he analyzes these efforts consists of two segments of unequal length: the shorter portion culminates with consciousness identifying the knowledge it seeks with self-knowledge; it is followed by the second part, disproportionately longer, which examines the shapes consciousness takes as it attempts to justify its claim to self-knowledge. The movement through these two unequal phases ultimately yields the conclusion that the project of metaphysics inevitably fails, owing to its

5   M: 56/MM: 80. Miller here uses "patterns" for "*Gestalten*," but earlier in the Introduction where Hegel uses "*Gestalt*" Miller renders it with "shape." For Hegel's "*Gestalt*" I use "shape" throughout. "Shape of consciousness" must be distinguished from what we can call the "form of consciousness," the set of formal features that define Hegel's unique phenomenological conception of consciousness, discussed in the second section of the paper. The single, abiding form of consciousness contrasts with the plurality of shapes of consciousness. They are many due to the epistemic agent's epistemic resourcefulness in the face of its continual failure to achieve its aim.

6   For a detailed discussion of Hegel's phenomenological method, see K. R. Dove's two papers, "Hegel's Phenomenological Method," *Review of Metaphysics*, 23/4 (June, 1970) and "Die Epoche der Phenomenologie des Geistes," *Hegel-Studien, Beiheft* (Bonn: Bouvier Verlag, 1974). The line of demarcation that Hegel maintains between the perspective of consciousness and that of the phenomenologist has come to be called the "hermeneutic" or "phenomenological" difference. See, for example, Johannes Heinrichs, *Die Logik der Phänomenologie des Geistes* (Bonn: Bouvier Verlag, 1974), and Alan White, *Absolute Knowledge: Hegel and the Problem of Metaphysics* (Athens, OH: Ohio University Press, 1983). The ancient roots of Hegel's recognition of the indispensable role of this contrast to his phenomenological project extend beyond Socratic elenchus to Aristotle's refutation by demonstration, introduced in *Metaphysics*, Bk. 4, chapter 4 in response to one type of skeptical objection to the principle of non-contradiction. The refutation relies on this internal/external distinction, exploiting the skeptic's commitments while refraining from imposing any of its own. For Aristotle's use of this internal/external distinction or "phenomenological difference" in his *Nicomachean Ethics*, see Ronna Burger, *Aristotle's Dialogue with Socrates: On the "Nicomachean Ethics"* (Chicago: University of Chicago Press, 2009), especially 72.

fatal adherence to a set of premises rooted in the structure of consciousness. In the short argument consciousness founders because its structure is found to be logically incompatible with self-knowledge; in the long argument consciousness tries to avoid this logical difficulty by conjoining self-knowledge with the signature Hegelian concept of Spirit. Yet, in doing so, it confronts an inconsistent triad of the structure of consciousness, Spirit, and self-knowledge, and thus comes to grief again. The *Phenomenology* tracks, in Hegel's famous formula, "a highway of despair."[7]

The Structure and Trajectory of Hegel's Phenomenological Argument

As the inquiry progresses over the course of nearly five hundred pages, the *Phenomenology* covers a seemingly all-encompassing content. Even before covering the first quarter of the work, its topics already range from sensation, perception, and the search for explanatory scientific laws to life and desire, the existential struggle for recognition, lordship and servitude; from stoic detachment and self-consuming skepticism to despair over the failure of asceticism, this unhappiness assuaged only by surrender to a mediator who is acknowledged as representing transcendent authority. In the vast remaining bulk of the book, Hegel turns his attention to membership in ethical, socioeconomic, political, moral, and religious community, closing with a brief retrospective surveying the steps that have led to the outcome of the inquiry.

A quick glance at the table of contents shows this wealth of content ordered in eight chapters, which are articulated into a tripartite division: Consciousness, Self-Consciousness, and Reason, with this last dividing in turn into four successive subsections: Reason, Spirit, Religion, and Absolute Knowing.[8] This schematic outline maps the trajectory of the

---

7   M: 49/MM: 72. Actually, it is not Miller but Baillie who in his translation (*The Phenomenology of Mind*, Harper Torchback, 1967, 78) uses "highway" instead of "way," which is more literal than poetic, since the German is simply "*Weg der Verzweiflung*." Hegel begins the paragraph by underlining this despair, stating that natural consciousness will prove to be "not real knowing."

8   Imposing upon the contents of the *Phenomenology* a tripartite arrangement of eight chapters, three divisions, and four subsections of the third division, Hegel uses Roman numerals for the eight chapters, single capital letters for the three major divisions—A. Consciousness, B. Self-Consciousness, and C.

two main phases of the argument as a whole.[9] The far shorter phase, comprising the first four chapters, starts with Consciousness and peaks fairly quickly with the move to Self-Consciousness. At this point, Hegel observes, consciousness first enters "the native realm of truth."[10] The advent

Reason— and double capital letters for the four subsections of Reason, respectively, AA. Reason, BB. Spirit, CC. Religion, and DD. Absolute Knowing. Each of the eight chapters treats a distinct subshape of consciousness of the divisional shape to which it belongs. The first three, under the division heading Consciousness, deal, respectively, with sensation or what Hegel calls Sense-certainty, Perception, and Understanding, in which the epistemic agent claims to have theoretical knowledge of reality by means of explanatory scientific laws. The other above-listed topics—life, desire, life-death struggle for recognition, lordship and servitude, stoicism, skepticism, and unhappy consciousness—Hegel packs into the fourth chapter, the shape of Self-consciousness, which doubles as the second main division. Of the 435 pages of the Miller translation, all these contents treated in the first four of the eight chapters take up only 79 pages, occupying no more than a mere fifth of the total page-length. Hegel's treatment of the different types of sociality or community in the fifth, sixth, and seventh chapters that fall under the heading of Reason take up the remaining space of the *Phenomenology*, with the final, very brief eighth chapter, Absolute Knowing, devoted to closing the argument as a whole. Uniquely in this tripartite scheme, the term "reason" does triple duty, since it serves not only to name a specific subshape investigated in chapter five, but also to designate the third and final genus division as well as its first double-letter subsection. This organization of the contents, with approximately 80 percent of the book devoted to the analysis of the four-fold character of Reason, is a further indication that Hegel intends his phenomenological approach to stand as an alternative to the Kantian critique of reason. For an extended discussion of Hegel's use of Kantian language in his treatment of Reason in chapter five of the *Phenomenology*, see my paper, "Reason, Idealism, and the Category: Kantian Language in Hegel's *Phenomenology of Spirit*," in *The Linguistic Dimension of Kant's Thought*, eds., Frank Schalow and Richard Velkley (Evanston, IL: Northwestern University Press, 2014).

9   It is assumed throughout that in the *Phenomenology* Hegel puts forward a single, albeit complex line of argument. Not all readers accept this premise. For a detailed, extensive effort to substantiate the claim that the *Phenomenology* is a coherent whole guided by a general conception, see Michael N. Forster, *Hegel's Idea of a Phenomenology of Spirit* (Chicago: University of Chicago Press, 1998).

10   M: 104/MM: 137.

of Self-Consciousness simultaneously shifts the focus of the inquiry to self-knowledge, which could encourage the view that Hegel intends to identify them. Support for this belief would be forthcoming, if Self-Consciousness were able to justify its claim to self-knowledge. For then self-knowledge would receive its adequate expression in the shape of Self-Consciousness, and the argument of the *Phenomenology* would reach an affirmative conclusion when consciousness, configured as Self-consciousness, realizes metaphysics. Instead, the failure of Self-Consciousness to make good on its claim belies the impression of its identity with self-knowledge. Rather than bringing the argument to a successful close, chapter four on Self-Consciousness serves, therefore, as the decisive pivotal link to the longer segment, which must continue probing the prospects for self-knowledge beyond the boundary set by Self-Consciousness. If consciousness is going to keep alive what from this point forward is its pursuit of self-knowledge, it has to revive its efforts by assuming the new shape of Reason. The treatment of the four subsections of Reason makes up the whole of the second phase of the argument, sprawling across nearly four-fifths of the work and home to its increasingly rich content.

Hegel's Phenomenological Conception of Consciousness: Epistemic, Normative, and Teleological Difference

Before turning to the main line of argument of the *Phenomenology*, some additional remarks might help clarify Hegel's conception of consciousness, so essential to his inquiry.[11] One could think of consciousness simply as awareness or wakefulness; in Hegel's usage, however, it is something much more specific. Its primary sense is cognitive, or even more precisely, epistemic. As already noted, at its core it is a structure of opposition between

---

11 Hegel dedicates only a few paragraphs of the short, but indispensable eleven-page Introduction to the *Phenomenology* to this task of elucidating the phenomenological conception of consciousness. Most crucial of all are those at M: 52–54/MM: 75–78. For it is in these paragraphs that he explains with admirable clarity and concision the epistemic, normative, and teleological differences that together constitute the formal structure of consciousness at work throughout his entire analysis.

two poles, the object as it is for consciousness and the object as it is independent of its relation to the cognitive agent—a contrast, as Hegel sometimes puts it, between knowing and truth.[12] This structure of opposition functions as the framework for the quest for metaphysical knowledge under investigation. Knowing is presumed to be a relation to an object; however, while this epistemic relation is essential to consciousness, the relation is merely a contingent property of the object itself.[13] Let's dub this modal asymmetry the "epistemic difference."

Hegel's inquiry aims to determine whether the knowledge project undertaken within the horizon of this epistemic difference can succeed.

12 M: 52–53/MM: 76. Hegel speaks sometimes of the contrast between for itself and in itself. In one of the most well-known and important passages in the Introduction, he writes that consciousness "differentiates something from itself to which at the same time it relates itself . . . there is something for consciousness, and the determinate aspect of this relating, or the being of something for a consciousness, is knowing. However, from this being for an other, we distinguish being in itself; what is related to knowing is also distinguished from knowing, and also posited as being external to, outside, or independent of this relation; the aspect of this in itself is called truth" 52-53/76. For a detailed analysis of this phenomenological concept of truth, see R. Aschenberg, "Der Wahrheitsbegriff in Hegels *Phenomenologie des Geistes,*" in *Die Ontologische Option*, ed. Klaus Hartmann (Berlin: DeGruyter, 1976).

13 With his comment on Kant's conception of the "Ding an sich" in the Bremen Lectures of 1949, Heidegger indicates that Kant operates with this idea of the object as it is in itself: "Das Ding an sich bedeutet für Kant: der Gegenstand an sich. Der Charakter des 'Ansich' besagt für Kant, dass der Gegenstand an sich Gegenstand ist ohne die Beziehung auf das menschliche Vorstellen, d.h., ohne das 'Gegen,' wodurch er für dieses Vorstellen allererst steht. 'Ding an sich' bedeutet, streng kritisch gedacht, einen Gegenstand, der keiner ist, weil er stehen soll ohne ein mögliches Gegen-für das menschliche Vorstellen, das ihm entgegnet." Martin Heidegger, Bremer Vorträge 1949, *Gesamtausgabe* 79, p. 16 (Frankfurt: Klostermann, 1994). Nowadays, this construal of the object as in itself—originally Kant's thing in itself of "transcendental realism"—is sometimes conveyed by expressions such as "mind-independence," "metaphysical realism," or most simply "realism." If we use "realism" to designate the view that the property of being in such an epistemic relation is a contingent relational property of what is to be known, then Hegelian phenomenology is concerned with investigating the prospects of the metaphysical quest characterized by its unquestioned commitment to realism.

In pursuing its goal, consciousness, Hegel's name for the knowledge claimant, operates with the traditional idea of knowledge as justified true belief. To win justification for a claim to know the truth requires appeal to an epistemic norm, a criterion specifying what counts as epistemic justification. Any theory of the traditional conception of knowledge will supply this criterion by dint of giving an account of what knowledge is—the class characteristic determining what it is to be included in the class of knowers.[14] As knowledge of knowledge, an epistemology necessarily claims reflexive self-knowledge. In addition to possessing an epistemology, consciousness also operates with the distinction between attributing knowledge to another and attributing it to oneself. In first-person self-attribution, consciousness thus claims self-knowledge in two senses—not only the reflexive self-knowledge of epistemology, but also knowledge of itself as a member of the class of knowers.[15] In the *Phenomenology*, while consciousness, whose knowledge

14 A successful epistemology has to satisfy two conditions of adequacy: 1) it must be sufficiently comprehensive so as to make a place for itself as an instance of the very conception of knowledge it proposes; and 2) to meet this demand for self-referential inclusiveness, it has to supply an account of self-knowledge in this self-reflexive sense. An epistemology that satisfies these conditions of adequacy will, consequently, have to include an account of knowledge as reflexive self-knowledge and its knowledge about knowledge will have to conform to the very conception of reflexive self-knowledge it conceptualizes.

15 Adapting the language of set-theory—employing the tripartite distinction among class or set, class member, and class characteristic—one can think of knowledge attribution, both first- and third-person, as asserting class inclusion: the attributor, in identifying a member of the class of knowers, implies thereby that he knows the class characteristic, what it is to be a knower, thus implying further that he has knowledge of knowledge.

The use of a set-theoretical construal here does not entail a commitment to using the conceptual and technical apparatus or the symbolic notation of mathematical set theory. The more modest aim is to exploit the ensemble of ordinary notions of class, class member, and class characteristic to clarify knowledge attribution: knowledge is the class characteristic, and to attribute knowledge to an epistemic agent is to claim that he instantiates the characteristic and hence is a member of the class of knowers. With first-person self-attribution, one not only claims to have such self-reflexive self-knowledge; what is unique in this case is that one also includes oneself in the class of those who have

claim is under investigation, adopts this first-person perspective, the third-person perspective is reserved for the phenomenologist as spectator.

Given the Socratic strictures governing his spectator stance, the phenomenologist, in his examination of consciousness, must refrain from introducing any epistemic criterion of his own. Were he to claim to know what real knowledge is, he would in effect become a pretender to the throne of metaphysics. The phenomenologist leaves it to consciousness to play epistemologist—it must devise its own epistemic criterion—and simultaneously to assume its role as the candidate whose claim to membership in the class of knowers needs to be justified. This duality between an epistemic norm providing the measure of genuine knowledge, and a candidate, the knowledge claimant—let's call it the "normative difference"—has both poles anchored in consciousness.[16]

Accordingly, one can reformulate Hegel's thought experiment as the examination of the prospects of first-person epistemic self-evaluation under the condition of epistemic difference.[17] The project is a dynamic one, in which, it will turn out, consciousness repeatedly fails to pass epistemic muster by its own lights, and this dynamism points to one last contrast essential to Hegel's conception of consciousness, which will be labeled the "teleological difference." Consciousness understands itself, to begin with, as only potentially a member of the class of knowers. Moving from potential to actual membership is an achievement. Consciousness must

such reflexive self-knowledge. I, the epistemologist, know of myself that I instantiate the class characteristic articulated by the theory of knowledge I endorse.

16 As Hegel insists at M: 53–54/MM: 77, where he states that "what is essential to maintain throughout the entire investigation," is that all evaluative epistemic standards "fall within the knowing that we are investigating, and consequently, we do not have to import criteria or apply our own bright ideas or thoughts in the investigation."

17 M: 53–54/MM: 76–77. Imputing this epistemic responsibility to consciousness serves Hegel's purpose of enforcing the phenomenological difference: Only consciousness undertakes, from the internal point of view, its dynamic project of first-person epistemic self-evaluation within the framework of epistemic difference.

establish that its candidacy lives up to the dictates of its very own epistemic norm; it must demonstrate that it instantiates the class characteristic necessary and sufficient for membership in the class of knowers. Each time consciousness fails to accomplish that end it must regroup and try again, revising not only its knowledge claim, but ultimately its criterion of evaluation as well.[18]

The standard that consciousness initially furnishes for itself at each stage takes the form of a theory of truth, which is its preconception of the object as it is in itself.[19] However, for its first-person self-evaluation, consciousness needs to appeal to more than a theory of truth; it must also provide an account of epistemic justification, which determines whether its claim to know can be credibly stamped as real knowledge. Its standard of justification is correspondence: if the object as consciousness encounters or represents it corresponds to the object in itself, i.e., according to consciousness' own pre-delineated theory of truth, then it can legitimately claim to possess real knowledge.[20] Consciousness operates, then, with two interrelated criteria: on the one hand, the primary truth criterion, its preconception of mind-independent reality and, on the other hand, the secondary criterion of epistemic justification, which is correspondence between its preconception of truth and the object as consciousness actually encounters it. Only if its encountered object corresponds to its preconceived truth, can consciousness secure its successful candidacy, having satisfied its self-imposed standard of epistemic justification.

To determine for itself whether or not correspondence obtains, consciousness must compare its representation of the object as it encounters it

---

18   M: 54–56/MM: 76–78.
19   At M: 53/MM: 77, Hegel writes: "Consciousness gives its standard to itself... the moment of truth . . . Thus, in what consciousness from within itself declares to be the in itself or the true, we have the standard that it itself puts forward to measure its knowing."
20   M: 53/MM: 77. "If we call knowing the concept, the essence or what is true, however, that which is or the object, the examination consists in seeing whether the concept *corresponds* to the object. But if we call the essence or the in itself of the object the concept, and understand the object by contrast as object, namely as it is for another, then the examination consists in seeing whether the object *corresponds* to its concept" (emphasis added).

with its theory of truth. To evaluate its knowledge claim in light of its two-fold standard of truth and correspondence, consciousness must, therefore, be aware not only of the object but of itself as well. Self-consciousness in this sense is built into the very project of consciousness itself.[21] This conception of self-consciousness would dovetail nicely with an ordinary understanding of self-knowledge as introspective reflection. But it would fail to explain why, although all shapes of consciousness must engage in this familiar sort of reflection,[22] Hegel only labels one of them "Self-Consciousness." There must be something more distinctive about Self-Consciousness as a unique shape that enables it to perform its pivotal linking function in the argument of the *Phenomenology*.

The Phenomenological History of Consciousness: The Main Argument

In describing the object of his phenomenological inquiry, Hegel speaks of the "history" of consciousness; however, he does not pretend to be concerned with recounting events that actually happened.[23] Two of the most well-known discussions in the book are inspired by fictional works, one dealing with Sophocles' *Antigone*, the other with Diderot's dialogue, *Rameau's Nephew*.[24] The vignette of the lord-servant relation, to which Hegel devotes only a few pages, has no historical pedigree, even if it is perhaps the most influential passage, thanks to Marx and his followers, who transformed it into the basis for a metaphysics of human nature and of history.[25] Hegel's "history" of consciousness is, as one could say with Rousseau,

21 Hegel expresses this sense of self-consciousness at M: 54/MM: 77–78.
22 In chapter II, Perception, Hegel officially characterizes this kind of introspective self-awareness as "reflection," to which consciousness itself for the first time acknowledges it resorts to account for its mistakes. M: 71-72/MM: 98–99.
23 M: 50/MM: 73
24 On Sophocles' *Antigone*, M: 261, 284/MM: 322, 348; on Diderot's *Rameau's Nephew*, M: 298, 318/MM: 365, 387.
25 This tradition of the reception of the *Phenomenology* began with Marx, whose notebooks from the 1840s, first made public in 1927—now known as the *Economic and Philosophic Manuscripts of 1844*, also as the *Paris Manuscripts*—docu-

conjectural or hypothetical.[26] All of its contents are chosen and configured with an eye towards their epistemic significance alone; they are ripe for phenomenological analysis solely as attempts by consciousness to attain metaphysics.

In the drama that Hegel famously denotes "the dialectic of experience,"[27] one shape of consciousness after another passes in review making up a sequence of deficient efforts. Each subsequent endeavor of consciousness to justify its knowledge claim incorporates "lessons learned" from previous attempts, avoiding predecessor errors rather than repeating them even as it innovates and makes novel, shape-specific mistakes of its own. Hegel's diagnoses of the failures composing this procession reveal a typical pattern: within any one shape, consciousness progresses from the weakest to the strongest versions of the knowledge claim under scrutiny, while maintaining allegiance to the prevailing preconception of truth. In the transition from one shape to the next, the previously prevailing theory of truth is abandoned in favor of a new one.[28]

ment his reading of the *Phenomenology*, which concentrates its attention almost solely on the subsection of chapter IV dealing with the lord-servant relation. This tradition culminates in Alexandre Kojève's influential lectures on Hegel in the decade following the publication of Marx's early writings. Excerpts from the 1947 French publication of Kojève's lectures, which contain his lecture notes together with some of their transcriptions, were translated into English and published in 1969, shortly after Kojève's death in May, 1968. See Alexandre Kojève, *Introduction to the Reading of Hegel*, ed. Allan Bloom, trans. James Nichols (New York: Basic Books, 1969).

26 See Jean-Jacques Rousseau, *The First and Second Discourses*, ed. Roger Masters, trans. Roger and Judith Masters (Bedford: St. Martin's Press, 1964), 92, 103.

27 M: 55/MM: 78.

28 M: 55–57/MM: 78–81. According to Hegel's retrospective glance from the vantage point of the immediate successor shape, Self-consciousness, the conception of truth common to the subshapes of the first major shape, Consciousness, is that truth resides in the object that is presumptively other than the cognizing subject. By contrast, with the transition to the novel, second major shape of Self-consciousness it is proclaimed that only now for the first time consciousness has entered the "native realm of truth," since truth is now located in the cognitive subject itself, with the implication, which cannot be overemphasized, that from this point forward the knowledge sought can only be self-knowledge.

The first phase of the argument, which begins with the analysis of the shape called Consciousness, owes its brevity to the epistemic agent's quick realization that its cognitive encounters, contrary to what it presumes, can never afford it direct access to its object. Rather, they are unavoidably mediated by its own perceptions and conceptualizations; and since its perceptions are theory-laden, consciousness soon realizes that its claims accurately to represent the object in itself turn out to be claims to know an object of its own theoretical conjuring. Hence, consciousness is compelled to conclude that knowledge, if attainable, must take the form of self-knowledge.

Consciousness proves incapable of obtaining self-knowledge, however, in its new guise of Self-Consciousness. The fundamental problem plaguing consciousness in this new, second major shape is its commitment to the thesis that knowledge has to default to self-knowledge for the sole reason that, according to its theory of truth, there is and can be nothing to be known other than itself; yet, as a structure of opposition, consciousness must adhere to the premise that knowledge is of an object in itself, independent of and other than consciousness. Self-consciousness maintains a theory of truth that rejects any objective reality other than itself; nevertheless, as consciousness it must grant just such a realm of objectivity shot through with otherness. If knowledge can only be self-knowledge, yet knowledge must be of a mind-independent object, then self-knowledge cannot be achieved in the shape of Self-Consciousness.[29]

29 Because consciousness in the shape of Self-consciousness no longer assumes that the object it confronts is the locus of truth, Hegel now characterizes Consciousness as desire (M: 105/MM: 139). Consciousness seeks its epistemic satisfaction by proving that it itself, not the object it immediately encounters and presumes is other, is the one, sole truth. To establish that its claim possesses the justifying property of correspondence, it must demonstrate that the only object in itself is itself and itself alone. It cannot abide the otherness it immediately encounters, and must eliminate it, even though, due to epistemic difference, it cannot help but presuppose it.

This justificatory task compels Consciousness as desire to adopt an utterly negative attitude towards its object, and as Self-consciousness to establish the identity of the object with itself, the assumed locus of truth. It has to destroy or annihilate the desired object altogether, leaving no competitor for the title of truth. But this strategy is self-defeating, because the desire relation is a ne-

As the argument of the *Phenomenology* pivots from this immediate upshot of its shorter segment to the longer, consciousness in the third and final major shape of Reason inherits this challenge: how can the

cessary condition of Self-consciousness, and to annihilate the encountered object of desire destroys the desire relation. No proof of the claim to be the sole truth is forthcoming since, as Hegel asserts, the object of desire must be, if Self-consciousness is to be: "Desire and the self-certainty obtained in its satisfaction, are conditioned by its object; for self-certainty comes from sublating this other: that the sublating might be, this other must be." (M: 109/MM: 143) Hegel's descriptions of the various subshapes of Self-consciousness that involve fear of death, violence, subordination, destruction, and nothingness, characteristic of the existential life-death struggle for recognition and the lord-servant relation, as well as the stoic indifference, the skepticism, and ascetic misery with which the chapter ends, are a function of this destructive imperative.

It might be thought that Self-consciousness has an alternative non-destructive route open to it. If its desired object were but another self-consciousness like itself, it could identify itself with the object, relate epistemically only to itself as sole truth, and thereby attain self-knowledge. Yet, this gambit assumes the rejection of the identification, intrinsic to consciousness, of the object, what is in itself, with otherness. This rejection is in fact implied by the treatment of the encountered object of desire as another self-consciousness. For, logically speaking, this is to acknowledge it as an individual, i.e., a numerically different but eidetically identical entity, a differentiated instance of same kind. (For a reconstruction of Hegel's account of the logic of individuality, see my "Ways of Being Singular: The Logic of Individuality," in *Hegel's Theory of the Subject*, ed. David Gray Carlson (London: Palgrave Macmillan 2005), 85–98.) This option in effect adumbrates the concept of spirit—not accidentally introduced here for the first time—as reciprocal recognition (M: 110, 111/MM: 145). If Consciousness in the shape of Self-consciousness could avail itself of this option, Hegel's thought experiment would end here with the epistemic agent achieving self-knowledge and thus successfully completing its quest. What blocks Consciousness from adopting this strategy under the auspices of Self-consciousness and instead compels it to trek through the long argument in the successive shapes of Reason?

Here's the rub. Recall that Self-consciousness emerges as a result of the falsification of the thesis of its predecessor shape that truth is other than Consciousness. The premise of the entire account of Self-consciousness is the opposing conception that the truth lies instead solely in the knower. Built into the very conception of the shape of Self-consciousness, therefore, is the as-opposition of consciousness and self-knowledge be conjoined free from contradiction?

As a shape of consciousness, Reason exhibits all its formal features: starting from the epistemic difference between consciousness and its presumed mind-independent object, it must justify its knowledge claim by establishing correspondence between the two sides of this opposition through a process of self-evaluation in which it measures itself against standards of its own provenance. What is unique and peculiar about Reason's theory of truth, however, is that it implies the denial of the opposition of consciousness! For, according to Reason, it belongs to the very nature of the object in itself that it is identical to the object as encountered by consciousness.[30] A knowledge claim is justified if and only if the object encountered is the truth. Consequently, it is in principle impossible for the object as it is in truth to fail to correspond to what it is for consciousness and vice-versa. But this excludes the epistemic difference that defines consciousness as a structure of opposition. Reason's bi-conditional theory of truth, therefore, entails the elimination of consciousness as the privileged condition for attaining knowledge.

sumption that these two truth theories form an exclusive disjunction, which in turn requires Self-consciousness to persist in assuming the otherness of the object immediately given to it.

For an account of the *Phenomenology* that places in the interpretive center the violence endemic to Self-consciousness as desire, see Peter Kalkavage, *The Logic of Desire: An Introduction to Hegel's Phenomenology of Spirit* (Philadelphia: Paul Dry Books, 2007). Taking his cue from the definition with which Kojève begins his "famous commentary" on the *Phenomenology*, "Man is self-consciousness," Kalkavage devotes his efforts to exploring "*what self is* for Hegel, what follows from the identification of human nature with selfhood understood as self-consciousness, and why, as Hegel says at one point, 'self-consciousness is desire'" (xiii). Desire, on his reading of Hegel, "is aggressive or violent: the impulse to negate. This impulse recurs throughout the journey of consciousness" (109). Violence thus plays a key role in "the drama of man as self-consciousness" (110).

30 Hegel refers to this unity or identity as "the category." He uses this Kantian expression, because for Kant, as Hegel reads him, a category or pure concept is constitutive of the objectivity of the object. For an analysis of Hegel's account of Reason (the first subsection of Reason), which attends especially to its Kantian resonance, see my "Reason, Idealism, and the Category: Kantian Language in Hegel's *Phenomenology of Spirit*," *supra* note #8.

This logical consequence has its full impact when combined with the strict limitation of all knowledge claims to those of self-knowledge; for, it conjoins to Reason's theory of truth the critical qualification that the object of knowledge can only be the self. Three crucial implications follow. The first is ontological: Ultimately the sole object of knowledge can only be the self-knowing knower; but at a minimum, that exclusive object can have only those properties, whatever they turn out to be, that are constitutive of the self of the knower. The second is an epistemological implication: Knowledge of this exclusive object consists entirely in discerning precisely what those characteristics are that constitute its self. To attain self-knowledge, consciousness has to learn about the nature of its self; again ultimately, they must at least include epistemic properties. Finally, the requirement governing rational self-knowledge has an additional, anti-dualist ontological implication: It is not possible for there to be two different selves, one of which is the object as encountered and the other the self as it is in itself. Reason can justifiably claim self-knowledge if and only if what it encounters does not imply a real or true self that is alien to the self it takes itself to embody. ·

Hegel joins these three implications together in his preliminary sketch of the shape of Reason. Under the heading "idealism," he first characterizes Reason as "the certainty of being all reality."[31] Given the reduction of

31   M: 140/MM: 179. This principle of idealism states Reason's theory of truth. As the immediate successor to the previous shape of Self-consciousness, Reason must start from the premise that knowledge is self-knowledge, and its idealist claim, therefore, is not just that it knows reality—the claim of every shape of consciousness—but that it is itself the very comprehensive reality that it claims to know. Hegel offers a bi-conditional formulation for Reason's pre-delineated theory of truth: "what is in itself only is insofar as it is for consciousness, and what is for it is also in itself." By encapsulating Reason's idealism with the Kantian expression, "the category," he encodes the principle that "self-consciousness and being is the same essence," which will for the duration serve as Reason's measure of its epistemic success. This uniquely idealist conception of categorial truth is utterly formal, leaving undetermined until further notice the features that self and reality have to have if the claim consciousness as Reason makes to self-knowledge is to measure up to its self-imposed standard of categoriality. Due to this initial emptiness of categorial truth, the question remains open as to the steps Reason will have to take to supply content to the categorial form in order to justify its claim to self-know-

knowledge to self-knowledge, there is, in principle, no reality to be known other than the reality of the self of Reason, whatever—again by Reason's own lights—it discovers itself to be. Reason's idealism is tantamount to the claim that it itself is the very comprehensive reality that it claims to know. Precisely as a shape of consciousness, however, Reason still presumes the epistemic difference between what is for consciousness and what is in itself; and that supposition of mind-independence stands in stark conflict with Reason's defining theory of truth, according to which there is and can be no such irreducible difference.

The decisive step in the long argument of the *Phenomenology* is taken when Reason attempts to solve the problem it inherited from Self-Consciousness by taking on the shape of Spirit. The meaning of this quintessentially Hegelian term, *Geist*, is expressed in Hegel's pithy formula, the "I that is we and we that is I."[32] "Spirit" designates this royal we, and when one says "we know," the royal we stands in for every knower. Incorporating Spirit into the phenomenological inquiry extends new hope to the seeker of self-knowledge by suggesting the following strategy. First, the object of the epistemic agent's knowledge claim must be an I. Since the one claiming knowledge is himself an I, the epistemic relation is in the broadest sense a social relation among I's or selves. If, furthermore, the claimant can justifiably hold that in knowing the object he has achieved self-knowledge, then the encountered object must be not merely an I, but one that is the same as the knowledge-claiming I. Of course, the object-I cannot be numerically the same as the knowledge-claiming I; after all, there must be a difference, so the identity can only be that of sameness in kind. An I that is We must be a differentiated instance of the same kind as its fellow I's. Consequently, there must be a property or set of properties that both the object-I and the knowledge-claiming I instantiate that make them members of the same class.[33] But

ledge. Still, it is already clear that Reason, if it is to achieve self-knowledge, will have to take matters into its own hands, progressively determining both its self and reality, which categorically are the same, in order finally to bring both into accord with the formal demands of categoriality.

32 M: 110/MM: 145.

33 Since set theory permits a null set or singleton, a we cannot be a class in strict set-theoretical terms.

their joint instantiating of a shared class-characteristic cannot be only for the phenomenological spectator looking on at the members of the class from his external point of view. It must be known from the internal point of view: Spirit implies the participants' reciprocal recognition, and they enjoy that epistemic mutuality because the class characteristic they share is a relational property, a function of their interaction with one another. Spirit provides an interpretation of Reason's claim to be all reality: it assumes the shape of a self that knows itself in the object that is constituted by the interaction of all the members of the same class to which it knows itself to belong. This is what Hegel means in stating that Spirit is "aware of itself as its world and of its world as itself."[34]

If the epistemic agent under phenomenological scrutiny were simply unalloyed Spirit, metaphysics at this point would become actual, with self-knowledge achieved in the form of class members' reciprocal recognition, finally freed from the inconsistency stemming from the conjunction of self-knowledge and the opposition of consciousness. But Spirit is still a shape of consciousness, and thus is tainted by the epistemic difference between consciousness and the alien object it claims to know. The long argument of the *Phenomenology* will end with this core diagnostic claim: the very idea of spiritual self-knowing as a shape of consciousness is self-contradictory.

Hegel reaches this conclusion by inspecting a variety of ethical, moral, and religious configurations, all of which exhibit this intractable difficulty of an alien reality that frustrates the metaphysical claim to spiritual self-knowledge. In Reason's first spiritual shape, ethical community (*Sittlichkeit*), the members of the We share common characteristics through their willing conformity to law, which codifies the rules governing their interrelations and defining their law-bred role-identities. The class members know themselves in and through their relations to one another, precisely because who they are, spiritually, is determined by the same set of rules they all accept and enact. The problem, however, is that ethical community, reflecting the structure of consciousness, its opposition between that which is given or in itself, and that which is dependent upon human positing, is constituted by two conflicting codes of law. Hegel exposes this difficulty in his memorable

34   M: 263/MM: 324.

interpretation of the tragic clash between Antigone and Creon, who individualize the irreconcilable conflict between the family, governed by divine law grounded in a transcendent inscrutable authority, and the city ruled by human law.

In the immediately following subshape of Spirit, Hegel shows that the relations within and between state and civil society suffer their own forms of opposition reflected in a variety of experiences of alienation between natural and conventional selfhood. Markets, whose rules determine the social roles the individuals perform in their interactions, create both artificial needs and the desire for wealth, the conventional means of exchange and measure of value necessary for their satisfaction. In demanding conformity to their constitutive rules, social and political institutions highlight the contrast between the givens of nature and the imperatives of convention that mold and so transform or suppress the former. A turn to piety provides no path of liberation from worldly alienation; for faith's postulation of another world, in which the individual seeks the certainty of knowing his true self, only heightens his awareness of the self he must presume to be false, inescapably rooted as it is in this world from which he wants to flee. Nor, finally, can the alienated spirit overcome its internal division by claiming for itself an enlightened universal self that transcends all natural as well as conventional differences. Reason's idealist claim to be all reality now sparks the practical demand for revolutionary action to found a political order corresponding to that universal selfhood, which makes families, markets, and private civil institutions, owing to their lack of sufficient universality, strictly impermissible. Enforcing the prohibition against them entails terror. This is the terrible price consciousness as Spirit pays for its attempt to complete its quest for self-knowledge by abolishing all differences among selves that frustrate the realization of its political project.

In the final shape of Spirit, the moral view of the world, which lies beyond the limits of political idealism, Hegel uncovers yet another manifestation of the opposition of consciousness standing in the way of Spirit's self-knowledge. Here the imperatives of the moral law valid for all rational beings, which consciousness claims to find within its own rational self, conflict with the reality of brute nature, both internal and external. This independent, alien domain of reality, which simply will not bend exhaustively to the demands of moral duty, presents the ultimate obstacle to moral self-knowledge that Spirit cannot overcome. Consciousness insists that its moral self is the sole reality; to justify its claim would require completing the never-ending task of the moralization of nature and naturalization of morality.

Renewing for the last time its quest to achieve metaphysical knowledge, Reason initiates a final attempt, in the shape of Religion, to reconcile spiritual self-knowledge with the formal opposition of consciousness. Despite avoiding all its predecessors' mistakes, this gambit too proves unsuccessful, bringing to a close the long segment of the argument and with that the main argument of the *Phenomenology* as a whole. Religious consciousness claims knowledge of itself as Spirit, hence self-knowledge of its membership in the class of self-knowers. While construing religion in these terms through his phenomenological lens, Hegel at the same time exploits the traditional view of divine omniscience,[35] inferring that the core claim of consciousness as Religion is to know itself to be God. This is a new formulation of what, if achieved, would amount to the attainment of metaphysics. For if divine omniscience is perfect knowing, God would be the successful epistemologist, who attributes to himself the justified true belief that he is a member of the class of self-knowers, because he knows that he instantiates the class-characteristic defining self-knowledge as determined by his own true, warranted theory of it.

In its most complete shape as the religion of revelation, the bold claim of Religion is tantamount to the first-person assertion, I am God. This assertion in fact encapsulates a set of three interrelated claims: consciousness knows what God is, namely self-knowing spirit; consciousness knows of a human being who knows himself to be the incarnation of God; and consciousness knows that having knowledge of that incarnate God is its own attainment of self-knowledge. In short, consciousness claims to know itself

---

35 Hegel does not always use the term "God" (*Gott*). He often uses, for example, the more formal expression, "absolute essence" (*absolute Wesen*) M: 410-411/MM: 495–96. For an analysis of the argument of Religion, chapter VII of the *Phenomenology*, see my "Religion and Self-Knowledge in Hegel's *Phenomenology of Spirit*," in *American Dialectic* Vol. 3/1 (2013), 69–92.

to be the self-knowing incarnate God. The grand claim of the religion of revelation, in other words, is that the religious knower, in knowing himself to be God incarnate, has at last grabbed hold of the holy grail of metaphysics.

Why, then, does this final shape of religious consciousness fall short? For the simple reason that the religion of revelation, as a shape of consciousness informed by the oppositional framework, reifies its object, transforming what it claims to know as its very self into an alien being. It claims that God appears to it in the guise of a single, living human being, instantiating natural, rather than solely spiritual properties, subject to the vicissitudes of space, time, and natural decay. With the death of the would-be divine human, members of the spiritual community are no longer eyewitnesses to his presence; they must resort to the cognitive medium of representation, a "mix of thought and sensation," to imagine the departed incarnate deity.[36] They can only aspire to liken themselves to his purely spiritual image, looking with hope to a future in which they too will undergo the same transfiguration. Until that time, or rather until time is extinguished, the once incarnate God remains beyond, of another kind, not constituted through interaction with the fellow members of the class and not one with whom they can completely identify. Religion is

36 The members of the community of the faithful realize that their unhappiness is due in part to their mistaken attribution of natural properties to a being that they at the same time assume to be purely spiritual. They can attempt to avoid that error by representing a being whose natural, sensory properties are contingent, but whose essential properties are spiritual, although doing so would raise a new question about the contingency of incarnation. This leads religious consciousness to seek God through historical inquiry, attempting to recover the lost presence by tracing it to its past. In doing so, Religion combines the use of naturalistic imagery—the relation of father and son, for example—with a moralizing account, which moves from a story of creation, loss of innocence, expulsion, and evil, to alienation and suffering, death, and finally resurrection. In all of this, individuals are still attempting to differentiate themselves as individuated members of the same class (M: 462–73/MM: 555–68), not, however, by conceptualizing the logic of self-relation, but by fashioning the representation of the object as self-knowing Spirit (M: 460–62/MM: 554–55).

left bereft of a justification for its ambitious claim to spiritual self-knowl-edge.[37]

The Closing Argument of the *Phenomenology*: Absolute Knowing

The phenomenological investigation of Religion leads to the diagnostic in-sight that its failure to achieve self-knowledge of Spirit is due solely to its at-tempt to do so under the auspices of epistemic difference. Further progress in the quest for metaphysics is impossible, since the only way to avoid the otherwise insoluble problem is to jettison the opposition of consciousness al-together as the privileged framework for knowledge. Yet, one last shape of consciousness emerges from this conclusion, which Hegel labels "Absolute Knowing." Should this highfalutin name be taken to suggest, to the contrary, that consciousness can finally achieve success in establishing metaphysics? Hegel nowhere states or even implies that Absolute Knowing should be con-strued to designate the knowing of the absolute as of an object, whether the totality of being or the highest being. In one of the two passages where he actually uses the expression "the absolute," he likens it, disparagingly, to a black hole-like abyss that swallows up all distinctions—echoing the sarcasm of his well-known comment in the Preface to the *Phenomenology* about "the night in which all cows are black."[38] If success of the project under investiga-tion in the *Phenomenology* is still defined from the internal point of view of consciousness, as it has been all along—the achievement of metaphysical knowledge within the framework of epistemic difference—the terminal chap-ter on Absolute Knowing offers a negative answer.[39]

If, on the other hand, success is understood from the external, phe-nomenological point of view—diagnostic insight into the causes of the nec-essary failure of the metaphysical knowledge project under scrutiny—then Hegel's thought experiment has conducted a successful probe with a final unequivocal result. Its end is not aporetic. Absolute Knowing, as the final

---

37   M: 473–78/MM: 568–74.
38   M: 9/MM: 22.
39   This would mean that Hegel has reached, by his own distinctive Socratic means, concurrence with Kant's conclusion about the impossibility of meta-physics.

shape, is immunized against the one remaining, but fatal mistake of its predecessor, Religion: it recognizes that it cannot consistently hold that spiritual self-knowledge is knowledge of a relation-independent object in itself. But given the consciousness-based definition of knowledge, Absolute Knowing is, as Hegel states, no knowing at all.[40] Its achievement consists, rather, in an act of recollection through which it reconstructs for itself an etiology of the path that has led to the demise of the quest for metaphysical knowledge. It sloughs off at last the opposition of consciousness and ceases to be a shape of consciousness at all. In its retrospective glance, it converges with the phenomenological point of view and shares in the phenomenologist's non-metaphysical enlightenment.[41]

40 ". . . the phenomenology of spirit is the science of consciousness, the exposition of it . . . consciousness has for its result the Concept of science, i.e., pure knowing . . . Pure knowing as concentrated into this unity has sublated all reference to an other and to mediation; it is without any distinction and as thus distinctionless, ceases to be knowledge." Provided that "pure knowing" and "absolute knowing" can justifiably be treated as synonyms, absolute knowing is no knowing at all. G. W. F. Hegel, *Hegel's Science of Logic*, trans. A. W. Miller (London: George Allen & Unwin, 1968), 48–49, 69.

41 On closer inspection, Absolute Knowing consists in retrospective insight concerning the following five elements: a) the self-reflexive character of epistemology; b) self-knowledge as first-person self-ascription of the class characteristic specifying what it is to be a knower; c) epistemic difference constitutive of consciousness that implies a commitment to realism; d) the concept of Spirit, implying self-knowledge as mutual recognition through rule-mediated interaction; e) the inconsistent triad of consciousness, Spirit and self-knowledge, rendering metaphysics logically impossible.

Hegel concluded his Introduction to the *Phenomenology* with this final sentence: "In pressing forward to its true existence, consciousness will arrive at a point at which it rids itself of its semblance of being burdened with what is alien in kind, with what is only for it and is as what is other, or where appearance becomes identical to essence, so that the presentation of it coincides at precisely this point with the authentic science of spirit; and finally, when consciousness grasps this its essence, it will signify the nature of Absolute Knowing itself" (M: 56–57/MM: 80–81). Reason's categorial theory of truth, proclaiming the elimination of epistemic difference, first marks this point at which in principle consciousness rids itself of the semblance of what is alien in kind. When Reason assumes the shape of Spirit, the *Phenomenology* as the science of the experience of consciousness becomes the science of the expe-

Conclusion

The argumentative path of Hegel's thought experiment, internalized by Absolute Knowing, terminates in the recognition that the pursuit of metaphysics is doomed to failure: If this knowledge is presumed to be of the object as thing in itself, then knowledge of the unchanging truth about being, of reality not in a partial sphere but as a whole, is strictly speaking impossible. But this is the wisdom that, according to tradition-bred definition, philosophy is purported to seek. Indeed, the Platonic Socrates, at the beginning of the tradition, finds the only worthwhile life to be one erotically driven to strive for wisdom, by an examination of opinion that aims to replace it with knowledge. Until this epistemic goal is achieved, philosophers in the Socratic mold at least have human wisdom, awareness of the fundamental questions and self-knowledge of their ignorance of the answers. The Socratic is vulnerable, however, to a radical skeptical attack that leverages Hegel's phenomenological result: If the wisdom philosophy seeks is simply identical with metaphysics, and that has been found to be impossible, the very idea of human wisdom is undermined as well, for the philosopher's animating desire is in vain. Such skepticism might allow the illusion of philosophy to persist, but only at the price of willful blindness to its absurdity. The Hegelian phenomenologist, however, can rescue the Socratic from this threat by denying the skeptic's identification of wisdom with metaphysics. He can show at the same time that this radical skepticism is ensnared in its own dilemma. If the skeptic makes an absolutely global claim about the impossibility of knowledge as such, he faces self-destruction in the form of self-referential inconsistency. If, on the other hand, he confines himself to claiming only the impossibility of wisdom within the framework of

rience of consciousness in the shape of Spirit. Absolute Knowing is the final shape in that it adequately understands that the necessary and sufficient conditions for knowledge are strictly incompatible with epistemic difference. Thus, a knowledge claim that is justified owing to its correspondence to the essential content of categorial truth inherited from Religion—namely that truth is self-knowing Spirit—is absolutely impossible within the horizon of consciousness. An epistemic agent, if he really does know, knows himself to be self-knowing Spirit. If he possesses such self-knowledge, he also necessarily knows that his knowing cannot be informed by the structure of the opposition of conscious-

consciousness, he merely mimics the insight of the phenomenologist. In that case, the skeptic belongs with his fellow Socratics in their achievement of genuine human wisdom, which retains its vitality provided it directs its philosophical eros towards a non-metaphysical wisdom.[42]

ness. In short, he comprehends the following exclusive disjunction: either he knows, or he operates epistemically entirely within the framework of consciousness, but not both. To appreciate this disjunction is to have achieved Absolute Knowing.

42 This paper purposely prescinds from the question, which has preoccupied scholars for quite some time, of the system-theoretical role of the *Phenomenology* in the Hegelian corpus. Rather than interpreting the book as but an early version of his more mature system of philosophy, many take Hegel's comments about the book, primarily those found in the prefatory and introductory discussions to his *Science of Logic*, as evidence that he assigns it a propaedeutic function, more specifically an introduction to philosophy understood as science. Further clarifying Hegel's idea of phenomenology as the "deduction of the concept of science," is the thesis that the principal obstacle to philosophic science is the "natural assumption" rooted in the opposition of consciousness, to which Hegel refers with the first words of the Introduction to the *Phenomenology*. Hegel's phenomenological intention consists in eliminating that one barrier barring entry to philosophy as genuine knowledge. The reconstruction presented in this paper is consistent with this thesis about the system-theoretical role of the *Phenomenology*, since the thought experiment Hegel conducts results in the failure of consciousness to attain metaphysical knowledge, and in the emergence of Absolute Knowing, which is the diagnostic insight into the structure of consciousness as cause of the failure. To assume the stance of Absolute Knowing is to leave behind the natural assumption that the wisdom the philosopher seeks, like all knowledge whatsoever, can be pursued only within the oppositional framework of consciousness. Liberated by the *Phenomenology* from that cramped view, philosophy can now proceed to pursue non-metaphysical wisdom, whose starting point must be indeterminacy, since it remains to be determined what such knowledge will ultimately look like. For a detailed account of this propaedeutic function of the *Phenomenology* that pays careful attention to the evidentiary support in Hegel's texts, see William Maker, *Philosophy Without Foundations: Rethinking Hegel* (Binghamton: SUNY Press, 1994). In two recent extensive commentaries on the *Phenomenology* and the *Science of Logic*, respectively, Richard Dien Winfield lays out in detail the arguments consonant with this interpretation of the *Phenomenology*'s system-theoretical role. See *Hegel's Phenomenology of Spirit: A Critical Rethinking in Seventeen Lectures* (Lanham, MD: Rowman and Littlefield,

2013), and *Hegel's Science of Logic: A Critical Rethinking in Thirty Lectures* (Lanham: Rowman and Littlefield, 2012). The earliest reference to Hegel's "non-metaphysical" intention for his systematic conception of philosophy as science, as far as I know, is in Klaus Hartmann, "Hegel: a Non-metaphysical View," in *Hegel: A Collection of Critical Essays*, ed. A. MacIntyre (Notre Dame, IN: Notre Dame Press, 1972).

Poetry, Philosophy and Faith in Kierkegaard's
Philosophical Fragments
Ann Ward

In *Philosophical Fragments*, Kierkegaard, under the pseudonymous author-ship of Johannes Climacus, explores the relationship between philosophy and faith by contrasting Socrates and "the god" as teachers. Socratic ques-tioning, Climacus argues, causes the recollection of truths that were already in the learner. Learning is thus re-affirmation of the self and discarding of the teacher. The god, on the other hand, is a savior who brings knowledge of truth that was beyond the learner. Learning is the discarding of self as one accepts what only the god can give. Scholars such as Jacob Howland argue, however, that for Climacus philosophy and faith are more consistent than at first appears, and that faith may actually be the perfection of So-cratic reason rather than its negation.[1]

This chapter explores how Socratic philosophy and religious faith in *Fragments* are brought together and also how they are drawn apart. Climacus initially tries to bring philosophy and faith together by giving a rational ac-count of why the core belief of Christianity, that the god becomes human,

---

1   See Jacob Howland, *Kierkegaard and Socrates: A Study of Philosophy and Faith* (New York: Cambridge University Press, 2006), 4–7. For the consistency of philosophy and faith in Kierkegaard's *Fear and Trembling* which also seems to pull them apart, see for example Merold Westphal, "Kierkegaard and Hegel," in *The Cambridge Companion to Kierkegaard*, Alastair Hannay and Gordon D. Marion, eds. (Cambridge: Cambridge University Press, 1998), 108–10, 121; and Edward F. Mooney, "Understanding Abraham: Care, Faith, and the Ab-surd," in *Kierkegaard's Fear and Trembling: Critical Appraisals*, Robert L. Perkins, ed. (Tuscaloosa: University of Alabama Press, 1981), 100–01, 109. Also see Thomas L. Pangle, *Political Philosophy and the God of Abraham* (Baltimore: The Johns Hopkins University Press, 2003), 179–81.

is necessary. The most significant way, however, in which Climacus brings philosophy and faith together is through his understanding of the condition necessary for grasping the truth brought by the god. This condition involves becoming aware of our ignorance, an awareness that is also brought about by the type of Socratic dialectic described in Plato's *Apology of Socrates*. Yet, Climacus' understanding of philosophy and faith also diverge. Thus, I argue that in *Fragments* Christianity's beginning point in the existence of god is not open to rational demonstration but rather presupposes faith. Moreover, I argue that although the condition for learning the truth may initially bring Socratic dialectic and faith together, it is actually a locus for their difference. I also explore Climacus' understanding of the tension between faith in creation *ex nihilo* and the philosophic understanding of the eternity of the universe.

I conclude with reflections on how *Fragments*, as a work of poetic art, can mediate between the pedagogical experiences of philosophical learners and those of religious learners. *Fragments* can be considered a work of poetic art rather than a treatise because Kierkegaard chooses to conceal his authorship in his pseudonym, Johannes Climacus. As poetic art, *Fragments,* I argue, can have both a Christian and a Socratic relationship to the reader. I also argue that as poetry *Fragments* mediates between philosophy and faith in another way as well. In positing the god as the unknown, passionate subjectivity beyond the person, Christianity unfolds in *Fragments* as a poetic account of the philosophic condition of the awareness of the unknown as a missing part of the self.

Recollection v. Rebirth

Climacus begins chapter one of *Fragments* with the question: "Can the truth be learned?"[2] Acknowledging that this is a Socratic question, Climacus thus begins with the problem of the concept of learning raised in the Plato's *Meno* (PF 9). After four failed attempts to define virtue, Socrates reassures

2   Soren Kierkegaard, *Philosophical Fragments, or a Fragment of Philosophy*, Howard V. Hong and Edna H. Hong, eds. and trans. (Princeton: Princeton University Press, 1985), 9. All subsequent citations will be taken from this edition, and will be in parentheses within the text as *PF* followed by page numbers.

Meno, the interlocutor who gives his name to the dialogue, that he still wishes to pursue with him the question of what virtue is. In response, Meno asks, "How will you look for it Socrates, when you do not know at all what it is? How will you aim for something you do not know at all? If you should meet with it, how will you know that this is the thing that you did not know?"[3] Socrates responds sympathetically by claiming, "I know what you want to say Meno [...] that a man cannot search either for what he knows or for what he does not know? He cannot search for what he knows—since he knows it, there is no need to search—nor for what he does not know, for he does not know what to look for" (*Meno,* 80e).

In the above exchange between Meno and Socrates, a number of conditions toward truth are revealed. The first is the condition of the wise, or those who know. Knowers will not search for truth because they already know it and hence learning, for them, is unnecessary. The second condition is that of the ignorant or the non-knowers. Non-knowers are more complex, however, as they can actually take two forms. The first and most apparent form of the non-knower in the exchange above are those who know they are ignorant and hence need to learn the truth, but fear that learning is impossible. For instance, if we do not know what virtue is before we begin, how will we know or have confidence that we have found it in the end. The irony brought out by this condition is that it seems you have to have knowledge of something before you can learn it. The second and less apparent form of the non-knower, implied in the exchange between Socrates and Meno above but made more explicit in Socrates' account of his interrogation of the politicians, poets and artisans in Plato's *Apology of Socrates*, are the ignorant who lack knowledge of their ignorance.[4] If they remain unaware of their need to learn, they will never begin the search for truth. The goal of Socratic questioning, as described in the *Apology*, is to give the questioned this crucial knowledge of ignorance, a knowledge more likely to arouse hostility toward Socrates rather than love.[5]

---

3   Plato, *Meno*, G. M. A. Grube trans. (Indianapolis: Hackett Publishing Company, 2002), 80d. All subsequent citations will be taken from this edition.

4   Plato, *Apology of Socrates*, G. M. A. Grube, trans. (Indianapolis: Hackett Publishing Company, 2002), 21d, 22c, and 22d–e. All subsequent citations will be taken from this edition.

5   See Plato, *Apology*, 21d, 24b. Also see Plato, *Meno*, 80a–b.

The search for truth requires knowledge of ignorance. But even with knowledge of ignorance how can we begin the search if we do not know what we are looking for? As Meno says, "How will you aim for something you do not know at all? If you should meet with it, how will you know that this is the thing that you did not know?" (*Meno*, 80d). Human learning which seeks to grasp the truth appears to be an impossible activity. To resolve this problem and keep the idea of the search for truth alive, Socrates, Climacus argues, develops the theory of recollection. According to Climacus:

> Socrates thinks through the difficulty by means (of the principle) that all learning and seeking are but recollecting. Thus the ignorant person merely needs to be reminded in order, by himself, to call to mind what he knows. The truth is not introduced into him but was in him. Socrates elaborates on this idea, and in it the Greek pathos is in fact concentrated, since it becomes a demonstration for the immortality of the soul—retrogressively, please note—or a demonstration for the pre-existence of the soul. (*PF* 9–10)

Climacus thus refers to Socrates' claim in the *Meno* that, "searching and learning are, as a whole, recollection" (*Meno*, 81d). By recollection Socrates means that the learner, when questioned in the right way by the teacher, remembers truths that they knew but had forgotten. The teacher does not impart or give knowledge, but rather reminds the learner of the knowledge in their souls that they had forgotten was there. Learners, therefore, do have knowledge of the truth they are looking for before they "learn" it, as it were.

In arguing that the theory of recollection resolves not only the problem of learning for Socrates but also serves to demonstrate the immortality of the soul, Climacus moves from reference to the *Meno* to Plato's *Phaedo*. In the *Phaedo*, Socrates argues that when we sense two equal things in this world, such as two equal sticks and stones, if we think about them in the right way we are reminded of the "Equal Itself," or the idea or form of the Equal.[6] This

6 Plato, *Phaedo*, Eva Brann, Peter Kalkavage, Eric Salem trans. (Newburyport, MA: Focus Classical Library, 1998),74a–b. All subsequent citations will be taken from this edition.

same process of recollection holds for all of the ideas or forms; whenever we consider particular manifestations of a thing in this world, such as particular manifestations of beauty, if we contemplate them correctly we are reminded of the universal classification, such as the idea or form of beauty itself, that groups the particulars into a class.[7] The knowledge in the soul, therefore, that the learner recollects is knowledge of the universal ideas or forms. But, where did we get this knowledge of the ideas or forms such that we can be reminded of them when considering their particular manifestations? Socrates concludes that the soul must have acquired knowledge of them before we were born, and then "forgot" this knowledge when entering our body upon birth. This shows that the soul, thinking the universal ideas, must exist separate from the body prior to birth, and that the process of recollecting entails overcoming the inhibiting factors of the body after birth.[8]

Climacus argues that with the theory of recollection Socrates presents himself not so much as a "teacher" but rather as a "midwife" instead (*PF* 10). As midwife, Socrates helps the learner bring forth or give birth to truths that were in them rather than himself, and as such Socrates is the inessential or "accidental" member of the pair (*PF* 11). Climacus thus argues:

> [T]he ultimate idea in all questioning is that the person asked must himself possess the truth and acquire it by himself. The temporal point of departure is a nothing, because in the same moment I discover that I have known the truth from eternity without knowing it, in the same moment that instant is hidden in the eternal, assimilated into it in such a way that I, so to speak, still cannot find it even if I were to look for it, because there is no Here and no There, but only an [...] (everywhere and nowhere). (*PF* 13)

7   Plato, *Phaedo*, 75d. Also see Paul Stern, *Socratic Rationalism and Political Phi-losophy: An Interpretation of Plato's Phaedo* (Albany: State University of New York Press, 1993), 197–98; and Ann Ward, "The Immortality of the Soul and the Origin of the Cosmos in Plato's *Phaedo*," in *Matter and Form: From Natural Science to Political Philosophy*, Ann Ward, ed. (Lanham, MD: Lexington Books, 2009), 26.

8   Plato, *Phaedo*, 75c–d, 76c. Also see Plato, *Meno*, 81b–e.

Socrates, therefore, once he has helped the learner reveal the knowledge that was concealed in their souls, does not seek credit for having taught anything. Indeed, one of the truths that Socratic questioning attempts to have brought to light is that sentimentality toward the "teacher," or the moment of contact between teacher and learner, is an illusion; who the teacher is and the point in time in which the learner is questioned by them is of no significance to the learner, because truth is in the learner. This leads Climacus to assert that for Socrates, reminding another of the truth within them "is the highest relation a human being can have to another." (*PF* 10) Reminding is highest because it is impossible for one human being to give to another human being something new or other than themselves that is not already within them. Thus, Climacus says, "In the Socratic view [...] self-knowledge is God knowledge" (*PF* 11). The suggestion is that the highest form of human knowledge is knowledge of the self—of the truth within the self and that the truth is within the self—and not knowledge of the other or the higher than the self, such as the god as distinct from the human. Socrates thus posits an equality between himself and other human beings, or between "teacher" and "learner," such that he "does not exclusively and conceitedly cultivate the company of brilliant minds [...] but philosophized just as absolutely with whomever he spoke" (*PF* 11).

The alternative to Socrates that Climacus poses is the god. As a teacher, the god, for Climacus, differs from Socrates in four significant ways. First, the god is essential to the learner and hence the moment in time they come into contact will never be forgotten by the learner.[9] For the learner the god is essential because the learner does not have the truth within them but rather, as Climacus says, "untruth" (*PF* 14). The second difference is thus that the god is not simply a "midwife" of an idea that was already in the learner, but rather is a teacher in the precise sense in that the god gives or brings truth to the learner. The god teaches the learner what they do not know, and hence one suspects that the truth the god brings is of a different type than that which is within the learner of recollection.

Climacus characterizes the state of untruth, through one's own fault,

9 *Philosophical Fragments*, 13.

as sin: "this state—to be untruth and to be that through one's own fault—what can we call it? Let us call it *sin*" (*PF* 15). Sin is thus the human incapacity or lost ability to learn, through their own fault. What does Climacus mean by "through [their] own fault?" He appears to mean that human beings, because of what they are, cannot acquire or regain this ability to learn by their own devices or through human reason alone, but rather require the aid of the god. This leads us to the third way in which the god in Climacus' account differs from Socrates. Not only does the god bring truth to the learner but the god also brings the condition to learn the truth. According to Climacus, "the condition for understanding the truth is like being able to ask about it." (*PF* 14). The condition, therefore, for acquiring the ability to learn is being able to ask, "What is truth?" Since we will only ask "What is truth?" if we learn that we don't know it—that we are in fact in a state of untruth—the condition that the god gives us is knowledge of our own ignorance.

The fourth way in which the god differs from Socrates is that when the god gives the learner the preparatory condition and then the truth itself, the learner is reborn in the sense that they become a person different from what they were before; previously they lacked the truth, but now they have it. According to Climacus:

> Just as the person who by Socratic midwifery gave birth to himself and in doing so forgot everything else in the world and in a more profound sense owed no human being anything, so also the one who is born again owes no human being anything, but owes that divine teacher everything. And just as the other one, because of himself, forgot the whole world, so he in turn, because of this teacher, must forget himself. (*PF* 19)

Climacus suggests that Socrates, as "midwife," causes the learner to give birth in the sense that they recollect and hence bring to light the truth that was already in them. Learning, in the Socratic sense, is thus reaffirmation of the self and the discarding of the teacher. The god, on the other hand, as "savior," causes the learner to be "the one born" in the sense of learning a truth that was other than or outside of the self, becoming thereby a new and different person than they were before. Learning is thus a discarding of the self as one receives the truth and hence the new life that the god and only the god can give.[10]

In this contrast between Socrates and the god as teachers, Climacus initially appears to draw a sharp distinction between philosophy and faith. In the religious view, for lack of a better term, learning is dependent on the god who must give us the condition for learning the truth and the truth itself. Divine revelation is thus absolutely essential and human reason, due to sin, is severely limited. In the philosophic view, learning is a process whereby we recollect, with the help of Socratic questioning, truths already within our souls. Truth, it seems, is accessible to human reason alone and revelation is superfluous.[11] Climacus' apparent implication is that it is difficult to reconcile Socratic rationalism with faith in divine revelation. This conflict is perhaps related to the different concepts of truth utilized by the philosophic and religious paradigms. The philosophic learner recollects universal ideas or truths accessible to human reason alone, whereas the religious learner, by contrast, appears to embrace a passionate subjectivity or particularity beyond the universal. The god, it seems, can be felt but not thought.

The Reasonableness of Christianity?

In chapter two of *Fragments*, Climacus attempts to give a rational account of why it is necessary that the god appear as a human being among human beings. Thus, after drawing philosophy and faith apart in chapter one he attempts to bring them together in chapter two by showing that the core belief of Christianity, that god becomes man, is reasonable, even while the god is love and hence is felt if not thought. Climacus begins by considering the different motives that Socrates and the god have for teaching. According to Climacus, Socrates teaches or questions his interlocutors because, like his interlocutors, he needs them to recollect the truth within himself. Just as the teacher is for the learner, the learner is the occasion for the

10 See Timothy P. Jackson, "Arminian Edification: Kierkegaard on Grace and Free Will," in *The Cambridge Companion to Kierkegaard*, Alastair Hannay and Gordon D. Marion, eds. (Cambridge: Cambridge University Press, 1998), 235.
11 See Howland, *Kierkegaard and Socrates*, 30, 46, 48.

teacher's self-understanding (*PF* 24). The difference, therefore, between teacher and learner is minor, as both Socrates and his interlocutors learn through the relationship.

The motive for the god to teach is quite different from that of Socrates. The god is perfectly self-sufficient and thus does not, as Socrates does, need pupils to understand himself, suggesting a radical inequality or lack of re-ciprocity between the god as teacher and the human learner; the learner needs the god but the god does not need them in return (*PF* 24). Climacus thus speculates:

> What, then, moves him [the god] to make his appearance? He must move himself [...] But if he moves himself, then there is of course no need that moves him, as if he himself could not endure silence but was compelled to burst into speech. But if he moves himself and is not moved by need, what moves him then but love, for love does not have the satisfaction of need outside itself but within. (*PF* 24)

Climacus, in the above passage, implicitly draws a distinction between human love and divine love. Human love is derived out of deficiency or need and is a feeling of lack, and it is generated by a beloved who appears beautiful and good. Divine love, on the other hand, flowing from a being without need or lack, appears to be derived from something like abundance or overflow—it is love out of sufficiency—and is generated from within the lover, who is god, and not the beloved. The god, in other words, loves for what he is—love, which is the god's essential nature—not for what we or the human beloved are.

The end the god wishes to achieve in becoming a teacher is similar to the motive, namely love, as the god desires that human beings, in gratitude for having received truth from the god, love the god in return. According to Climacus, "The love [of the god] [...] must be for the learner, and the goal must be to win him, for only in love is the different made equal, and only in equality or in unity is there understanding" (*PF* 25). Mutual love will overcome the inequality between god and human and thus a secondary motive of the god emerges: to make human beings equal to the god, which means possessing an equality of understanding with the god. Another distinction between human and divine love in Climacus' account therefore emerges. Human love involves sexuality and unhappy love, felt by both lover and beloved, is the failure to unite bodily. Divine love, on the other hand, seeks understanding or intellectual unity—to be of "one mind," as it were, and hence to think the truth together—and unhappy love, felt much more deeply by the god rather than the human—is the failure of intellectual unity.[12] Notice that the god is portrayed here not simply as love but also mind. As mind the god is infinitely superior to the human being. Given this radical inequality between teacher and learner, it seems that no true and thus happy love is possible between god and man.

Climacus argues that an equality or unity between god and man, if only imperfectly, could be brought about in two ways. The god could elevate human beings to himself, or the god could descend to human beings. The key problem with unity brought about by the ascent of the human learner is that the learner would receive a gift from the god that they could never repay. Yet, for the sake of their happiness the learner would have to be deceived or remain ignorant of this unredeemable debt, or in other words ignore the fact that the inequality between god and human has *not* actually been overcome.[13] Such ignorance, however, on the part of the learner would make the god unhappy.[14] The god wants human beings to live in the light of truth, or to be fully aware of their situation, which means being fully aware of their inferiority to the divine. Climacus indicates that the real difficulty is that human beings must attain unity with the god while still understanding that there is a distinction between the human and the divine. The god's task, in other words, involves seemingly irreconcilable contraries: human beings must be united with the god at the same time that they are taught the truth, namely that human beings are radically separate from or inferior to the god. Teaching human beings involves the simultaneous combination of unity and separateness, equality and inequality.

Given the difficulties of unity through the ascent of the learner, Climacus argues that the only possible option is unity through descent of the divine teacher. The god, however, can descend in two ways. The god could

12   Kierkegaard, *Philosophical Fragments*, 25–26.
13   Ibid., 29.
14   Ibid., 29.

descend in his own form as god to human beings. There are, in turn, two problems with this form of divine descent, according to Climacus. First, human beings would glorify the god as the superior when the god wishes to glorify human beings; the god is love and the human is the beloved.[15] Climacus indicates the second problem when he says, "There was a people who had a good understanding of the divine; this people believed that to see the god was death" (*PF* 30). For the human being, looking on god means death just as "the shoot of the lily is tender and easily snapped" (*PF* 30). In these passages Climacus suggests that if human beings were to become fully aware of a being so superior to human beings—the god in the form of the god—this would lead human beings to a desire for death; human beings would be overcome by self-loathing and hatred for their inferiority.

The second way the god could descend to avoid producing this self-loathing in human beings for their insufficiency as human, is to descend not in the form of the god but in the form of the human, and the lowliest of human beings at that, the servant and sufferer.[16] In other words, the god must make himself appear inferior to most other human beings, and at their weakest point, while an infant. Climacus gives the following poetic account of this type of divine descent:

> Look, there he stands—the god. Where? There. Can you not see him? He is the god, and yet he has no place where he can lay his head [...] The form of the servant was not something put on. Therefore the god must suffer all things, endure all things, be tried in all things, hunger in the desert, thirst in his agonies, be forsaken in death, absolutely the equal of the lowliest of human beings—look behold the man! (*PF* 32–33)

The story of the god's descent in human form seems to be the story of Christianity, and Climacus, in telling it, attempts to give it a logical necessity.[17] If the god exists he is love, meaning the god loves human beings. The

---

15 Ibid.
16 Kierkegaard, *Philosophical Fragments*, 31.
17 See Ann Ward, "Socratic Irony and Platonic Ideas? Kierkegaard's 'Critique' of Socrates in *The Concept of Irony*," in *Socrates: Reason or Unreason as the Foun-*

god's love for human beings is a desire for intellectual unity or a meeting of minds between the two, and thus the god must close the gap between the god and the human while still maintaining the distinction between them. Indeed, this appears to be the truth that the god is teaching, that man is not the highest being but rather the god is. The god can only close the gap between the god and the human without destroying the human, by appearing in the form of the human, indeed the lowliest of human beings.

Passion and the Paradox

In chapter two, as we have seen, Climacus attempts to give an account of Christianity that demonstrates its rational necessity, thereby bringing philosophic rationalism and faith together. In chapter three, however, Climacus revises this account to show that it actually relies on a beginning point that cannot be rationally proven, namely the existence of the god. To show that the existence of the god is an assumption that is a product of faith rather than reason, Climacus turns to an analogy with Napoleon and his works. According to Climacus:

> If one wanted to demonstrate Napoleon's existence from Napoleon's works, would it not be most curious, since his existence certainly explains the works but the works do not demonstrate *his* existence unless I have already in advance interpreted the word "his" in such a way as to have assumed that he exists [...] If I call the works Napoleon's works, then the demonstration is superfluous, since I have already mentioned his name. If I ignore this, I can never demonstrate from the works that they are Napoleon's but demonstrate (purely ideally) that such works are the works of a great general etc. (*PF* 40–41)

dation of European Identity, ed. Ann Ward (Newcastle: Cambridge Scholars Publishing, 2007), 173–72; and C. Stephen Evans, *Passionate Reason: Making Sense of Kierkegaard's Philosophical Fragments* (Bloomington: Indiana University Press, 1992), 16, 19–21; but see Howland, *Kierkegaard and Socrates*, 29; and David E. Mercer, *Kierkegaard's Living Room: The Relation Between Faith and History in Philosophical Fragments* (Montreal and Kingston: McGill-Queen's University Press, 2001), 63–64, 71.

Climacus suggests that if we were to observe the battlefield at Waterloo and see many dead human beings strewn across it, we would naturally ask whose doing or work this was. We could answer General Wellington, Tsar Alexander I, or we could answer General Napoleon. How would we know it was Napoleon? Because we already know that he exists, who he is, that he was there on that day and what he did. Climacus' point is that we could not prove with certainty that Napoleon exists simply by objectively observing his works. On the contrary we would call such works Napoleon's works based on our prior knowledge that Napoleon exists, who he is, and what he does or did.

As Napoleon is to his works, so the god is to his. Thus, Climacus asserts:

> God's works, therefore, only the god can do. Quite correct. But, then, what are the god's works? The works from which I want to demonstrate his existence do not immediately and directly exist, not at all. Or are the wisdom in nature and the goodness or wisdom in Governance right in front of our noses? Do we not encounter the most terrible spiritual trials here, and is it ever possible to be finished with all these trials? But I still do not demonstrate God's existence from such an order of things. (*PF* 42)

Climacus indicates that observing what we believe are the god's works cannot rationally demonstrate the god's existence. For instance, we observe the beauty and order in the natural world. We naturally ask, Whose works or creations are these? Although medieval Christian theologians such as Thomas Aquinas answer that they are the works of the god, others do not. The ancient Greek philosophers answer that they are no one's works, as the universe is eternal and not created in time. Modern evolutionary biologists, on the other hand, answer that they are the products of natural selection. The indemonstrability of the god's existence from what are believed to be the god's works brings to light that faith, including Christian faith, has an unphilosophic beginning point.[18]

18   See M. Jamie Ferreira, "Faith and the Kierkegaardian Leap," in *The Cambridge Companion to Kierkegaard*, ed. Alastair Hannay and Gordon D. Marion (Cambridge: Cambridge University Press, 1998), 209–10.

In chapter four Climacus illustrates that not only is Christianity's beginning point rationally indemonstrable, but so is its end point or core belief—that the god becomes human. Thus, despite his long narrative in chapter two that suggests that if the god exists and he is love it is a logical necessity that he become human, Climacus now argues that the "paradox"—the eternal (god) becoming historical, and hence born in time becoming flesh—requires the dismissal of reason or the understanding. According to Climacus:

> [W]hen the understanding and the paradox happily encounter each other in the moment, when the understanding steps aside and the paradox gives itself, and the third something, the something in which this occurs (for it does not occur through the understanding, which is discharged, or through the paradox, which gives itself—consequently *in* something) [...] that happy passion [occurs] to which we shall now give a name. We shall call it *faith*. This passion, then, must be that above mentioned condition that the paradox provides. (*PF* 59)

Climacus thus argues that faith—the condition given by the god (the paradox) for grasping the truth that only the god (the paradox) can bring—is "not a knowledge" but a passion (*PF* 62). Again, strictly speaking we feel the presence of the god (in human form), we do not know him.

Socrates and the Unknown

The rational indemonstrability of the god's existence, for Climacus, results from his notion of what the god is. The god, for Climacus, signifies the concept of the unknown (*PF* 39). As the unknown, it is that which "thought itself cannot think," and hence is "the frontier which is continually arrived at [...] the absolutely different" (*PF* 37, 44). Climacus says of the unknown, "[d]efined as the absolutely different, it seems to be at the point of being disclosed, but not so, because the understanding cannot even think the absolutely different" (*PF* 45). The concept of the unknown, therefore, points to that which is beyond reason's limits and is thus incomprehensible to it, but which reason nonetheless thinks is there. Since reason, understood

Socratically, thinks the universal, it would appear that the unknown which is absolutely different from reason, to which the name "the god" is given, is a passionate particularity or subjectivity beyond the universal.

Climacus, however, says of Socrates, "[h]e constantly presupposes that the god exists [...] If he had been asked why he conducted himself in this manner, he presumably would have explained that he lacked the kind of courage needed to dare to embark on such a voyage of discovery without having behind him the assurance that god exists" (*PF* 44). Pointing to the Socrates of the *Apology* rather than the *Meno*, Climacus seems to suggest that Socrates always kept the unknown, or that which he knew he was ignorant of, before him when he philosophized.[19] Keeping "in mind," as it were, what he did not know, Socrates sought to give his interlocutors the condition that resembled his own; knowledge of ignorance.

Thus, although initially highlighting the gap between Socratic philosophy and the god as the unknown in chapter three, Climacus also brings them together by pointing to the Socrates of the *Apology*.[20] The point of contact between Socrates and the god in Climacus' account is the condition for learning the truth. Climacus, in chapter one, describes the condition for learning the truth as "being able to ask about it," and hence as acquiring knowledge that we lack truth and need to seek it. For Climacus, it is the god that gives this condition, which is called "faith" in chapter four. In the *Apology*, it is Socrates who gives the necessary condition. Of one of his interlocutors Socrates says, "I [...] tried to show him that he thought himself wise, but that he was not," and to all those to whom he speaks he tries to show that "human wisdom is worth little or nothing."[21] In this way, Socratic questioning or dialectic acts in the same way as the condition, or "faith," given by the god.[22]

---

19 Plato, *Apology*, 21d.
20 But see Ferreira, "Faith," 208–09.
21 Plato, *Apology*, 21d, 23a. Howland argues that as Socrates is the occasion for his interlocutors to acquire knowledge of their own ignorance, so the god, understood as distinct from the human but speaking in oracles through the Pythia, is the occasion for Socrates to acquire knowledge of ignorance and is the ultimate warrant for Socratic philosophizing. See Howland, *Kierkegaard and Socrates*, 59, 66–67.
22 But see Jackson, "Arminian Edification," 236–37.

Yet, if we consider the relation of Socratic questioning in the *Apology* to the purpose of Socratic questioning in the *Meno*, Climacus' concept of the condition for learning the truth can also be a locus for drawing philosophy and faith apart. In the *Apology*, Socratic questioning, if successful, can lead to knowledge of one's own ignorance and an understanding of the human condition as that of non-knowers who think we know. Socrates, in other words, teaches us that we don't know what we think we know and hence that the truth is not within us. In the *Meno*, on the other hand, Socratic questioning, if successful, can lead to knowledge of one's prior knowledge as we recollect universal truths that are already in us, and we come to understand the human condition as that of knowers who don't know we know. Socrates thus teaches that we all in fact have the truth within us but have forgotten that this is the case.[23]

The positions of the *Apology* and the *Meno* with respect to the purpose of Socratic questioning seem irreconcilable. However, if we consider the two dialogues together, perhaps the teaching is as follows. Socrates first encounters persons who are ignorant but don't know this. His questioning teaches them that they don't know what they think they know, and in acquiring such knowledge of their ignorance Socrates' interlocutors can discard the false opinions about truth that they hold. Yet, this discarding of false opinion would then make possible the second stage of Socratic questioning, illustrated in the *Meno*. In the *Meno* the purpose of Socratic questioning is to allow the interlocutor to recollect the universal truths or ideas that were in their souls but which they had forgotten and had been obscured by the false opinions which they had previously held. Having swept away our false opinions, Socratic questioning can help us bring to mind the universal truths we do hold. The crucial difference with Climacus' account is that for Climacus, acquiring knowledge from the god of one's own ignorance or awareness that one is actually in untruth, does not lead one to the recollection of universal truths accessible to human reason alone, but rather opens one up to, or gives one faith in, the possibility of a passionate subjectivity beyond the universal.

---

23   For a similar relation between the Socrates of Kierkegaard's *Concept of Irony* and the Socrates of *Philosophical Fragments*, see Ward, "Socratic Irony and Platonic Ideas?," 171.

Eternal v. Historical

Climacus draws philosophy and faith apart again by grounding faith in an historical way of thinking in contrast to the attempt by philosophy, focusing the philosophic perspective of the *Meno*, to transcend history and grasp something eternal. In what is titled the "Interlude" between chapters four and five of *Fragments*, Climacus argues that philosophy seeks to grasp the necessary understood as the non-historical, or that which does not come to be and pass away in time but rather simply *is* always (*PF* 74). The necessary does not come into existence because this would mean there was a time when it did not exist and hence was unnecessary. The necessary, as that which simply *is* always, are the eternal and unchanging essences or nature of things, or what in Platonic dialogues are called the ideas or forms, that do not come to be in time but rather transcend time. These necessary essences are the only things, in the strict sense, that can be fully known, and hence are not believed in as subjects of faith. Therefore, according to Climacus:

> One does not have *faith* that the god exists, eternally under-
> stood, even though one assumes that the god exists. That is im-
> proper use of language. Socrates did not have faith that the god
> existed. What he knew about the god he attained by recollec-
> tion, and for him the existence of the god was by no means his-
> torical. (*PF* 87)

Faith, in contrast to philosophy, reaches for the historical, or for that which comes to be and passes away in time, and as historical is unnecessary.[24] The historical is unnecessary because coming into existence means that it did not exist prior to coming to be and might not have come to be, and as an actuality that came to be from non-being, the historical, according to Climacus, is the possible rather than the necessary (*PF* 73–74). The result of the possible, or non-being, becoming actual, is that an uncertainty attaches to every historical fact that comes into existence; it could have come into existence in another way or it could not have come into existence at all.[25]

---

24   Also see Mercer, *Kierkegaard's Living Room*, 65–68, 75–76.
25   Ibid., 79.

Because of this uncertainty Climacus asserts, "Any apprehension of the past that thinks to understand it thoroughly by constructing it has only thoroughly misunderstood it" (*PF* 79). The historical, in other words, cannot in the strict sense be known but rather only believed in; we can only have faith that a possibility, such as the god becoming human in time, actually came into existence. Climacus thus argues:

> [F]aith pertains not to essence but to being, and the assumption that god exists defines him eternally, not historically. The historical is that the god *has come into existence* (for the contemporary), that he has been one present by *having come into existence* (for one coming later). But precisely here is the contradiction. In the immediate sense, no one can become contemporary with the historical fact [...], but because it involves coming into existence, it is the object of faith. (*PF* 87)

The deeper question that Climacus seems to be pointing to in these passages is whether the universe is eternal or comes to be in time. Philosophy, Climacus suggests, which seeks rational knowledge of truth, must begin with the assumption of the eternity of the universe; that the universal ideas or natural essences that are the cause of all things in our world never come to be and pass away but always *are*.[26] The philosopher, therefore, does not believe in *creation*, or that both the universe and the cause of the universe—the god, or the eternal—came to be in time, and does not believe in creation *ex nihilo*, or the concept that the god creates the universe from nothing.[27] The concept of creation *ex nihilo* is inconsistent with the philosophic search for rational truth because, as Climacus argues, it would entail a fundamental uncertainty in the order of things that would make knowledge, in the strict sense, impossible.[28] Philosophy, therefore, in pushing to transcend time to understand and make known things that are timeless, can give human beings a certain comfort or

26 Also see Pangle, *Political Philosophy*, 30–31.
27 Ibid., 35–39.
28 Also see Lucretius, *On the Nature of Things*, in *The Longman Standard History of Ancient Philosophy* (New York: Pearson/Longman, 2006), 460.

security in the knowledge that our world will never pass away and our home will always be our home.[29]

Faith, in contrast to philosophy, embraces the notion that the universe and the cause of the universe—the god, who becomes human—came to be in time.[30] In doing so Climacus suggests that the faithful dismiss the understanding and embrace the irrational and the uncertain. The implication is that the person of faith lives with a tremendous insecurity and anxiety that the universe, devoid of any universal forms or natural essences that precede and therefore limit the god, can change at any moment. Climacus goes so far as to describe faith that the god and his universe has come to be in time as "the terror of the paradox" (*PF* 70). For Christians, because the god came to be in time this means he also passed away in time—the imagery of the cross—and for the person of faith simply, if the universe came to be in time this means it will also pass away in time; our world will end and our home will disappear.

Poetry between Philosophy and Faith

I wish to conclude by reflecting on how poetry can mediate between the pedagogical experiences of philosophic learners and those of religious learners as they are presented in *Fragments*. Kierkegaard, in *Fragments*, chooses to conceal his authorship in his pseudonym Johannes Climacus. *Fragments*, therefore, is not a treatise but rather a work of poetic art. Moreover, in the opening of the Preface Climacus describes it as a work offered "by one's own hand, on one's own behalf, at one's own expense" (*PF* 5). Thus, as poetry, *Fragments* invites the reader to have a personal encounter with the author in much the same way that the religious learner encounters the god such that the god is essential to the learner. Climacus reiterates the necessity of the personal encounter between the god and the religious learner in chapter four of *Fragments*. Here, Climacus contrasts the student of philosophy with the follower of the god come to be in time, or the embodied god, in the following way. According to Climacus, "If I comprehend Spinoza's

---

29 Also see Epicurus, *Letter to Herodotus*, in *The Longman Standard History of Ancient Philosophy* (New York: Pearson/Longman, 2006), 450–51.

30 Also see Pangle, *Political Philosophy*, 40–47.

teaching, then in the moment I comprehend it I am not occupied with Spinoza but with his teaching" (*PF* 62). The teaching of the philosopher, in other words, is accessible to human reason and once grasped by reason the student focuses on the teaching and not the teacher. The truth that the philosopher teaches, to the extent that it can be grasped by reason, stands above any particular human being; it is a universal truth that both teacher and learner can think at the same time, and the learner loves the universal "idea" and not the teacher. The teaching of the embodied god, in contrast, has a very different impact on the learner. Climacus thus argues:

> [I]f we assume that the structure is as we have assumed, (and unless we do, we go back to Socrates), namely, that the teacher himself provides the learner with the condition, then the object of faith becomes not the *teaching* but the *teacher*, for the essence of the Socratic is that the learner, because he himself is the truth and has the condition, can thrust the teacher away. Indeed, assisting people to be able to do this constituted the Socratic art and heroism. Faith, then, must constantly cling firmly to the teacher. But in order for the teacher to be able to give the condition, he must be the god, and in order to put the learner in possession of it, he must be man. This contradiction is in turn the object of faith and is the paradox, the moment. (*PF* 62)

For Climacus, the truth that the embodied god teaches—I am the god and a human being, the eternal and the historical, the universal and the particular—is not accessible to human reason, but can only be held to by faith. Yet, since it is not accessible to reason, it cannot be separated from the teacher or thought independently by the learner. The embodied god does not give the learner a simple universal to think, but what appears to be a combination of universal and particular or a higher, more absolute particularity beyond the universal which cannot be known in the strict sense but only felt.[31] The learner, therefore, is "stuck," as it were, to the embodied

---

31 Ward, "Socratic Irony and Platonic Ideas?," 173. For a discussion of faith as positing the god and the follower of the god as a higher individuality beyond the universal, see Kierkegaard's *Fear and Trembling*, Howard V. Hong and

god; they cannot move to a universal separate from or beyond the divine teacher. Faith, therefore, is not believing in what the embodied god says, for example the Sermon on the Mount, but simply that the embodied god is—the god become human.

Fragments, however, as poetry, not only invites the reader to have a personal encounter with the author in much the same way that the religious learner has a personal encounter with the god which is essential, but it also distances the reader from the author. If the author is understood as Kierkegaard rather than his pseudonym, when the reader proceeds to have a personal encounter with Climacus they discard Kierkegaard in much the same way that the philosophic learner discards the teacher. As a work of poetic art, therefore, *Fragments* can have both a Christian and a Socratic relationship to the reader.

As poetry, *Fragments* mediates between philosophy and faith in another way as well. Climacus, turning to the perspective of the *Apology* and leaving the *Meno* aside, opens chapter three by claiming:

> Although Socrates did his very best to gain knowledge of human nature and to know himself [...] he nevertheless admitted that the reason he was disinclined to ponder the nature of such creatures as Pegasus and the Gorgons was that he still was not quite clear about himself, whether he (a connoisseur of human nature) was a more curious monster than Typhon or a friendlier and simpler being sharing something divine. (*PF* 37)

Climacus suggests that for Socrates to acquire knowledge of what the human being is, and hence self-knowledge, he must acquire knowledge of what the human being is not, or that which is lesser and greater than the human, if only to rule it out. Yet, of the god, or the greater than human,

Edna H. Hong, eds. and trans. (Princeton: Princeton University Press, 1983), 55, 73; and Ann Ward, "Abraham, Agnes and Socrates: Love and History in Kierkegaard's *Fear and Trembling*," in *Love and Friendship: Rethinking Politics and Affection in Modern Times*, Eduardo A. Velasquez, ed. (Lanham, MD: Lexington Books, 2003), 308–13.

Climacus muses, "But what is the unknown against which the understanding in its paradoxical passion collides and which even disturbs man in his self-knowledge? It is the unknown. But it is not a human being [...] or anything else that he knows. Therefore, let us call this unknown the god" (*PF* 39). The nature of god, therefore, as an unknowable, passionate subjectivity beyond the universal that thought desires to think but cannot, ensures that the Socratic quest for knowledge of self and other, or knowledge of the self through knowledge of the whole, will be a task of a lifetime as it can never be fulfilled. Yet, Climacus pairs this desire to know the god for the sake of self-knowledge with the desire to know the erotic part of the self. According to Climacus, "It is the same with the paradox of erotic love. A person lives undisturbed in himself, and then awakens the paradox of self-love as love for another, for one missing" (*PF* 39). Love for another, such as the god, appears to signify or be an image for the love we have for the missing but unknown part of the self.[32] It seems that the god and the story of Christianity as told by Climacus, and other stories which flow from the god, is a poetic account of the philosophic condition; faith, as an awareness of the unknown as a passionate subjectivity beyond the self, is a metaphor for the awareness of the unknown as a passionate subjectivity within the self.

32   But see Howland, *Kierkegaard and Socrates*, 69, 103–04, 113–16, 123, 126–27.

World Enough and Time: Immortal Longings, Tragedy, and Comedy in *Antony and Cleopatra*

Mary P. Nichols

Shakespeare's *Antony and Cleopatra* is situated in a time and place of world historical change, the end of the Roman republic and the beginning of the Roman empire. The Roman republic exists in the play only in imperfect memory, for its defenders failed in their attempt to preserve self-government by assassinating Julius Caesar, and a new Caesar, Julius's heir Octavius, emerges as the "sole sir o' th' world" by the end of the play (5.2.119).[1] The old order has broken down, and new orders are not yet clearly in sight. As many commentators have noticed, Shakespeare includes anachronistic allusions to Christianity in this play that ends in 31 BC, not long before the birth of Christ. Cleopatra's attendants refer to three kings, and a star in the east (1.2.28; 5.2.307), for example, almost as if the pagan world of the play were preparing for the good news of Christianity.[2]

In this time when everything seems uncertain and anything possible, love is not confined to a proper Roman family or found only in the libertine dalliances outside of it, although both are alluded to in passing in the play (e.g., 2.3.4–7; 2.6.68–70). Rather, Antony and Cleopatra experience

---

1   Citations to the play are to the Arden edition of Shakespeare's *Antony and Cleopatra*, ed., with an introduction, by John Wilders (New York: Routledge, 1995).

2   J. L. Simmons, *Shakespeare's Pagan World: The Roman Tragedies* (Charlottesville: University of Virginia Press, 1973), 109–63, esp. 113–14,124, 136, and 162; John Alvis, *Shakespeare's Understanding of Honor* (Durham, NC: Carolina Academic Press, 1990), 180–95; Jan H. Blits, *New Heaven, New Earth: Shakespeare's* Antony and Cleopatra (Lanham, MD: Lexington, 2009), e.g., 158, 181–83, and passim.

"eternity" "in [their] lips and eyes" and "none our parts so poor,/But was a race of heaven" (1.3.36–38). From the outset, the lovers reject any measure or "bourn" for their love (1.1.16; see also 1.1.2). In the face of all impediments, their love will find "new heaven, new earth," Antony claims, using an expression that Shakespeare takes from the Book of Revelation (1.1.17; Revelation 21, 1–4). Antony and Cleopatra's love carries them beyond time and place, and even leads them to expect their reunion after death (4.14.51–55; 5.2.227–28 and 299–302).[3] As Cleopatra approaches her end, she speaks of her "immortal longings" (5.2.280).

No time is ever enough for a love that stretches to eternity. Nor is even the wide world of the play—extending as it does from Rome to Egypt—large enough for the lovers. When Coriolanus is exiled from Rome in the play bearing his name, he asserts in his pride that he will find "a world elsewhere" (3.3.135),[4] but he inevitably returns to attack Rome. His world is Rome. Antony and Cleopatra's world, in contrast, is always elsewhere, for there is no place in the world for their infinite love. Unlike Coriolanus, who cannot escape his world, Antony and Cleopatra cannot find one that is theirs. Antony would let "Rome in Tiber melt," and Cleopatra would "Melt Egypt into Nile!" for the sake of their love, but then they would have no place to go (1.1.34; 2.5.78). Without time and space, the lovers themselves cannot keep their shapes, or know themselves or each other. The jealousies and distrust that therefore drive their relationship lead to their defeat and suicides. Antony eventually senses that he "cannot hold [his] visible shape" but is as "indistinct as water is in water" (4.14.1–14), and Cleopatra thinks that with her suicide she can become "fire and air," while giving her "other elements to baser life" (5.2.288–89). Their love appears to belong to elements that cannot sustain it. In the first section of this essay, I explore the tragic consequences of Antony and Cleopatra's infinite love.

3   As Wilders points out, Shakespeare's Antony and Cleopatra experience a transcendence that is not found in Plutarch, from which Shakespeare adapted many aspects of his play. "Introduction," *Antony and Cleopatra*, 61.

4   Quotations and references to plays other than *Antony and Cleopatra* are to *The Riverside Shakespeare,* ed. G. Blakemore Evans (Boston: Houghton Mifflin, 1974).

Shakespeare nevertheless includes unmistakably comic elements in his play, as many critics have noted, especially those who understand the play to foreshadow the coming of Christianity and the promise of ever-lasting life as relief from the sting of death. G. Wilson Knight, for example, observes that the "brighter elements" in the play "serve to diffuse a glory over death." Antony and Cleopatra find "not death but life."[5] In the second section of my essay, I discuss the play's comic elements, and argue that they do not depend primarily on an expectation of an afterlife, but rather on a playfulness (and joy) in this life that the soul's transcendence makes possible. The lovers' revels, their "gaudy nights," their witty turns, and self-mockery continue even unto their deaths (see 3.13.188). Unlike Caesar, who sees only that Antony and Cleopatra "waste" the "lamps of night in revel" (1.4.4–5), Antony knows that Cleopatra cannot be "idleness itself" because "[her] royalty/ Holds idleness [her] subject" (1.3.93–95). The lovers play, it seems, without wasting time. And, in turn, time does not waste them, at least in Shakespeare's portrayal, as it does his tragic Richard II (*Richard II* 5.5.49). Time appears to be on their side, at least when they command idleness rather than yield to it. It is only then that Antony and Cleopatra can "mock the midnight bell" (3.13.199). Antony's words to Cleopatra, of course, are ambiguous. Mock they may, but the bell chimes.

The comic elements that Shakespeare includes in this tragedy come to fruition in his comedies, to which I turn in the last section of this essay. Whereas Antony and Cleopatra imagine being "married" only in death, and Cleopatra is drawn to images of sterility (e.g., 1.5.79–81; 3.13.163–72),

---

5 G. Wilson Knight, *The Imperial Theme* (London: Methuen, 1965), 199 and 262. A. C. Bradley does not include *Antony and Cleopatra* among Shakespeare's four greatest tragedies, *Hamlet, Lear, Macbeth*, and *Othello*. *Oxford Lectures on Poetry* (Oxford: Oxford University Press, 1909), 282, 284–85, and 304. Wilders observes that what the Romans see as a tragedy is regarded as an apotheosis by Cleopatra, who experiences death less as a defeat than "a kind of victory"; "Introduction," *Antony and Cleopatra*, 3; 47–48. Also see Maurice Charney, *Shakespeare's Roman Plays* (Cambridge: Harvard University Press, 1961), 141; Paul A. Cantor, *Shakespeare's Rome: Republic and Empire* (Ithaca: Cornell University Press, 1976), 183; Allan Bloom, *Love and Friendship* (New York: Simon and Schuster, 1993), 321.

Shakespeare's comedies celebrate marriage and generation. It is not that lovers in the comedies experience no desire for the infinite. Orlando in *As You Like It*, for example, proclaims that he will love Rosalind "for ever, and a day." His formulation indicates self-awareness, and even self-mockery, for no day could be added to "forever." Rosalind answers in kind when she teasingly commands him to "Say 'a day' without the 'ever'" (4.1.145–46). But neither is rejecting the longing for eternity. In fact, their very playfulness in confronting that longing hastens their commitment to each other in marriage. The love that transcends time supports a love that takes place in time, for the "day" of their mortal lives.

Unlike the political orders of Rome and Egypt, where there are "absolute" queens and masters (e.g., 3.6.8–11 and 5.2.115–16), in Shakespeare's comedies fathers—and rulers—become matchmakers, but in the end recognize the limits of their rule in the freedom of the lovers themselves. It is a freedom that proceeds from the transcendent character of the human soul that love reveals, even as it qualifies perfect knowledge of oneself and others. In the comedies, Shakespeare lets us watch love develop through the playfulness of courtship, where lovers endure the trials of love, find joy and commitment in marriage, and often look forward to ruling in a "brave new world" that checks the oppressions of the past in the name of human freedom (*Tempest*; *As You Like It*; *Midsummer Night's Dream*; *Much Ado About Nothing*). Thus I argue that Shakespeare's comedies fulfill the comic promise that he makes in the tragedy of *Antony and Cleopatra* by pointing the way to a "new earth" that he finds entailed in Christianity's promise of a new heaven. It is the liberal political orders that his comedies presage that recognize the extent to which our immortal longings transcend the world, and consequently allow space for the play and joy that proceeds from that transcendence and overflows into temporal life.

Infinite Love and the Demands of the World: The Makings of Tragedy

The Romans criticize the excess of Antony's love, which overflows all measure. They believe that a man "like plated Mars" has "become the bellows and the fan to cool a gypsy's lust" (1.1.1–10). Antony falls short of himself, they think, when Cleopatra draws him away from the political and military excellence for which he is renowned (1.1.58–60; 3.10.26–27; 3.13.147--8).[6] Even the lovers themselves experience their love as overflowing all measure, although they delight in the experience. When Cleopatra teases Antony by asking how much he loves her, he tells her that there is "beggary in love that can be reckoned" (1.1.15). To the Romans overflowing indicates excess, to Antony it means generosity, abundance, a love flowing from a fullness of soul rather than from need (or "beggary"). One of the Roman soldiers, in trying to describe Antony's generosity, says that he "continues still a Jove" (4.6.29–30). The divinity that he imitates transcends the needy gods of pagan antiquity, such as Venus who seduces Mars, and Mars who falls for her seductions (e.g., 1.5.19; cf. Aristotle, *Nicomachean Ethics* 1142b15–18).

Later in the play, one of Caesar's followers refers to Caesar in terms of godlike bounty, for the Roman conqueror "is so full of grace that [it] flows over on all that need." Given the context of his praise of Caesar—he is trying to give Cleopatra false hope of Caesar's generosity so that she will submit to his will (5.2.23–28; 5.1.61–66)—his words ring false. Caesar expects to be "kneeled to" "for grace," but will use force if she does not comply (5.2.28 and 34–38). Cleopatra suspects Caesar's pretense: "he words me, girls, he words me," she tells her attendants (5.2.190). His duplicity, however, gives Shakespeare the opportunity to contrast him with Antony, who better illustrates the godlike bounty that is falsely attributed to Caesar.[7] Indeed, Antony acts as "a mine of bounty" even to a friend who betrays him (4.6.23 and 33). Shakespeare shows us his generosity in his treatment of his household servants, whom he wishes to serve as well as they have served him (4.2.18–19).[8] And Cleopatra imagines that there is no winter

---

6 Like the Romans, Plutarch emphasizes Cleopatra's harmful effect on Antony. According to Plutarch, Cleopatra seduces Antony, awakening vices and quenching whatever spark of goodness he had; *Plutarch's Lives of the Noble Grecians and Romans*, Vol. 6, trans. Sir Thomas North (New York: AMS Press, 1967 [1579]), 24 and 29. Janet Adelman, "Appendix A: Plutarch and Shakespeare," *The Common Liar* (New Haven, CT: Yale University Press, 1973), 173. See also Alvis, *Shakespeare's Understanding of Honor,* 182–83.

7 Adelman comments that "Octavius overflows only in expediency," *The Common Liar*, 124; also 128.

8 Scholars have seen parallels between the banquet Antony holds before what he supposes may be his last battle and the Last Supper; Blits, *New Heaven,*

in his bounty, but rather an autumn that grows by reaping (5.2.85–87; see also 4.6.29–30), almost as if there were reserves in his soul that could never be exhausted and that therefore made an infinite bounty possible.[9]

If Antony's bounty were as infinite as Cleopatra describes it, however, how could it stop with Cleopatra? Would not his very virtue, and not just the political necessities that are brewing in Rome in his absence, recall him to Rome, where he can exercise his virtues by ruling, and by triumphing over those who oppose his rule? Although Antony tells Cleopatra that Rome is nothing to him, and "here is my space," he also would break his "strong Egyptian fetters" so that he can return to Rome (1.1.34; 1.2.122). After he has gone, Cleopatra imagines herself fishing, and every fish she draws up an Antony, to which she will say, "Ah, ha! You're caught" (2.5.10–15). But if every fish is an Antony, no one of them is Antony. Antony escapes her. We do not know whether Cleopatra knows this, or even whether she would want it otherwise. After all, her comparison between Antony and the fish she pulls from the water is playful. Cleopatra rejoices that Antony "comest . . . smiling from/ The world's great snare uncaught" when he returns from battle. It is in this instance that she refers to his "infinite virtue" (4.8.17–18). What preserves Antony's freedom from the snares of the world also preserves it from her own snares.[10]

New Earth, 157–59. Shakespeare found a similar scene in Plutarch, but adapts it for his purposes. There is no suggestion in his source that Antony wishes to serve his servants. Rather Antony simply asks them to fill his cups as much as possible that night, for it may be his last; Plutarch, 78.

9   In *Romeo and Juliet*, Shakespeare makes the connection between love and the experience of the soul's infinite bounty even more explicit, when Juliet tells Romeo, "My bounty is as boundless as the sea, / My love as deep; the more I give to thee,/ The more I have, for both are infinite" (2.2.133–35).

10   Enobarbus understands something like this as well. When Cleopatra first approached Antony from her barge on the river Cyndus, he recounts, adorned with all the splendors that nature and wealth can endow, all other people flock to the banks of the river to get a glimpse, while Antony alone sits in the marketplace "Whistling to the air; which, but for vacancy,/Had gone to gaze on Cleopatra too/And made a gap in nature" (2.2.202–15; 221–28). In spite of her allure, Antony does not go immediately to gaze upon Cleopatra; something of himself remains in reserve. Enobarbus' observation about the impossibility of vacancy applies to the human soul. Had he understood this fully,

When Cleopatra praises Antony as "the demi-Atlas of this earth" (1.5.24), she suggests that the man she loves has a scope that goes well beyond Egypt as well as Rome. She loves "the greatest soldier of the world," her "man of men" (1.3.39; 1.5.75), but the greatest soldier in the world does not remain in the thrall of an Egyptian queen. For Antony to be himself—and loved by Cleopatra—he must perform the deeds that manifest who he is and show him worthy of being loved. Cleopatra recognizes this as well, and she finally urges him to return to Rome to deal with problems there for the sake of his honor (1.4.99–100). Antony consoles her—and himself—with the thought that his exploits will win kingdoms for her (1.3.69–72; 1.5.45–49; cf. 3.6.8–10). But his conceit is as illusory as his claim that his space is simply where he stands in Egypt. With his departure for Rome we see his tragedy unrolling.

Whereas Cleopatra describes Antony's infinite bounty and infinite virtue, Antony's friend Enobarbus tries to capture Cleopatra's appeal when he describes her to the Romans: "Age cannot wither her, nor custom stale/Her infinite variety" (2.2.245–46). Cleopatra's infinite variety keeps Antony's love alive. This is her gift to him. There is no tiring of Cleopatra because she is always changing. She is one "Whom everything becomes, to chide, to laugh/ To weep," Antony says. He loves all the ways in which Cleopatra shows herself, "whose every passion fully strives/ To make itself, in thee, fair and admired" (1.1. 50–52). That Cleopatra herself is never fully manifest in any of the ways she shows herself allows the lovers to play, or to "sport." Dismissing the serious matters that messages from Rome might reveal, Antony asks Cleopatra, "What sport tonight?" (1.1.48). There seem to be unlimited possibilities that they share, represented at various times in the play as feasting, drinking, and revelry, sports such as fishing, and even "wander[ing] through the streets and not[ing] the qualities of people" (1.4.3–5; 2.5.15–23; 1.1.45–55). They imagine themselves seeing without being seen, although no disguise enters their picture, as it does in Plutarch's.[11] In playing, the lovers are acting, as we see in their teasing each

he might not have been disloyal to Antony and gone over to Caesar. That is, he would have known that Antony is "Antony yet" (see 3.13.97–98), and not simply the puppet of Cleopatra (cf. 3.11.54–61 and Plutarch, 69).

11 Plutarch refuses "to reckon up all the foolishe sportes they made," for to do so would itself be foolish. He does report that Antony and Cleopatra would

other. And when they are acting, something of themselves, the actor as opposed to his actions, remains hidden. Other actions remain possible for them, other streets to wander, other qualities of people to note. Lovers cannot perfectly locate each other, not in spite of but precisely because of their shared activities.

Cleopatra asks her attendant Charmian to seek Antony out, "If you find him sad,/Say I am dancing; if in mirth, report/That I am sudden sick" (1.3.4–6). Thus she would unsettle him, appearing opposite to him and thereby drawing him away from his present mood. Present pleasures must yield to indeterminate future ones. She knows that "to cross him in nothing," as Charmian recommends, is "the way to lose him" (1.3.10–11).[12] Antony's first wife, Fulvia, also attempted to cross him, and by so doing to lure him home, first by going to war against Antony's brother, and then joining his brother in waging war against Caesar. But she cannot compete with Cleopatra. Antony wishes Fulvia's demise, although he later laments her death. He perceives that "She's good," only after she is "gone," and thus "The hand could pluck her back that shoved her on" (1.2.93–97; 2.2.100–01; 1.2.133–34). A woman of infinite variety, however, is "gone" while still alive, beckoning her lover with the future that her infinite variety promises, and that human life in time makes possible. As Enobarbus observes, "Other women cloy/ The appetites they feed, but she makes hungry/ Where most she satisfies" (2.2.246–48).

Even starker than the contrast between Cleopatra and Fulvia is that between Cleopatra and Antony's second wife, Caesar's sister Octavia, a woman of "holy, cold, and still conversation" (2.6.124–25), whom Antony

"go up and down the city" at night, disguised like slaves and servants and "peere into poore mens windows and their shops, and scold and brawle with them," 29. Shakespeare transforms the account into something more elevated, something that could even describe his own poetry.

12 Pretending to be the shepherd Ganymede pretending to be Rosalind in *As You Like It*, Rosalind tells her lover Orlando that once they are wed, "I will weep for/ nothing, like Diana in the fountain, and I will do that/ when you are dispos'd to be merry; I will laugh like a hyen, and that when/thou are inclin'd to sleep" (4.1.153–56). Whereas Rosalind speaks in play, warning her future husband to beware of her deceptions, Cleopatra acts out the image of herself she gives Charmian. In spite of Cleopatra's proclaimed "infinity variety," in comparison to Rosalind she is simple.

marries for the sake of a political alliance with her brother. Antony tells Octavia that he has "not kept [his] square; but that to come/ Shall all be done by the rule" (2.3.6–7). But Antony has from the beginning disavowed rules or measures. The Romans hope that Octavia's beauty, wisdom, and modesty can settle Antony's heart (2.2.251–52). Of course, Antony's heart cannot be settled, and he returns to Egypt and the unsettled and unsettling Cleopatra. It seems right that Octavia return to Rome rather than remain by Antony's side.

A downside of Cleopatra's "infinite variety," however, is that Antony cannot be sure he knows her—and therefore whether she can be trusted. As Antony well knows (3.13.121–25), before she was with Antony, she had been with Julius Caesar, and before that with Pompey. Since Cleopatra has had many lovers before Antony, why not another after Antony, perhaps Octavius Caesar himself? Or, if the "scarce-bearded" boy, as she refers to him with disdain (1.1.22), is not her type, perhaps one of his lieutenants, who might win favors for her from his master? After Antony's major defeat by Caesar at Actium, we see her sending Caesar word by one of his lieutenants that she "kiss[es] his conquering hand" (3.13.78–79). Can we be sure she is temporizing? Antony is not, and becomes infuriated. "Not know me yet?" she asks him (3.13.162), but how could he "know" her if she is always changing? When Antony observes earlier that Cleopatra is "cunning past man's thought" (1.2.152), he may say more than he knows. Cleopatra is indeed "past man's thought."[13]

Life would be simpler, to be sure, for beings simpler than Antony and Cleopatra. Upon his return to Rome, Antony describes such a simpler being to his fellow Romans when they show considerable curiosity about exotic Egypt. The Egyptian crocodile, he tells them, is shaped like itself; it is as broad as it has breadth; it is as high as it is, and is of its own color. It lives by what nourishes it, and its tears are wet (2.7.41–50). No crocodile could fail to meet Antony's criteria for what a crocodile is, even if they do not

---

13 Blits points out that Cleopatra is the only title character in a Shakespearean tragedy without a soliloquy. "She is always on stage but never transparent," and "typically remains hidden even when in full public view"; *New Heaven, New Earth*, 142. See also Bradley, *Oxford Lectures*, 301. Adelman argues that the uncertainty we have about Cleopatra extends to all the major events of the play; *The Common Liar*, 15–16, and 22.

capture anything unique to crocodiles. When the Roman Lepidus hears Antony's description of the crocodile, he comments that "it is a strange serpent." But his wits are dulled by wine, as Antony points out (2.7.49–53). The crocodile Antony describes is not as strange as a human being. It is shaped like itself, whereas human beings might lose their shapes, as Antony claims happens to himself (4.14.13–14). Nor are they always of their own color: soon after Antony describes the crocodile, the Romans' "cheeks" are "burnt from drinking," and they are not themselves (2.7.120–25; also 2.7.4). Unlike the crocodile, a human being can act like or unlike himself, as Antony is said to do, and can even say this of himself, as Antony does.[14] And so his actions can become a source of shame to himself, as they do for Antony (1.1.57–59; 2.2.6–8; 81–84; 95–97). There is no variety in the crocodile, and even when the elements go out of it, it "transmigrates," that is, it becomes another like itself (2.7.45–46).

Nor does calling human tears wet, as Antony does those of the crocodile, reveal much about them. Antony's tears when leaving Cleopatra to go to Rome may be "excellent dissembling," Cleopatra claims, for they may be tears for Fulvia (1.3.76–86). And Enobarbus can suppose that Antony's tears for Caesar—and for Brutus—show merely that "that year" he "was troubled with a rheum" (3.2.54–59). As to Cleopatra's tears, Enobarbus does not know what to name them, for he "cannot call her/ winds and waters sighs and tears; they are greater storms and tempests than almanacs can report" (1.2.154–56). Just as Cleopatra is beyond what any art can capture (2.2.200–01), she is beyond report, at least that of an almanac. Her insistence that Antony fight Caesar's forces by sea rather than by land, which is beyond any reasonable calculation of what Antony and his forces can accomplish, finally seals their doom.

Antony follows Cleopatra's advice in spite of the warnings of his men. His "war-mark'd footmen" think that Antony is rejecting "the way that promises assurance," trading "firm security" for "chance and hazard" (3.7.44–48). In other words, Antony is true to his and Cleopatra's love,

---

14 Even Coriolanus, whose "nature," his enemy Aufidius suggests, is "Not to be other than one thing, not moving/ From the casque to th' cushion," is persuaded by his mother to "perform a part/ [He] hast not done before" (*Coriolanus* 4.7.41–45; 3.2.109–10), even if he is not a great success at it.

which is more like the hazard of the sea than the certain footing of land. Antony supposes that if they fail at sea, they can then fight on land (3.7. 52–53). In Antony's mind, one choice now does not preclude another one later. It is almost as if he were dealing in infinite possibilities. The battle is lost when Cleopatra, after insisting on being present, flees the fighting with her Egyptian fleet. Antony, to his shame, follows with his. Their defeat by Caesar leads eventually to their suicides. Antony's comes first, when Cleopatra has it reported to him that she has taken her life, a ruse she supposes that will make Antony regret his anger at her, but he resolves to follow her again. She does not foresee in time the effect that her message will have on him. For his part, Antony does not remember that the shifty Cleopatra is "ever a boggler" (3.13.110). This is one time that he should not trust her.

Antony imagines them together after death, "hand in hand," "Where souls do couch on flowers," and Cleopatra imagines herself joining him (4.14.51–55; 4.14.100–02; 5.2.282–86; 294–95). They may question death ("where is thy sting?"), but by the events of the play Shakespeare questions whether the lovers can be together "in love" without the actions that make them loved, actions that take place in particular situations and political contexts.[15] Their dilemma is a universal one, for human beings live in particular times and places, whereas love unmoors them from their familiar worlds when promising new heavens and new earths. At a dramatic moment in the play Antony asks his friend, who happens to be named Eros, whether he can still see him, for Antony "cannot hold [his] visible shape," becoming as "indistinct as water is in water" (4.14.10–11). The very insecurity to which love gives birth threatens love itself. Human beings cannot live indefinitely at sea. Antony's loss at sea weakens his ability to win on land.

Comic Elements in *Antony and Cleopatra*

Given the parallels in the play between the transcendence of this world that the protagonists seek, and the transcendence promised with the coming

15 See Cantor, *Shakespeare's Rome*, 164. Cantor refers us to *Troilus and Cressida*, where Troilus explains the "monstruosity" of love—"that the will is infinite and the execution confin'd, that the desire is boundless and the act a slave to limit" (3.2.81–83).

of Christ, some scholars have found in the play a warning against Christianity. If Christianity turns human beings toward the infinite, and away from the limits of time and place, it would only exacerbate human tragedy. More particularly, it is argued that Christianity is a religion more appropriate for the rule of a godlike Roman emperor who requires meekness and submission from his subjects rather than proud self-regard.[16] Subjection to absolute political authority becomes even easier if one imagines future happiness in heaven. The play, from this perspective, announces the demise of human virtue and achievement, agency and responsibility, whether because human beings live subject to authoritarian rule, or in light of eternity.[17] In the former case, Rome has no "room" for more than just one man, as Cassius feared (*Julius Caesar* 1.2.150–57); in the latter case, no such room is needed. As Cleopatra says in response to Antony's death, "Young boys and girls/are level now with men. The odds is gone,/And there is nothing left remarkable beneath the visiting moon" (4.15.67–70). It is a high price to pay for "universal peace."[18] Such readings of the play suggest the tragedy of Rome, and even the tragedy of the West.

Although Shakespeare is aware of the dangers that attend the demise of one world and the rise of a new one, especially when the new one looks up to an absolute master, his outlook on the future of the West, I argue, is

16 E.g., Blits, *New Heaven, New Earth*, 1–5, 8–9; Cantor, *Shakespeare's Rome*, 220–21, note 18.

17 As the defeated Antony approaches his end, his soldiers hear strange music and one of his men explains that the god Hercules whom Antony loved is leaving him (4.3.21–22). The episode suggests the departure of pagan religion, making way for the coming of Christ, but it also indicates the demise of ancient virtue. Hercules departs. Shakespeare adapted this detail from Plutarch's life of Antony, but Plutarch associates the strange music with Bacchic revels; Plutarch, 78. By substituting Hercules for Bacchus, Shakespeare suggests a more heroic Antony than Plutarch's, and also a greater loss to the world. See Alvis, *Shakespeare's Understanding of Honor*, 185.

18 When Octavius proclaims near the end of the play that "the time of universal peace is near" (4.6.5), one can hear Shakespeare speaking through him, and giving his phrase a different meaning. The universal peace is not the Pax Romana of the Empire, but the peace brought by Christ to those who believe in him. See Simmons, *Shakespeare's Pagan World*, 113–14,124, 136, and 162; Alvis, *Shakespeare's Understanding of Honor*, 180–95.

not as bleak as this view suggests. Not only does the play seem less tragic than other Shakespearean tragedies, as scholars have noted, and the deaths of the protagonists as triumphs of life, but the infinite longings of their soul engender a playfulness throughout the play that has more to do with how they live than with what they expect from the afterlife. Beings with a stake in this world, moreover, are ill fit to be subjects of a despot. Shakespeare's allusions to Christianity in the play, I argue, suggest not only a religion of otherworldly salvation, but also an appreciation of life in this world, and are consistent with a comedy that elevates rather than demeans.

Early in the play, Shakespeare gives a comic tone to life in Egypt when he introduces Cleopatra's attendants, Charmian and Iras, as they ask a soothsayer to predict their fortunes. He can read only "a little" "in nature's infinite book of secrecy" (1.2.10–11). It is fitting, then, that everything he says is ambiguous. While an audience expecting a tragedy would find the soothsayer's predictions about Cleopatra's attendants ominous, they themselves interpret them optimistically. When he claims, for example, that Charmian will outlive her mistress, she assumes this means that she will have a long life—not that Cleopatra's will end shortly. When he tells her that her fortune thus far is fairer than that which will approach, she supposes merely that she will have many bastards and is delighted. In an infinite world, there are many possibilities, and they are not all tragic. Some are comic, as Charmian imagines when she hears the soothsayer's predictions, and even though they are not realized for her in this play, Shakespeare includes them. Charmian even supposes that she might have a child at fifty, to whom Herod of Jewry would pay homage (1.2.29–30). In time, all things are possible, even a miraculous birth, and its recognition by temporal authority. Due to the uncertainty of what we will confront in the course of time and how we will confront it, we know too little of ourselves to know that our lives are tragic. It is appropriate that the soothsayer in *Julius Caesar* speak of disaster on a specific and imminent date, the Ides of March, whereas the soothsayer in *Antony and Cleopatra* speaks in vague terms that do not necessarily portend ill. Nature's secrets are infinite. Infinity leaves room for comedy.[19]

19 Adelman connects the great variety and multiplicity of the play—its relatively short scenes, its quick changes of setting, its many minor characters—with comedy. Whereas in Shakespeare's tragedies, the play's structure typically fo-

Shakespeare uses the mystical language of the Book of Revelation to comic effect in Antony's death. When Antony's men find him dying, they observe that "the star has fallen" and "time is at its period," just as an Angel in Revelation swears that time will be no more (4.14.107–08; *Revelation* 10:6). But Shakespeare undercuts their notion that Antony's death signals the end of the world by comically prolonging his act of dying. In spite of the guards' pronouncement that the end has come, Shakespeare gives Antony more time. One factor that distinguishes comedy from tragedy is the pace at which time travels. The fast movement of tragic events gives them a sense of inevitability, even when they follow from choices the protagonist makes.[20] The slow motion of dramatic pacing, by contrast, makes the play seem less tragic. Time of course can prolong suffering, as Antony says after he hears of Cleopatra's death, "All length is torture" (4.14.47). Length of time, however, also allows other choices to be made, others actions to occur. The results that follow do not seem inevitable.[21] In

cuses attention on the protagonists, the world of *Antony and Cleopatra* "is an enormously crowded place," in which there are "several versions of experience, among the comic and satiric as well as tragic"; *The Common Liar*, 42–49. Although Adelman connects the end of the play with the "romances" of Shakespeare's last plays (166), she argues that the effect of the play's variety is to intensify the tragic experience rather than to qualify it: the tragedy is more moving because "it can take the criticism of comic structure and nonetheless survive"; 40–52, esp. 52.

20 Romeo and Juliet kill themselves immediately upon believing that the other is dead. Hamlet walks into Laertes' trap with a sense of inevitability, and four deaths—his mother's, Claudius's, Laertes', and his own occur within a few lines of Shakespeare's play (5.2.302–360). Macbeth's inability to control time, he knows, will be his undoing (1.7.1–7 and 5.5.19–28). Lear experiences himself as if he were bound on a wheel of fire (4.7.45–46). Time is not the tragic hero's friend.

21 In *As You Like It*, Rosalind is given considerable time to trifle with Orlando, or rather educate him in the ways of love (3.2.343–429 and 4.1.38–199). It is in comedy—not tragedy—that there is time to reflect on how time moves differently in different human experiences, as Rosalind does (3.2.299–333). In that same play, Jaques describes the slow movement of human life through its seven ages (2.7.139–66). There is time for many ages. In *The Winter's Tale*, Shakespeare introduces the passage of sixteen years with the chorus Time, whose words presage the coming of spring (4.1). Time has many seasons.

Shakespeare's play, Antony resolves to die "at once" (e.g., 4.14.83), but his death is slow in coming.

In the first place, Antony asks his friend Eros to help him die by thrusting a sword into his side. But this early assisted suicide fails, because Eros turns his sword upon himself to escape the sorrow of Antony's death (4.14.95–96). Antony has more time than he planned. Might he reconsider? He claims that he has learned how to die from Eros's example (4.14.103–04). But might he not have learned the importance of life from Eros's decision to sacrifice himself rather than to help him die? Or might a message come from Cleopatra revealing her deception in time to prevent his suicide? Antony is given time, but falls upon his own sword. Even so, he has more time, for his wound does not immediately kill him. He must ask the members of his guard to end his life, but they refuse in turn (4.14.109–14).

Antony may in effect ask death where is its sting, but for death to be stingless it must come. Antony's difficulty in finding death also follows a figure from *Revelation*, where it is said that at the end of time "men [shall] seek death, and shall not find it, and shall desire to die, and death shall fly from them" (*Revelation* 9:6). Shakespeare's dramatization of the flight of death from Antony's grasp suggests that the Book of Revelation is as ambiguous as the soothsayer's predictions. The flight of death at the end of time keeps time alive. Although the very title of that book of the Bible suggests revealing, its mystical language keeps its revelations elusive and mystifying. And by fleeing Antony, death gives him time to learn that Cleopatra is still alive. Although he has already inflicted on himself a mortal wound, he can "importune death awhile" for one last kiss of Cleopatra (4.15.16-21). It is not that "the greatest soldier in the world" (1.3.39) makes himself ridiculous by failing to execute his own death;[22] as long as death flees Antony, he remains alive. The flight of death, metaphorically speaking, allows the living to experience the joys of this life, just as Antony lives for another kiss. Transcending the anger he had shown previously at Cleopatra's actions, the generous, perhaps even forgiving Antony does exactly this. Shakespeare thus uses *Revelation* itself to suggest a comic vision, which qualifies the play's tragedy. As he completes his story of the lovers'

---

22 This is suggested by Wilders, "Introduction," *Antony and Cleopatra*, 45; see also Simmons, *Shakespeare's Pagan World*, 149.

ends, he makes his comic vision even more substantial. Life is not merely prolonged, but life can be filled with happy moments even in the face of death.

When the dying Antony is brought to Cleopatra, she comes to his bidding no more quickly than has death. She has taken refuge in her monument (built to be her tomb), lest she be taken by Caesar's forces and brought to Rome. She assumes there is time—and rightly—for Antony to be hoisted up to her in her monument before he dies. As Cleopatra and her attendants struggle to draw Antony up, Shakespeare draws love down to earth by staging a physical representation of its elevating power. The discrepancy between human aspiration and our earthly existence does not preclude elevation in this life, however comic. The invisible, in this case the elevating power of love, with Shakespeare's help becomes visible to the human eye.

The dying Antony himself jokes that his hoisting must be "quick, or I am gone" (4.15.32). He will not long be "quick," or alive, even if Cleopatra "quicken[s]" his lips with kissing (4.15.32 and 39–41). Life itself is quick, even if his death is not. When Antony reaches her, "all" present, like a chorus in a tragedy, observe "Ah, heavy sight" (4.15.42, see also 4.14.108). But since they too pun—Antony was a heavy load for hoisting—it may be they speak like a chorus in a comedy. "Sport indeed," Cleopatra says, perhaps speaking for the playwright as much as for herself (4.15.30–42). Later, Cleopatra imagines that Roman comedians will ridicule them on stage, with Antony "brought drunken forth," and "Some squeaking Cleopatra boy my greatness/ I' the posture of a whore" (5.2.215–20). Shakespeare's comedy, however, is of another sort, for he does not mock Antony and Cleopatra's aspirations. It is Octavius, not Shakespeare, who "laugh[s]" at Antony, as when that "old ruffian" challenges him to single combat (4.1.4–6). Rather, throughout their repartee, Shakespeare allows Antony and Cleopatra to laugh at themselves, in situations in which their laughter expresses their love. Cleopatra accepts her lover as a heavy load, for example, and Antony wants her to be quick about it since he does not have long to live.

When Antony dies, finally, Cleopatra proclaims that she will also take her life. But she too in effect importunes death a while as she considers what to do. Time gives her options. She listens to messengers from Caesar and considers what they propose.[23] Cleopatra then meets Caesar himself. Although Caesar has not demanded a reckoning from her, she presents him with "a brief [or catalogue] of money, plate, and jewels/[She] is possessed of," and calls her treasurer in to confirm that she has "reserved to [herself] nothing." When her treasurer arrives, however, he contradicts her: she has reserved enough to purchase back what she has made known. Her "brief" is too "brief" to cover all that is hers. She denounces his betrayal, calling the man who revealed that she has not made all she has manifest a "soulless villain." She was merely reserving, she tells Caesar, some "lady trifles," "im-moment toys," for Caesar's sister and wife "to induce their mediation" in her behalf once she is taken to Rome (5.2.137–74).

Of course, Cleopatra may be equivocating with Caesar. She has already told one of Caesar's men that she would take her life before she would be brought to Rome and "chastised with the sober eye/ Of dull Octavia" (5.2.53–54). Comradery between Cleopatra and these Roman matrons is laughable, except to one like Octavius who does not fully grasp what a for-eign object Cleopatra is (see 5.2.111). Plutarch says that her holding back some of her possessions puts Caesar off-guard: he is deceived into thinking that she is anticipating her future in Rome rather than planning suicide.[24] But Shakespeare does not make her intentions clear. The episode in the play indicates how little we know of Cleopatra—her intentions, her pos-sessions, and her reservations. Her statements of subservience to Caesar in this scene—referring to him, for example, as her lord and master (5.2.114–16 and 189)—are similar to her compliance with his messenger earlier. Her question to Antony, "Not know me yet?" echoes until the end of the play. More generally, the scene underscores the truth about the human soul—that like Cleopatra it holds in reserve as much as it makes known (if such reserve could be calculated any more than can love). It is "reserve" that makes the soul capable of infinite variety as well as of infinite

23 Antony may expect her to join him after death, but he does not expect it to happen immediately. His dying advice concerns her earthly life—how she should seek both safety and honor with Caesar (4.15.47–50).

24 Plutarch, 85. Blits argues that Shakespeare's Cleopatra had set this scene up with her treasurer for this very purpose. In Plutarch, Blits points out, the trea-surer is there "by chance," whereas in Shakespeare's drama Cleopatra calls him in to play his part. 204–06.

bounty. Without any reserve, love would remain "beggary," to use Antony's phrase. Love would be reduced to need. We can know that there is such a reserve, even though this reserve makes it difficult—in fact impossible— to perfectly know ourselves and those we love. In other words, we can know enough for love to be possible. And when Antony asks Eros whether he can still see him, Eros refuses to affirm Antony's dissolution, addressing him as "noble lord" (4.14.1). At a time when Antony hardly knows himself, Eros knows enough of the man, not only his "visible shape," to sacrifice his life to keep Antony alive.

When Cleopatra learns that her move to Rome as Caesar's captive is imminent, she sends for a "rural fellow," or Clown, who brings her a basket of figs with a poisonous snake concealed within (5.2.232–43).[25] Like rural fellows in some other Shakespearean comedies, such as Lancelot Gobbo in *Merchant of Venice* or Dogberry in *Much Ado about Nothing,* the clown speaks one malapropism after another. Cleopatra's exchanges with the Clown further delay her death, and she must bid him farewell more than once (5.2.260; 277). Death seems to flee her as it does Antony, for she has difficulty in getting rid of the Clown, as he stays to talk about "the worm." His malapropisms are as ambiguous as the soothsayer's earlier predictions. To warn Cleopatra that the asp is a deadly snake, he says that "its biting is immortal" (5.2.245–46). But if Cleopatra meets Antony after death, as she hopes, the Clown's misuse of the word might reveal the truth. Before leaving Cleopatra with his gift, the Clown observes that "the worm is not to be trusted except in the keeping of wise people," for "there is no goodness in the worm" (5.2.264–66). But is there evil in the worm either, if it only "does its kind" (5.2.261–62), or acts according to its nature, as the Clown says? The worm bites all alike, or at least with no discrimination between those whom it should and should not bite. That is why it must be entrusted only to the wise.

25 Cleopatra's physician tells Caesar that "She hath pursued conclusions infinite/ Of easy ways to die" (5.2.353–55). Plutarch reports only that Cleopatra considered "all sorts of poisons" before determining that the biting of an asp caused the least pain. 75. If Cleopatra pursued "infinite" ways, however, she would never be able to decide on one or to draw a conclusion. In Shakespeare's play, she cannot really know that the asp is her best choice.

Cleopatra tells her attendant Iras that in bringing her the snake, the Clown "brings [her] liberty" (5.2.236). But a being capable of infinite variety is already in a sense free, for he—or she—is not limited to being any one thing. But freedom does not guarantee wisdom. If freedom is evidenced when something of oneself is held in reserve, wisdom is evidenced by one's choices and deeds, or metaphorically, by what one can write in one's brief when one comes before one's lord and master. It is this infinite potential of the human soul, which is realized and revealed over the course of a human life, although only imperfectly in any finite existence, that allows Shakespeare to write comedies as well as tragedies. And it is because of the soul's freedom that wisdom is both possible and necessary.

In the same breath that she imagines her death as brave and noble, Cleopatra asks, "is it sin/To rush into the secret house of death/Ere death dare come to us?" (4.15.84–86). This is the only occurrence of "sin" in the play. Cleopatra's question remains unanswered, but it lingers. A human being who dares to rush to death presumes a godlike control over life and death.[26] He refuses to endure, in the words Edgar spoke to his father in *Lear*, his "going hence," just as he endured his coming hither (*King Lear* 5.3.9–11). Cleopatra is not wise enough to be trusted with the worm. Those who are sufficiently wise, however, are those with no use for it. Whether or not the Clown himself is wise enough to see this, he does not take responsibility for others. He leaves the snake with Cleopatra. He recognizes freedom, and leaves wisdom a question.[27] The snake may tempt, but it is

26 Thomas Aquinas writes that suicide is forbidden because "it belongs to God alone to pronounce sentence of death and life." It is also "contrary to the inclination of nature, and to charity whereby every man should love himself." *Summa Theologica*, Question 64, Article 5. That is, suicide is sin because one's life on earth—and not simply eternal life—is good. Cf. Cantor, in contrast, who connects the "sin" of suicide with the belief in an afterlife: when death becomes desirable because life is worthless, this selfish act must be forbidden as sin. Roman suicide, in contrast, affirms the value of life—especially a certain kind of life: it is not life that is worthless but life without liberty. *Shakespeare's Rome*, 166–67.

27 Shakespeare highlights Cleopatra's freedom and her choice, when the asp does its job only in its own time. She commands "the poor venomous fool" to "Be angry and dispatch" (5.2.304–05).

up to us to resist temptation. The play that begins with an allusion to the new heaven and earth of *Revelation* ends with an allusion to *Genesis*, and the freedom that God gave our first parents—the freedom to choose.

After Antony dies, Cleopatra dreams that she sees him: his face was like the heavens and in it a sun and a moon that lighted the earth; his legs bestride the ocean; his reared arm crested the world; and he could be heard as rattling thunder (5.2.75–85). Shakespeare's model for the appearance of Antony in her dream is the "mighty angel" in the *Book of Revelation*, who comes down from heaven, whose face is like the sun, whose voice is answered by thunder, and who stands upon both land and sea (*Revelation*, 10.1–6). It is in this context that Cleopatra attributes to Antony a bounty without winter, an autumn that grows by reaping. When the Roman Dolabella, to whom Cleopatra reports her dream, denies that there ever was or could be such a man, how can he be so sure?[28] Cleopatra exclaims that Dolabella "lies up to the hearing of the gods!" (5.2.92–94). Even if there is no such man as the one who bestrides the ocean in Cleopatra's dream, her love stirs her to dream of such a man, and to imagine such transcendence. In nature, there is no autumn that does not yield to winter, nor life that does not yield to death, but in nature beings simply "do their kind." If that were the case for human beings, there would be neither tragedy nor comedy.

Where then, does Shakespeare's play leave us, with his comic rendering of Antony's and Cleopatra's deaths? The final step of my argument shows how the play's treatment of marriage and generation points to Shakespeare's comedies.[29]

---

28 Adelman, although she does not connect Cleopatra's dream with Christianity, argues that the structure of the play itself, such as the shift from short scenes to longer ones, leads us progressively to identify with the viewpoint of the lovers and thus prepares us to give our assent to Cleopatra's dream. *The Common Liar*, 157–66.

29 Others also turn to Shakespeare's comedies in the context of discussing *Antony and Cleopatra*. Simmons's brief suggestions are consistent with those I elaborate here, for example. *Shakespeare's Pagan World*, 152. I am indebted to Alvis's thoughtful interpretation, although his interpretation sees a greater contrast between the otherworldly aspects of Christianity and the civil character of the marriages in the comedies that "takes precedence over the transcendent." *Shakespeare's Understanding of Honor*, 191–95.

Locating Shakespeare's Politics in Shakespeare's Comedies

When Antony determines to follow Cleopatra in death, he proclaims that he will be "A bridegroom in [his] death, and run into't/As to a lover's bed" (4.14.100–02). Through Antony's words, Shakespeare echoes another passage from Revelation, where the holy city, the new Jerusalem, is "prepared as a bride trimmed for her husband" (*Revelation* 21:2).[30] The better life Antony imagines is with Cleopatra as his bride, even if it cannot be in the world they inhabit on earth. And Cleopatra calls out to him just before she dies, "Husband, I come. Now to that name my courage prove my title!" (5.2.286–87). Although marriage between them has never arisen as a possibility during the play, they now, each independently of the other, imagine their marriage in death. That marriage will be one of love, and their virtue will prove them worthy. At least, Cleopatra hopes that her courage will earn her the title of Antony's wife.

The play thus ends with a vision of love that finds expression not only in the immortality of the soul but also in marriage. Marriage as the expression of love seems foreign to the world that Antony and Cleopatra inhabit, as Shakespeare presents it in the play. Among the Egyptians whom we meet there are no married couples; there are not even married men (see 1.2.61–66), although there is a eunuch. In the Rome of the play, Antony is the married man, first to Fulvia, whom he wishes gone, and then to Octavia, whom he marries for "the occasion," and soon abandons (2.6.133). Caesar, for his part, arranges that marriage for political reasons. Marriage is present in the play, but never as an expression of love or a way toward human fulfillment. The new Jerusalem for Shakespeare includes a conception of marriage that unites a man and a woman in love.[31]

---

30 Blits, *New Heaven, New Earth*, 181.

31 A more complete treatment of Roman marriage would have to consider that between Coriolanus and Virgilia in *Coriolanus*, and that between Brutus and Portia in *Julius Caesar*. A measure of the difference between these marriages and those characteristic of Shakespeare's comedies is that the Roman marriages do not emerge in these plays from courtship. The marriage of Henry V to the French princess could be considered a marriage of convenience, inasmuch as with their marriage France recognizes Henry's claim to the French throne. But even this marriage of convenience involves an extensive scene of courtship while negotiations take place offstage (*Henry V* 5.2).

So too does Shakespeare allude to the generation of children through marriage as a good the characters of his play do not experience. In one of his angry moments when he believes that Cleopatra has betrayed him, Antony rails that for her he has forgone the begetting of lawful issue (3.13.112). History tells us that Antony did have several children with Octavia, but Shakespeare omits them from his play, collapsing their marriage into a brief moment before Antony abandons her. As a result, Antony is able to lament that his choosing Cleopatra over Octavia means that he has no legitimate progeny. Antony and Cleopatra also had several children, but we learn of them primarily from Caesar, who speaks disdainfully of them as bastards (3.6.7–8). Cleopatra may imitate the Egyptian goddess of generation (3.6.17), but in Shakespeare's play, she acts almost as if she had no children.[32] Although she does request from Caesar that he let her keep Egypt for her son and heirs (3.12.16–19; 5.2.18–19), she later wishes without hesitation the "memory of [her] womb" destroyed, along with her own life and her "brave Egyptians all," had she betrayed Antony (3.13.163–72).[33] The only other image that Shakespeare gives us of Cleopatra as a mother involves the serpent of Egypt as it does its work, with Cleopatra holding it like "[her] baby at [her] breast,/That sucks the nurse asleep" (5.2.308–09).[34] A marriage in death, as the lovers imagine for themselves, would be without progeny. In all these ways, Shakespeare suggests that we look beyond Rome and Egypt, for human orders that give greater place to love's fulfillment in

32   Alvis, *Shakespeare's Understanding of Honor,* 192.

33   Bradley observes that "the threat of Octavius to destroy her children if she takes her own life passes by her as the wind." *Oxford Lectures,* 301.

34   In Plutarch, the asp simply bites Cleopatra in the arm; 87. Cleopatra's holding it to her breast is Shakespeare's invention. Adelman suggests that the change reminds us of the fecundity associated with Egypt; *The Common Liar,* 64. She connects the references to Antony's abundance to images of Egypt, and especially of the overflowing Nile. She finds "no middle ground" between "a world of lavish overflow and the attendant risk of serpents," on one hand, and "a world of measure and the attendant risk of sterility," on the other. 130. That is why, for example, she associates the snake at Cleopatra's breast with fecundity rather than with sterility, and assimilates Antony's generosity to the overflow of the Nile. From this she concludes that "the only way to fertility is through dissolution." 129–30. In her view, Shakespeare understands human life in light of non-human nature, which is indifferent to morality.

marriage and generation within families. Time does not end with Antony and Cleopatra. The world historical transition that is taking place in Antony and Cleopatra's world, Shakespeare indicates throughout the play, is not merely from the Roman Republic to the Empire, but from pagan religion to Christianity.

In Shakespeare's Christian settings, kings are at most God's "anointed" and not gods themselves (e.g., *Richard II*, 1.2.37–41). Absolute rule of one human being by another violates this truth. Christianity supports limited government. Good rulers (such as Shakespeare's Henry V) demonstrate bounty in ruling, but this includes acknowledging the responsibilities of others for their actions (e.g., *Henry V*, 4.1.124–89). In Shakespeare's comedies, parents may try to act as matchmakers for their children, especially their daughters, but their offspring often take things into their own hands (e.g., *Midsummer Night's Dream*, *Merry Wives of Windsor*, and *Merchant of Venice*). The young assert their freedom, but happily bind themselves in marriage. And those marriages typically look forward to generation and children, which bind them even further, even as they give birth to lives beyond their own. Theirs is a happiness possible for beings who live in time and who accept time's limits as a condition of their happiness.

In the comedies, there is often an extended role for courtship, in which men and women become acquainted with each other before the commitment of marriage. The guises of courtship—sometimes literally disguises as in *As You Like It* and *Twelfth Night*—allow greater insight than the sight provided only by the eye (see *Much Ado About Nothing* 1.1.187–92). Courtship may not lead to perfect knowledge in the comedies, but it leads to marriage. Antony and Cleopatra, in contrast, have consummated their love in illegitimate offspring before the play begins, and they remaining courting, even until the end of their lives. The needs of the lovers in Shakespeare's comedies move them to love and their love begets their bounty— not only to each other, but to their children, to the future, and to the political orders that they will inhabit and in some cases rule. Marriage and generation weds need to generosity.

Rosalind, in *As You Like It*, for example, thinks of "her child's father," when she thinks of Orlando (1.3.11). The recalcitrant Benedick in *Much Ado*, when he finally acknowledges his love for Beatrice, is reminded that "the world must be peopled" (2.3.242). In the *Tempest* Prospero calls forth goddesses of marriage and fertility to bless the union of Miranda and Ferdinand (4.1.57–138), and the deities of *Midsummer Night's Dream* bless the issue of the marriages once the newlyweds retire for the evening (5.1.401–14). In *As You Like It*, Hymen, the god of marriage, "peoples every town" (5.4.143). In his comedies, Shakespeare uses pagan divinities, paradoxically, to affirm for human couples a happiness from marriage and generation that the divinities themselves do not experience from their own coupling. His pagan divinities, in effect, acknowledge their own lack in their very acts of bounty. They are defective gods, even if Shakespeare's poetry shows them at their best.

Shakespeare's comedies, which celebrate love's fulfillment in marriage and generation, offer an alternative to the "universal peace" made possible by an absolute ruler such as Octavius Caesar (4.6.5). Whereas the low comedy that ridicules immortal longings and love's aspirations understands human beings as fit for the rule of despots, a comedy that celebrates love and marriage fosters a view of human beings as able to participate in a political order that has space for self-government, just as men and women exercise self-rule in their choice of each other. In these ways, Shakespeare attempts to give direction to the new heaven and new earth proclaimed by *Revelation* with a conception of love based on bounty as well as need, a conception of the soul that is both free and capable of wisdom, a conception of marriage based on love, and a politics that finds in the soul's freedom both limits to rule and support for self-government. All these changes, in turn, make possible a new sort of comedy whose mockery of human aspirations occurs only in the larger context of their joyous affirmation.

Consistent with Christianity's view of the transcendent human soul, in *Antony and Cleopatra* soul cannot be perfectly located in a particular place or time, just as it cannot be perfectly located in place and time. This freedom places limits on our knowledge of ourselves and others, but also serves as a bulwark against despotism. Cleopatra is often called in the play, especially by her lover Antony, simply "Egypt." This naming not only unpeoples Egypt, as Cleopatra threatens to do by sending away all her subjects with messages to Antony (1.5.79–81). This naming also belies Cleopatra's infinite variety. That is why when Antony calls her "false soul of Egypt," he must be in part right. All naming of soul is in part false. The soul remains in reserve, even when a lover like Cleopatra claims she reserves nothing. It is a treasurer like Shakespeare who calls her to account.

Part III -
Telling Stories About Cities and Souls

The Deluge Myth in Plato's *Laws*:
Philosophical Music and Intoxicant
Scott R. Hemmenway

At the beginning of Book III of Plato's *Laws*, the Athenian Stranger tells a story about an ancient flood so devastating that the only survivors are a few scattered mountain herdsmen, who then, over an immense stretch of time, move off of the mountains to resettle and progress through different forms of regimes up until the settling of Lacedaimon (676a–683b).[1] The stated goal of this narrative is to ascertain the "origin of the political regime" (676a) or "the first genesis and change of political regimes" (676c) in the service of the conversation that the three interlocutors are having about laws. The following reading of this passage, which will be called the Deluge Myth, has three aims. The first is to use it as an example of a type of story I call a myth of political origins in order to address the question of the philosophical significance of such mythic discourse. In abstract terms, a myth of political origins posits and explores a remote time long before cities in order to think through what human nature is and why and how political association is needed and suited to that nature. Additionally, an analysis of the development through the first few stages of political association attempts to further illuminate basic political questions and thus how they ought to be answered. The Athenian Stranger's myth has both of these features: a look

---

1   Translations, with some modifications, are from Thomas Pangle, *The Laws of Plato*, translation, notes and an Interpretive Essay (New York: Basic Books, 1980); also consulted was R. G. Bury's translation from the Loeb Classical Library, *Plato: Laws*, 2 vols. (Cambridge: Harvard University Press, Loeb Classical Library, 1934).

at man's pre-political origins,[2] namely, life for the survivors of a devastating deluge, and an analysis of the transition back into political life and of the need for legislation, namely, the evolution they undergo through four distinct kinds of regimes. This myth thus affords the opportunity to ask whether and how a myth of political origins can be part of a philosophical inquiry—does the projection in thought to the events of a remote time contribute to an understanding of what law is, for example?[3]

Problems in answering this latter question for the Deluge Myth introduce the second aim of this paper, which is to understand how the myth fits into the drama of the *Laws*. Plato writes in the form of dramatic dialogues, and so the assessment of any type of discourse has to take into account the dramatic context within which it is found. The Stranger's recourse to mythic discourse could be explained by the particular opinions and characters of his interlocutors, the course of their conversation, and where the Stranger wishes to take them, rather than by any doctrine about the place of myths of political origins in political inquiry. The question of the drama of the *Laws* might seem to be more puzzling than in other Platonic dialogues because the bulk of the work reads like an exposition of a code of laws that hardly seems to need the literary structure of a conversation between characters. Of more immediate concern is the appearance that some sections, or topics of conversation, are not obviously related to what precedes or follows them; in other words, although all are certainly relevant to the subject of laws, the movement from one topic to the next does not always seem to flow as a real or even as an imitated conversation would.[4] The Deluge

2   Friedländer calls it a "pre-formation" of the state in Paul Friedländer, *Plato: The Dialogues, Second and Third Periods*, trans. Hans Meyerhoff (Princeton: Princeton University Press, 1969), 409.

3   See Lachterman's review of Drombrowski, *Plato's Philosophy of History,* for the interesting suggestion that the Athenian Stranger's rhetorical aim in telling his story puts it more in the company of Hobbes' *Leviathan* and Rousseau's *Second Discourse* than in that of "factual" history: David Lachterman, "Review of *Plato's Philosophy of History*, by D. Dombrowski," *International Studies in Philosophy* 16 (1984): 84–86, at 86.

4   This is the kind of evidence that some interpreters use to argue that the *Laws* is incomplete or unfinished, or that Plato was struggling against a form of writing that he had outgrown. For a good treatment of this and other "misconceptions about the *Laws*," see Eric Voegelin, *Plato* (Baton Rouge: Louisiana State University Press, 1966), 215–23.

Myth begins rather abruptly after putting "a capstone on the argument about wine" (674c); and further, although this quasi-historical viewpoint leads to examinations of the ancient regimes of Sparta, Persia and Athens, it is not clear how starting from the survivors of a deluge contributes to these subsequent discussions. My second aim is to argue for a continuity of the myth with the conversation surrounding it and thus to illuminate in particular why and how the Stranger uses his myth dramatically or dialogically. The main feature of this argument is a consideration of the discussions of music and drunkenness that precede it.[5] One of the many things that the Stranger does in these foregoing sections, according to my interpretation, is to give us tools for interpreting his use of myth. In a word, the myth seems to be designed to function as a kind of poetry and intoxicant for Kleinias and Megillus.

The third aim is simply to confirm my hermeneutic assumption that the other two aims are necessary to each other and are appropriate to Plato's text. By this I mean that with respect to the reading at hand, we learn more than how the Athenian Stranger employs mythic discourse to help Kleinias and Megillus understand something; we also learn how myths of political origins can work to provide philosophic insight into such matters as cities, regimes, and laws. Plato's style of writing might present philosophy in such a way that interpreting drama and understanding things, i.e., philosophizing, mutually illuminate each other.

The Deluge Myth as a Myth of Political Origins

A myth of political origins as I conceive of it has as its general characteristics the following major structure. First, human beings are imagined in a situation or condition that is devoid of political structures as we know them, a pre-political state, as it were. Commonly, a mythic device is used for separating the present from that other time, whether it is some great expanse of time or some cataclysmic event. Second, the need or occasion

---

5   Partial justification for treating these topics together is what the Stranger says right at the end of the Deluge Myth: "We have come now once again, as if according to a god, to the point at the beginning of our dialogue about laws where we digressed and fell into the topics of music and drunken carousals" (682e).

for political association is described and the narrative thus has the capacity to account, sometimes in several stages of development, for why and how human association changes into forms that are distinctly political. The perspective that such a structured story offers thus makes possible the addressing of questions like what is human nature such that it requires a city, what regime is most appropriate for men, or what is law—as the Athenian Stranger puts it, "Now what we've been saying, and all that is still to follow from it, has been said as a means to our coming to understand what need the men of that time had for laws, and who was lawgiver for them" (679e–680a). Some other Platonic myths that also fit this general description more or less are the Promethean myth from the *Protagoras* (320c–323c) and the myth of the reversing cosmos from the *Statesman* (268d–274e).

The *Laws* myth uses an ancient deluge to reduce humankind to a small remnant, thus beginning a new epoch, and then posits a great expanse of time to separate us from these ancestors of ours. The survivors of this flood were stranded and isolated mountain herdsmen, while the cities and civilized men below them were all destroyed. Instead of some other disaster, like the fires mentioned in the *Timaeus* (22a), this particular natural destruction has the theoretical advantage that the population left behind is, politically speaking, a relatively clean slate.[6] These people are even without any "memory" of "city, regime, and legislation" (678a), and "so it is from these men so disposed that all the things we have came: cities, regimes, arts, and laws, as well as much virtue and evil" (678a). These mountain herdsmen, consequently, are essentially pre-political,[7] and so by narrating

6   Cf. Benardete: "By choosing the flood, the Stranger chooses the survivors, whose way of life establishes the beginning of political life. In light of this choice, the cause of political change is identified with the cause of the vanishing of the city. The city thus comes to be from the noncity." Seth Benardete, *Plato's "Laws": The Discovery of Being* (Chicago: University of Chicago Press, 2000), 91.

7   There is one problem concerning the unexplained origin of the traditions about gods and human beings that they are said to accept so uncritically (679c); if some unnamed ancient poet or legislator were responsible for these traditions, then their political character would already be partly formed and this would in turn affect their potential to accept further political forms.

how cities developed for them gradually over a long time, the myth attempts to provide an insight into the origin and nature of political association.

Before charting that development, however, the Stranger takes some time to paint a portrait of these primitive people and their way of life, and it seems that he is intent on its being a rather idyllic picture.[8] It is perfectly consistent with their lack of political sophistication that these herdsmen were fairly primitive technologically, but the Stranger goes out of his way to insist that all the arts be lost to the waters.[9] He also associates the arts with not only politics, but with any and all possible source of conflict between them.[10] The very beginning of his description sets the tone: they "lack experience in the arts, and especially in the contrivances that city dwellers use against one another, motivated by the desire to have more, the love of victory, and all the other mischief they think up against each other" (677b).[11] Although the god-given and peaceful molding and weaving arts provide essential livelihood, the art of metals is specifically mentioned as having disappeared, and when it is claimed that the arts that depend on metals are also gone and then said that "civil war and war were destroyed during that time" (678e), it is implied that weapons and the means for producing them are gone. Also absent is any need or occasion to fight: there is plenty of land,

---

8   See Barker for a comparison of this "golden 'state of nature'" with the similar city of swine of the *Republic* and for a comment on Plato's ambiguity about this "paradise of the hills." Sir Ernest Barker, *Greek Political Theory: Plato and his Predecessors* (London: Methuen & Co., 1918), 356–57.

9   Benardete has a different take on the significance of the loss of *technē*: "The immediate connection between the end of book 2 and the beginning of book 3 consists in the parallelism between the Stranger's denial that thoughtfulness can be at the beginning of any animal, and his thesis that the arts in their full development are not found at the beginning of political society"; *Plato's "Laws,"* 88.

10   Another connection to a state of nature theorist is made by Benardete: "The connection the Stranger makes between the arts and immorality recalls Rousseau, but the Stranger does not offer any argument. He deepens the puzzle by linking the disappearance of wisdom (σοφία), whether political or of another kind, with the disappearance of tools"; ibid., 94.

11   By contrast, Protagoras has mankind acquiring the *technai* from Prometheus independently of the political problem of injustice and its solution.

no transportation, and plenty of food.[12] In fact, their isolation makes them especially friendly when they do see one another. And finally, they have neither wealth nor poverty to induce "hubris, nor injustice, nor again rivalries and envy" (679c).[13] What follows these conditions is a rather positive portrait of their goodness or virtue which is worth quoting in full:

> Shouldn't we go on to say that the many generations who passed their lives this way were less practiced and less knowledgeable in the arts generally than those who lived before the flood or those who live now, and especially as regards the arts of war? They didn't know all the present-day arts of war on land or on sea, or in a city all by itself, which are called lawsuits and civil wars, and in which every sort of contrivance of words and deeds is devised in order to do mutual mischief and injustice. So, for the reason we already have explained, shouldn't we say that they were simpler and more courageous and also more moderate and in every way more just? (679d–e)

With the two provisos that perfect virtue, as well as perfect vice, are only possible with city life (678b) and that the Stranger has substituted a very un-Athenian virtue—naïve simplicity—for wisdom, it appears as if the general shape of this myth points toward the complete corruption of our virtue with the introduction of politics.[14]

12 The slight ambiguity over whether herding or hunting provides them with food and how there might be game at all (677e and 679a) is a hint, I think, that the Stranger would like to but cannot altogether avoid mentioning a practice that involves aggression and weapons. See the later description of hunting and its relation to courage and war at 823b–24a.

13 The moral effects of wealth and poverty are, of course, a major theme of the later legislation; see, e.g., 736e–737b.

14 See also Zuckert: "The Athenian agrees with Clinias that human beings become hostile after they have organized themselves into cities. But, he suggests, they do not view each other antagonistically before they are organized into discrete political units. He posits something like a modern 'state of nature' to counter Clinias' initial claim that war is necessary and natural"; Catherine Zuckert, *Plato's Philosophers: The Coherence of the Dialogues* (Chicago: Chicago University Press, 2009), 73.

The rest of the myth follows the gradual descent from the mountain tops to the sea once enough time has passed for the survivors to get past their fear of the water and lowland. There are four forms of regimes that this genesis of the political life passes through.[15] The first is called "dynasty" and classified as a "type of regime," but actually only characterizes the initial and almost apolitical condition of the mountain herdsmen: independent households or clans guided by "habits and so-called ancestral customs" (680a) and ruled by elders whose authority is hereditary. This primitive patriarchy is also called "the most just of kingships" (680e). The Stranger uses Homer as a "witness for the fact that such regimes come to be sometimes" (680d), quoting some lines that describe the household of the Cyclops. The Stranger's attribution of justice to this "regime" and his generally peaceful portrait of their life can be maintained only because Kleinias is not familiar with the events told of in Homer's poem; Megillus, on the other hand, is aware that "in his mythologizing [Homer] attributes their ancient or primitive habits to their savagery" (680d).

In observing the move from mountain top to foothills and the corresponding introduction of the second type of regime, the Athenian Stranger first mentions "cities" (680e) and remarks that they have come upon "the origin of legislation" (681c). The exact nature of this change, "this transformation of regime" (681d), represents the move to political association for these human beings, but the story about why and how it occurred has some odd twists and turns. The shift from herding to farming as they descend is plausible; however, the reason they start living in close proximity is that they need "one common, large dwelling [built] by erecting defensive walls of stone around themselves on account of wild beasts" (681a). This external threat that forces cooperation is similar to the one that Protagoras tells of in his myth, and he similarly glosses over the possible complexity of social cooperation required even for the practice of simple *technai* and that might actually provide a more

---

15 All four stages are mentioned at the end of Book III in the Stranger's summary of the discussion so far: "the Dorian armed camp, both the hill-dwellings of Dardonus and the settlement on the sea, and the first people who were the survivors of the catastrophe . . ." (702a2–5).

plausible explanation for the emergence of politics.[16] In contrast to Protagoras' myth, however, the Stranger's account resolves the differences between these people forced to live together without having to appeal to Zeus for justice. The conflict is described as one mainly of customs and habits due to different temperaments, named orderly and manly, and the long period of mutual isolation. Again, unlike the very difficult task that the Eleatic Stranger envisions for the statesman,[17] a peaceful blending and compromise of these two types of human being is achieved by some "lawgivers" who cooperate with the chiefs or leaders of the incoming clans. These lawgivers thus bring about the change of regime from a plurality of dynasties to an aristocracy or kingship, "while they themselves will live in (or manage)[18] the changing regime" (681d). The ambiguity over the ruling status of the original legislators is matched by the vagueness of the selection process of the legislators and the approving of their selection of laws. One cannot help noticing that the description of this process resembles the difficult task of establishing a colony of diverse peoples that will soon face Kleinias as a legislator for Magnesia. The Athenian Stranger will later say that this part of founding a new settlement is almost a Herculean labor that requires an exceptional tyrant and/or legislator (707e ff.); the transition for these primitive people is achieved, however, almost effortlessly. The third regime occurs as the people venture down onto the plain and out to the shores of the sea. It is associated with the city of Ilium told of in Homer, but almost nothing is said about the reason for the change in location beyond population pressure—except, of course, that they were forgetting their fear of water (682c)—nor about the forms of the corresponding political changes. The only thing we learn about this "third scheme of regime" is that in it are mixed "all forms and experiences of regimes and cities" (681d). The

16 *Protagoras* 322b. See also the structure of the healthy city in the *Republic* for the political implications of the practice of *technai* (*Republic* 369–72), discussed in Scott R. Hemmenway's "The *Techne*-Analogy in Socrates' Healthy City: Justice and the Craftsman in the *Republic*," *Ancient Philosophy* 19 (1999): 267–84.

17 *Statesman*, 306a-311c.

18 The word οἰκήσουσιν can be translated either as "they will rule" (Pangle) or as "they will live under" (Bury translation).

significant change is the introduction of war.[19] Taking up the myths about the Trojan War, the Athenian Stranger asserts that "others undertook a military expedition against this one, and probably came by sea, since now everyone was making use of the sea without fear" (682c–d). The Stranger's narrative of this war is particularly negative, and he concentrates on the domestic trouble that occurred for the Achaeans: the "civil unrest of the young" (682d). Internal dissension (στάσις) seems to go hand in hand with external war.[20] In fact, he seems to invent the story that the Dorian invasion of the Peloponnesus was peopled by exiles from this civil war. The city of Ilium, which "boldly stirred up the Trojan War" (685c), and the Achaeans' cities torn apart as a result of waging a ten-year siege, however, characterize this third state in which very little is said about the source of such great evils.[21]

The fourth regime is that of the Dorians who reclaimed the Peloponnesus, and it is here that the Athenian Stranger notes that having arrived at the settling of Lacedaimon they are in a position to begin anew and evaluate what has and what has not been nobly settled in this city, "a second attempt at an investigation into lawgiving," as Megillus calls it (683b). And it is here that what I consider to be the myth of political origins ends and a very different kind of investigation begins. As is obvious from my mention of other Platonic myths and my emphasis on the peculiarities and mythic qualities of the Stranger's story, I do not think that this account is Plato's definitive doctrine on Greek historical-political origins. Just how he

19   It is not made clear whether this recent fearlessness is actually due to ignorance or bravery. Strauss suggests that the loss of an awareness of the ultimate frailty of human endeavors has allowed these men to take their cities seriously enough to dedicate themselves to them, which includes risking their lives for them; Leo Strauss, *The Argument and the Action of Plato's Laws* (Chicago: University of Chicago Press, 1975), 41. Benardete comments, "The Stranger now returns to war, but war is no longer at the beginning of political life. There is political life before there is the polis and war"; *Plato's "Laws,"* 89.

20   See the earlier discussion of the two forms of war at 629c–e and the surrounding criticism by the Stranger of laws and regimes oriented towards war.

21   Friedländer suggests that one of the purposes of this presentation of stages is to support the later hypothesis that every regime is only ever corrupted by some internal force; *Plato*, 411. Although I think this is true for the third stage, I do not see how it applies to the first two stages.

meant us to understand it will now be explored by observing how the Athenian Stranger means Kleinias and Megillus to hear it and be affected by its peculiar power.

The Deluge Myth as Intoxicant

As already noted, the Deluge Myth is begun rather abruptly after they put "a capstone to the argument about wine" (674c). In fact, the obscurity of the change in topic is only exaggerated by the fact that, just previous to suggesting a capstone to the "discussion of the use of drunkenness" (673d), the Athenian Stranger had proposed to move on to the other half of the choral art, namely gymnastics for the body, now that they had completed the first half, namely music for the soul (672e–673d). Not only is the suggestion of a discussion of gymnastics seemingly ignored in favor of an unheralded telling of the myth, but the form in which the subject is proposed is almost inconsistent with the former division of the choral art into song and dance (654b).[22] The argument I now put forth to explain this difficult transition is that the discussions of both music and drunkenness form a suitable preface to the myth because the Stranger uses mythological discourse as both poetry and intoxicant.[23]

---

22 My speculation on the sudden introduction and dropping of the subject of gymnastics is that the Stranger is not hinting at the shift to the contents of Book III, but testing Kleinias and Megillus on how well they have understood that body and soul cannot be separated in education into music and gymnastics. Compare Socrates' explanation to Glaucon of a similar point in the *Republic* (410c–412b). See Strauss, *The Argument and the Action,* 37, Pangle, "Interpretative Essay," 422–23, and Benardete, *Plato's "Laws,"* 86. The general approach taken by these three is to note that gymnastics is concerned with the body and that the political issues raised in Book III are closely related to our corporeal existence, for example, war and the origin of the city.

23 See Voegelin for an interesting and very different interpretation of the significance of the long discussion of the customs of social drinking; *Plato,* 240–41. He sees this digression, which has baffled interpreters, as a good example of Plato's new literary technique of presenting problems symbolically. Benardete compares getting drunk to "the prelaw state of human beings," namely the prepolitical condition of disorder that law has to handle; *Plato's "Laws,"* 35–36.

The inquiry into the custom of getting drunk that takes up the bulk of Books I and II is actually the third attempt that the Athenian, the Spartan, and the Cretan make at evaluating laws. The first two are focused on Cretan and Spartan customs, e.g., of gymnastics and common meals, and they both degenerate into mere "controversy" (638d). It seems that several factors interfere with the Stranger's getting their examination of laws off onto the right foot, and a brief summary of some of them will be helpful in getting a picture of what kind of obstacles the Stranger faces in attempting to raise the conversation to a philosophic level, both in the third attempt with the discussion about drunkenness and then with his myth. First, there is a certain amount of piety and patriotism that prevents both Megillus and Kleinias from being comfortable with the kind of radical questioning in which the Stranger wishes to engage them. Second, their age and the force of habit have made their opinions rigid. Third, neither Spartans nor Cretans are known for experience in any kind of sophisticated conversation, much less philosophy.[24] And fourth, both conceive the business of politics to be aimed primarily at war and human virtue to consist in the strength to endure pain and to resist tempting pleasures. The topic of drunkenness allows the Stranger, because of the other two's inexperience with it and its seeming remoteness from any serious legal custom, quite a bit of leeway to circumvent these obstacles, all the while challenging some of their views. The Athenian Stranger also says that their investigation will illustrate the "correct method for our inquiry into all such things" (638e), the main feature of which is that one should seriously consider any communal activity only as directed by the "correct ruler" (640a). Part of the reason that some of what the Stranger says about properly conducted drinking parties is so odd is, I believe, that the description is meant also to refer to the form of social intercourse that the three of them are presently engaged in.[25] Being

24 Even if Kleinias and Megillus are untypically well-disposed to Athenians and hence their loquaciousness (641e–643a).

25 In support of this self-referentiality, Pangle notes two hints that the conversation depicted in the Laws is itself a "banquet"; "Interpretative Essay," 403–404. His interpretation, however, of what intoxicates the old men is "a lengthy private discussion of the forbidden pleasure of drunkenness and drinking parties." Strauss similarly says, "Could wine, or at any rate the vicarious enjoyment of wine through a conversation about wine, have this rejuvenating effect

guided into a philosophical conversation for Megillus and Kleinias will be like getting drunk under careful supervision.

The first of two potential political benefits of intoxication is in the context of drinking parties designed to test citizens for the "natures and habits of souls" (650b); more specifically, drunkenness offers the seemingly paradoxical occasion for practicing the virtue of moderation, understood as the ability to be victorious over pleasures. Wine is a drug that makes us bolder and hence less fearful of the opinion of others, and, thus intoxicated, one might give in to pleasures one would find shameful when sober. The Stranger asserts that tests could be set up for strength in resisting, for example, the pleasure of sexual desire or the attractiveness of injustice (649d), although he does not really explain how these are engineered; I have a hypothesis, but it will have to wait until our discussion of poetry. The most interesting detail of the elaboration of these parties is how the Stranger describes the effect of wine. At first he says that it makes pleasures, pains, and emotions more intense, but opinions and prudent thoughts flee, and hence the disposition of the soul becomes more childlike (645d–646a), but later he claims that it makes the drunk man "more cheerful . . . swell with an opinion of his own power . . . and filled with complete license of speech, supposing himself to be wise; isn't he filled with freedom and total fearlessness" (649b). These effects of intoxication are just what the Stranger needs for his interlocutors to feel in order to loosen them up from their age, belligerence, rigid opinions, hesitancy to talk, and shamefulness. What could serve as such an agent for intoxication?[26] My proposal: a carefully measured and administered amount of philosophy, just enough to induce the exhilarating and heady feeling of supposing that one knows or understands something important without being threatened (restricted by shame

(cf. 645e3–8)?"; *The Argument and the Action*, 20–21. I believe, as will be stated below, that a more important intoxicant is philosophy or its mythic imitation.

26 Compare Clark's general discussion of the use of philosophy as medicine in the *Laws*, and in particular wine as a drug (φάρμακον) that the Stranger applies to Megillus and Kleinias; Randall Baldwin Clark, *The Law Most Beautiful and Best: Medical Argument and Magical Rhetoric in Plato's Laws* (Lanham, MD: Lexington Books, 2003), 119. These remedies he classifies as examples of the use of magic as opposed to reason, while I view, for example, myth as instrumental to reason.

or loyalty).[27] I believe that the Stranger can be observed throughout the whole conversation of the *Laws* to be administering this drug, but a particularly good example is the telling of the Deluge Myth. A myth of political origins can be a measured dose of philosophy: it offers a suitably large and freeing perspective and an easy and satisfying explanation for how lawgiving came to be. Kleinias and Megillus seem to follow the narrative very positively, and part of the pleasure they feel is the intoxicating potential of its simple and comprehensive explanatory power.

As with the drinking parties that are tests for moderation, however, there is a danger to intoxication: philosophy can tempt one by means of the pleasure of knowing to adopt an ignoble or shameful opinion. The temptation with respect to believing that one has already understood the origin of law is nicely illustrated later in the *Laws* when the Stranger exposes Kleinias to a sophistical account of the origin and truth of legal conventions (889e–890a). Given Kleinias' own opinions about the legitimacy of mere strength,[28] one could easily imagine him being seduced into believing a relativist account of the distinction between nature and law and the type of story that attends it—a good example would be Glaucon's version in the *Republic* of justice being a contract among the weaker (358e–359b). The Stranger, a philosopher immune to the drunkenness that theory can produce, guides Kleinias so that he is not tempted to say or assent to anything really shameful. The myth of the genealogy of the city that the

27 Strauss, by contrast, speaks about the mental dulling due to intoxication: "And wise men would need wine, in order to participate fully in the 'symphony' of the city; their mind must lose something—we do not know how much—of its clarity"; *The Argument and the Action*, 33. See also Whitaker, who says, "In other words, the hesitating of the old to sing and dance may not be due only to stage fright. They may also balk at the message they must give to the young, a message they themselves may doubt, i.e., a message they may think is a lie [e.g., about the relation between the just and pleasant life]. Drinking then, not only loosens their sense of shame so that they will exhibit themselves in public. It also may muddle their mind, making them more willing to believe in the pleasant message that they may not be so accepting of in their more just and sharp-eyed sober state"; Albert Keith Whitaker, *A Journey into Platonic Politics. Plato's Laws* (Lanham, MD: University Press of America, 2004), 35–36.

28 See 626a, 690b, and 715a.

Stranger will offer is a more sober account, one that allows Kleinias to taste the intoxicating power of knowledge without getting so drunk that he says or reveals that he thinks that shameful and base desires are all there is to political reality.

The second of two potential political benefits of intoxication is explained later in Book II in conjunction with the Dionysian chorus of elders. The role that wine plays here is to help the older men get over their shame at performing in front of others, a natural moderation that comes with age. In other words, wine is a "drug that soothes the austerity of old age" and makes the stiffer (σκληρότερον) character of the soul softer (666b–c). The more venerable of the citizens are thus "encouraged" to take part eagerly in the politically valuable festivals (666a). Both Kleinias and Megillus are elderly gentlemen and therefore require some kind of intoxicant to loosen them up so that they will participate in "playing at this moderate old man's game concerning laws" (685a). I believe that the intoxicant or medicine that Kleinias and Megillus need is philosophy, an intoxicant whose potentially maddening effects require careful supervision. After all, if one drinks too much, he "becomes filled with license of speech, doesn't listen to those around him, supposing he has become capable of ruling others as well as himself" (671b). I have already indicated that the Stranger's myth is like a wine diluted with the proper amount of water; it has the power to soften these Dorians enough to move them away from their rigid opinions and toward a suitably playful theoretical standpoint, without driving them mad with the presumption of superior wisdom. What now needs exploring is the discussion of music and poetry that an intoxicant could encourage the old men to sing.

The Deluge Myth as Music

Under the guise of explaining how "correctly used wine parties" provide the additional benefit of a "safeguard for education," namely, why it is that it is a good thing that wine can encourage old men to participate in public performances of music, the Stranger engages his interlocutors in discussion of a whole range of topics connected to education, including the choral arts, imitation, and the proper criteria for judging poetry. As with the discussion of drinking parties, I think much of what the Stranger is talking about applies to the education that Megillus and Kleinias require, both to become more virtuous themselves and to understand virtue so that they are then able to engage in a more sophisticated and intelligent conversation about laws. The appeal of poetry and the effect of its regular singing are powerful formative tools for habituating young souls to virtue, and the telling of the Deluge myth works in a similar way as soothing music for the Dorians.

Early in the *Laws*, we are made aware that Kleinias' and Megillus' conception of virtue is based on the idea of fighting fears, i.e., courage, and resisting pleasures, i.e., moderation (see 626e & 633c–634a). A virtue based on consonance, not struggle, is the aim of education in this section of the discussion. In other words, the passions can be trained or habituated to love and hate what reason says one should love and hate, and thus pleasure and pain can be positive forces in the psychology of virtue instead of things to fight and overcome. The "correctly trained pleasures and pains" (653c) are the ones associated with music, and so the Stranger needs to explain how it is that music moves the soul.

Although the Athenian does not clearly distinguish them in his explanation, there are actually several distinct kinds of pleasures that music affords. The first is associated with the natural proclivity of children to move and vocalize. For humans, this pleasure can be enhanced by doing these in rhythm and harmony, and hence we have dance and song. The choral art, or music, can be used in the education of the young, therefore, because, like play, it is pleasant. The connection to virtue is made through a second quality and pleasure of music: it is imitative. Humans, especially young ones, are fascinated by and delighted with imitation.[29] Imitative play was earlier mentioned as helpful in technical education; for example, young farmers play with miniature tools that are imitations of the real ones (643c). In a moral education, the imitation will naturally be of good and virtuous men, and thus the Stranger asserts that "choral performances are imitations of characters" (655d). Not only can posture and tune be an image of a man's comportment, but his deeds and speeches can be depicted in the words of songs. Consequently, the young can be brought to behave and enjoy behaving in a virtuous manner if they are given good music, i.e., fine songs and dances, to perform and watch.

---

29   The mention, at 658c, of children's preference for puppets is an indication of this.

This argument depends on the premise that one assimilates to what one enjoys; hence the need for extreme care with music, "for in making a mistake, one is greatly harmed because he becomes well-disposed to evil habits" (669b–c). There is a further complication, however, to this assimilation. A third pleasure of music, one that is available to those already formed or educated, is the enjoyment of performing or watching imitations of characters that are like themselves. This means that if one is already virtuous, then watching or performing fine music will only reinforce one's habitual liking of one's own virtue. However, if one's "nature and habits" are in conflict with each other, although shame would restrain a public admission, one could actually delight in the imitation of wicked characters and so be made worse by the natural assimilation (655d–656b). Consequently, music is not only useful for the formation of the young and for reinforcing the training of the old, it can also be used to expose character defects if one can find out what imitations someone secretly enjoys.

Although the Athenian Stranger does not make the following connection explicitly, he has now furnished enough material to fill out the sketchy picture of the tests for moderation that "correctly used wine parties" were designed to perform. The ignoble pleasure that can safely be indulged on such occasions is the enjoyment of performances of imitations of shameful characters. "Natures and habits" can be revealed and tested by the singing or reciting of different kinds of poems in a situation where shame has been relaxed. At one point much later in the conversation we learn of a possible dissonance between what Kleinias really thinks and what he should be afraid or ashamed to admit in a more public setting. Much to the Athenian's dismay, which is indicated by his swearing, Kleinias does not believe that the unjust man is necessarily unhappy (662c). Although admittedly shameful, a courageous man who is successful in attaining the good things of life in an unjust manner nonetheless leads a pleasant life, according to Kleinias.[30] By forcing this admission, not an unexpected one given what we already have learned about Kleinias, the Stranger has managed to expose a dissonance in Kleinias's nature and habits that could leave him susceptible to

30 See Zuckert for an interesting speculation on Plato's choice of Kleinias' name, namely that of Alcibiades' father and son; *Plato's Philosophers*, 71, n39.

the corrupting influence of ignoble poetry.[31] A myth, for example, that idealized the naturally strong man and his power to get whatever he wants—a sophist's myth about the origins of convention—might tempt him, and he might secretly find pleasure in a story that he would be ashamed to admit when sober.[32]

What I shall now suggest is that the Deluge Myth that the Stranger tells can be seen as a fine song designed to substitute for what Kleinias might secretly enjoy more. When the Stranger insists that the poets are "to write poems correctly by portraying the postures and songs of moderate, courageous, and entirely good men in rhythms and harmony" (660a), that could be a description of the aim of his own mythological discourse. More specifically, a type of character is depicted in the myth which it would benefit Kleinias to take pleasure in hearing imitated. We saw that the primitive herdsman was peaceful and friendly, and further he was found to possess all the virtues, except wisdom, to a high degree. This character is hence a good antidote to what Kleinias or Megillus might have thought was most essential about the virtues of a man fit for the natural war that exists between all cities, indeed between all men (626a–d). His moderation, in particular, is not based on restraint, but an easy consonance between accepted customs and his simple passions. His goodness or virtue is such that it ought to command the Dorian's respect and thus works to represent a salutary model for the origin or principle of man's political nature for them. If Kleinias and Megillus did not take pleasure in this imitation, it would certainly be good for them to be encouraged to join in the singing of it at regular festivals until they did.

To the objection that the Stranger's myth is hardly a work of music, it must be conceded that it is not composed in meter or accompanied by

31 Although Kleinias is apparently astonished by the sophist's account of the origin and nature of convention (890b2), such a reductionist theory is actually not so far removed from his own stance on the political legitimacy of mere strength. Strauss notes this and refers to 626a3–5, 690b4–8, and 715a1–2; *The Argument and the Action*. 145.

32 In the aforementioned example of the Athenian's later exposing Kleinias to an account of the origin of convention, Kleinias does express disapproval. Perhaps this is due to the salutary effect of the Stranger's myth of the origins of laws that has persuasively presented a more noble vision of virtue.

harmony. And it also does not have the "grace" of Homer and the "urbane qualities of his lines" (680c) which the Stranger actually quotes to support his own story. As with the appeal to Homer as a source of information about the divine cause for Cretan laws at the very beginning of the dialogue (624a), the poets are often the ones to whom one turns for inspiration about the origins of things. This is not necessarily because of the reason that the Stranger gives for the poets' divine voice, i.e., that "they hit upon many things that truly happened" (682a). Instead, their history does not have to be accurate, for they are able to capture or illuminate something of the truth about the human soul through their inspired visions of fantastic far-away places and times. The philosopher's mythologizing is perhaps less beautiful, yet it is less hit-or-miss. In spite of the fact that this myth is expressed in prose, it functions as a form of poetry because of its capacity to evoke images of human character and deeds. And as in Homer, the essential truth of stories of ancient times lies not in whether things actually happened as they are told, but primarily in what they teach about the human soul, its virtue, and its place in the cosmos. The Athenian Stranger's poem may not be in a form suitable for a choral performance at a public festival, but, as an imitation of virtuous men, its performance ought to be enjoyed by Kleinias and Megillus.

Conclusion

Space limitation allows me here only to assert that confirmation of my reading of the myth as intoxicant and poetry, as well as a myth of political origins, can be found in the investigation of the settling of Sparta, the look at the ancient regimes of Persia and Athens, as well as the founding of the city in speech which takes up the rest of the conversation. I conclude with some general speculation on the drama of the *Laws*, myths of political origins, and Plato's style of writing.

The Athenian Stranger narrates a story about an ancient series of events as "a means to . . . coming to understand what need the men of that time had for laws, and who was lawgiver for them" (679e–670a). This myth has been interpreted as part of a broader effort to engage his interlocutors in as philosophical a conversation as possible about laws, and I believe this effort extends through the entire work. The multifaceted kinds and directions of discourse that the Stranger employs reflect his acute diagnosis and treatment of Kleinias' and Megillus' philosophical limitations. The use of a myth of political origins, where laws get washed away and gradually reappear as man moves from mountain to sea, is a particularly effective rhetorical treatment and is especially illuminated by a look at what the Stranger says about drunkenness and music. Mythic discourse has the potential to be an intoxicant and enchanter of the soul. It can be both maddening and soothing, liberating and captivating, emboldening and moderating. One can observe the Stranger exploiting these powers in his deft telling of the deluge and its consequences for mankind. This is the sort of thing one learns by attending to the drama of a Platonic dialogue like the *Laws*.

But are myths of political origins then just poetry and intoxication? What do they have to do with philosophy? With understanding what law is? One way to read Plato's dialogues as more than demonstrations of philosophic rhetoric is to attempt to see in them an image of philosophy. In the present case, thinking about subjects like political regimes and laws might have to involve complex psychic—and even "non-rational"—responses to stories about origins. At least in this case, that is what Plato's style of writing suggests.

A version of this paper was given to a panel, organized by Denise Schaeffer, at the meeting of the Northeast Political Science Association in Boston, November 2004. The project was completed with support from Eureka College in the form of release time.

On Founding:
City and Soul in *A Midsummer Night's Dream*
Michael P. Zuckert

A Midsummer Night's Dream presents a set of disparate social worlds and plot lines held together only by Theseus. The lovers belong to the society of his court and flee his Athens to escape the law he threatens to visit upon Hermia if she fails to marry as her father demands; by the day of Theseus' marriage Hermia is to decide what fate she chooses—to marry the man selected for her, to enter upon the life of a nun, or "to die the death." As it turns out, however, she needs do none of these, but is free to marry the man of her choice, but this too occurs on Theseus' wedding day with Theseus' permission. The "rude mechanicals" belong to *Midsummer Night's Dream* only so far as they too orbit around Theseus, for they appear in order to prepare a dramatic production for Theseus' wedding. Finally, the inhabitants of the third major world of the play, the fairies, are lurking in the vicinity of Athens only to help celebrate the wedding (2.1. 70–74; 138).[1]

Theseus is thus the center of the play, holding all else together. Shakespeare very decidedly set it in Athens and made Theseus the ruler of this Athens. He thereby brought into his play Theseus and his reputation as the founder of Athens. According to Plutarch, the chief source for the life of Theseus, the Thesean founding of Athens was also the founding of the first democracy and perhaps the first institution of political life proper. As Plutarch puts it, "Theseus was the first, who, as Aristotle says, out of an inclination to popular government, parted with the regal power" (*Life of*

---

1   William Shakespeare, *A Midsummer Night's Dream*, New York, New American Library (Signet Classic), 1963.

Theseus, paras. 24–25).[2] The significance of Theseus as founder of Athens, of democracy, of politics itself is testified to by great authorities, ancient and modern, including, as Plutarch indicated, Aristotle, who affirmed that despite the naturalness of the political association, "the one who first constituted [a city] is responsible for the greatest of goods" (compare *Politics*, 1253a 30; cf. 1252b 15–24 with Plutarch on Theseus' founding activity, paras. 24–25).

Focusing attention on Theseus also brings to the fore the "Machiavellian connection," because the Florentine treats Theseus as one of his four "highest examples" of the new prince in the new principality, i.e., of the bringer of "new modes and orders" (*The Prince*, ch. 6).[3] In bringing Theseus into his play, then, Shakespeare allows *Midsummer Night's Dream* to become the site of a sustained consideration of Machiavelli's confessedly highest theme—new modes and orders, or foundings.

A Midsummer Night's Dream (*MND*) also presents the oldest event ever staged by Shakespeare. The founding of Athens precedes the Trojan War (as in *Troilus and Cressida*) to say nothing of the events of Roman history. As oldest, *MND* is, at least in one sense, first in the Shakespearean corpus. Its priority is underlined by the character of the event portrayed—not merely the oldest, but the founding, not only of Athens, but of politics as such. *MND* is both the introduction to the Shakespearean corpus and a central locus for Shakespeare's reflections on Machiavelli and Machiavellian themes.

Plutarch

Machiavelli identifies Theseus as one of his most illustrious founder-princes, yet he was certainly not the first to make Theseus and the founding of Athens a subject for reflection. The most important source on Theseus was Plutarch. Theseus' was the first biography in *The Parallel Lives*. He too recognizes Theseus' firstness. Plutarch pairs Theseus with Romulus, the

---

2 Plutarch, *The Lives of the Noble Grecians and Romans,* Dryden translation (Chicago: University of Chicago Press, The Great Books, 1952).

3 Niccolo Machiavelli, *The Prince*, Harvey Mansfield translator (Chicago: University of Chicago Press, 1998).

semi-mythical founder of Rome. The founding of Athens is thus for Plutarch the central event in Theseus' varied career. He has accordingly artfully arranged his narrative to shed its light on this act above all. There are three elements to Plutarch's account: Athens before Theseus, Theseus before Athens, and the Thesean founding itself, an event resulting from a conjunction of imperatives implicit in the first two topics. Pre-Thesean Athens, marked by both internal and external crises, was not a happy place. The most evident sign of crisis was the humiliating necessity Athens was under to pay to Crete a tribute every nine years of seven young men and seven young women. The most famous, as well as "the most dramatic" version of the story has it that the fourteen youths were to be thrown into the labyrinth, there to be killed by the Minotaur, the half-man, half-bull who lived in the heart of the maze.

Athens suffered humiliation not only at the hands of the potent and organized Minoans, but was unable to protect its very borders from the depredations of bandits and marauders. (Plutarch, sects. 7–12). Internal weakness lay behind the Athenians' inability to deal successfully with these various external powers. The king was Aegeus, reputed father of Theseus, but his kingdom was weak and his rule shaky. Athens was not a city—it was rather a mere scattering of villages, clans in the Attic countryside. These were neither physically united nor at peace with each other (Plutarch, Sect. 24). Moreover, there was great rivalry, even for the nominal authority that Aegeus held. His brother Pallas had fifty sons, who "hoped to rule the kingdom after Aegeus." But Aegeus was concerned that they would not wait for nature to follow its course. Even before the birth of Theseus, "Aegeus was mortally afraid . . . of the sons of Pallas . . . who were plotting against him" (sect. 3). Those plots broke out into open rebellion when, years later, Theseus arrived in Athens and was acknowledged by Aegeus as his heir (sect. 13).

Part of Aegeus' weakness had been due to his lack of an heir: he was "despised . . . for his childlessness" (sect. 3). Aegeus was also vulnerable because of his own questionable descent. The sons of Pallas accused him of being "only an adopted son of Pandion [with] no ties of blood to the house of Erechtheus" (sects. 3 and 13). The background against which the issue of descent is so important is relatively clear: Athens was a hereditary monarchy of the patriarchal sort, organized into clan groups where the claim to supreme fatherhood was unclear and subject to contest. Political authority was indistinguishable from familial authority in the father, or in the chief father of what was now an extended clan structure. It was this very imperfect structure of authority that was responsible for the crises, internal and external, of pre-Thesean Athens.

Plutarch sees the greatness of Theseus in his transformation of this very imperfect patriarchal monarchy into a genuinely political community, but Theseus first attempted to find his place within this traditional structure. The early history of Theseus, as told by Plutarch, is centered on how little able Theseus was to succeed in this venture. Plutarch recounts the traditional tale of Theseus' birth—the child of an almost casual one-night stand between Aegeus and Aethra, daughter of the King of Troezen. Aegeus was long-gone from Troezen by the time Theseus was born, a circumstance that contributed to uncertainty over his parentage (sect. 2). The sons of Pallas were enraged when Theseus "was declared the successor . . . since he was," they believed, "a mere immigrant and a foreigner" (sect. 13). Despite Aegeus' willingness to own him as his son and despite the fact that Theseus had proven his prowess on his journey from Troezen to Athens, putting down a bevy of bandits and other unsavories (sects. 6–12), Theseus was met at every turn by resistance to his ascent to the kingship. Having become aware of how difficult it would be to make good any claim to rule under the traditional (hereditary) form of legitimacy, it is no wonder that Theseus attempted to display his prowess in Herculean exploits, culminating in his expedition against the great and terrifying bull of Crete.

Somewhere along the way Theseus came to realize he could not succeed on the basis of prowess alone. After his return from Crete, he undertook the reforms of Athens for which he is most remembered. Plutarch is conveying in his narrative how pressed by the necessity, i.e., by the weakness of his situation, Theseus was on the eve of these reforms. The traditional patriarchal order was not going to make a place for him.

In his account of the pre-founding part of Theseus' life Plutarch emphasizes Thesean qualities, which, in retrospect, can be seen to have specially fit him for his founding activity. Not only did he combine "physical strength . . . courage and a resolute spirit" with "good sense and intelligence," but he was a particularly public-spirited man. As opposed to the great villains on the Troezen road, "who did not apply [their] gifts of nature to any just or useful purpose," Theseus "fell upon these villains . . . not for any wrong done to himself, but for the sake of others" (sect. 6; and comparison). Theseus not only possessed this apparently inherent drive to serve the common good, but he also displayed a natural talent or calling for justice. Each of the villains he encountered in his travels had a characteristic way of visiting violence on his victim. To each one Theseus responded in kind. He "always paid back those who offered him violence with the very same treatment that they had intended for him" (sect. 11). Plutarch tellingly comments that Theseus thereby "punished the wicked," and, by "meting out to them the same violence they had inflicted on others," he was subjecting them to "a justice that was modeled on their own injustice" (sect. 11). From the outset, then, Theseus was a champion of justice and reciprocity.

The limitations of his situation and his natural tendency to justice seem to have combined to provoke Theseus to what Plutarch calls "a wonderful and far-reaching plan." Upon his return from Crete and his discovery of the death of Aegeus, Theseus instituted his four-part reform. First, from the scattered villages of Attica he made a city; he concentrated the population of the different clans together in one city, larger, more powerful, with one set of public institutions (sect. 24). He did not stop with the Attic clans that recognized each other as blood relations; he "invited people from every quarter to settle there on equal terms with the Athenians" (sect. 25). This was in part an effort to make the city still larger and presumably more powerful, more capable of policing its own borders and defending against the likes of Minos; it is also an extension of the initial impulse to gather in one place peoples who do not have a natural bond of connection, or who have only a very attenuated one. As a result of this extension of the policy of gathering, the city and the family are emphatically not coextensive in the new Athens.

Theseus not only expanded Athens in this horizontal way; he also effected shifts of a vertical sort: "he established a commonwealth which embraced all sorts and conditions of men." Authority is no longer limited to the nobles or the wealthy. But he did not produce a city that was mere "disorder and confusion." To prevent that "he was the first to divide the city into three distinct classes" and placed political power in a balance among these classes. Indeed, he developed a regime tilted toward empowering "the numerical strength" of the "artisans" (sect. 25). A pre-requisite to all these reforms, however, was that Theseus "lay down his own royal power," tenuously inherited from Aegeus, an offer he had made to lure the new citizens into the new city. In place of the kingship Theseus held only the chief-generalship.

Theseus thus transformed the old clan-centered patriarchal monarchy of Aegeus into a political community, where community no longer followed family and where authority no longer fell to the fathers as fathers. A new way of sharing power and of consent replaced the old patriarchy.

According to Plutarch's account, then, Theseus is a great benefactor. Yet Plutarch does not hesitate to blame Theseus as well. Somewhat surprisingly, Plutarch indicts Theseus for parricide. "Theseus, in his forgetfulness and neglect of the command [to fly a signal flag on the ship returning from Crete] can scarcely, by any excuses, or before the most indulgent judges, avoid the imputation of parricide" (*Comparison*, 48). Perhaps I am an overindulgent judge, but I would hesitate to impute parricide to Theseus—carelessness, yes, inconsiderateness, maybe, but parricide? Plutarch's strong claim makes sense only when we notice that in overturning the traditional patriarchal order he killed the authority of the fathers as such, and thus in a manner killed his father and all fathers.

Plutarch has another charge against Theseus as well: "The faults committed in the rapes of women admit of no plausible excuse in Theseus. First, because of the frequent repetition of the crime; for he stole Ariadne, Antiopa, Anaxophe the Troezenian, [and] at last Helen." Although it seems rather strong to refer to many of these episodes as rapes, Plutarch touches on a running motif in the story of Theseus—his way with women and his way of abandoning them. "It is to be suspected," Plutarch surmises, "these things were done out of wantonness and lust" (*Comparison*, 48). Theseus' parricide was an essential part of his founding activity; one wonders whether his "wantonness and lust" are also. In founding the city and politics, Theseus undermined the sovereign authority of the family over society and of the father over the family. The family is the institution formed in order to and via the control of erotic forces: in the family eros is strictly limited and channeled in approved (hallowed) paths. From the outset Theseus fails to respect the erotic boundaries established by the family. What Plutarch relates about Theseus at the time of his journey to Crete seems to have been true of him his whole life through. "There is a story, too, that he was commanded by an oracle from the god at Delphi to make Aphrodite his guide and beg her to accompany him on his voyage" (sect. 18; cf. sect. 20–21). That is, Theseus took Aphrodite, but not Hera for his guide. This is another way of saying that his overturning of patriarchy also involved an unchaining of eros. Plutarch did not approve, but he suggests in his own narrative that this unchaining of eros was a perhaps a necessary by-product (and cause?) of Theseus' political innovations.

Machiavelli

Machiavelli's presentation of Theseus echoes the chief themes of Plutarch's account so closely that it seems likely that Machiavelli had the Greek's discussion in his mind when he formulated his own views on founder-princes. Plutarch's narrative is dominated by four themes: (a) the situation of Athens prior to the Thesean founding; (b) the qualities and situation of Theseus that made him particularly fit to be the founder; (c) the reforms he instituted; and (d) the crimes he committed, especially the crimes against the family (parricide and rape) implicit in his founding activity. Machiavelli's discussion contains the same four elements, recognizable as parallel to Plutarch's, but all four transformed in very significant ways. The four appear in Machiavelli as opportunity, virtú, armed prophecy, and fratricide, respectively.

In his discussion of the "opportunity" presented to his founder princes, Machiavelli picks up a theme present in Plutarch's account, and, characteristically, radicalizes it. Plutarch makes a decisive part of his story the internal and external weakness of Athens. Had Athens been thriving, Theseus would not have been tempted nor Athens been so open to his great reforms. In Machiavelli's pages this theme becomes much larger. He is presenting an account of the origin of political societies in the form of the account of his founder-princes. All the foundings have in common one precedent situation—the deep misfortune, even misery of those who become the "matter" for the new forming instituted by the founder. The initial situation is one of misery. Machiavelli thus shifts emphasis from Plutarch's account. The initial situation in Plutarch is patriarchal monarchy, the failings of which indeed produced the crisis (opportunity) Theseus faced, but Plutarch does not suggest anything so universal as Machiavelli does—the universal misery without political life. Like Aristotle, he firmly connects the emergence of the city to the pre-existence of natural social formations, families, clans, villages. Machiavelli is silent about family, clan, and patriarchy. Machiavelli instead moves more in the direction of Hobbes's notion of a state of nature, a generalized condition of misery and weakness.

Machiavelli's depreciation of patriarchy and his radicalization of the initial misery are related to the strongest affirmation he makes as to what is natural: "And truly it is a very natural and ordinary thing to desire to acquire" (14). The desire to acquire, productive of conflict and inherently dissociative among human beings in a world of scarce resources, replaces for Machiavelli the Aristotelian principles visible in Plutarch's account. The city is natural in the sense that it is the final term in a progression of natural associations; nature works to knit human beings together, not to dissociate them. The Machiavellian reformulation of the character of the "occasion" facing Theseus thus betokens a very fundamental shift in his understanding of the origins in particular and of nature in general.

Machiavelli also echoes Plutarch's treatment of Theseus in his teaching about the virtue of the founders, but again he severely changes Plutarch's point. Theseus possessed virtue according to Plutarch, especially the classic virtues of ancient moral philosophy—courage, practical wisdom, and especially justice, understood as devotion to the good of others and a firm sense of the appropriateness of reciprocity, or equality. His virtues, according to Plutarch, fit him for his founding activity, for he grasps the essential point that justice involves a kind of reciprocity that allows individuals to relate on the basis of their deeds and not on the basis of blood and family role alone. Theseus can found a city because of his prior grasp of justice. Machiavelli's great founders are also men of virtue, with the greatest founders possessing three virtues in particular. "Their excellent virtue enabled the opportunity to be recognized." They possessed that excellence that enabled them to see that the misery of the people was not merely misfortune, but was laden with possibility. But their innovations are not instituted in the first instance for the sake of their people, but "so as to found *their* state and *their* security" (emphasis added). The misfortune of the people put into their hands "the matter" onto which they could "introduce any form they pleased." Only a people deep in misery is so open to fashioning or reforming. The name of the virtue that allows the founder-princes to see in misery a great opportunity is ambition. Since the great founders in the first instance serve their ambition, there is no question of justice or some other other-regarding quality being for Machiavelli, as it was for Plutarch, one of the defining virtues of the founders.

The second great virtue of the founders appears to be strength of imagination. They can imagine a new form in which the matter they find about them might be cast. They, as opposed to the general run of mankind, can "truly believe in new things" even when they do not "have a firm experience of them." The great founders are those whose strength of mind can carry them beyond present experience to a vision of an after-life, a world not seen but which yet might be.

Finally, the great founders must possess one further virtue—a ruthlessness that enables them to respond to the fact that their people, however miserable their lives may be, will always lose faith in the founder's vision of new modes and orders. "The nature of peoples is variable; and it is easy to persuade them of something, but difficult to keep them in that persuasion. And thus things must be ordered in such a mode that when they no longer believe, one can make them believe by force." Above all, the founders must be able and willing to "use force" rather than to "beg" or "pray" (Italian: *pregare*).

Machiavelli's three great virtues, ambition, imagination, and ruthlessness, bear little resemblance to any notion of virtue in Plutarch or in Christianity. Machiavelli in Chapter 6 of *The Prince* is much less interested than Plutarch in the details of the new modes and orders introduced by his founder-princes. His focus is rather on what appears to be the most decisive action of the founders, the use of violence against their own people that requires the founders to be "armed prophets," that is, to possess and be willing to use their "own arms." The new prince must not only keep his people "in the faith," but he must also, like Moses, "eliminate those who had envied" him. The use of force against rivals and waverers renders the founders "powerful, secure, honored, and prosperous." The terror induced by the prince leads, according to Machiavelli, not to hatred but to "veneration" of the prince. The terror opens the people to the new fashioning the founder imposes, and promotes the necessary (if not sufficient) condition for the maintenance of the new order, veneration or reverence. Machiavelli is appealing here to the psychology associated in modern times with hostage-takings and terrorism. Sometimes hostages come to identify with their captors, to "root" for them, sometimes shift allegiance entirely to them. Machiavelli has in mind the complex psychological reaction that follows from the situation of the terrorized people in which is first aroused the greatest fear and feelings of helplessness and powerlessness, together with the feeling of awe that goes out to the power able to instill that fear, the fear and awe combined with gratitude when the anticipated destruction does not come. The combination of these passions prompts the feeling of reverence that leads the people to see the founder not as a great villain but as a man of divine power and a great benefactor.

The result of the founding activity is not only benefit to the founders but "their fatherlands [too] were ennobled . . . and became very prosperous." The founders' activity is the basis for the common good. Machiavelli's emphasis on terror reflects his notion that not nature but only compulsion makes human beings virtuous enough to sustain civil life.

> Nature has so constituted men that, though all things are objects
> of desire, not all things are attainable; so that desire always exceeds the power of attainment, with the result that men are ill
> content with what they possess and their present state brings
> them little satisfaction. (*Discourses* I. 37)[4]

Given the dissatisfactions of human life, the natural tendency to discontentedness, human beings require an equally forceful passion (fear) to induce them to curb, although never to suppress, their desires.

Thus Machiavelli's focus on the utterly formative character of violence or terror. Despite the fact that he emphasizes the necessity to use force against one's own people, Machiavelli forbears from calling his great founders criminals in *The Prince*, but in the *Discourses* he dwells much on the fratricide that he defends as necessary to the founding activity. The founder, so far as he must use force against his own people, his brothers, is indeed necessarily guilty of something very akin to fratricide. The emphasis

4   Niccolo Machiavelli, *Discourses on Livy*, trans. Harvey Mansfield and Nathan
    Tarcov (Chicago: University of Chicago Press, 1996).

on fratricide is Machiavelli's way of speaking of the necessary character of the founder's activity in the face of nature's dissociative mandate: only by turning against one's own with violence can society be made.

Shakespeare

Both Shakespeare's Theseus and his Athens are recognizable if modified forms of the Theseus and the Athens presented in Plutarch's *Lives*. The Athens we see at the opening of the play is not in such deep crisis as Plutarch's Athens. Theseus has already won Athens' freedom from Cretan hegemony; he has already ascended to the dukedom (kingship) and, it seems, his father is already dead. He has already conquered the Amazons, and indeed the play opens with his resolve to marry the conquered Amazon queen. Yet in the decisive matter the Athens of *MND* is the same as the Athens Plutarch depicts prior to the Thesean founding. In Shakespeare's Athens the fathers rule: according to Athenian "ancient privilege," or Athenian "law" (1.1. 41, 44; IV; 158) the children belong to the fathers, and the fathers may "dispose" of them as they will. This power to dispose of the children is exactly what it would be over any piece of property: "she is mine, and all my right of her / I do estate unto Demetrius" (1.1. 97–98). The patriarchal law is not one law among many in Athens; it appears to be the law of laws. Theseus owes his dukedom to the operation of the patriarchal hereditary principle, and more significantly, the law of patriarchy sets an absolute bound to his power; as Theseus tells Hermia in the crucial opening scene: "by no means may we extenuate" the patriarchal law that requires her to marry as her father demands (1.1. 120; cf. 56). Theseus does not merely bow to the patriarchal law, but he explains and defends it:

> To you, your father should be as a god,
> One that composed your beauties, yea, and one
> To whom you are but as a form in wax
> By him imprinted and within his power
> To leave the figure or disfigure it. (1.1. 47–51)

The child belongs to the father as to its source. Just as God or gods are the ultimate source, so the father is the immediate source of the being of the child. What the source (her father) has made he can destroy; it is the same principle that establishes the right of the gods to dispose of human beings as they will. That Theseus owes his position to the patriarchal principles of the Athenian regime is underlined by one of the most striking changes Shakespeare makes on his original source: he names Hermia's father Egeus. For Theseus to be duke Egeus must be dead; but the continuing rule of the fathers, and Theseus' dependence on the patriarchal principle are indicated by the continuing presence and sway of his father in the guise of Hermia's father. Egeus lives on because in Athens fathers as such rule.

Shakespeare's Theseus is also the Theseus of Plutarch. He is the same man who abandoned Perigenia, "whom he ravished," who "broke his faith" with Aegles, Ariadne, and Antiopa—the same women of whom Plutarch tells the same sad story of seduction and abandonment (2.1. 78–80). As in Plutarch, he takes pride in his kinship to Hercules and suggests the same emulative impulse Plutarch had emphasized (5.1. 44–47). The one important difference that we see is that Shakespeare's Theseus is from the first moments of the play much more eager to marry than the Theseus of tradition ever was.

That change results from the fact that Shakespeare's Theseus at first sets out to rule within and under the ancient patriarchal order: he requires an heir. Moreover, Shakespeare's firm placement of Theseus as actual ruler of patriarchal Athens gives a deeper sense to Theseus' war against the Amazons than Plutarch does. The Amazons are women who live as much without men as possible, who are not subject, in other words, to patriarchy. The principle of patriarchy requires the subjection of women as much as children, however, and the triumph of patriarchal Athens against the anti-patriarchal Amazons can be seen as the consolidation of the victory of the patriarchal principle over Amazonian (female) independence or non-subordination. Shakespeare's Theseus is thus a great champion of patriarchy.

The action of *MND* is essentially the same as the action in Plutarch's "Life of Theseus": Theseus overturns the patriarchy. Towards the end of the play, Egeus demands "the law, the law [upon Lysander's] head" (4.1. 158). This time, however, Theseus responds quite differently from the way he did in the opening scene: "Egeus, I will overbear your will" (4.1. 182). What Theseus could not do to even a small degree at the beginning he can do altogether by the end. By overruling the father and the patriarchal law

Theseus re-founds the regime. Just as in the traditional account, Theseus replaces the ancient patriarchy with a much more democratic principle; he takes the "rude mechanicals" into his polity also, recognizing their role, or better put, giving them a role, a part to play in the polity. The naturalness of the drama metaphor shows how readily the workmen's play and its acceptance can serve as stand-in for the more explicitly political point Plutarch makes. Shakespeare has made their play a metaphor for the new political enfranchisement of the artisan class. Athens is transformed from a community of fathers, ruled by the law of the fathers, into a city of artisans—carpenters, weavers, tinkers, and the like. The central event of *A Midsummer Night's Dream*, the founding of Athens as a political community, is the same as the central event of Plutarch's narrative, and the same that Machiavelli made thematic to his discussion of Theseus.

Shakespeare has clearly changed much from what things were in Plutarch. This is not to say that all is well in Theseus' Athens, however. In Shakespeare's Athens all the crises are erotic crises; the political has been transposed into a far different key. Although Shakespeare gives essentially the same action as Plutarch (and Machiavelli in his way), the overturning of patriarchy and the establishment of politics proper in its place, *MND* treats this action almost entirely as one involving love and marriage. Understanding that transposition is the key to understanding the play.

The crises in *MND* are crises of love and their solution requires the overturning of Athenian patriarchy. It is only as the play proceeds, however, that we come to understand how the crises of love and the eros-inspired overturning of patriarchy are strictly paralleled on the political plane. While some Shakespearean plays reveal a deep tension between love and politics (e.g., *Romeo and Juliet, Troilus and Cressida, Antony and Cleopatra*) in *MND* he presents their deep similarity, so that the one can serve more or less as stand-in for the other.

The most pressing love crisis of the play centers on Theseus himself. The very opening scene reveals the extraordinarily unsatisfactory situation in which he finds himself. He awaits eagerly the "nuptial hour" set for him and Hippolyta, and bemoans the length of time he must wait until the new moon:

> O methinks, how slow
> This old moon wanes! She lingers my desires,
> Like to a stepdame, or a dowager,
> Long withering out a young man's reverence. (1.1 3–6)

Time passes slowly for someone eagerly anticipating the future. But Hippolyta sees time very differently.

> Four days will quickly steep themselves in night,
> Four nights will quickly dream away the time. (1.1. 7–8)

Time goes quickly for one dreading the future; such is the disparity in the situation of the two as they look forward with eagerness or reluctance to the upcoming marriage.

The nuptial moon is not for Hippolyta what it is for Theseus, the presider over nights of love, but rather a threatening "silver bow / New bent in heaven. . . ." Cf. parallel moon references, 2.1. 156: "the cold moon"; 2.1. 161–62: the "chaste beauty of the wat'ry moon" quenches "Cupid's fiery shaft"; 1.1. 169–70: "Cupid's . . . best arrow with the *golden* head" in contrast to the "silver bow" Hippolyta invokes.

The dominant character of the opening exchange between Theseus and Hippolyta is just this contrast in mood and attitude. He is expectant, she is reluctant; she sees their marriage as "solemnities," he responds by calling for "merriment." This seems a direct response to her mood, for he wants Philostrate to

> Awake the pent and nimble spirit of mirth,
> Turn melancholy forth to funerals (I.i. 13–14).

It is her melancholy he seeks to turn out, but his awkward reference to "funerals" reminds both her and the audience of one reason for the melancholy: she and her people have just been conquered in a war with much loss of life. As an Amazon, moreover, it is unlikely that she welcomes the opportunity to become the wife of the duke who has just defeated her, especially within the patriarchal context of Theseus' Athens. As victor in war he may claim a right to make her his own, but there is no reason to suppose she accepts or favors this claim.

> Theseus senses the difficulty:
> Hippolyta, I wooed thee with my sword,
> And won thy love doing thee injuries.
> But I will wed thee in another key,
> With pomp, with triumph, and with reveling. (I.i. 16–19)

He claims to have won her love, but the whole context belies his claim; he senses that "doing injuries" does not in fact win love, and promises a new tack. But the central item of his new style of courting, "triumph," can only serve to remind her of the galling subjection in which she finds herself.

What is most remarkable about the initial situation of Theseus and his bride-to-be is his abrupt realization of how unsatisfactory that situation is. Theseus wants not merely her, but her love. He has conquered her and can dispose of her body as he will; he can force her to marry him, but he cannot force her to like it or to love him. But, he suddenly sees, it is her love, not merely her presence in his bed that he seeks. His attempts to bring her to a more willing participation through forced merriment do not promise well for him, either. Nonetheless, by the end of the play he finds a way. The last scene opens with a marked contrast to her coolness in the first scene. She addresses him as "my Theseus" in the opening line of the last scene and in her very last sentence of the play she makes clear how far she has changed. To Theseus' announcement that Thisbe returns to "end the play" (within the play) and thus to free the newlyweds for bed, she responds, "I hope she will be brief" (5.1. 316–19). The play is to help "wear away this long age of three hours / Between our aftersupper and bedtime." It is to ease the "anguish of a torturing hour" before the newlyweds may retire to their nuptial delights. Hippolyta's "I hope she will be brief" says it all: she has come to view time just as Theseus did at first. Just as Shakespeare's Theseus overturns the old patriarchal order and establishes a new kind of politics, so he achieves his heart's desire, the love of his beloved. Like Plutarch and, in a more extreme form, Machiavelli, Shakespeare shows a Theseus impelled by his circumstances to seek a new path—subordinated in his public capacity by the patriarchal limitations on his authority and frustrated in his private desires for love.

Much light is shed on Theseus' initial situation by the lovers Hermia and Lysander, who are abruptly dragged before the Duke by the vexed patriarch Egeus (1.1. 22). The two lovers are, in a sense, the complement to Theseus and Hippolyta. Their love is mutual and legal authority is being invoked to keep them apart, while in the case of the prince and his bride, the love is not mutual and legal authority is being invoked to press them together. Both pairs of lovers, however, are examples of the failure of love to find its fulfillment. For Theseus and Hippolyta, love fails to achieve reciprocity, while Lysander and Hermia instance requited love falling prey to external circumstance. Within the play they are the clearest case of the "crossed lovers" about whom they lament toward the end of the scene.

Even more to the point, however, the two lovers speak to Theseus' situation in a very direct way, for Egeus details how Lysander won the love of his daughter, a topic on which Theseus apparently needs guidance. He gave her "love tokens," he sang to her "verses of . . . love," gave her gifts which expressed his love (1.1. 27–36). Lysander won her love by wooing her, that is, by showing her his love for her, his desire for her and for her love for him. Love is paradoxical: it is the desire for the desire of the other and is won with the display of the desire for the other and, even more, the desire for the other's desire. Love is infinitely dialectical, it seems.

The two sets of lovers thus reveal a great deal about the character of love and, among other things, they reveal the inadequacy of the patriarchal order. If love is desire for the desire of the other, it can never be commanded, as both Theseus and his father-surrogate Egeus attempt to do. The character of human love proves that human beings are not objects of the sort that could rightly be property of the sort that patriarchal theory posits. In the case of love of non-human things, the possession or enjoyment of the object is the fulfillment of the love, but in the case of human love only the requital of love can fulfill love. And this can never be commanded, deeded, or sold; human love must be free, and human beings are thus in this decisive respect free beings, seeking and recognizing the freedom of others.

Shakespeare shows the audience in the opening moments of the play wherein the fundamental defect of patriarchy lies and why, therefore, it can and must be superseded. The Thesean overcoming of patriarchy at the end, then, is the fulfillment of a necessity indicated at the beginning. How far Theseus understands this lesson, so relevant to his own situation, is not altogether clear. He not only agrees to enforce the patriarchal law; he also eloquently defends it. But he does modify the law. As Egeus initially appeals to it, the law provides that he may "dispose of" his daughter either in marriage to whomever he chooses or "to her death" (1.1. 42–44). Yet when Theseus restates the law he adds a third option—"to abjure forever the society of men." He does not offer her what she wants, legal permission to marry the man of her choice, but he mitigates substantially the law as originally stated. The mitigation is in the direction of recognizing the free nature of love and of human beings in that it allows an alternative between death and marriage to a mate chosen by another: "O hell! To choose love by another's eyes!" (1.1. 140). That third option no longer requires that love be commanded—if one is willing or able to live chastely, that is, without the fulfilling of love, one can, under Theseus' amendment to the old law, avoid having one's love be commanded. One does not have the right to choose, but one has the right not to be commanded. Theseus thus effects a substantial modification of the patriarchal principle, but he does not overturn the patriarchal principle, for it maintains that only the father's choice can "dispose" of the child into love.

What might Theseus' half-way measure signify? On the one side, it seems to represent his realization of the inappropriateness of the patriarchal order's notion of authority in general and of love in particular. He sees that love cannot be commanded, and thus that humans are not the sort of beings posited in his own version of patriarchal theory. Humans do not simply belong to their source; they are not simply property. The "form" they have stamped upon them, even if it does derive from the father, is the form of, let us say, rational being, self-directed and free being. Yet, on the other hand, Theseus owes his own position as Duke to the patriarchal authority principle, and cannot overturn that principle without challenging the entire order on which his position depends. It may be a position with many limitations— witness both his personal frustration vis à vis Hippolyta and his public subordination to the law of laws of Athens—but it is one he cannot overcome.

Attention shifts almost immediately to the third set of lovers, or would-be lovers, Demetrius and Helena. Demetrius presses his case for Hermia, against which Lysander defends by attempting to discredit Demetrius and the merits of his claim to Hermia:

> Demetrius, I'll avouch it to his head,
> Made love to Nedar's daughter, Helena,
> And won her soul; and she, sweet lady, loves,
>
> Devoutly dotes, dotes in idolatry,
> Upon this spotted and inconstant man. (1.1. 106–10)

Demetrius, "spotted and inconstant" Demetrius, speaks to the Thesean situation too. Theseus is a "spotted and inconstant man," as both Shakespeare and Plutarch inform us. Demetrius' (and Theseus') inconstancy reminds of another way in which love can fail—not through failure ever to reach reciprocity, not through external impediment, but through the very evanescence of love itself.

"Spotted Demetrius" was perfectly successful in his courtship of Helena—he "won her soul." But in the winning he seems to have lost his taste for the chase. Both Demetrius and Theseus raise the puzzling question (to be raised even more emphatically later on in the woods), what makes love perdure? Is there anything in the nature of love itself that implies lastingness? As a desire, as a seeking for an absent good, why should not the achievement of the sought object quench the desire? Demetrius won Helena's soul via wooing her, but he fails to understand love as the title to love, for he urges Lysander to "yield [his] crazed title" to Hermia to his own "certain right" (1.1. 91-92). He believes that Egeus' preference for him establishes his right in matters of love. He falls short of both Lysander and Theseus in his understanding of love, for he believes it is nothing but desire for possession of the other. Demetrius, in other words, understands love in the mode of Egeus' patriarchal theory. He thereby shows himself to be unworthy of love and distinctly lower in rank than Lysander, despite their relative equality in birth and wealth. Contrary to what is frequently said of the young lovers, there is in fact a great and very relevant difference between the two men. They are not interchangeable. The inconstancy of love points to a deeper explanation of the half-way character of Theseus' modification of the patriarchal law. A full-scale reform would enfranchise the freedom of love, but the freedom of love, if love is by its nature as moon-like and inconstant as the play presents it, is profoundly upsetting of social life, and profoundly unsatisfactory for individuals as well. From deep personal experience, then, Theseus, the inconstant lover, understands full well the insufficiency of the two chief alternatives—love constrained (as in the patriarchal law), or a love freed (as in the woeful inconstancy of love). He cannot or will not (as a responsible ruler) attempt to overturn the patriarchal order because constraint of human eros is necessary for human social life. Theseus' parting words in the scene suggest his awareness of the inadequacy of the solution he has forged. He asks Demetrius and Egeus to come with him—he has "some private schooling for [them] both" (1.1. 114–15). What this schooling is we are never told, but we might surmise that he will attempt to convince them voluntarily to give up their legal claims (1.1. 120). He does not contemplate going further in modifying the law (the lawful control of eros remains necessary), but he can hope to prevail on them to allow freedom a fuller reign in this case at least. It is noteworthy that he does not ask to speak to Lysander or Hermia at this time. They either must give way, if the others do not, or they will be the beneficiaries of Theseus' persuasive power, if he can prevail on Egeus and Demetrius in this conference. Obviously, he does not prevail, for they both continue to press their legal rights even after the conference.

Theseus thus understands that his modification of the ancient law is not in itself sufficient. This realization must be reinforced when he notices Hippolyta's reaction to the whole proceedings. Upon pronouncing for a last time the options Hermia faces, Theseus prepares to depart. "Come, my Hippolyta. What cheer, my love?" (1.1. 122). She obviously does not approve of the proceedings, and Theseus must see that he continues to make no progress on his "Hippolyta problem," for he has just given legal support to the very forcing of love that she herself is oppressed by.

A City of Artisans: Love and Politics in Shakespeare's Athens

Plutarch's Theseus was the first to empower the artisans, but Shakespeare's artisans are present not as citizens but as actors. They bring into the play yet another feature of Athens, although not one that either Plutarch or Machiavelli emphasizes, Athens as the first home of the drama. That

Shakespeare the dramatist takes an interest in this side of Athens beyond that taken by his more narrowly political predecessors should come as no great surprise. Yet the ease with which the workmen's drama can serve as metaphor for the political transformation of Athens under Theseus shows that Shakespeare is not so much abandoning the political focus of his predecessors as broadening it.

The artisans are part of the systematic transposition of the story of Theseus from the straightforward key of politics in Plutarch and Machiavelli to the (metaphorical) key of love; their opening scene makes clear why that transposition is possible and what it signifies. The connection between the artisans and the world of Theseus' court proves to be yet deeper and more intricate than the merely formal link via their preparation to participate in the "merriments" and "reveling" of Theseus' wedding. They mean to put on the play of "the most lamentable comedy, and most cruel death of Pyramus and Thisbe" (1.2. 11–13). The two lovers they mean to portray are remarkably like lovers Shakespeare portrays elsewhere (Romeo and Juliet) and like the pair of lovers who come to be central to *MND*, Lysander and Hermia. For all three sets of lovers are prime instances of the thesis Lysander and Hermia put forward: "The course of true love never did run smooth." More than that, "true lovers have ever been crossed"; it is "an edict in destiny" that love will fail, will be

> momentary as a sound,
> Swift as a shadow, short as any dream, (1.1. 144–54)

even a "mid-summer night's dream." Their vision of love is intrinsically tragic:

> The jaws of darkness do devour it up:
> So quick bright things come to confusion. (1.1. 148–49)

In the first scene love seems firmly on course to fail just as they predict— their love but also the loves or aborted loves of Theseus and Helena as well.

Pyramus and Thisbe are paradigmatic of the tragic failure of love, paradigms especially of the love of Lysander and Hermia (no less than of Romeo and Juliet). Within all three pairs the lovers are kept from each other by authority of the fathers. All three pairs resolve to flee the patriarchal authority, with Hermia and Lysander imitating Pyramus and Thisbe quite directly: they leave the patriarchal city for the freedom—and danger—of the wood. In light of the precedent of Pyramus and Thisbe and the general law of love outlined in the "course of true love" duet, it would seem that Lysander and Hermia are on their way to yet another tragedy of love—Romeo and Juliet all over again perhaps.

But, of course that does not happen. Just as *MND* portrays the Thesean conquest of patriarchy, so it shows the overcoming of the tragedy of love. *MND* is the quintessential comedy of love—the course of true love does (ultimately) run smooth, and the end of the play holds out the sparkling promise of all fairy tales (cf. 5.1. 409–10). *Midsummer Night's Dream* begins as though it will be yet another tragedy of love, but concludes a comedy. The artisans in their play of *Pyramus and Thisbe* do much the same—they take a tragic tale of love and turn it into a comedy (1.1. 12; cf. 5.1. 57, 65–70). What Shakespeare does in *MND* at large, the artisans do in small. Their *Pyramus and Thisbe* is a microcosm of *A Midsummer Night's Dream*.

If that is so, then Peter Quince, the author and director of *Pyramus and Thisbe*, stands as a parallel to Shakespeare himself, a comic parallel, to be sure. The appearance of a figure of Shakespeare himself is a most rare event. In this, the chronologically first play of his corpus, Shakespeare steps forth, in delicious disguise, to take a little bow. (The only other fairly clear appearance of the author is in the play that stands at the end of the corpus, *The Tempest*, where Prospero appears as another avatar of Shakespeare.) Quince's task is to prepare a play suitable for a wedding celebration; according to the current scholarly consensus, this was Shakespeare's task as well, for *MND* was most likely commissioned and originally performed for a wedding party at the home of a noble family. At first sight, Quince's selection of the story of Pyramus and Thisbe seems incompetent—he chooses to present one of the classic tragic tales of love, one of the stories Hermia and Lysander had in mind when they spoke of "crossed lovers," a story very unsuited for a wedding. Yet Quince and his mates manage to stage the tragic tale of Pyramus and Thisbe in such a way as to take the sting of tragedy out of it; by destroying the dramatic illusion on which theater rests they make their play less able to represent the world, and thus less able to be taken to present the truth. Their mis-represented tragedy thus becomes a comedy—and serves its purpose extremely well. It entertains, but more importantly, it assures the newlyweds that the truth of love is not tragic.

Indeed, only a play that brings the tragic potential of love onto stage and then neutralizes it can be so assuring of the non-tragic promise of marriage. When seen this way, the closeness of the parallel between Shakespeare's deed and Quince's becomes all the more apparent. Shakespeare, of course, outdoes Quince, for he draws the teeth of the tragedy doubly—once in "Pyramus and Thisbe," and once in his very different kind of transformation of the tragedy of love into comedy in the main story.

Quince is not merely a master playwright, but a master director as well. Drawing on the quite unpromising materials supplied by the Athenian workmen he must cast his play and organize his production. His greatest challenge comes from his "star," Nick Bottom, the weaver. Bottom poses difficulties for Quince from the very moment Quince begins to cast the play. Bottom is assigned the part of Pyramus, a character of whom he has never heard, for he wishes to know if that is "a lover, or a tyrant." His first protest against Quince's ordering of things comes when he pronounces that his "chief humor is for a tyrant" (1.2. 22, 29). That is to say, he not merely prefers to play the tyrant, but he has the "humor" or disposition of a tyrant. The model tyrant for him is "Ercles": a particularly declamatory speech is identified by him to be "Ercles' vein, a tyrant's vein" (1.2. 41). That identification of himself with Hercules and of Hercules as a tyrant is particularly interesting in the broader context of the play, for just as in Plutarch's "Life of Theseus," so in *MND* there is a close connection between Hercules and Theseus. Hercules is Theseus' "kinsman," and the object of the latter's emulative exertions, including war against the Amazons, in imitation of his cousin (5.1. 47). Bottom seeks to play Hercules as Theseus does (or did). This line of thought leads up to the following suggestion: in the "rude mechanicals" sub-plot Bottom stands as surrogate for Theseus. While Theseus himself goes not into the wood until everything important and transformative has happened, his two surrogates do go, and both are exposed to and transformed by the fairy-magic at work there. Perhaps the deepest magic of the play lies in the peculiar kind of "action at a distance" it portrays: Theseus is cured of his inconstancy along with or via his first avatar, Demetrius, and of his tyrannous humor along with or via his second avatar, Bottom. That is how the chief action of *MND* can be the Thesean founding of Athens as made possible by the escape from the city into the magic wood, an escape in which Theseus himself does not participate. Bottom, on behalf of himself and Theseus, confesses or proudly lays claim to "the humor of a tyrant." Even though he is far more likable and benign than the run-of-the-mill tyrant, nonetheless, on reflection, that seems not a bad self-characterization. His first four speeches all contain imperatives; where Quince asks questions or makes statements in the indicative mood, Bottom issues commands. He refuses to allow Peter Quince to proceed in his own genial way, but commands Quince to "call" the actors names, then interrupts him before he can do so, and has him instead "say what the play treats on" as a prelude to calling the roll. Then he interrupts Quince again to comment on the play and insist that Quince "call forth" the actors, even though Quince was obviously about to do that very thing without further prompting. Finally, he commands Quince to "name what part" he is to play. He is, in a word, a very bossy man, who insists on being in control. Quince reveals his philosophic disposition in not losing patience with this "control-freak."

Bottom's attempts to engross all (or almost all) the parts in the play for himself reveals even more the nature of the tyrannical humor. He would be not only Pyramus but Thisbe and the lion as well; he would play Thisbe "in a monstrous little voice" to his own Pyramus, carrying on all parts of the dialogue himself: "Thisbe, Thisbe!" "Ah Pyramus, my love dear!" (1.2. 54–55). At bottom, the tyrant does not merely wish to command all, but to be all; the core of the tyrant's soul is the desire to overcome the limits of his own finitude. Thus the tyrant does not hesitate at murder. But, of course, the tyrant cannot be all. The tyrant-actor would destroy the play by taking all the parts; the tyrant-murderer would destroy the community by eliminating all others. In practice the tyrant seeks not to eliminate all others but to have all others dependent on his will; to be recognized by them, but not have to recognize them in turn. The tyrant absolutizes himself and overcomes his finitude by refusing to recognize any limitation on his will. He accepts neither law nor a segregated and limited role in the community. Above all, he refuses to accept the principle Quince insists that Bottom accept. "You can play no part but Pyramus" (1.2. 85, cf. 56). Quince enforces the principle, "one man, one part." Translated into broader social and political terms, this is the Platonic principle of justice (or at least of moderation): one man, one job. Quince as director, i.e., as ruler of this quasi-polity, is a Platonic statesman.

Bottom posed the tyrant, his preferred role, as the alternative to the lover. Love or tyranny—these seem to be the fundamental alternatives. In posing that set of alternatives Bottom firmly connects his scene back to the opening scene of the play, and at the same time helps us to understand the transposition from the key of politics to the key of love, which is the defining feature of *MND*. The tyrant and the lover really do have something essential in common. The lover seeks the love of the other; the tyrant seeks the love, or the recognition of others, too. Both attempt to overcome their solitude and finitude in the other. But the two differ significantly as well: the lover who understands love in its fullness seeks the perfect mutuality and equality of love; the tyrant seeks to gain love without giving it. The lover and the tyrant differ in that one seeks as much symmetry as possible, while the other aims at complete asymmetry. Shakespeare shows us, however, that the tyrant is caught in a web of self-contradiction. He seeks recognition by others without recognizing them as others. He must both obliterate and recognize the otherness of the others.

Shakespeare shows us, in other words, that political life is just as problematical as love, and in just the same way. Political life bears the recurrent danger of falling into tragedy—the unrealizable self-contradiction of the tyrannous urge of the soul. Bottom reveals that the human soul is beset with a deep-lying tendency to tyranny, the most obvious political manifestation of which, of course, is the recalcitrance human beings have towards justice, that is, the disposition to render to the other his or her due.

Political life that is not tyrannous is thus like love; it rests on the same kind of mutuality. Thus within *MND* love can be a surrogate for politics, and Shakespeare can retell the story of the founding of Athens by telling the story of the comedy of love. The clearest model for treating the tyranny-in-the-soul is Quince's "taming" of Bottom. Quince must get Bottom and the others to be just in the sense of being moderate, in particular, in the sense of recognizing differentiation and even hierarchy. He must get the Bottoms to stay in their places. Does he succeed? The answer must be yes, although the taming of Bottom also requires the finishing touch supplied by the fairy-magic that transforms him into an ass, or rather that makes manifest to him (and others) his asininity but that at the same time mates him with a goddess. Quince succeeds with Bottom first by being firm with him, by imposing on him the rule of "one man, one part." Quince succeeds because he combines authority and wisdom, the authority of his directorship and the wisdom of his knowledge of the nature of plays (and societies) and the nature of his actors and their parts. But he does not merely impose himself on Bottom and the others. As he tells Bottom:

> You can play no part but Pyramus,
> For Pyramus is a sweet-faced man; a
> Proper man as one shall see in a
> Summer's day, a most lovely gentle-
> Manlike man; therefore you must needs
> Play Pyramus. (1.2. 85-89)

Quince's implicit point is that Bottom is suited by his virtues and good qualities to take on the part of Pyramus, with his virtues and good qualities. It is, indeed, a kind of flattery of Bottom, but above all, it is a kind of recognition of him for his virtues.

Quince's mode of governing Bottom neatly parallels the new departure Theseus takes in Athens as a whole. For in enfranchising the many, and recognizing them as participants in the mutual ruling of the city, Theseus, in effect, recognizes all the Bottoms of Athens. Thus Theseus overcomes his own tyranny and in instituting political life proper institutes a mode of relating more like the love he seeks and finally wins from Hippolyta. The political leader/lover that Theseus becomes recognizes and accepts the differences—of persons and functions (e.g., arts)—in the community but works to make them a unity. The model of this action is the weaver, who makes a whole out of different threads. Bottom's own art thus contains the paradigm for the solution to his own tyrannous humor.

Peter Quince thus plays a role in the civilizing of Bottom, but, of course, not the sole role, for his experience in the wood needs to be considered as well (but will not be considered here). But if Quince somehow stands in for Shakespeare, then Shakespeare too must play a political role. Is it an accident that the city that originated politics also originated the drama? Is there not some point to Shakespeare's use of the drama as a metaphor for the political founding of Athens? If the political problem is the tyrant lurking in the human soul, and if the necessary solution to that is an education in moderation, then Shakespeare suggests that drama can supply just what the soul requires—a training in getting outside oneself and into the other. It can serve as a model, as it does for Bottom, of how articulated differentiation can make a satisfying unity—the dramatist's art is at least as much a model as the weaver's art. The drama can, for example, reveal the inherent beauty of the just soul, can demonstrate more consistently than "real life" the rewards of justice and moderation, and the penalties of immoderation and imprudence as in Shakespearean tragedy. *MND* is a good example: the tyrannous impulses of Theseus are transformed as he comes to understand the need for mutuality in love and of consent and shared authority in politics. He becomes more just and he (as well as the others) benefit from it. He wins the love he seeks and, ironically, by instituting genuine political relations through renouncing some of his power and sharing it he arguably improves his political situation as well: he frees both himself and the city from the tyranny of patriarchy. The old patriarchal law of laws in Athens gives way to the new democratic political order.

Shakespeare, Machiavelli, Theseus

In building his new modes and orders on the people, Shakespeare's Theseus could be said to follow Machiavellian advice:

> When a prince who founds on the people knows how to command and is a man full of heart, does not get frightened in adversity, does not fail to make other preparations, and with his spirit and his orders keeps the generality of people inspired, he will never find himself deceived by them and he will see he has laid his foundations well. (*Prince*, ch. IX, 41)

Machiavelli is far more sympathetic to the popular or democratic side of Theseus' project than Plutarch was. Despite that fact, Shakespeare's vision of Theseus and of the foundation of politics is far closer to Plutarch's than to Machiavelli's, although, in truth, Shakespeare departs significantly from both.

We can now draw some tentative conclusions about Shakespeare and Machiavelli on political founding. *MND* is by and large a critique of

Machiavelli. Nevertheless, Shakespeare's rendition of the founding of new modes and orders contains four elements quite parallel to the four in his two important predecessors. To the Machiavellian doctrine of opportunity, i.e., of the misery of the original situation, Shakespeare has the corresponding notion of the tragedy of patriarchy. To the Machiavellian teaching of virtu, Shakespeare counters with the notion of the ethical. To the Machiavellian notion of armed prophecy, Shakespeare has the parallel of divine weaving. And finally, to the Machiavellian doctrine of fratricide, Shakespeare has the parallel of bestiality. The explication of these four elements requires forays into parts of *MND* more or less untreated thus far, but the center of Shakespeare's anti-Machiavellianism can be grasped on the basis of the first topic alone. I limit myself to that.

Like Plutarch and Machiavelli, Shakespeare locates Theseus' bringing of new modes and orders in the context of an opportunity. For both Theseus and substantial segments of his populace the status quo is profoundly unsatisfactory. Like Plutarch and unlike Machiavelli, however, Shakespeare presents the status quo ante as patriarchal order, and the difficulties which conduce to the re-founding as flowing from the prevalent patriarchal order. In emphasizing the antecedent patriarchal order Shakespeare clearly conceives the pre-history of politics far more in the mode of Plutarch, and behind him of Aristotle, than of Machiavelli.

Yet Shakespeare departs substantially from Plutarch in his diagnosis of the source of the unsatisfactoriness of the patriarchal order. He strikingly fails to bring out the internal and external political weakness stemming from the patriarchal principle of authority as Plutarch had done, and instead emphasizes the tragic character of patriarchy. It is based on a false theory of human being and repeatedly culminates in one or another form of the tragedy of love. Patriarchy is untrue to the truth of human freedom and thus it treats both family and political relations falsely. Human subjectivity, as revealed especially in the nature of love, requires both a different family and a different political order.

Shakespeare's alternative to patriarchy is just as much an alternative to Machiavelli, however. The Machiavellian theory of opportunity betokens the original misery of the human condition, a misery reflecting the dissociative force of nature. Shakespeare rather affirms the naturally associative force of love. Human beings seek and find themselves in the other, and while this has infinite potential for going wrong, it also points to the deeply natural—and ultimately political—character of human sociality. Human beings do not need to be made sociable via terror as Machiavelli holds; they are sociable, but that sociability requires proper institutions in order to flourish. Bottom in his tyrannical humor is Shakespeare's way of showing the self-contradiction of Machiavelli's position. In one sense Shakespeare has anticipated the rejoinder Rousseau will make to Machiavelli's disciple Hobbes: the founders are already thoroughly social in their drive for fame, i.e., recognition by others. Unlike Rousseau, however, who attempts to develop a theory of mankind as truly solitary, Shakespeare insists on primitive sociality. That sociality points toward, although it does not compel of itself, mutuality, free choice in love, and a politics of consent. That is, Shakespeare points to the fundamentally moral foundation; morality is not, as it was for Machiavelli, a secondary derivative from the necessities of forced sociability.

Shakespeare's teaching on the "opportunity" contains in a nutshell the core of his judgment of Machiavelli on new modes and orders. The other topics are variants on the theme, or in some cases themes required by Shakespeare's very different grasp of what the foundations of political order involve or require.

Shakespeare's Critique of Philosopher Kings in *Love's Labour's Lost*

Lee Ward

Shakespeare is often seen in certain circles as a proponent of Platonic political philosophy.[1] In this chapter I wish to challenge this notion by arguing that in *Love's Labour's Lost*, the play in which Shakespeare deals most directly with philosophy, he is deeply critical of perhaps the most distinctive feature of Plato's political theory—namely, the proposal for philosopher kings in the *Republic*. In this comedy the King of Navarre and a small group of courtiers withdraw from active politics, not to mention normal social life, in order to dedicate three years to intensive philosophic study. Shakespeare's comic genius in this play punctures the moral and intellectual pretensions of these would-be modern philosopher kings.

Love's Labour's Lost presents a two-fold critique of Platonic philosophy both in terms of the philosopher kings of the *Republic* and with respect to what Shakespeare takes to be, following Aristophanes, the ridiculous asceticism associated with the philosophic life epitomised by Socrates. For Shakespeare the philosopher kings signify the extremism of a vision of philosophic education that is austere and unerotic. Knowledge, the poet suggests, requires a robust dose of sensuality and recognition of the erotic attachments that support healthy social and political life. In the person of the King of Navarre, the ostensible protagonist of the play, Shakespeare

---

1   Allan Bloom, *Love and Friendship* (New York: Simon & Schuster, 1993), 269, 408; Leon Craig, *Of Philosophers and Kings: Political Philosophy in Shakespeare's Macbeth and King Lear* (Toronto: University of Toronto Press, 2001), 4, 21, 251; Allan Bloom and Harry V. Jaffa, *Shakespeare's Politics* (New York: Basic Books, 1964), 7.

also evokes the image of the bitter religious wars in Europe through the unmistakable parallel to the famous Huguenot King Henry IV, who abjured his Calvinist faith in order to secure his rule of Catholic France. It is rare in Shakespeare's plays to portray living political figures, not to mention an actual king as a central character. Unlike Prospero, the fictional Duke of Milan surrounded by his books on a desert island in *The Tempest*, the King of Navarre in *Love's Labour's Lost* is a recognizable political figure to Shakespeare's audience. Shakespeare presents his real King of Navarre as the embodiment of the ascetic tendencies in Platonic rationalism that only contribute to the religious fanaticism of early modern Europe bitterly divided on sectarian grounds. By drawing on the context of Henry IV, Shakespeare introduces Christian theology as a radicalizing element added to classical philosophy that converts the austere warrior philosophers of the *Republic* into the ridiculous, misogynistic feudal scholar monks of *Love's Labour's Lost*. He also, however, follows the classical poet Aristophanes in portraying negatively the apolitical Socratic existence by presenting an argument for poetic moderation that critiques Socrates' secession from normal political and social existence. As with Aristophanes' savage satirizing of Socrates in his play *The Clouds*, in which philosophy is cast as an activity on the fringe of decent society, Shakespeare also presents the philosopher as a figure of ridicule with a cultish following of disciples. Through the course of the education and romantic interplay in *Love's Labour's Lost* Navarre realizes that philosophic rationalism does not transcend sectarianism or supply the moderate principles of civil law necessary for human flourishing. Rather it is love or *eros* that Shakespeare offers as the vivid political metaphor symbolizing the importance of charity, tolerance, and consent.

The central claim in *Love's Labour's Lost* is about the superiority of poetry over philosophy. This is a unique comedy insofar as it does not conclude with the standard happy coupling. In fact, Shakespeare ends this play with a number of failed or suspended courtships. The comic spirit, however, is expressed in the victory of poetry over philosophy in several senses. First, Shakespeare's poetry corrects the excesses of philosophical asceticism. Pleasure and love, the core concerns of poetry, assume natural sociability, and thus support moderate juridical principles that do not do violence to the human material in society. Second, the centrality of oaths and promise-keeping in the play raises serious questions about the source of moral obligation (whether it is external with God and law or in the internal order of soul) and reveals Shakespeare's concern that in early modern Christianity, philosophy has often been subsumed by theology to produce a fanatical approach to morality and punishment.[2] In contrast to the brutalizing alliance of rationalist philosophy and sectarian religion, Shakespeare offers the possibility for a poetic reconstruction of community on the basis of friendship, consent, and healthy erotic attachments. Finally, Shakespeare's claim for the superiority of his poetry over Plato's philosophy derives from his capacity to bring the abstract philosophy of Plato and the historical reality of religious sectarianism in Europe together in the dramatic setting of Navarre's court, a feat only made possible by the poet's imaginative art. Indeed, the erstwhile philosopher kings of *Love's Labour's Lost* are given the opportunity to experience Shakespeare's poetic education with the promise to acquire a measure of political and religious moderation.

A Philosopher King in Navarre?

Love's Labour's Lost is unique among Shakespeare's plays in several senses. Few of them literally begin with a king's speech and none are living kings familiar to Shakespeare's contemporaries. Thus, the psychology of rulers is clearly a theme of the play. However, Navarre stands out among Shakespeare's kings in that he alone explicitly dedicates himself and his companions to a period of contemplative life. In order to understand Shakespeare's intention in this play we have to consider both the Platonic account of philosophy and the significance of religious sectarianism in Europe of Shakespeare's time.

Arguably the two most memorable presentations of philosophy in antiquity were Plato's account of philosopher kings in the *Republic* and

---

2   Pangle argues convincingly that Shakespeare's contemporary Cervantes also exhibited deep concerns about the "militant tendencies" in modern religion in *Don Quixote*. Thomas L. Pangle, "Preliminary Observations on the Theologico-Political Dimension of Cervantes' *Don Quixote*," in *Natural Right and Political Philosophy: Essays in Honor of Catherine Zuckert and Michael Zuckert* (South Bend, IN: University of Notre Dame Press, 2013), 383–99, at 390.

Aristophanes' comic critique of Socrates, hero of the Platonic dialogues, in his play *The Clouds*. The peak of Plato's argument for the city in speech in the *Republic* is the famous statement that: "Until philosophers rule as kings in their cities, or those who are nowadays called kings and leading men become genuine and adequate philosophers so that political power and philosophy become thoroughly blended together, while the numerous natures that now pursue either one exclusively are forcibly prevented from doing so, cities will have no rest from evils."[3] In the *Republic* Socrates argues that philosophers enjoy perfectly ordered tripartite souls by virtue of their education in moderation, courage, justice and wisdom. Their claim to rule is based upon their unique intellectual capacity to rationally apprehend "divine patterns" of justice that can be applied to the affairs of the city. Philosophic rule rests on the notion that not all great political questions can be resolved, or even understood, solely on the basis of experience.[4] Philosophers emerge from the rigorous education in music (poetry) and gymnastics (physical education) that produced the spirited warrior class of tough, austere and unsentimental soldiers. Control of sexual passions is central to the early philosophic education of the *Republic*, in which public control of erotics famously culminated in the ritualized eugenics program in Book V. Socrates' insistence in the *Republic* that the poets, especially Homer, need to be censored in order to discourage superstition among the warriors reveals the deep rivalry between poetry and philosophy over which will provide the authoritative teachers on moral issues.[5] By this account, it is only a select few among the warrior class who will ever go on to pursue a full philosophic education including the study of mathematics, astronomy, and practice in dialectics (Rep 522e–541b).

The ease with which philosopher kings are created in the free-flowing and abstract character of *logos* in the dialogue of the *Republic* belies a number of difficult practical and logical problems in Plato's account. To start,

---

3   Plato, *The Republic*, trans. C. D. C. Reeve (Indianapolis: Hackett Publishing 2004 [380bce]), 473c8–d5. Hereafter in notes and text, "Rep" and Stephanus number.

4   Mary P. Nichols, *Socrates and the Political Community: An Ancient Debate* (Albany, NY: State University of New York Press, 1987), 123.

5   See Rep 376d–403d.

philosophic education presupposes conditions only made possible by the class structure of the city in speech. This chicken and egg problem is compounded by Plato's assertion that any non-tragic reading of politics depends upon the possibility of philosopher kings. Yet, as Socrates admits, in most actual cities philosophers are dismissed as useless or vicious (Rep 487d). Moreover, Socrates suggests that the contemplative life is so enjoyable and satisfying that philosophers would likely need to be coerced to serve the city as rulers. Finally, even within the rarefied dialectical structure of the *Republic* philosophic rule inevitably corrupts and leads to the terrible decline of regimes into tyranny in Books 8 and 9.

Aristophanes' comic counterpart to Platonic philosopher kings presents another set of problems for the possibility of philosophic rule. His play *The Clouds* reminds us that the actuality of philosophy in the *polis* was Socrates, not the exalted Guardians of the *Republic*. Aristophanes ridiculed Socrates' philosophic school or "thinkery" as a magnet for followers who resemble a fanatical religious cult marked by contempt for honest work, and thus are condemned to a life of poverty and petty crime.[6] The portrait of philosophy skilfully and caustically drawn by Aristophanes is a profoundly communal activity. Perhaps Aristophanes' sharpest insights relate to his sense of the fundamentally sectarian instincts among philosophers and their disciples who typically hive themselves off into warring schools. Aristophanes' Socrates is also a ridiculous figure expounding quack science and pedantic nonsense. The one prominent common link between the august philosopher kings of the *Republic* and the ridiculous denizens of Socrates' thinkery is asceticism. The deep austerity and anti-materialism of the philosophic life in both instances presents philosophy in terms of a quasi-religious experience. As we shall see, the ascetic tendency of philosophy is a theme that Shakespeare draws upon in *Love's Labour's Lost*.

However, in this play Shakespeare sidesteps the twin problems of coercion and crushing poverty by focusing on the second of the two possibilities put forth in the *Republic*; namely, an existing ruler who genuinely

---

6   Aristophanes 1984 [419bce]. "Clouds," in *Four Texts on Socrates*, trans. Thomas G. West and Grace Starry West (Ithaca, NY: Cornell University Press, 1984), 115–76.

philosophizes.[7] The philosopher king of *Love's Labour's Lost* is not a son of the Greek *polis*, but rather a scion of the early modern feudal aristocracy. Scholars are largely agreed that "Ferdinand" the King of Navarre is almost certainly based upon King Henry of Navarre.[8] Indeed, the name Ferdinand never appears in the dialogue of the play, and thus Shakespeare's audience in the 1590's understandably assumed that the King of Navarre is their contemporary Henry. He was ruler of the strategically located principality of Navarre bridging northern Spain and southern France. From 1589–1610 he was also King Henry IV of France, becoming the first of the Bourbon line through inheritance from his father's side. In a period of intense religious war and theological controversy, Henry was a veritable lightning rod for conflict, the figure at the center of a perfect storm of political and religious hatred. That is to say, as the Protestant King of Navarre who abjured his Calvinist faith in order to secure the throne of Catholic France, Henry was a symbol of the religious schisms then ravaging Europe in Shakespeare's time.

Henry was popular in England in the early years of his reign when Queen Elizabeth I sent English troops to support him in his civil war against the Catholic League. However, his July 1593 conversion to Catholicism was seen as a betrayal to Protestants in England and across Europe. There is little doubt that Henry's abjuration of Calvinism was very much on Shakespeare's mind, as he has the Princess of France at one point in the

---

7   Hibbard also sees the parallel between Navarre and Plato's philosopher kings; G. R. Hibbard, "Introduction" *Love's Labour's Lost: The Oxford Shakespeare* (Oxford: Clarendon Press, 1990), 22–23. I agree with Craig that Shakespeare considered "Plato's texts and problems," especially "the relation between philosophy and political power," but I reach a very different conclusion from Craig with respect to Shakespeare's position in the quarrel between philosophy and poetry (Craig, *Of Philosophers and Kings,* 251).

8   Hibbard, "Introduction," 49; Richard David, "Introduction," *Love's Labour's Lost: Arden Edition* (London: Methuen & Co. 1956), xxviii. Rupert Taylor, *The Date of Love's Labour's Lost* (New York: AMS Press,1966), 23. For good biographies of Henry IV, see Ronald S. Love, *Blood and Religion: The Conscience of Henry IV 1553–1593* (Montréal & Kingston: McGill-Queen's University Press, 2001); David Buisseret, *Henry IV* (Boston: George Allen & Unwin, 1984); Desmond Seward, *The First Bourbon: Henry IV, King of France and Navarre* (London: Constable & Company, 1971).

play cry "Saint Denis to Saint Cupid!"[9] This allusion to Saint Denis recalls not only the patron saint of France but also the town of St. Denis which was the site of Henry's official conversion.[10] Most scholars conclude that *Love's Labour's Lost* was composed as early as 1594 and first performed at court in 1597. Thus it is thought to have been written after Henry's abjuration. The question for us, then, is why did Shakespeare write a comedy that had as its central character a French king and notorious religious convert, who supposedly dedicated his entire court to the study of philosophy and the contemplative life? The answer lies in the text of the play to which we now turn.

What is Philosophy?

Navarre's opening speech sets the scene for the play by laying out the basis for a certain conception of philosophic rule and contemplative community. There are two main elements in Navarre's account of philosophy, which are in considerable tension with one another. The first element is Navarre's statement about the relation between philosophy and politics: "Let fame, that all hunt after in their lives,/ Live register'd upon our brazen tombs,/ And then grace us in the disgrace of death;/ When spite of cormorant devouring Time,/ Th' endeavour of this present breath may buy/ That honor which shall bate his scythe's keen edge,/ And make us heirs of all Eternity" (1.1.1–7). Here Navarre sets out a philosophical alternative to the Machiavellian promise of eternal fame through the glorious and memorable achievements of political rule with daring and *virtù*. With Navarre, Shakespeare introduces us to a ruler who seeks fame from the reputation of the intellectual life of his court, or "little academe" (1.1.13). By transforming his court into a venue "still and contemplative in living art," Navarre seeks the Machiavellian end of fame and glory through decidedly unpolitical, even apolitical, means. Why does Navarre believe that turning his court

9   All quotations from *Love's Labour's Lost* are from William Shakespeare, "Love's Labour's Lost," *The Riverside Shakespeare*, ed. G. Blakemore Evans (Boston: Houghton Mifflin Company 1974 [1597]), 179–216. The Princess's call is from Act 5, scene 2, line 87. Hereafter in text simply act, scene, and line number.
10   Love, *Blood and Religion*, 287–88.

into a philosophic academy will make them "heirs of all eternity"? Achieving eternity could mean fame for participating in rational apprehension of the timeless and unchanging Platonic ideas or forms. The profundity of knowledge about these basic principles of intelligibility would contrast with the relative banality of the temporally limited accounts of reality that pass for wisdom in normal political judgment. Navarre's triumphalist opening remarks could also signify his presumption that experiencing a period of intense philosophic study will result in exemplary rule by him. In either possibility, Shakespeare's association of the desire for fame with the drive for intellectual purity places philosophy, at least in part, in service to political goals.

The second major element in Navarre's opening speech has to do with Shakespeare's explanation of the relation between philosophy and *eros*. Navarre radicalizes the already considerable austerity woven into Plato's account of philosopher kings. Navarre exhorts his men as "Brave conquerors" to engage in war with their "own affections" (1.1.9). While Navarre insists upon the three-year vow in his academy dealing with celibacy, fasting, and sleep deprivation, he offers no reason why these strictures are actually necessary for philosophic education. Navarre's assumption appears to be that asceticism is not only instrumental to, but rather the core experience of, philosophic education. The hostility to sensuality among these would-be philosophers is decidedly monkish and theological. Indeed, Shakespeare presents this asceticism as fanatical and worthy only of ridicule or contempt. For instance, one rule of Navarre's Academy is that "No woman shall come within a mile of my court . . . on pain of losing her tongue" (1.1.120). As Breitenberg observes, Navarre and his men unite in opposition "to the idea of women as linked to a debased corporeality."[11] In addition to the stark misogyny underlying Navarre's philosophic project, Shakespeare's allusion to such savage punishments reminds his audience of Europe's brutal religious wars and persecutions.

The deep conflict between knowledge and *eros* in Navarre's presentation of philosophy is problematic on several levels. First, it is not at all clear that Navarre and his followers have fully thought through the difficulty of

11   Mark Breitenburg, *Anxious Masculinity in Early Modern England* (Cambridge: Cambridge University Press, 1996) 136–37.

constructing a community by artifice on the basis of a purely intellectual understanding of moral obligation. Most of Navarre's companions are unaware that there is any difficulty here at all. Longaville boasts that "The mind shall banquet though the body pine," while Dumaine insists "To love, to wealth, to pomp, I pine and die/ With all these living in philosophy" (1.1.25, 31–32). Only Berowne, the voice of poetry amongst the philosophers, rebels against the attempt to expel all forms of sensuality and erotic attachment from the community of philosophers: "O, these barren tasks, too hard to keep,/ Not to see ladies, study, fast, not sleep!" (1.1.47–48). As Berowne implies, there is something profoundly unnatural about a community devoid of erotic and political attachments, arguably the two most powerful forms of human connection. This is in effect a community of artifice united through an act of sheer will expressed by compact rather than pleasure and affection. Moreover, Shakespeare has Navarre and his courtiers, with the exception of Berowne, adopt the style and rhetoric of religious fanatics, although their pledge is ostensibly to a philosophical truth rather than a confessional one. Indeed, Navarre's project seems to depend on the possibility that philosophical rationalism can in fact transcend sectarian differences. Perhaps this points to Navarre's motivation insofar as there is some logic to the Huguenot King confronting the challenge of ruling a Catholic people by turning to philosophy.

While Navarre and his men present their philosophic project as, at least in part, in service to political goals, it seems to result in the formation of a strangely apolitical community bound by rules adopted from monkish extreme discipline. Shakespeare's philosophic court at the opening of *Love's Labour's Lost* is more bookish than the authentic Socratic experience of engagement with other citizens in the *agora*. In this sense, Shakespeare's account of philosophy more closely resembles the budding philosopher Guardians of Books 5 and 6 of the *Republic* than in the dialogic activity of the Socrates portrayed in the dialogues. The one common theme uniting the ideal of philosopher kings with the life of Socrates, the hero of the Platonic dialogues, is an abiding asceticism and distrust of material needs and desires. It is the ascetic core of what he takes to be Platonic philosophy that Shakespeare, like Aristophanes before him, identified as the fertile source of comedy. Under the poet's skilful hand, these moralistic and ascetic philosophers cannot help but succumb to perjury and hypocrisy.

What Is a Little Perjury Among Friends?

Love's Labour's Lost foreshadows the state of nature portrayed by Thomas Hobbes and John Locke. The action and dialogue take place entirely out of doors in a natural setting suffused with the latent possibility, and suppressed reality, of political artifice. Strangely in a play populated by kings, lords, and ladies, the presence of sovereign power is initially quite obscure, but soon after the opening scene political reality and erotic necessity puncture the philosophic pretensions of Navarre and his men. The scheduled arrival of the Princess of France and her retinue is the first intrusion into the bucolic academy. Reflecting upon his harsh decree banning women from the court, Navarre sighs "What say you lords? Why this was quite forgot" (1.1.141). With the Princess condemned to holding court *alfresco*, the inhospitable king exhibits his first instance of the philosopher's neglect of political duty as Shakespeare presents the conflicting tendencies when philosophic dogmatism confronts practical diplomacy. The second early challenge to the viability of Navarre's philosophic court comes from the clown Costard's apprehension by the Spaniard Armado for consorting with Jaquenetta in violation of Navarre's strict orders against fraternization. However, the penalty of a year's imprisonment for being "taken with a wench" (1.1.288) is reduced by the king to a one week fast with only "bran and water" (1.1.301). Clearly, the threat of dire punishment was little deterrent to fairly harmless "crimes" driven by erotic attraction. The ascetic code of conduct underlying Navarre's contemplative society begins to unravel practically as soon as it is promulgated.

Indeed, the very first serious questioning of Navarre's project arose from the nature of the oath binding the community of scholars. Berowne's reluctance to sign on to the three-year commitment on such harsh terms exposed the problematic features of the oath. Extension of the celibacy principle to its logical limits would mean no generation of new life, a fate in keeping with the sterile and unerotic condition of the academy. Berowne's aversion to the dogmatism of the oath signifies his awareness that political reality requires recognizing certain necessities. As he claims: "Necessity will make us all forsworn" (1.1.149). There is the political necessity for the small principality of Navarre to establish good relations with its powerful neighbor France. And we know from the historical context of the play, there was also the necessity to recognize religious sensitivities in the meeting of a Protestant king and a Catholic princess.

As Shakespeare was well aware, oaths can be associated with both civil law and religious vows. Oaths often blur the distinction between the civil and religious spheres. With Navarre and his court this is certainly the case. The social compact normally contains elements that are purged from Navarre's community, especially that mixture of law and *eros* contained in the marriage vow. As Berowne's reluctance to sign the oath reveals, covenants can also expose the limits of friendship. The central problem Shakespeare sets before us revolves around the question: Is a vow to philosophise fundamentally misguided? Here Shakespeare foreshadows Jean-Jacques Rousseau's charge that with their social compact theory Hobbes and Locke turn every individual in the state of nature into a philosopher.[12] The Princess ridicules "Navarre and his book-men" (2.1.227) for apparently failing to understand that social bonds are largely emotional, erotic, familial, and possibly even sectarian too.[13] But even if pleasure is the natural support for obligation, hedonic considerations do not establish who or what vouchsafes an oath or what punishment there is for promise-breaking. This, properly speaking, raises the philosophic question of soul. Oaths could be enforced by external agency such as God or the civil authorities. Strangely Navarre makes no mention of God directly, but he does affirm the value of severe punishments including imprisonment, mutilation, and death. Audiences could not help but be aware of the connection between Henry of Navarre's abjuration of Calvinism and Navarre's perjury

12 Jean-Jacques Rousseau, trans. Roger D. Masters and Judith R. Masters, *The First and Second Discourses* (New York: St Martin's Press 1964 [1750, 1754]), 102.

13 Here is a wonderful example of how religious sectarianism could confound natural *eros* in the sixteenth century, taken from the memoirs of Margaret Valois, actual Catholic wife of Henry IV: "The king my husband being followed by a handsome troupe of lords and gentlemen, as honorable as the finest gallants I've ever seen at court; and there was nothing less than admirable about them, *except that they were Huguenots*"; Felicia Hardison Londré, "Elizabethan Views of the "Other": French, Spanish and Russians in *Love's Labour's Lost*," in Londré, *Love's Labour's Lost: Critical Essays* (New York: Garland Publishing, 1997), 325–41, at 328, emphasis added.

in the play.[14] Oaths can also be enforced by internal factors, most notably concern for the order or harmony of one's soul. While Navarre and his followers soon come to the realization that the pleasure of contemplating one's glory and fame pales in comparison to the joys of romantic love, it is only through the course of the play that they gradually become aware, however imperfectly, that proper order of one's soul is crucially dependant on *eros* in the form of attachment with, and openness to, another self.

The turning point in the play is the wonderfully improbable and comic discovery scene in which Navarre and his courtiers each inadvertently expose their desire for one of their French female visitors. Navarre in love with the Princess, and Berowne in love with Rosaline, are especially tormented souls far removed from the well-honed psychic balance of Plato's philosopher kings. Berowne exclaims: "This love is as mad as Ajax. It kills sheep; it kills me, I a sheep" (4.3.6). Navarre moans: "O paradox! Black is the badge of Hell,/ The hue of dungeons, and the school of night;/ And beauty's crest becomes heaven's well" (4.3.250). The discovery scene creates a new basis for the union of Navarre and his men—that is as a community of hypocrites equally false to their promise. The basic contradiction confronting these perjurers is not lost on them. How can those who have broken faith be trusted to honor new pledges? Berowne queries: "If love makes me forsworn, how shall I swear to love?" (4.2.105). Longaville complains of his love Maria: "Did not the heavenly rhetoric of thine eye . . . Persuade my heart to this false perjury?" (4.3.60). However, it is precisely in the idea of "heavenly" or divine beauty that Longaville discovers the romantic casuistry to set his conscience at peace: "If by me broke, what fool is not so wise/ To lose an oath to win a paradise?" (4.3.70).

Yet it would be to Berowne, spokesman for poetry in the play, that Shakespeare leaves the most complete and powerful "salve for perjury" (4.3.284). In his famous Promethean Fire speech Berowne offered the men a series of arguments to defend forsaking their oaths. First, he advances the unnaturalness of ascetic philosophy and the extreme privations it seems to require: "To fast, to study, and to see no woman–/Flat treason 'gainst the kingly state of youth" (4.3.288). If it were wrong for healthy young men to act upon their desires, then why did nature or God make these desires

14 Hibbard, "Introduction," 51.

so powerful? Second, Berowne insists upon the erotic ground of education. Romantic love emerges as the experience that provides the mirror to the self for one only becomes fully cognizant of one's soul through intimate connection with another: "From woman's eyes this doctrine I derive:/ They sparkle still the right Promethean Fire;/ They are the books, the arts, the academes,/ That show, contain, and nourish all the world,/ Else none at all in aught proves excellent" (4.3.347-51). We notice the link Shakespeare establishes between romantic love and the mythical discovery of the arts and sciences with the important difference being attribution not to a male hero/god, but rather to a mortal female lover. "Beauty's tutors" allow for self-discovery through erotic attachment to another self as mirror of the soul: "For where is any author in the world/ Teaches such beauty as a woman's eye?/ Learning is but an adjunct to ourself,/ And where we are, our learning likewise is" (4.3.308-11).

Berowne articulates the explicit link between love and poetry, insisting that love "hath taught me to rhyme, and to be melancholy" (4.3.12-3). For Berowne romantic love is a form of education superior to the study of books because love animates the soul and enhances the perceptive powers of all of the senses. The cloistered book knowledge of Navarre's court is, according to Berowne, "leaden contemplation" that never leaves the brain of "barren practicers" (4.3.318, 322), but "love, first learned in a lady's eyes" gives "to every power a double power,/ Above their functions and their offices" (4.3.324, 328–29). Berowne also acknowledges the religious commitments implicit in Navarre's oath, but reverses the thrust of Navarre's original reasoning to come to the conclusion that *eros* or love is the instrument that the divine employs to produce justice in the world: "And when love speaks, the voice of all the gods/ Make heaven drowsy with the harmony . . . And plant in tyrant's mild humility" (4.3.341–45). However, Berowne also identifies the problem of theological and doctrinal conflict pitting the Old Testament against the New, the God of the Law against the God of Love. In words reminiscent of St Paul's appeal to a higher law in *Romans* 13:8, Berowne proclaims: "Let us lose our oaths to find ourselves,/ Or else we lose ourselves to keep our oaths./ It is religion to be thus forsworn:/ For charity itself fulfills the law,/ And who can sever love from charity?" (4.3.358–61). The upshot of Berowne's Promethean Fire speech is that pleasure and love, the major themes of poetry, resolve conscience better than philosophical rationalism or dogmatic piety. Poetry is also, however, concerned with mercy and compassion, the proper characteristics of religion, at least when it is not distorted by dogmatic speculation. The reciprocity central to romantic love connects knowledge and self-knowledge, even as the social dimension of education lends itself more naturally to poetic representation than philosophic contemplation.

The Turn to Poetry

Navarre and his followers' courtship of the French ladies revolved around a series of poetic interludes that punctuate Act 5. There was, of course, a foreshadowing of this turn to poetry in Act 4. For example, the sonnet-writing (and reading aloud) exercise of Navarre and his men was central to the unfolding of the discovery scene. When the men sought surreptitiously to woo they did so through verse, not by writing a systematic treatise on love. There was also the interception of Armado's letter to Jaquenetta, which was perhaps unintentionally poetic due to the malapropisms of the "fantastical" Spaniard who plays the unwitting jester to Navarre's court. Navarre, like his namesake Henry IV, courts France and marginalizes Spain. Another dramatic interlude in Act 4 involved the Princess and the deer hunt. On one hand, this scene is clearly a light-hearted metaphor for Cupid's arrow striking the smitten King of Navarre. However, there is also a darker allusion to the slaughter of innocents in France's savage religious wars, as the Princess confesses: "Glory grows guilty of detested crimes,/ When for fame's sake, for praise, an outward part,/ We bend to that the working of the heart;/ As I for praise alone now seek to spill/ The poor deer's blood, that my heart means no ill" (4.1.31-5). Darker, violent imagery is seldom far beneath the surface in *Love's Labour's Lost*, as for example when we are reminded that even the delightful Cupid, image of love, was assassin to a sister of Katherine, the object of Dumaine's affection: "He made her melancholy, sad and heavy, so she died" (5.2.14–15).

In Act 5 theatrical and poetical representation is embedded into the courtship of the Navarrese men and the French ladies. As we recall from Berowne's Promethean Fire speech, the play advances the idea that the romantic exchanges made possible by the dramatic devices of Act 5 are themselves the means to knowledge of being and of the self. The first dramatic intervention was the Muscovite performance. Boyet, the elderly lord attending on the French Princess, sets the scene by relaying the details of the plan that he has overheard. Disguised "like Muscovites or Russians" Navarre and his men will visit the Princess' *alfresco* court: "Their purpose is to parley, court, and dance,/ And everyone his love-feat will advance/ Unto his several mistresses, which they'll know/ By favors several which they did bestow" (5.2.121–25). In order to pursue their love interests, Navarre and his men have recourse to theatrical dramatization. While the adoption of ridiculous foreign characters certainly adds to the comic value of the scene, the audience is left to wonder why the men do not court their ladies openly? In one sense, they are damned by their own dogmatic philosophic project. The royal edict is still in place, and thus they disguise themselves in order to conceal their hypocrisy. Navarre later admits his regret and indeed shame about his inhospitable conduct toward the Princess: "O you have liv'd in desolation here,/ Unseen, unvisited, much to our shame" (5.2.357–58). Alternatively, the Muscovite disguise is perhaps a ham-fisted test of the ladies' virtue, or even a playful attempt to delight the ladies upon exposure later.

The Muscovite scene does not go as Navarre and his men had planned. The ladies forewarned, disguise themselves in order to give the men a taste of their own medicine. This leads to the second discovery scene, which returns to the theme of perjury, when the men discover that they have sworn oaths of undying love to the wrong women. The ladies decide to be uncooperative and downright standoffish about the whole affair, as Rosaline recommends tormenting their hapless suitors: "Let us complain to what fools were here/ Disguis'd like Muscovites in shapeless gear" (5.2.302). The Muscovite scene also, however, reveals that Navarre and his men are the products of an imperfect education and have a defective view of poetry, seeing it solely as instrumental to attaining their goal, namely possessing the beloved. Shakespeare suggests that the men are not yet aware of the possibility of genuine self-forgetting produced through open exchange and mutual respect.

This sense of the inadequacy of Navarre's understanding of poetry is only heightened by his response to the second major poetic interlude in Act 5, the pageant of the Nine Worthies. The guiding spirit behind the Nine Worthies is a collection of secondary characters including Armado, his page Moth, Holofernes the scholar, the curate Nathaniel, the constable Dull, and the clown Costard, who combine to produce a theatrical performance for the Princess. Under the leadership of Armado the troupe's efforts are open, sincere and amateurish in the best (and original) sense of the word. When Navarre tries to cancel the performance pleading its low quality, the Princess demurs insisting: "That sport best pleaseth that doth least know how" (5.2.516). The idea behind the Nine Worthies, familiar to Shakespeare's contemporaries, was edifying tales about great men of virtue; each of them heroes, three of whom were traditionally from pagan antiquity, three from the Jewish Bible, and three Christians.[15] Several important points emerge from the performance of the Nine Worthies in *Love's Labour's Lost*.

First, we only witness an incomplete collection of worthies. In this play within a play the action is interrupted and ultimately aborted after the appearance of only five of the heroes. Moreover, the traditional grouping of three in each set (classical, Jewish, Christian) is broken with four pagans Hector, Pompey, Alexander and Hercules, and only one Jewish champion Judas Maccabeus. Pompey and Hercules replace the more standard Caesar.[16] No Christian worthies appear, perhaps again reflecting the shadow of religious war in Europe too divided over religious doctrine even to agree upon a list of Christian worthies. Second, the pageant presents an argument for the superiority of the active life over the contemplative life. The worthies signify a venerable view that practice of exemplary virtue in political life is the genuine source of eternal fame, rather than the cloistered and cultish existence of Navarre's Academy. It is not surprising then that Navarre was so dismissive of the players: "I say they shall not come" (5.2.514). In contrast to Navarre's pompous "book-men," the pageant of worthies offers the "sweet war-man" Hector, of whom Armado says "when he breathed, he was a man" (5.2.662). The cruel mockery of the players by Navarre and his men reveals once more the inadequacy of Navarre's understanding of poetic education, which is meant to moderate cruel and vindictive passions. Indeed,

15 For a fuller discussion of the idea behind the concept of the Nine Worthies, see William C. Carroll, *The Great Feast of Language in Love's Labour's Lost* (Princeton: Princeton University Press, 1976), 229–35.
16 Ibid., 229.

Navarre and his men expose a profound disrespect for poetry and the principle of reciprocity central to the power of poetic arts. Holofernes, the scholar playing Judas Maccabeus, delivers perhaps the most moving line in the entire play when he responds to the taunting by Berowne and Dumaine: "This is not generous, not gentle, not humble" (5.2.628). The Navarrese lords do not even seem to be aware of their own contradiction when they mock the very ideal of immortality in others that they themselves sought with the establishment of the Academy in the first place.[17] Poetry demands self-reflection upon confrontation with representation of other selves.

While the turn to poetry in *Love's Labour's Lost* is unmistakable, this play is not itself a traditional or standard comedy, which typically concludes with a spate of happy couples coupling. The Nine Worthies parallel Pyramus and Thisbe, the play within a play in *A Midsummer Night's Dream*.[18] But whereas Pyramus and Thisbe was a mock tragedy of ill-starred love that indirectly reflected the nascent self-confidence of the Athenian *demos*, the Nine Worthies in *Love's Labour's Lost* is suspended prior to completion due to two intrusions: reports of Jaquenetta's pregnancy (and Armado's demonstrably broken vow), and Marcade's arrival with the news of the death of the French King. The spectre of death and the promise of new life combine to puncture fatally the dramatic illusion of the Nine Worthies' pageant. Navarre's courtship of the Princess fails, or at least is suspended, by this intrusion of mortality even as his insensitivity, or rather callousness, in the Princess's moment of grief could not but bode ill for love-making: "Yet since love's argument was first on foot,/ Let not the cloud of sorrow justle it" (5.2.747). It is little surprise that the Princess rebuffs his entreaties with the argument that this is not the time "to make a world-without-end bargain" (5.2.789). Rather, all of the men are prescribed by their lady loves a one-year cooling-off period in order to allow the French maidens to mourn the dead King. Navarre is condemned to a year in a "forlorn and

17 Anne Barton, "Introduction to *Love's Labour's Lost*," *The Riverside Shakespeare*, ed. G. Blakemore Evans (Boston: Houghton Mifflin Company, 1974) 174–78, at 176.

18 For a good discussion of the poetic power and political meaning of the Pyramus and Thisbe performance in *A Midsummer Night's Dream*, see Jan Blits, *The Soul of Athens: Shakespeare's A Midsummer Night's Dream* (Lanham, MD: Lexington Books, 2003), 174–92.

naked hermitage" as a means to an "austere and insociable life" (5.2.799), while the sharp-tongued Berowne is ordered by Rosaline to "seek the weary beds of sick people" in hospital as penance for his rudeness (5.2.822).

The characters in *Love's Labour's Lost* are peculiarly aware that they are part of an atypical comedy. Unsurprisingly, Berowne exemplifies this self-consciousness: "Our wooing doth not end like an old play: Jack hath not Gill" (5.2.875). Indeed, he goes further to point to the structural limits of drama by insisting that a twelve-month waiting period is "too long for a play" (5.2.878). Politics and filial piety obstruct erotic attachment, and we are reminded that mourning periods, like marriage ceremonies, are the purview of the churches. This is a hard lesson for Navarre and his men, but the conclusion of the play indicates that perhaps the romantic education of the Princess and her ladies is also incomplete. The assignment of mortifying missions is probably not the best idea, given that Navarre and his men (with the exception of Berowne) are already inclined toward morbid asceticism, and thus these assignments will possibly just intensify their worst traits. The sense that *Love's Labour's Lost* is a unique case among Shakespeare's comedies, a comedy really only *in potentia*, is perhaps confirmed by the closing song, an appendix to the pageant of the Nine Worthies, performed by the Cuckoo and the Owl. These symbols of spring and winter, as well as youth and age, not to mention wisdom and marital infidelity, practically get the last word with a dialectical exchange that confirms the incomplete or *aporetic* character of the play. This is arguably fitting, for only a comedy that is truly aware of the limits of comedy can fully capture Shakespeare's comic spirit.

Conclusion

Shakespeare's *Love's Labour's Lost* shares much in common with Aristophanes' brutal satirizing of Socratic philosophy in *The Clouds*. The element that Shakespeare added to the Aristophanic comic mix is mockery of a sitting European monarch, not just ridiculing an eccentric busybody in the *agora*. Through the comedic action of the play, Shakespeare illustrates that the Platonic conception of a philosopher king in Christian Europe is an ideal prone to capture and manipulation by religious and theological extremists. Navarre's project to transcend religious sectarianism through philosophic rationalism was doomed from the start, as philosophic reason is drawn to serve the cause of religious fanaticism precisely because of ascetic tendencies within Socratic philosophy itself. For Shakespeare the superiority of poetry over philosophy rests on the premise that pleasure and *eros* can transcend religious and ideological cleavages. *Love's Labour's Lost* demonstrates Shakespeare's conviction that his poetry has the power to bring together philosophy (Plato) and historical and religious context (Henry IV) in a manner that reflects universal principles of justice, moderation and reciprocity. A century before John Locke's *Letter on Toleration*, Shakespeare adumbrated a vision of a post-sectarian, tolerant Europe assuming nascent form in the romantic education of the Huguenot King of Catholic France. The comic possibilities confronting Navarre in *Love's Labour's Lost* point to a spirit of accommodation that is natural to poetry, and thus makes possible what seems impossible in the rigid categories of dogmatic philosophy and theology.

Shakespeare's belief in the superiority of poetry over philosophy also entails a certain, albeit qualified, claim about the superiority of the active over the contemplative life. The worthies and great heroes of pagan antiquity, who represent one vision of the most admirable human beings, were not philosopher kings. But Shakespeare's rejection of philosopher kings does not in itself demonstrate that he believed that poetry simply can validate the goodness of political life. In the Myth of Er, Plato's spectacular poem about the afterlife that practically concludes the *Republic*, the soul of Odysseus (arguably the political man *par excellence*) chooses the quiet life of a private man as the most just life (Rep 620c). Shakespeare leaves us to wonder uncertainly if at the end of *Love's Labour's Lost* Navarre, in renouncing ascetic philosophy in favor of romantic love, has truly learned to accept the responsibilities of a just king.

Part IV – On Writing:
Philosophy and Poetry in Dialogue

Kant on the Philosopher's Art:
Architectonic and Spirit
Richard Velkley

The Sublime Inscription

Citing a passage from Johann Segner's *Naturlehre*, Kant in section 49 ("On the Powers of the Mind which Constitute Genius") of the third of his *Critiques*, the *Critique of Judgment* (1790), links nature as the object of speculative reflection to the aesthetic category of the sublime. Segner writes about an inscription above the temple of Isis, Mother Nature, which reads: "I am all that is, that was, and will be, and no mortal has lifted my veil." Kant comments: "Perhaps nothing more sublime has ever been said, or a thought expressed more sublimely" than by this inscription, and adds that Segner "made use of this idea in an ingenious (*sinnreich*) vignette in order first to imbue the pupil, whom he was about to lead into the temple, with the sacred thrill (*heilige Schauer*) that is meant to attune the mind to solemn attentiveness (*das Gemüth zu feierlicher Aufmerksamkeit stimmen soll*)."[1] In Kant's estimation this gnomic utterance surpasses or at least equals in sublimity his pronouncement in the *Critique of Practical Reason*: "Two things fill the mind with ever renewed and increasing admiration and reverence, the more often and more steadily one reflects on them: the starry heavens above me and the moral law within me."[2] Indeed the

---

1 *Kants gesammelte Schriften*, Deutsche Akademie der Wissenschaften (Berlin: Walter de Gruyter, 1902– ; henceforth *KgS*) V, 317. For translations from the third *Critique* I employ Kant, *Critique of Judgment*, trans. Werner S. Pluhar (Indianapolis: Hackett Publishing, 1987), which has the pages of the Akademie edition in the margins.
2 *KgS* V, 161–62. *Critique of Practical Reason*, trans. Mary Gregor (Cambridge: Cambridge University Press, 1997), 133–34. Translation slightly altered.

praise of Segner's vignette suggests that nature's eternal concealment of her secret exceeds in sublimity the wonder Kant ascribes to the realms of nature and morality in his dictum, for of these forms of infinity he writes "I do not need to seek them and merely conjecture them as though they were veiled in obscurity or in the transcendent (*im Überschwenglichen*) beyond my horizon; I see them before me and I connect them immediately with the consciousness of my existence." Nature in this passage is immense but intelligible since the principles of mathematical science have brought "at last the clear and henceforth unalterable insight into the structure of the world (*Weltaufbau*)."[3] I can attain these correct estimates of these sublime matters only through an exercise of reason employing a well thought-out method, without which the same objects inspire thoughts leading to the errors of astrology, enthusiasm, and fanaticism.

Furthermore, of the "two things" that fill the mind, nature's intelligible immensity is overshadowed by the supersensible dignity of the moral law. The countless worlds negate my importance as an animal destined to give up its power of life, but the moral law elevates my worth infinitely as personality, since morality reveals my independence from animality and the whole sensible world. By contrast, Segner's inscription suggests that nature has an unfathomable secret that trumps both celestial mechanics and rational autonomy, at least through its power to inspire sacred thrills, for what is in play is nature in the reflective sense of the supersensible common ground of mechanism and morality, thematic in both parts (aesthetic and teleological) of the third *Critique* as the highest object of speculative thinking. Revealingly the comment on Segner relates that highest object not only to the aesthetic judgment of the sublime but to the realm of fine art, for the thrill-evoking utterance is an inscription on a temple. Architecture as fine art has in turn a kinship with architectonic, not just by etymology, since Kant near the end of the *Critique of Pure Reason* (Doctrine of Method, chapter 3, "The Architectonic of Pure Reason") writes "by an architectonic I understand the art of systems (*Kunst der Systeme*)."[4]

---

3   *KgS* V, 163.
4   *Kritik der reinen Vernunft* (henceforth *KrV*) A832/B860. For translations from this work I employ Kant, *Critique of Pure Reason*, trans. Norman Kemp Smith (New York: St. Martin's Press, 1965).

In what follows I explore the kinship between the art of philosophic architectonic and fine art, understanding both as products of genius and its animating force, spirit, as Kant expressly says in *Anthropology from a Pragmatic Point of View*.[5] The concentration is on the Architectonic chapter of the first *Critique*, in which one discerns a number of pointers toward the inquiries of the third *Critique*. The earlier writing poses problems that the latter writing addresses. In particular, the Architectonic chapter raises the question of whether philosophical architectonic rests on wholly intelligible grounds, and it is connected by an essential if not obvious thread to the third *Critique*'s account of how the communicable structure of fine art as based on "aesthetic ideas" surpasses conceptual determination.[6] Philosophic architectonic and fine art are accordingly linked as revealing nature's eternal self-concealment. Exploring this linkage serves to elucidate how Kant's account of fine art has important self-reflexive moments.

Architectonic Art

An architectonic is the doctrine of the scientific in our knowledge, but it is not the system of science itself. It is what raises ordinary knowledge to the rank of science by transforming a mere aggregate (*Aggregat*) of knowledge into a system.[7] Architectonic falls under transcendental doctrine of method, but as an art of methodical transformation of knowledge there are no transcendental rules governing its practice. These statements point toward what Kant says about the power of judgment in the introduction to the third *Critique*, insofar as this faculty has no legislative domain (*Gebiet*) of its own, unlike understanding and reason, which legislate over nature and freedom. The power of judgment does have an a priori subjective principle of its own, purposiveness, guiding the reflective search for laws which are contingent with respect to pure transcendental laws, and this reflective activity

5   *KgS* VII, 224–27; *Anthropology from a Pragmatic Point of View*, trans. Robert B. Louden (Cambridge: Cambridge University Press, 2006), 119–23.
6   See Alfredo Ferrarin, *The Powers of Pure Reason: Kant and the Idea of Cosmic Philosophy* (Chicago: University of Chicago Press, 2015), for excellent discussions of Kant's conceptions of architectonic, system, and the idea of philosophy.
7   *KrV* A832/B860.

makes possible a transition (*Übergang*) from nature to freedom by proposing a supersensible substrate that underlies both.[8] Such unification of domains serves the interest of reason in discovering grounds for regarding the realization of freedom in the sensible world as possible. To promote this interest is what Kant adduces as the ultimate systematic rationale for the critique of the power of judgment and its principle of purposiveness, for such critique is the necessary propaedeutic to articulating the system that unites theoretical and practical employments of reason into a whole.[9] One could say that the architectonic of the first *Critique* points toward the third as the fulfillment of its methodological project. In other words, the third *Critique* is the critical account of the possibility of the art which is the architectonic of the system of reason. The realm of application for the power of judgment is art (*Kunst*), corresponding to nature for the understanding and reason for freedom, according to the chart that concludes the introduction.[10] To restrict the meaning of this term to fine art is not warranted and nothing should exclude its embracing architectonic art. The third *Critique* practices and exemplifies this art, although its own practice qua art is broached only indirectly, chiefly by way of detailing the characteristics of fine art.

The architectonic chapter describes how the government (*Regierung*) of reason demands a system of philosophy because it requires that knowledge must serve the essential ends of reason. Philosophy is defined as the science of the relation of all knowledge to the essential ends of human reason, of which the highest is the whole vocation of man as expounded by moral philosophy.[11] With respect to these ends the philosopher is the lawgiver of human reasons and not the artificer thereof (*Vernunftkünstler*). Of the philosopher-lawgiver Kant says "he nowhere exists" for philosophy as the highest legislation is still an unrealized idea. Nonetheless "the idea of his legislation is to be found in that reason with which every human being is endowed," and by examining the structure of common human rationality one can discover what it prescribes regarding systematic unity. Architectonic is concerned accordingly with uncovering the idea of the legislation

8   *KgS* V, 174–79.
9   Ibid., 179.
10   Ibid., 198.
11   *KrV* A839–40/B867–68.

latent in human reason. "By a system I understand the unity of the manifold modes of knowledge under one idea."[12] The task of architectonic is to determine "the form of a whole," which encompasses the scope of the content of a system as well the relative positions of its parts. The idea of that form outlines the various legislations of reason and the relations between them, but it is subordinate to reason's highest end; all parts of the system are related to that end and to each other through their relation to that end. The whole is thus articulated (*gegliedert*) like an animal body which develops from an inner principle, and is not composed externally as an aggregate.

There is a certain tension between architectonic as concerned with an idea of legislation and its product, the system of reason, as organic being. It is not clear that the legislator is to the artificer as organic being is to aggregate. One has to say that the idea of system is not itself a form of legislation and that it is the product of an art, although it is not a mere artifact. The third *Critique* carefully distinguishes fine art from mere artifice, for fine art appears to be a product of nature, since indeed it is the product of a natural gift, spirit (*Geist*), which is not constrained by rules, and through which "nature gives the rule to art" by its creation of exemplary works.[13] This is a prime case of Kant's reflective account of nature as free and spontaneous, distinct from nature as phenomena governed by universal laws. The inspiration of the genial creator with spirit gives birth to works that are beautiful wholes, not mere aggregates. Art produced by mere imitation lacks spirit, and it does not enliven the mind by initiating a wealth of associations to which no concept can be adequate. I shall come back to the concept of spirit later.

The product of architectonic cannot be called fine art without qualification, although Kant's language invites the comparison. Indeed he appears to work hard to prevent the collapse of the distinction. Thus the system of the various modes of knowledge must not be a "rhapsody." But does not this just mean that architectonic is a higher form of art than "rhapsody"? The term "rhapsody" is used earlier in the *Critique* to characterize a haphazard, empirical search for the pure concepts of reason, contrasting with their systematic derivation from a common principle, the faculty of

12   Ibid., A832/B860.
13   *KgS* V, 306–08.

determinate judgment, but the text does not warrant applying the term "art" to the discovery of the principle of the deduction.[14] The architectonic artist differs from both the rhapsode and the artificer, and is akin to Socrates although he renounced all writing including poetry. In the *Jaesche Logic* one reads "The artificer of reason, or as Socrates calls him the philodoxus, strives only after speculative knowledge, without caring how much his knowledge contributes to the ultimate end of human reason."[15] One who seeks to establish this contribution strives for wisdom. "Philosophy is the idea of a perfect wisdom which shows us the ultimate ends of human reason." But more than Socrates, Plato is the thinker behind Kant's account of the architectonic artist, for he avows his debt to Plato for the word "idea" to designate the systematic whole of reason. Plato understood ideas as causally productive of living beings, whereby he "rightly discerns proof of an origin from ideas" or that ideas must in some sense be originative.[16]

Elsewhere Kant ascribes "enthusiastic" genius to Plato as well as to Rousseau, as they employ ideas of reason beyond the limits of experience, and claims one can learn much from them.[17] In the *Critique* he says, "If we set aside the exaggerations in Plato's methods of expression, the philosopher's flight from the ectypal mode of reflecting upon the physical world-order to the architectonic ordering of it according to ends, that is, according to ideas, is an enterprise which calls for respect and admiration."[18] At the same time, Kant rejects what he calls Plato's claim to possess something like a divine understanding, for which archetypes are individual objects of pure intuition.[19] Nonetheless reason's need for ideas of architectonic ordering must be defended against empiricism and metaphysical "indifferentism." This is to acknowledge reason's inevitable erotic character, manifest in its drive to conceive the world in terms of productive-organizing archetypes, wherewith it discloses at the same time its own artistic-poetic nature. Kant makes a confession of his own eros for metaphysics: "We shall

14 *KrV* A51/B106.
15 *KgS* IX, 24.
16 *KrV* A317/B374.
17 *KgS* XV, ref. 921.
18 *KrV* A318/B375.
19 Ibid., A568/B596; A5/B9.

always return to metaphysics as to a beloved one with whom we have had a quarrel."[20] This avowal contains a note of unease, reflecting a troubled past in which the speculative philosopher has been drawn by the beloved into dialectical error. Perhaps his quarrel with the beloved has been a quarrel with himself, as the speculative thinker has been seduced by his own genial poetic tendencies.

Monogram and System

The tension one saw between legislative and organic language can be related to this internal quarrel, as can a couple of figurative terms used to characterize architectonic: monogram and *generatio aequivoca*. Both terms express something ambiguous about the idea of system. The latter requires a *schema*, an outline or monogram of the whole and its division into parts; this monogram discloses a derivation from a single supreme end, making organic unity possible, unlike a science having merely technical unity as based on a set of contingent and optional ends. The a priori unity established by architectonic contrasts with the technical unity derived from empirical ends whose number cannot be foreseen.[21] But in another context, the discussion of the "Ideal of Pure Reason" in rational theology, Kant gives a different coloring to "monogram."[22] He first characterizes the "ideal of reason" as grounded in an idea or rule of reason, for which the ideal is the complete determination in an individual, and then opposes the rational ideal to ideals of sensibility which are mere products of the imagination. "No one can give an intelligible account of them; each of them is a kind of *monogram*, a mere set of qualities determined by no assignable rule, and forming rather a blurred sketch drawn from diverse experiences than a determinate image— a representation such as painters or physiognomists profess to carry in their heads, and which they treat as being an incommunicable shadowy image of their creations or even of their critical judgments."[23] Such monograms or sensible ideals are perhaps a step lower than attempts to realize the ideal

---

20   *KrV* A850/B878.
21   Ibid., A833–34/B861–62.
22   Ibid., A567–71/B595–99
23   Ibid., A570/B598.

of reason in an example from the field of appearance, "as, for example, a wise man in a romance," which are impracticable and have "something absurd" about them. It is striking that the term "monogram" has such a lowly status in one context but has an exalted role in fulfilling the essential ends of reason in another context. Or does the exalted version betray some kinship with the lowly one? Let us note that the monogram of the idea of a science or knowledge that has the form of system is also called a *schema*, so it must be compared to another passage in the *Critique*, the account of the schematism of the pure concepts of the understanding.[24] The *schema* or monogram of the idea of a system of knowledge lacks the firm foundation of the *schemata* in the pure concepts of reason, which *schemata* carry out the a priori application of the pure concepts to pure intuition. The idea of a system, by contrast, precedes the working out of the system, and in its first form the *schema* of the idea is seldom adequate to the idea. Thus "this idea lies hidden in reason like a seed in which the parts are undeveloped and are hardly recognizable even under microscopic observation."[25] The idea is like a living thing requiring cultivation of which architectonic is the art or culture. The idea cannot appear on the scene fully formed and with its final form fully knowable, and accordingly the founder of a science cannot adequately determine his idea. He and "often even his latest successors" are groping about for an idea which they have never succeeded in making clear to themselves. One should not explain and determine the science according to their description, but according to "the idea, which one finds grounded in reason itself out of the natural unity of parts that the founder has brought together."

But Kant's further description of this process makes it sound less organic. The early stages are not like cultivation, since "only after we have spent much time in the collection of materials somewhat rhapsodically at the suggestion lying hidden in our minds, and after we have indeed assembled the materials in a merely technical fashion, does it first become possible for us to discern the idea in a clearer light and to devise a whole architectonically in accordance with the ends of reason."[26] Therefore the

24 Ibid., A137–47/B176–87.
25 Ibid., A834/B862
26 Ibid., A834–35/B862–663

first *schema* or monogram is like a blurred sketch or shadowy image; yet it has all the same a peculiar organic character. Kant writes: "Systems seem to be formed in the manner of lowly organisms, through a *generatio aequivoca* from the mere confluence of assembled concepts, at first imperfect then gradually attaining completeness, although they one and all have had their *schema* as the original seed in the sheer self-development of reason."[27] What sort of formation is this? To illuminate the meaning of equivocal generation one can turn to two other instances of it. In the second (B) edition Transcendental Deduction Kant writes that an explanation of the agreement of the categories with experience in terms of grounding these concepts in experience commits one to an empirical derivation of their origin or *generatio aequivoca*.[28] Is then every case of empirical origination one of equivocal generation? Kant's reference is to a concept in contemporary biology of the production of organized beings by mechanical processes in crude, unorganized matter, as is evident from section 80 of the third *Critique*.[29] He calls this an absurd hypothesis unlike "the daring adventure of reason" in the supposition of a *generatio univoca* in which all organic life derives from a common organic ancestor, thus a version of evolution of species. But oddly Kant describes this mode of generation in terms hardly distinguishable from *generatio aequivoca*, as he writes of "mother earth, like a large animal, as it were," giving birth initially to "creatures of less purposive form" who generate better adapted beings. Kant claims "experience does not show an example" of this. Given his view of these hypotheses as either absurd or improbable, it is all the more interesting that he speaks of such generation in the realm of knowledge or the self-development of reason. His use of the analogy underlines the mysteriousness of the process and the hiddenness of the origin. Also, since the empirical origination of categories was described as both a "rhapsody" and *generatio aequivoca*, one might be led to think that the origination of system in reason as *generatio aequivoca* is more like a rhapsody than Kant avows.

Furthermore other sources show that philosophy does not develop in human reason in an organic, unproblematic way. There is the dialectic

27 Ibid., A835/B863.
28 Ibid., B167.
29 *KgS* V, 419–20.

natural to reason in which transcendental illusion about the unconditioned spawns dogmatic metaphysics' despotic government over reason, whose empire gradually through internecine wars gives way to complete anarchy and "the nomadic, destructive incursions of the skeptics into civil society."[30] Before the discovery of critical philosophy brings an end to this disorder, the condition of reason is not merely one of "groping" but one of chaos and war. The history of speculative reason as dialectical is parallel to the history of reason in the practical sphere as propelled by unsociable sociability, such that conflict makes progress possible in both.[31] In both realms reason achieves self-mastery only through the encounter with difficulties, and in both realms reason makes the first steps of progress through development of technical skills for attaining contingent ends. In the final stage of its maturing reason uncovers a higher kind of art grounded in non-arbitrary ends. This art certainly involves, if it is not the same as, legislation. Kant writes "the endless disputes of a merely dogmatic reason thus finally constrain us to seek relief in some critique of reason itself, and in a legislation based on such criticism. As Hobbes maintains, the state of nature is a state of injustice and violence, and we have no option save to abolish it and submit ourselves to the constraint of law, which limits our freedom solely that it may be consistent with the freedom of all."[32] This leaves open for inquiry whether the legislation of reason is in need of supplementing or even directing by another art, perhaps a form of fine art or something like it.

The Idea of Philosophy

Following the passage on equivocal generation in the architectonic chapter, Kant takes up the difference between mathematical knowledge as based on construction of concepts in intuition and philosophical knowledge where a similar procedure of providing intuitive evidence to concepts is unavailable.[33] This bears on the question of whether and how philosophy can be learned.

---

30 *KrV* Aix.
31 Jane Kneller, *Kant and the Power of Imagination* (Cambridge: Cambridge University Press, 2007), 115–18.
32 *KrV* A752/B780.
33 Ibid., A836–37/B864–65, A844/B872; cf. A712–38/B740–66.

Both mathematics and philosophy are objectively rational forms of knowledge in that they have their first origin solely in human reason. But subjectively, in relation to the individual who possesses it, a mode of knowledge can be simply *historical* "if the individual knows only so much of it as has been given from the outside . . . whether through immediate experience or narration, or (as in the case of general knowledge) through instruction." One learns historically a system of philosophy, such as Wolff's, when one has "in one's head" all the principles, explanations and proofs of the doctrine. This imitative learning is the receptive parallel to the aggregative approach to forming a science. While such learning can take place in philosophy it is impossible in mathematics, for mathematical knowledge can be acquired only through principles of reason and in no other way; it cannot be subjectively historical. Mathematical concepts are knowable only through construction *in concreto* in pure intuition, whereby they are free of illusion and error. Philosophical concepts are not constructible and their relation to pure intuition is more questionable, such that their applicability to intuition is assured only by a special deduction, the transcendental. The status of philosophic concepts and the objectivity of philosophic knowledge are intrinsically controversial, and Kant does not presume to have ended all the controversy. Indeed "philosophy is the mere idea of a possible science, which nowhere exists *in concreto*, but to which by many different paths, we endeavor to approximate."

Whereas mathematics can be learned, "philosophy never can be learned, save in historical fashion; as regards what concerns reason, we can at most learn to *philosophize*."[34] One could learn philosophy only if the archetype of the system of philosophy lying in reason were to be realized in a *schema*, but perfect realization lies beyond human powers. "We can only learn to philosophize, that is, exercise the talent of reason in accordance with its universal principles." Yet efforts to attain clarity about the idea or archetype hidden in reason require reliance upon historical knowledge ("collecting materials almost rhapsodically") while one exercises the rational powers philosophically, so that Kant's dichotomy of historical learning of philosophy and learning to philosophize is untenable. Some remarks in the *Jaesche Logic* bear on this: "He who wants to learn to philosophize must... regard all systems of philosophy only as the *history of the use of reason*

---

34   Ibid., A837/B865.

and as objects for exercising his philosophic talent. The true philosopher, as a self-thinker, thus must make free, not slavishly imitating, use of his reason."[35] But Kant's own accounts of "The History of Pure Reason" and of the process of attaining the true system of reason show that a philosophical, non-imitative use of historical knowledge which is more than a mere "exercise" is not only possible but essential to philosophy.[36] The founders of sciences and their successors have left behind "the ruins of ancient systems," abandoned dwellings which supply essential materials for the final architecture of human knowledge, as Kant's use of Plato clearly evinces.[37] These "ruins" are to be "one and all organically united in a system of human knowledge." The architectural metaphor of ruins points again to the centrality of art in the systematic conception.

Kant offers a brief sketch of the philosopher who realizes the idea of the self-thinking architect of the true system of knowledge. He embodies not merely the "school-concept" (*Schulbegriff*) of philosophy, which seeks the logical perfection of knowledge and attains only an aggregative unity. Rather he personifies the "world-concept" (*Weltbegriff*) of philosophy which shows the relation of all knowledge to essential ends of reason.[38] The philosopher in this ideal sense, it could be said, is not solely one who knows the world but one who in a sense creates a world or cosmos of knowers organized for practical purposes. As legislator and teacher he uses the various scientists (mathematicians, natural investigators, and logicians), who are only "artificers," as instruments (*Werkzeuge*) to further the essential ends of reason. Kant says again that the ideal does not exist *in concreto* since philosophy is the mere idea of a possible science. The attainment of the ideal entails much more than the production of arguments in purely a priori fashion. It requires the actualization of an organic community among concrete thinkers and actors pursuing common ends, an historical actualization that needs knowledge of historical particulars. In this regard one should think of the epigram to the second edition of the first *Critique* taken from Bacon's *Great Instauration*, which begins "Of ourselves we say nothing (*De nobis ipsis*

---

35 *KgS* IX, 26.
36 *KrV* A852–56/B880–84.
37 Ibid., A835/B863, A852/B880.
38 Ibid., A838–39/B866–67.

silemus)" and continues "we lay the foundations not of some sect or doctrine, but of human utility and power."[39] The philosopher who has the idea of the whole of this project is a legislator surely but also an artist who constructs a plan and realizes it through prudent and effective communication, that is, through publication. In the architectonic chapter Kant says not much about the task of realization, and instead offers a scholastic division of philosophy into its principal legislations (metaphysics of nature and metaphysics of morals) and their sub-species. He seems to act more like an artificer than a philosophic architect-legislator. But he says that the distinct branches of philosophy must be presented "ultimately in one philosophic system" and that the attainment of this unification is called wisdom.[40] At the close of the chapter he underscore that the various sciences are only means to the system which serves essential ends of humanity. Thus metaphysics as the critique of reason concerns itself not only with the possibility of the sciences but with their use. In the speculative realm criticism's greatest use is to prevent errors, rather than to extend knowledge, and it does so by a "censorship which secures general order and harmony, and indeed the well-being of the scientific commonwealth" by keeping it focused on its supreme end which is practical.[41]

More clues about the nature of the final system of reason are found in the previous chapter, "The Canon of Pure Reason." Here Kant anticipates reason forming "a special kind of systematic unity, namely the moral," which he defines by means of the idea of a moral world: "a mere idea, though at the same time a practical idea, which really can have, as it ought to have, an influence upon the sensible world, to bring that world, as far as possible, into conformity with the idea."[42] The idea of the moral world unites moral perfection and happiness in the idea of the supreme good, making morality into a system.[43] In order to conceive its actualization, "the world must be represented as having originated from an idea" according to which "the investigation of nature tends to take the form of a system of ends, and in its

---

39   Ibid., Bii.
40   Ibid., A840/B868, A850/B878.
41   Ibid., A851/B879.
42   Ibid., A808/B836.
43   Ibid., A811/B840.

widest extension becomes physico-theology."[44] Here Kant provides the basis for the inquiries of the third *Critique*, with its reflective inquiry into nature as organized in such a way as to promote the realization of freedom, or the moral progress of the human species, according to concepts of purposiveness. The Critique of Aesthetic Judgment pursues this not only through the manifold connections it draws between aesthetic judgments and the receptiveness of the human mind to moral ideas, thus disclosing a purposive natural organization of human faculties for moral ends. It does so also through its true peak, the account of fine art, which reflects on how fine art comes into being through nature as purposive for human faculties (genius as nature giving the rule to art), and prepares the ground for the Critique of Teleological Judgment which reflects on how nature can be conceived purposively by analogy to art (nature as the work of a supreme artist). A crucial sentence is the following: "Nature, we say, is beautiful if it also looks like art; and art can be called fine art (*schöne Kunst*) only if we are conscious that it is art while it looks to us like nature."[45] Although the sentence is restricted to the aesthetic, it foreshadows the division of labor of the two parts of the third *Critique*: Part One regards art as though nature and Part Two regards nature as though art. The Kantian architectonic is fulfilled in Part Two by an artistic conception of nature as originating in an idea of reason and as organized to promote the highest rational end, as though nature were created by an intelligent being. This of course is only a reflective approach to nature which if regarded as theoretical and constitutive commits the error of anthropomorphic dogmatism. From a non-dogmatic standpoint the world of nature and human freedom, forming a whole, must be conceived as a work of art.[46]

The Spirit of Art and Philosophy

Closely allied to the view of nature as work of art is nature as itself artist, revealing its designs through the play of human passions and interests in

44 Ibid., A816/B844.
45 *KgS* V, 306 (sect. 45)
46 See Rachel Zuckert, *Kant on Beauty and Biology: An Interpretation of the "Critique of Judgment"* (Cambridge: Cambridge University Press, 2010), for fine discussions of these themes.

history. In various writings on history, Kant writes of nature's use of discord as unwilled by the human species to bring about human progress. *Toward Perpetual Peace* puts it thus: "Perpetual Peace is assured by nothing less than that great artist nature (*natura daedala rerum*) whose mechanical process makes her purposiveness visibly manifest, permitting harmony to emerge among men through their discord, even against their wills."[47] *Speculative Beginning of Human History* describes the goal of the historical development of the human as the remaking of the human by art, partly through natural forces and partly through human design. Kant writes that the ills afflicting the human species arise from a conflict between the moral species and the natural species, or between cultural progress and the human physical constitution, and the conflict will continue until "art so perfects itself as to be a second nature, which is the final goal of the human species' vocation."[48] But one has to note that this portrayal of nature as artist and the human as its ultimate work is the work of the artist Kant, who invents this image of nature as part of the fulfillment of the *schema* of the system of reason. Thus it is with wit and playfulness on a high level that Kant portrays himself, that is, the architectonic of reason as exemplified by him, in his accounts of natural and human artistry.

Anthropology from a Pragmatic Standpoint removes any doubt that Kant sees a kinship between philosophy and the talent for fine art. In the final sections of Book One on the cognitive faculty, he applies the term "genius" to all cognitive originality or inventiveness, although it may seem at first to have only a narrow range. "Now the talent for inventing is called genius, but we confer the name only on an artist, therefore only on someone who knows how to make something, not on someone who is acquainted with and knows many things." [49] But the term "artist" comprehends Newton and Leibniz as well as Leonardo da Vinci, as the genius is a person "of intense greatness, epoch-making in everything he undertakes." Furthermore Kant brings in "the architectonic mind, which methodically examines the connection of all the sciences and how they support one another," as a "subordinate type of genius, but still not a common one."[50] The architectonic

47   *KgS* VIII, 360.
48   *KgS* VIII, 117–18.
49   *KgS* VII, 224.
50   Ibid., 226–27.

genius is a kind of artist, although not a producer of fine art or at least not exclusively such. The genial talent of making and inventing is called spirit, defined as "the animating principle in the human being." It is limited to the animation of the cognitive faculty; otherwise Kant would be giving the pre-modern definition of soul. Spirit is the ability to arouse "interest by means of ideas" whereby "it sets the power of imagination in motion, which sees a great playroom (*Spielraum*) of similar concepts before it."[51] Strikingly, Kant accords a central role outside of fine art to imaginative play as initiated by ideas, in the artistic genius broadly defined to include scientific, philosophic, and architectonic forms. This language is related to what he says about "aesthetic ideas" in the third *Critique*: they are figures of the imagination in various media that set in motion a wealth of thought that no determinate concept can contain.[52] Such language underlines that the architectonic genius like the genius of fine art has a gift of communication, as spirit sets in motion the cognitive faculties of others. Kant in the *Anthropology* also makes the claim that nature provides the animating power, as he calls "genius the talent by which nature gives the rule to art." What Kant said of the seed of the idea of system in the architectonic artist, he says now of the animating source of the genial artist in general: "The man of genius cannot explain to himself its outbursts or even make himself understand how he arrived at an art which he could not have learned. For *invisibility* (of the cause of an effect) is an accessory concept of *spirit*."[53] This is generation that has no assignable cause, or it is *generatio aequivoca*.[54]

The third *Critique* states that in spirit's production of fine art, imagination breaks free from the laws of association that bind it in cognition, "creating as it were another nature out of the materials that nature gave

51 Ibid., 225.
52 *KgS* V, 313–19 (sect. 49).
53 Ibid., 226.
54 See Susan Shell, *The Embodiment of Reason: Kant on Spirit, Generation and Community* (Chicago: University of Chicago Press, 1996), 406 n18: "Like the artistic genius, Kant cannot explain how he arrived at his idea . . . ." There is "the problem of whether the idea is an 'invention' or a 'discovery.' . . . The difficulty comes in uniting the natural emergence of the idea (according to what are presumably mechanical laws) and its causeless origin in (or along with) freedom." Also see ibid., 224–32.

it."[55] This raises the question whether the "other nature" is not both the ground and the product of spirit, and also recalls the playfulness evident in Kant's description of nature's artistry remaking human nature, since Kant as the artist of this account is both author and product. It is related to the puzzle that was seen in the meaning of architectonic, where the system that legislates over the domains of reason does not include legislation for the art that invents the system. Such puzzles may lie behind Kant's claim that philosophy is the mere idea of a science that cannot exist *in concreto*, or as fully realized in individuals. The spirit making possible the uncovering of the idea of the system of philosophy has a source in the individual who is unable to account for it. Nature will not lift its veil, or step forward as mother earth to show whether it has given birth to the ideas of the architectonic. Such considerations may play a role in a limitation of philosophy Kant puts forward in the first *Critique*:

"Reason must not in its transcendental use hasten forward with sanguine expectations, as though the path which it has traversed leads directly to the goal, and as though the accepted premises could be so securely relied upon that there can be no need of constantly returning to them and considering whether we may not, perhaps in the course of the inferences, discover defects which have been overlooked in the principles, and which render it necessary either to determine these principles more fully or to change them entirely."[56]

55   *KgS* V, 314.
56   *KrV* A735–36/B763–64.

Doing Less More:
A Double *Apology* in Plato's *Euthydemus*
Gwenda-lin Grewal

The *Euthydemus* at first seems to be an ironic endorsement of the shallowest form of sophistry. Yet for all of its eccentric arguments—for instance, a proof that Socrates believes in sacrificing the gods to the gods—there are a number of peculiarities that suggest that, even at its most ludicrous points, the dialogue is more grounded than it looks. One such peculiarity is the kinship of the *Euthydemus* to the seven dialogues surrounding Socrates' trial and death. The *Euthydemus* shares its structure with Plato's *Crito*. Both are conversations with Crito alone, in which Socrates narrates a conversation he had with others. In the *Crito*, Socrates tells Crito about an imagined conversation he had with the Laws; it ends with the Laws' injunction that one cannot escape their brothers in Hades. In the *Euthydemus*, Socrates recounts his conversation with a pair of (imagined?) brothers, Euthydemus and Dionysodorus. He claims they are the wisest men alive because they can transmit the knowledge of the need for philosophy to anyone, even someone who is not interested. In practice, however, this entails something rather stylishly crude: the two of them dumbfound their interlocutors with their ability to win every argument by evasion (this seems to be their version of "knowledge of ignorance"). When one of them is losing, the other jumps in, as if they are identical—but only as winners. As losers, they must retain their separate identities. That they assume the place of the Laws in the *Crito* seems to imply that personified law and disembodied philosophy are somehow akin.

The content of the *Euthydemus* reveals something even more literal. There are allusions to the *Apology, Phaedo, Euthyphro, Theaetetus, Sophist,* and *Statesman* (in that order) in the first half of the dialogue. The first half is separated from the second by an interruption by Crito. Crito cuts in because he does not believe Socrates is accurately reporting the discussion he had with the young Cleinias, a cousin of Alcibiades and the beloved of Ctesippus. Cleinias is an easy target; he is much more malleable than the real Alcibiades. Socrates dares Euthydemus and Dionysodorus to demonstrate that they can engender in Cleinias the desire to pursue virtue (understood as philosophy). But the two brothers end up batting Cleinias around like a toy until he cowers at their feet. They have the knowledge, he has the ignorance; together, they produce knowledge of ignorance. But this is not exactly what Socrates had in mind. He resolves to demonstrate how Euthydemus and Dionysodorus ought to do it. That is to say, he will give a demonstration of "Socrates" conversing with Cleinias. What follows is *typical* Socrates, *typically* asking leading questions, which quickly lead to the more or less *typical* conclusion that "virtue is knowledge." After a fiery interruption by Ctesippus—he swoops in to defend Dionysodorus' accusation that he wishes for the death of Cleinias in wishing him to become wise, and so for him to lose his current identity—the discussion takes a turn toward generalship and the "kingly art." It is then that Crito interrupts the narration to accuse Socrates of fabricating Cleinias' answers. Crito's reaction suggests to the reader that Socrates is acting as if he were Plato—he is writing a script. Indeed, Cleinias' speech on generalship seems to have been lifted directly from Plato's *Statesman*. Moreover, the references to the *Apology*, *Phaedo*, *Euthyphro*, *Theaetetus*, and *Sophist* had preceded this, albeit somewhat out of order, as if Socrates were executed before he is even indicted.[1]

---

1   It is hard to resist the temptation to set the *Euthydemus* in Hades and to identify Euthydemus and Dionysodorus as the "brothers" of the Laws in Hades. At the end of the *Crito* Socrates says he hears the Laws as the Corybants hear the flutes; at the beginning of the *Euthydemus* he compares Euthydemus and Dionysodorus to the Corybants (277e).

The other references are as follows: Ctesippus refers to Dionysodorus' accusation as not even "holy to speak." Socrates then implores Ctesippus to treat Euthydemus and Dionysodorus as Menelaus treated Proteus. Ctesippus and Socrates must cling to the brothers' playful shape-shifting until they get serious. The *Euthyphro* ends with the same allusion (15d). Socrates tells Euthyphro that he is, like Proteus, not to be let go until he tells the truth about holiness and unholiness. In response to the accusation that Dionysodorus has

But before Socrates dies (and Euthydemus and Dionysodorus take over), an interesting revision of Plato's *Apology* occurs. In the *Apology* Socrates tells us that he is accused of ". . . making the weaker [*êttô*, "lesser"] *logos* stronger [*kreittô*, "greater"]" (Plato *Apology* 18b9–10, 19b6–c1, 23d6–7).[2] Socrates insists that this is an unjustifiable charge. He does so, however, by way of a rather strong *logos* that transforms his weaknesses into strengths. Socrates is weak, old, slow, poor, and only knowledgeable of his ignorance—at least, according to his own image of himself. Yet this defense (*apologia*)

falsely accused Ctesippus of wishing to obliterate his beloved, Euthydemus seizes on the problem of whether it is even possible to speak falsely. This is intended as a distraction to allow Dionysodorus to avoid having to make a direct reply. But the issue of speaking falsely eventually leads to that of contradicting, and then, to falsely opining. This is the subject matter of Plato's dialogue, the *Theaetetus*, which takes place after Socrates makes his journey to the court in the *Euthyphro*. Further, after Socrates resumes his discussion with Cleinias, the topic is whether there is some single art of making and using. A similar discussion is found in Plato's *Sophist*, which takes place on the day after Plato's *Euthyphro* and *Theaetetus*. The *Sophist* begins with Socrates inquiring of Theodorus whether sophist, statesman, philosopher are one, two, or three (217a3–10). He himself has just postulated that the philosopher appears in the guises of sophist and statesman, and sometimes, seeming madness, *manikôs* (216d1–3). It seems reasonable, then, to conclude that a hypothetical "*Philosopher*" would have completed the *Sophist* and *Statesman*. Instead, the *Theaetetus* is joined with the other two dialogues. Perhaps, then, there is a fourth. This is reinforced by the fact that there is a missing pair of interlocutors. In the *Theaetetus* Socrates converses with Theaetetus; in the *Sophist* the Stranger converses with Theaetetus; in the *Statesman* the Stranger converses with young Socrates. We are missing a dialogue between Socrates and young Socrates; Socrates even tells the Stranger in the *Statesman* that his turn will come to examine young Socrates (258a). The *Euthydemus*, for all its hints that Euthydemus and Dionysodorus are somehow thinking, or philosophy, incarnate certainly offers itself as a possibility.

See Seth Benardete, *The Being of the Beautiful* (Chicago: University of Chicago Press, 1984), xviii. Also, Leo Strauss, *What is Political Philosophy?* (Chicago: University of Chicago Press, 1988), 39–40—a passage which Benardete cites at xvi–xvii.

2 All translations are my own. Socrates is also accused of worshiping gods other than those of the city, a charge that is also addressed in the *Euthydemus* at 302c ff.

of his feebleness comes off as an elaborate self-aggrandizement, since to defend one's own weakness makes one greater than that weakness. It is this transformation of the weak into the strong that Crito perceives in Socrates' unnaturally erudite Cleinias. That philosophy may consist in a kind of willing self-abnegation reminds us of Plato's *Phaedo*, where Socrates tells his friends that they should not fear death (meaning, *his* death), because philosophy is just the "practice of dying and being dead" (*Phaedo* 64a). It is the goal of the philosopher not to exist, for it is only in this way that he can touch upon true truth, as one neutralized and unaffected by particular perspective.

Socrates had started his argument with Cleinias with "faring well (*eu prattein*)," which required being happy, which meant having goods, which required using them (278e ff.). Use was introduced because simply possessing goods did not take into account the subject's good disposition. Yet, from a certain point of view, having something always means having the potential to use it. One is never really wedded to what one has. If there is a distinction between oneself and it, one can always give it up. It is not so clear then, that one ever has it (for instance, does one ever "have" a baby?). Consequently, when the attempt was made to understand the goodness of the subject via the use of his possessions—i.e., the subject's function is to use his possessions in order to activate their goodness, and thereby his own goodness—another set of nominal conditions (another product) was generated by use for use. Socrates now has to add a new adverb in order to secure the goodness of using. Using must be done *rightly*. That is, it must be done well. The *eu* ("well") in *eu prattein* ("to fare well") has been pushed into another fold of the argument.

Cleinias quickly agrees to Socrates' addition of "rightly." Socrates commends him, "Beautifully indeed . . . you speak . . . ." (280e4) Beautifully, that is to say, not rightly. Socrates goes on, "For I believe, I suppose, it is other (*thateron*) than it should be, if someone uses any matter not rightly more than (*pleon...ê*) if he leaves it be. For the one is bad, while the other is neither bad nor good. Or don't we speak thus?" (280e5–281a1). Cleinias is said to "go along" with this. He had spoken beautifully (not rightly) at first; but since it is better, according to Socrates, to leave something be than to use it not rightly, Cleinias now agrees without saying anything at all. Socrates is about to transform the notion that it is better to leave something be into the more relative formula that it is better to "do less more." Perhaps he has already said too much. *Thateron*, which is crasis for *to heteron*, "the other," can be a euphemism for "bad." The sentence literally begins, "It is more (*pleon*) *the other* to use something not rightly . . ." "*The other*" makes the bad sound less bad. It leaves the bad alone by refraining from engaging it in speech. Badness is not tampered with, but left unexpressed—except by comparison. Cleinias seemed to have hit upon this earlier when he began to wonder (rather than to blush) at impasses in the argument. Wondering abstracted his soul from the *logos*, for blushing seemed to indicate he had taken the argument personally. By wondering, Cleinias could simply follow the *logos* wherever it went without letting his own interest get in the way. His subsequently beautiful speech was probably a Freudian slip. But Socrates' advice is complicated. He ends with, "don't we speak thus?" This might be translated as, "don't we claim (*phêmi*) thus?" That is, "isn't it conventionally held to be this way?" Leaving matters be might just mean going along with common opinion. It is not so clear that one can tell the difference between preserving reality and preserving the illusion of reality. It is a common injunction to say that one ought not to interfere with the way things are. Or, maybe it is just that this is how we, human beings, speak. Socrates started by saying "I believe, I suppose . . ." or "I think I think . . . ." This means, "I might not have this right—but I'm going to say it anyway." *Logos* by its very presence lacks knowledge with accuracy; one is led to voice because one is unclear about what is going on. Speech is even skewed when one thinks one knows what is going on, since if one were really knowledgeable there would be no need to talk. Speaking implies speaking not rightly. Still, Socrates suggests all this in a speech. It is not so clear that it is possible to simply let things be. The imperative of passivity—"let it be"—is already too active.

That there is either using not rightly or leaving things be seems to suggest that using rightly entails leaving things be. The aim has become one of neutralization rather than positive success. The subject's goal is to edit out his interest in using. Socrates gives several examples. The first concerns woodworking—"In the working and use concerning wood, is there anything else rightly accomplishing the using than knowledge of carpentry?" (281a2–4) Working and use are first combined, and then turned into verbs (to accomplish and to use). The source of the combination is knowledge of carpentry. One might wonder if an agent is even necessary, since knowledge leads straightway to success. Things are as good as done if one knows what one is doing. Carpentry does seem to work in this way. When one builds something, a method of putting it together becomes clear as one goes along. It is as if the process takes one over without one needing to make independent choices about how to proceed. In line with this, in the next example, knowledge becomes identical to accomplishing—"But surely, I suppose, even in the working concerning furnishings, the accomplishing is [a] knowledge with respect to using rightly" (281a4–6). The word "furnishings" could mean materials (e.g., wood) or tools (e.g., saws). Working concerning furnishings might be interpreted as "working concerning using." Agency has been folded into the material of the work. We are now concerned with knowledge of use, or knowledge of know-how, which is identified with the action of accomplishing. However, when Socrates applies the prior examples to the case in point, something changes. "Then . . . also concerning the use (*chreia*) of the goods we were first speaking of, both of wealth and of health and of beauty, did [a] knowledge lead the using rightly . . . and straighten up (make upright) the doing or something else?" (281a6–b1).[3] Instead of the adverb "rightly," Socrates uses the cognate verb, "to make upright," of which knowledge is now the subject. Knowledge seems to have acquired agency in its own right. The verb "to lead" (*hêgesthai*) might even be rendered "to consider," or "to think." Socrates omits being well born, having power and honors, the virtues and wisdom (good luck), which were also part of the list of goods— unless beauty is supposed to somehow confer these last seven items. It seems anachronistic that knowledge of using rightly could make one well born. However, that virtue is knowledge is certainly not unfamiliar in the Socratic canon. One thus has to wonder whether beauty means virtue as a whole. The status of knowledge changes still further in what follows— "Not only, therefore, good luck, but also doing well, so it seems, [the] knowledge provides to human beings both in every possession and doing" (281b2–4). In the former passage, "knowledge" did not have a definite article. It was unclear whether it was any old knowledge or Knowledge with a capital K. But Socrates now adds a definite article, "the," which suggests

---

3   One of the words for "use" (*chreia*) can also be translated as "necessity."

that there is only one knowledge that provides doing well to human beings. Knowledge, understood as all knowing, has transplanted wisdom entirely (it was previously said to be wisdom that supplied good luck). Knowledge gets its object with an accuracy that defies a subject's intervention; it supplies a "well" without any possibility of error. Yet, in its knockdown power, it looks more than automatic. It is too intelligent to remain solely an aid that assures that the subject acquires the good, but rather, it usurps the subject, and acquires a mind of its own. When one says that something accomplishes itself, one is moved to postulate something independent apart from the accomplishing. The verb "to accomplish" suggests that there is a subject that is doing the accomplishing. It is difficult to know what it would mean if things simply moved themselves without the motion originating in a concentrated source. At the same time, however, the success of knowledge depends on the disappearance of agency—or, one could say, upon a subject not interfering. When the subject interferes, knowledge becomes insufficiently object-oriented. Knowledge of the world is supposed to reflect the world rather than a particular (subjective) view of the world.[4] The solution is deification. Knowledge becomes a subject whose character as a subject provides only power, without obstacle. It invisibly moves, like breath. Appropriately, Socrates begins his next speech by swearing by Zeus—*ô pros Dios* (281b4–5). Typically, one might encounter, "*ô Zeus*," or "*pros Dios*," as an invocation of a god or a swearing by the god. But invoking one's swearing by the god is something else. Socrates is invoking the power we have of invoking an agent. To swear by "by Zeus" turns an oath to agency into an agent. This is emphasized by the fact that Zeus in its non-nominative forms bears a similarity to the word *dia* in

4   Especially in academic writing, an "I" is an unwelcome intrusion. It is better that one's work look as if it is the product of necessity rather than one's pen. Ironically, this suppression of the "I" (another version of "leaving things be") is carried out for the sake of the "I." The usual residue is the impersonal subject, "one."

5   It is interesting that Socrates had before called on Euthydemus and Dionysodorus, and then, Dionysodorus alone, with the words "oh Zeus" (276e). Here, he invokes Cleinias with "oh by Zeus." Rather than being Zeus himself, Cleinias is only Zeus' tool. His passive agreement has left him under the thumb of the god.

Greek (the accusative of Zeus, *Dia*, is identical). *Dia* means "through" or "on account of."[5] By "by Zeus" is to say on account of "the on account of."[6]

Socrates wonders if, oh by Zeus, "there is any benefit (*onêsis*) from the other possessions without prudence (*phronesis*) and wisdom?" Within the span of two pages, Cleinias has heard about the necessity of the good for happiness/virtue, happiness/virtue understood as knowledge, and (now) prudence as somehow linked to wisdom. He is receiving a compressed version of some of Socrates' most illustrious teachings. Prudence appears to have been what Socrates had meant by wisdom all along. Prudence gives one access to the good by honing in on it, and orchestrating how to act accordingly.[7] It is more like a disposition than a noun insofar as it adapts to various situations. Next to wisdom, however, it reduplicates the divide between the adverbial and the nominal—between having goods (wisdom) and being dexterous/good at having them (prudence). The pair replaces knowledge, which had at first become identical to necessity, only to have agency anonymously creep back in when it turned out to be the provider of good luck and doing well. Its splitting into prudence and wisdom leaves the subject as an object of reproach: "Would a human being be reproached possessing many things (*polla*) and doing (*prattein*) many things (*polla*) not having (*echein*) mind, or rather (*mallon*) [doing] a few things (*oliga*) having (*echein*) mind? Consider it in this way: would he not be off the mark less (*elattô*) doing (*prattein*) less (*elattô*), and, missing the mark less (*elattô*), do less (*êtton*) badly, and doing (*prattein*) less (*êtton*) badly, he would be less (*êtton*) miserable?" (281b6–c3)[8] Socrates begins neutrally. It is just the impersonal subject—some human being, who will go unnamed. The human being starts out behaving not rightly. He is either doing too much with nothing or not much with something. The implication seems to be that the human being would never have enough composure to do more than a handful of things. Thus, if he does less, he ought to be less reproachable (and

6   See also Plato, *Cratylus*, 413a.
7   See, for example, Plato, *Republic*, 348d, 396d; Aristotle, *Nicomachean Ethics*, 2.6.15.
8   The word for "reproach" in its optative form (*onaito*) is mistakable for the verb "to benefit," the noun of which Socrates had just used to refer to the "benefit" (*onêsis*) of the other possessions that prudence and wisdom supply. The latter verb can also mean, in a passive sense, "to be blessed."

so, happier). It is no longer that one does well by possessing goods, but instead, that one is deemed more or less unfortunate by something outside of oneself based on one's possessions and actions. But what Socrates says is absurdly indefinite. The question is: would a human being be reproached possessing many things (*polla*, muchly/intensely) and doing (faring) many things (*polla*, muchly/intensely) not having (being able with respect to) mind, or rather (more) [doing/faring] few things (*oliga*, in a little way/mildly) having (being able with respect to) mind?[9] The neuter plurals (not to mention, the verbs for "doing" and "having") are consistently ambiguous. On the one hand, they indicate doing something intensely or mildly—i.e., the quality, or the oomph, of the activity. On the other hand, they point to the object of the activity—i.e., its external measure, quantity, or goal. This division in aiming was already prefigured by knowledge breaking into prudence (oomph) and wisdom (aim).

The most straightforward option is: would one be reproached doing many things (intensely) not having mind or doing few things (mildly) having mind? Socrates is primarily interested in the case where one's mind is somewhere else. He is interested in subjects who fail to be subjects; subjects whose own intentions are not entirely under their control. A subject whose aim is off will miss the target less, if he aims at fewer things, or aims less intensely. He will thereby ameliorate an inevitably bad situation.[10] He will do good doing bad. If human beings are chronically unhappy, this would be a way of rendering them blessed without altering their status as human. Socrates' instruction to "consider (*skopei*) it thus" is a version of what he is suggesting. The command literally means, "look"—that is, look at an object in the world, external to you. But it comes to mean, "consider"—that is, look at an "object" in the world as if it were an object of your mind. Hypothesize. Don't take external reality as your aim with too much gusto. The previous argument prepared the way for this by illustrating the mind's

9 The neuter plurals here may be read substantively or adverbially. *Polla* can be rendered as the temporal, "often." In addition, *mallon* can mean "more" as well as "rather." The Greek could therefore be read as if Socrates were only posing a single option—"Would a human being be reproached possessing many things and doing many things having mind minorly (*oliga*) morely (*mallon*)?"

10 Cp. Aristotle *Nicomachean Ethics* 7.

ability to take as an object a thing that was not present. The consideration is this: would one not do/fare less (*elattô*) missing the mark (*exhamartanein*) less (*elattô*), and missing the mark (*hamartanein*) less (*elattô*), do/fare less (*êtton*) badly, and doing/faring less (*êtton*) badly, be less (*êtton*) miserable (*athlios*)? "Many" and "few" have been replaced by two words for the same word, "less," *elattô* and *êtton*. Socrates has economized his question. But *elattô* seems to point to a measured property of an object (an adjective); it means less in the sense of quantitatively small. *Êtton*, on the other hand, seems to point to the character of a subject (an adverb); it means less in the sense of weaker, or to a lesser extent. The shrinkage in diction leads to the ballooning of its scope. There is also a distinction made between "missing the mark (*exhamartanein*)" and "missing the mark" (*hamartanein*). The two words are more or less the same, but the *ex* (which means something like "out of" or "from") disappears with the appearance of *êtton*.[11] There are also two readings of "to do/fare less badly." Either less goes with badly, in which case one does/fares not as bad (meaning one fares better). Or, less goes with do/fare, in which case one does less, but badly and so, one really does more. The translation of "do" or "fare" seems to depend on whether one takes "less" as adverbial or nominal. "Miserable" (*athlios*), too, is dichotomous. In Homeric Greek it means "prize-winning" or "victorious," while in Attic it means "struggling" or "wretched." In the former case, the subject is described when he gains his object; in the latter, he is described in his pursuit of the object, i.e., as a subject. The split points to the bizarreness of Socrates' formulations. If one does not give one's all in an athletic contest, one hardly does better. Doing less would entail not caring about winning the prize, and so not being a contender. Of course, this all depends on one's aim (to win) being good. If one's aim is good, it is good to exert oneself (unless, perhaps, one thinks of the tortoise and the hare). Socrates seems to be trying to section off the intensity of an experience from its extension. He is concerned with isolating the subject's intrusion in what he does. When one's goal is incorrect, if one can instill it with minimal oomph, one will not be so bad off. But, if it turns out that not only all

---

11   If one attributes this to the reduction in externality implied by *êtton*, the following proportion results—doing is to faring as *elattô* is to *êtton* as *exhamartanein* is to *hamartanein* as object is to subject as nominal is to adverbial.

possessions can be used well or badly, but also that every action can be done well or badly, the activity of doing less will be no exception. If one does more of the less, one will keep oneself out of trouble; this is to read "more" quantitatively. On the other hand, if one does less, but in an excessive way (adverbially), one may in fact do too much. One may magnify the less so as to contaminate its smallness. We have such expressions as "less is more," "making a mountain out of molehill," and "the silent treatment," all of which entail the minimal being overblown by the intent of a subject. Socrates' argument seems to be riding on the quarantining of "more" and "less"; the more is only supposed to make the less lesser. Nonetheless, to Socrates' incredibly ambiguous question, Cleinias answers, "Entirely at least (*panu g'*)." Cleinias gives his answer his oomph in its entirety (*panu*), and then restricts it with a *ge* ("at least")—unless the *panu* sends the *ge* over the top, and renders it, "indeed" (another of its various meanings).

Socrates gives Cleinias a list of seven opposing conditions and traits. In each case, the condition or trait that is usually thought to be bad turns out to be better, when one's aim is bad. The first case is: who would more (*mallon*) do less (*elattô*)—poor or rich? That is, who does less more, someone having less or someone having more? The question is directed at external possessions. Since the poor have less resource than the rich, they will not be able to aim with so much power. Their slight circumstance leads to a reduction of their oomph. "More . . . or" is the ambiguous *mallon...ê*. Socrates could have easily used *pleon...ê* (he had in fact used this shortly before at 280e5). But *pleon* is less ambiguously more than *mallon*. In contrast, the *ê* taken with the comparative *mallon* can mean "rather than." The question could thus read, "do the poor do less rather than the rich?" In the latter interpretation, the focus is on the activity taken on its own; in the former (do the poor or rich more do less?), the activity is qualified, and the subject's condition (which is relative) is in question. It looks as if, when the subject of the action is not known, the degree of the subject's engagement in the activity is altered. *Mallon* brings this out because its definition is unwieldy.

Socrates gives six more examples: weak or strong, honored or dishonored, manly and moderate or cowardly, idle or hardworking, slow or quick, seeing and hearing bluntly or sharply. The list is parallel to his previous list of goods at 279a: being wealthy (vs. poor), healthy (vs. weak/sick), beautiful (noble) and equipped with respect to the things of the body (vs. ugly/shameful); being well-born and having power and honors (vs. being dishonored); being moderate, just (vs. unjust) and manly (vs. cowardly), and, finally, wisdom or good luck (vs. ignorance). In the revised list at 281c, Socrates omits beauty and justice, and adds hardworking (vs. idle), quick (vs. slow), and sharp (vs. blunt). These additions apparently replace wisdom.

Beauty would have been opposed to ugliness or shame. Given the way the argument goes, the lesser (and now superior) trait would have to have been ugliness. But those who are ugly may have an incentive to inflate themselves, due to their disadvantageous position. The ugly frequently harbor resentment of the beautiful. If one reads the opposite of beauty (nobility) as shame, this is even more apparent. Those who are ashamed hide under rocks (less) as often as they try to cover over their shame with aggression (more). In both cases, their action has to do with them having an exaggerated sense of themselves. What is more, beauty would have paralyzed the argument entirely. Beauty confers power. Attractive things/people can attract others with almost nothing to back them up. The more beautiful something seems, the less important its content is. One does not pit it against actuality; simply conceiving of it is sufficient. The oomph of beauty ostensibly satisfies without needing fuel from an alternative source; it has no calories. At the same time, however, the perfect internality of beauty is the very thing that stops it from ever being satisfying. Beauty signals the remove from the good (or, reality) that leaves one always hungry for more. One feels its intensity regardless of its being an object one could obtain, but from the moment one is under its sway one has already set sights on it as if it were a possibility. It forever gratifies because it inevitably produces oomph, but leaves one discontented because oomph is hard to separate from longing.

In the case of poor/rich and weak/strong, the bad option (which is now good) comes first. It is better to be financially and physically less resourceful if one's aim is going to be off. But when Socrates comes to "honored or dishonored," the order is reversed. Cleinias thinks the "dishonored" will do less more. Presumably one more does less being dishonored because one does not have a good reputation to support one's incorrect aiming. But the reversal of order in Socrates' question suggests that it is not at all clear that dishonor leaves one inept. Being dishonored introduces a motive for behaving excessively. The dishonored, like those who are ashamed, are frequently indignant. They magnify their inferiority. Their aim is thus harder to diminish because it is held with more intensity. Poor people and weak people might also be understood in this way, if they conceive of themselves as in a position of dishonor. Socrates had originally proposed a divide between the aim or goal (which was missed) and the oomph with which one aims at the goal. Incentive is a third thing having to do with a degree of self-aggrandizement; it is a hybrid of goal and oomph.

Socrates switches the order of the traits back when he comes to "idle or hardworking," just following "manly and moderate vs. cowardly." One might infer that there is some problem with virtue as well. This was first suggested by the omission of beauty (and its replacement, under Knowledge's authority, of the virtues). Beauty is in a way virtue entire. When we talk about a "good person," we mean someone who is good independent of any action—that is, in a way, regardless of content. To restrict his goodness to any one act would make him seem less beneficent than he is. The truly noble person is like a god in his unchangeable good will; he never looks to personal gain, and so he operates with the remove of the beautiful rather than the reality of the good. The particular virtues, on the other hand, seem to be inseparable from aiming to correct imperfections of person. Courage, for example, shows up when one faces adversity; moderation, when one faces temptation. Each virtue has an aim or end in mind that seeks to improve the subject's position. However, the goal of this argument is to throw a rock in front of the subject. The target is already contaminated, so that only virtues that can be combined to produce imbalance can be included.

Socrates pits manly (*andreios*, the standard adjective for "courageous") and moderate against cowardly. The cowardly are supposed to do less more than the manly and moderate. This is odd, since moderate people are usually thought to do less. Manly people, in contrast, push harder, and are more wrong, when their aim is wrong. Manliness alone would be so engaged in a showcase of the subject that it would not get the bad aim right, and so be better at aiming badly than cowardice. Moderation has to be added to manliness to make it more courageous than rash. Moderation is object-oriented; it assures that manliness will hit the right wrong, and therefore that cowardice (the lesser trait) will be more incompetently good. Socrates cannot be using "manly" as "courageous," because courage without proper measure of oomph and aim is impossible. Manly and moderate distill courage into a separate oomph and aim.

For a similar reason, justice is left out altogether. The unjust man already aims with all his oomph at the bad. It is not out of the question for a poor man to be a good man—even the dishonored man can be reinterpreted as good. But it is untenable to construe the unjust as good. The unjust man may have an interest in appearing to be good, but only while being bad. This makes him an even more untrustworthy candidate for this argument, since being good at being bad is the goal. He is all too willing to hit the wrong target, and would require something more than a modification of oomph to be more conditionally bad at hitting the bad. Wisdom, too, must be dropped, since its good aim is infallible. Socrates instead offers: idle vs. hardworking, slow vs. quick, and seeing and hearing bluntly vs. sharply. These are cases in which oomph and goal are easily divided. The traits that Socrates omits are those that do not submit to this division. Wisdom by itself is all aim; beauty is all oomph; and justice so succinctly ties oomph to aim that it is hard to determine where the one begins and the other ends. The omissions suggest that Socrates' division of oomph from aim is really impossible. Doing less more can always mean not just minimizing the less, but rather, infusing the less with more significance. It is always possible to develop an inferiority complex. It must be noted that, while Socrates' traits seemed to be left aside in the previous list of the goods—Socrates was not wealthy, powerful, beautiful or honored—the introduction of the imperfection of human aim rehabilitates them. Socrates is poor, weak, dishonored, and idle, often by his own admission.

The argument moves from poor, weak, and dishonored, which are all conditions for oomph, to cowardly, idle, slow, and blunt, which are all qualities of oomph. Blunt (vs. sharp) is coupled with the perceptions of seeing and hearing. Seeing and hearing are alternative forms of aiming. It is not as if one has them or one does not (e.g., in contrast to wealth). The perceptions already combine oomph (understood as capacity for aiming) and aim. Since there are a variety of perceptions, there seem to be a variety of attunements of aim for a single individual. In order to fail to hit the mark successfully one would thus have to turn down the oomph on every perception. But Socrates pairs seeing and hearing as if it were impossible for someone to be blind but not deaf. Seeing bluntly, moreover, does not sound as if it is a condition for which the political is required (e.g., in contrast to honor), unless one thinks of Oedipus. Greek tragedy is the place in which, no matter what the subject does, his aim will fail to hit the mark. Of course, tragedy is also the place in which, though everything under the sun goes wrong, the result is a laudatory composition.

Cleinias answers the first four cases by stating aloud the lesser option ("Poor," he said," "Weak," "Dishonored," "Cowardly"). But when Socrates comes to idle vs. hardworking, Cleinias is just said to "go along" (281c9). Cleinias becomes less than he was previously. In response to the final set of examples, Socrates reports that, "All such things we went along with one another" (281d1–2). Both Socrates and Cleinias finally relinquish their oomph to the argument.[12] It does not matter how much mental power they instill into it, it is inevitably aiming in a certain direction. But isn't this because they are seeing sharply? The success of the argument is part and parcel to the obliteration of the oomph of the interlocutors. Or rather, the obliteration of the oomph of the interlocutors is tantamount to their becoming wise. All of the goods that were listed as obviously good in the prior argument have now been shown to be bad. If one's aim (goal) is bad, it is good to be bad at aiming.[13] Things have thus been rendered worthless, because ambiguous. Nothing is by nature good. The only worth is that which is instilled when the subject collapses ambiguous things via ignorance or wisdom. By seeking to leave reality as it is, reality has become entirely relative. If ignorance (amathia) "leads" (or perhaps, "thinks," hêgesthai) objects, they become greater bads; if prudence and wisdom lead (think) them, they become greater goods (281d4–e1). The only reality is the comparative

---

12 The verb phêmi is used frequently in Socrates' narration. In contrast to eipein or legein, both of which mean, "to speak," phêmi means something more akin to "to claim." It seems to be the sign of decayed oomph. It does not lend a feeling of necessity to the logoi that are being spoken. The presence of the subject is felt more than the object of the argument. Cleinias brings this out when he cautiously responds to Socrates' assertion about the neutrality of the goods with, "'It appears,' he said (phêmi), 'so it seems, thus, as you are saying'" (281e1–2). Saying "it seems to appear" involves two degrees of skepticism.

13 Even the word "aim" is ambiguous in English. It could refer to the target or the approach of the target.

degree ("greater") that is bestowed upon neutral items by good or bad aim; a good aim is then the only thing that has a shot at being good.[14] Socrates and Cleinias have totally given in to an argument that makes the subject all-powerful.

But *amathia* had originally been introduced as the trait *amathês*, which had meant either "stupid" or "unlearned." The abstract noun *amathia* has a similar ambiguity; it can mean either "stupidity" or "unlearnedness." The former depends on an impregnable defect in the subject, the latter on a remediable deficit in the subject's acquisition of objects. One can thus be led by ignorance for worse or for better—badly or well (less badly). One might say that Socrates and Cleinias are being led by ignorance in a good way. The argument originated in their lack of knowledge about how to fare well, but its conclusion is meant to reveal something to them. They are somehow better off than they were previously, though they are no longer in control of the argument. The repetition of prudence as paired with wisdom seems to be the sign that wisdom suffers a similar ambiguity. Prudence has to assure that wisdom will be exercised in the right way; it is not hard to think of a situation in which someone who knows better does not do better, or someone wise uses their wisdom poorly (a political ruler, for example). Neither ignorance nor wisdom left to its own devices still guarantees goodness or badness. Neither can be cut free from the adverbial, which is to say both are inevitably qualified.

The verb that Socrates uses to refer to the ignorance or wisdom "leading" objects is *hêgesthai*, which he had also used to refer to knowledge's ability to use rightly. Its alterative meaning "to consider," or "to think," is suggestive. Socrates has been capitalizing on a possibility that had shown up in his account of using. Using was slippery; it kept generating new objects for use. Money pointed to this in the extreme—it is an absence of good that is thought to be good. One can bracket the particular goods that money can buy so as to reap a greater profit—greater, because money stands for not just one good but numerous, potential goods. The mind can thus magnify whatever lies before it, even if what lies before it appears to be nothing. It can make something out of nothing. If reality does not provide a wealth of substance, thinking burgeons thoughts. Thought can even

14 Cp. Immanuel Kant, *Groundwork for the Metaphysics of Morals*, paragraph 393.

intensify its own experience of its experiences. This is especially convenient when experiences are unpleasant. The solution is to simply take "perspective" on them. By making the world an object of reflection, something painful is mutated into something useful (*pathêi mathos*).[15] Reality becomes fiction; blushing is transformed into wondering; bad becomes good. This is precisely what Socrates does in this argument. Traits and conditions typically thought to be undesirable (being poor, weak, cowardly, etc.) have been revamped in a positive light. As a result, while the goal of the argument is to do less more, the argument itself is engaged in inflating the less. Once interest is taken out of the equation (e.g., because one will hit the wrong mark), one's interest becomes in taking one's interest out of the equation—in reducing the intensity with which one aims by increasing the intensity of one's concentration. Ironically, aiming to rid reality of the self thus leads to the mushrooming of the self. Isn't it strange that "to pay attention" means to try to intensely limit one's extension in the world?

Intensification—what one might call the power of reflection—is something with which tragedy, and poetry more generally, is intimately familiar. Tragedy relates horrible events (e.g., sleeping with one's mother and killing one's father), which the audience watches with pleasure. When one puts a frame around the bad, the bad suddenly becomes attractive. It becomes something one can love because it is not really being experienced. It is beautiful to observe, despite the fact that it would not be good to undergo. Poetry can even glorify humdrum details by knitting them with an eye to the necessity of events (*My Fair Lady* perhaps). The common becomes more or less than what it is by being downplayed or climaxed. In either case, the intensity of the subject is felt more powerfully as reality ceases to be what it is typically. There are poems that are meant to suck one in by seeming real (to make one lose oneself as subject). One's agency blends into the agency of the characters in the poem; one becomes more than one is because one becomes identical to all of the perspectives in the story. On the other hand, there are poems that are meant to make one think (to call attention to oneself as a subject). In this case, one's agency is highlighted. As the reality of an experience shrinks, one's experience of the experience expands. One experiences oneself as occupying a fundamentally different position than the characters of the

---

15 See the chorus of Aeschylus' *Agamemnon*.

poem, which makes one suspect that there is more to the poem than meets the eye (a crucial element, oneself, has yet to be included in the picture). The *Euthydemus* is an extremity of this. It begins with Euthydemus and Dionysodorus giving two arguments for *x* and not-*x*; Socrates follows with an argument for the good and an argument for the bad. The net output looks as if it is zero. Things have become value-neutral. Euthydemus and Dionysodorus size people down; they lessen them. But the resultant deficiency of subject matter compels the reader to increase his effort to understand. The reader's oomph is fueled by the oomph of the interlocutors having been sucked dry. One either gives up (in quite an exasperated way) or hangs on for dear life. The *Euthydemus* is playful but maddeningly so.

Socrates calls attention to this with his excessive treatment of the less. The goods of the city (wealth, health, and honor) get deprogrammed and the more Socratic goods (poverty, weakness, and dishonor) become the standard. Deprogramming convention is in a way classic Socrates. Socrates is always showing people that the opinions they take for granted have been built up to be something they are not. Socrates' enemies, however, interpret this as a kind of short-sightedness—e.g., Hippias in the *Hippias Minor*, who says, "Socrates, you are always braiding (*plexai*) some such *logoi*, and taking out whatever is most difficult in the logos, you hold onto this, fastening on a small thing, and do not contest with respect to the whole *pragma* about which the logos is" (369b8–c2). This is what Socrates' enemies refer to as his "playing (*paizein*)" (*Apology* 20d6, or 27a8, *paizontos*, "a player")—the very verb that Socrates uses to describe Euthydemus and Dionysodorus. Socrates' playing certainly caused an intense response from Athens. Yet, in the vicinity of Euthydemus and Dionysodorus, the Socratic mode looks much more palatable. Socrates has quite an easy time persuading Cleinias to pursue wisdom. Since the goods appear ambiguous without wisdom, it is only natural to conclude that everyone ought to seek to be as wise as possible. Wisdom is necessary to acquire ". . . much more . . . than money from a father . . . and from guardians and friends, both others and the ones saying they are lovers, both foreigners and citizens, asking and supplicating <them> to give a share of wisdom . . . [and it is] . . . nothing shameful . . . nor a cause for indignation, for the sake of this to minister to and be a slave to both a lover and every human being, wishing to do any of the beautiful services whatsoever, being eager to become wise . . ." (*Euthydemus* 282a8–

b6). The path to becoming wise consists in giving up one's agency to others, apparently under the assumption that some "share" of it will then be given back. One cannot harbor any resentment for being in a position of inferiority. One must be willing to perform slavish services to lovers and to everyone else. That is, one must be willing make oneself into an object of use in order to determine how one ought to use oneself. Such conduct certainly befits Socrates, who is as often pursuing his *eros* for young boys as he is his desire to improve their souls.

The language is strikingly similar to the language of the *Apology*. In the *Apology* Socrates repeats several times to the Athenian jury that he has been accused of ". . . making the weaker (*êttô*, "lesser") *logos* stronger (*kreittô*, "greater")" (18b9–10, 19b6–c1, 23d6–7). He claims that he is a much lesser thing than the *hoi polloi* make him out to be. Even the Pythian oracle (which prophesied that no man was wiser than Socrates) seems to Socrates to have blown him out of proportion (21b5–6). After hearing from the oracle that he was supposed to be the wisest man, Socrates made it his business to determine if this was true. He examined everyone he came across ". . . whether citizen or foreigner. . ." (23b6–7), and eventually concluded that the oracle must have meant that he was wiser only in a little thing—that, while other men think they know when they do not, Socrates does not think he knows (21d8–10). But he did not stop at this; since he thought the god meant that people become wiser when they realize how little human knowledge is worth, Socrates made a point to seek out everyone who had a high opinion of themselves in order to show them their inferiority. He "reproached" these people for making more out of less (29e7, 31a1, 41e6–7); that is, for caring about wealth and reputation and honor (what the city considers the goods) more than their souls (29e1; 30a10–b1; 31b5).[16] As a

---

16 In the *Euthydemus*, Socrates first concludes that the goods without the guidance of knowledge or ignorance are "worth nothing"; in the *Apology*, he ends by saying that people who suppose they are something but are really "worth nothing" should be "reproached," *Apology* 41e6–7. In the *Euthydemus* he then tells Cleinias that every man should make every manner of provision to be as wise as possible (282a5–6); in the *Apology* this is what Socrates himself exhorts every man to do. There is also a similarity in Socrates' subsequent instruction to Euthydemus and Dionysodorus to make "this youth" (Cleinias) wise and good (cp. *Apology* 29e1).

witness to his unflinching beneficence, he points out that he never asked for money (as do some of the other sophists). His "poverty" (31c4) of both mind and resource hardly make him a threat. In addition, he claims that he is "slow and old," while his accusers are "sharp and fast" (39b1–3). Still, despite these inferiorities (the very ones that he has been glorifying in the *Euthydemus*)—despite the fact that he is making an apology—the content and length of his remarks are quite grandiose. Both his presentation and its content are hardly minimal. Socrates' pursuit of and exhortation to knowledge of ignorance consumes his whole existence. At one point he declares that he would rather die than refrain from philosophy. What is more, knowledge of ignorance is itself a version of puffing up the less; knowing nothing is Socrates' greatest insight. It is therefore hard to understand what differentiates Socrates' excessive proclamations about his own minority from the moral righteousness he claims to remedy.[17]

In the *Euthydemus*, Socrates admits to Euthydemus and Dionysodorus that his speech is ". . . amateurish perhaps and scanty, though being spoken at length" (282d5–7). Its content is too slight for its largesse. Yet, in relation to the statements that Socrates makes to the Athenian jury, his remarks to Cleinias are condensed (much of Socratic philosophy seems to have been packed into 280e–283a). The *Euthydemus* presents the superiority of the less only hypothetically—would a human being [theoretically] be "reproached" doing many things (more) without mind (less) or few things (less) with mind (more)? That is, is it better to behave ignorantly and not know it or to have knowledge of one's ignorance? The human being who is at issue is clearly Socrates. Even the list of people from whom one ought to seek wisdom seems to be directed toward his audience—father and guardians (perhaps Crito and Socrates), friends—both others (Crito) and lovers (Cleinias and Ctesippus), and foreigners (Euthydemus and

17 There are outtakes. Death—which is of course on Socrates' mind in the *Apology*—is totally absent. In the *Apology*, Socrates cites death as *the* thing people (other than himself) render as more than what it is. The truth, according to Socrates, is that we do not really know if death is good or bad, but the *hoi polloi* are inclined to deem it evil. Oddly enough, Socrates spends the last few pages of the *Apology* speculating about how death is surely good, even if it is nothing. On the other hand, one can only assume it is also bad, when Socrates remarks that he would rather die than stop philosophizing.

Dionysodorus) and citizens (everyone other than Euthydemus and Dionysodorus).

What leads the Athenians to kill Socrates is thereby transmitted to an unwitting Cleinias; Socrates seems to have corrupted him. Cleinias painlessly agrees that the shameless pursuit of wisdom (i.e., Socratic philosophy) is the best way of life. But, Socrates cautions, being so shameless would only make sense if wisdom can be taught—"For this for us is still unconsidered and is not yet mutually agreed upon (*diômologesthai*) by both me and you" (282c1–4). The mutuality of the agreement is a strange requirement, since Socrates has just finished telling Cleinias that pursuing wisdom involves giving one's soul away to everyone for free. Cleinias quickly vouches for the fact that wisdom is teachable. This has an interesting parallel in the *Apology* as well. Socrates tells the jury that he never claimed to teach anyone anything, and that if someone claims he has learned from him, he is not telling the truth (33a5–6, b8–10). His aim—to make the youth as wise as possible—does not guarantee any concrete results. What is at stake is whether or not debasing oneself for wisdom—philosophy—is actually something one could exhort people to do. It is not surprising that Socrates is delighted by Cleinias' assertion that it is. Cleinias saves Socrates the trouble of his trial and execution. Socrates tells Cleinias that he has spoken beautifully and "done well (*eu poiein*)" (282c5–6). The conclusion is, then, that wisdom "makes (*poiein*)" a human being lucky and happy, so that it would appear that nothing else is necessary than "to philosophize" (282c9-d1).[18] Socrates follows this by asking Cleinias if he himself "has it in mind to do (*poiein*) this?" (282d2) Cleinias says he will do it as much as possible (*malista*, 282d3). He plans to make himself a superlative servant of philosophizing; he will humiliate himself to the utmost, since he believes that it will somehow lead to happiness. What had been only comparative goodness, Cleinias renders superlative. There is, in addition, an alteration in Socrates' terminology. The issue was how to "do well (*eu prattein*)." But, when Cleinias agrees to the teachable character of wisdom,

18 This is the second occurrence of a cognate of "philosophy." The first occurrence was *philosophia*, a noun, which Euthydemus and Dionysodorus claimed to be able to hand over to human beings (275a). Philosophy is here "to philosophize," a verb.

Socrates says that he "does well (*eu poiein*)." "To philosophize" is also articulated as something one "does" (*poiein*). One does (*poiein*) philosophy so one can do, *prattein*, well. In the very same sentence, Socrates uses *poiein* to refer to luck "making" a human being happy. *Poiein* gives us the English "poet"; it is more active than *prattein* (which gives us "pragmatic"). Applying the more to the less involves a certain beautification (poetizing) of reality. The argument had begun with the intent of neutralizing the subject; but the outcome is the aggrandizement of the subject as someone with superlatively neutral (Socratic) traits. Cleinias buys this poetic mutation at face value. He is willing to listen to Socrates. He addresses Socrates in the vocative twice ("Oh Socrates," 282c4, d3) in answer to Socrates' inquiries about teaching and philosophy. He seems to be avowing his devotion to Socrates' agency. His own agency is suppressed, despite the fact that what he is avowing to is his belief that he is capable of learning (of being an agent). Idolatry, like falling in love, shows its agency as awe. Cleinias for some reason believes he has the answers to all of Socrates' questions; he suddenly feels powerful. Yet his answers are manifestations of his having swooned for Socrates; his authority is the result of his being made powerless.

Euthydemus and Dionysodorus had neutralized Cleinias' agency completely; Cleinias could not speak by the time they were finished with him. Socrates, too, neutralizes the subject or agent, but in such a way that the subject rebounds as a sort of self-neutralizer. He offers this more grandiose portrait of what they do as his "example" to them (282d4–5). Philosophy (more of the less) has been laid down as a challenge to sophistry (less of the more). The standard sophists—the so-called "Sophists," such as Protagoras and Gorgias—are inclined to converse about virtue, happiness, and the good. Euthydemus and Dionysodorus, on the other hand, have shown themselves to be much more abstract; they are minimalists. They swoop in, perform an operation of logic-chopping, and then vanish. They are extremely pragmatic. Or rather, they seem to be choral—uninvolved in plot.

Socrates gives them two options: they can follow his example, and do what he just did by art, or the pair of them can exhibit the sequel to his argument. That is, they can show themselves to be poets or to be involved in the plot of Socrates' argument; they can be Platonic or Socratic. Either way, they are going to have to be manifestly more poetic than they have been previously. Doing what Socrates did, but by art, would have to mean pretending to be a co-learner with Cleinias. In other words, composing a dialogue. Presumably only one of them could do this, because they could not both be in conversation with Cleinias without seeming as if they were attacking him. But the alternative—to display the sequel—must be carried out by the two of them together. The sequel involves showing whether Cleinias needs to have multiple strings of knowledge or whether there is some singular knowledge that will of necessity make him happy and wise. It is not at all clear which option they choose. Dionysodorus, who is older, is said to begin earlier than Euthydemus. Then, if one of them begins, is he operating by art? On the other hand, Dionysodorus precedes Euthydemus, as if they are about to perform in a row. Yet, Dionysodorus does not seem to sequentially follow Socrates. Whatever they do is commenced in the vein of generation. They go in chronological order. Their historical genesis is their argumentative genesis. There is apparently nothing poetic about it.

This resiliency to poetry is precisely what Socrates has been demonstrating. Agency is elusive. If one calls it a noun one makes it less than it is, for its power consists in its ability to take on any verb; it is not as limited as a character in a plot. Yet, to resign it to the verbal is to give it too much oomph; it starts to be all over the place, and so, not really capable of concentration. It is not as liberated as a pure reflector (a chorus). Socrates had referred to Euthydemus and Dionysodorus' questions as "beautiful." The two of them did not offer anything good to Cleinias; they made him want to hide his face. Their prowess consisted in a sweeping elimination of reality. Socrates responds by demonstrating that the beautiful and the good (or the imagined and the real) are unthinkable apart from one another. Thinking has a power of degree. It can adjust its setting—turn itself up or down. It has the capacity to be very bright (where it may find itself annoyingly in the way) or very dim (where it all but disappears). It can read itself into a reflection or pull itself out. Euthydemus and Dionysodorus take this to mean that the mind's access to the good is inevitably confused. They then construe thinking as having the ability to discard and fabricate reality on a whim. Thinking is just poetizing; one can interpret as good whatever one likes. But they are scrupulous not to leave fingerprints. They endorse this poetic reflection so dramatically that it leads them to a kind of straight pragmatism. They are weirdly prudent. On the one hand, they disallow anything unambiguous; the mind has no contact with reality. On the other hand, the result is that the mind is the only reality, and therefore always in direct contact with it. Their antagonism of agency makes it possible for the agent to be totally at home in the world. One cannot yet know if they know this; they have never revealed themselves to be motivated by a desire to understand themselves, nor do they seem to care about the tension they create via their arguments. Cleinias, however, illustrates a motivation on their behalf when he proclaims how invested he is in debasing himself. The ambiguity of the good leads him to devote himself to unfurling it at all costs. Things are not just ambiguous but intensely ambiguous.

It is no wonder that Crito interrupts Socrates' conversation. He disapproves of Socrates' defense of staying in prison in the *Crito* as much as he disapproves of the implantation of Socratic philosophy in the young Cleinias. Crito is an intense supporter of *prattein*, not *poiein*. It is for this reason that Euthydemus and Dionysodorus are the appropriate teachers for him,[19] for in their utter remove from reality they end up being indistinguishable from it. The first half of the *Euthydemus* thus seems to be Socrates' attempt to defend philosophy in the face of sophistry, while at the same time showing that there is a kinship between the two, not only born out of a tie between the vacuous and the abstract but also between the ivory tower and the city. This is a threat as serious as the friendly face of Crito and as playful as the trials of Euthydemus and Dionysodorus. Socrates' apology must be double insofar as it knows of its own intensity. Philosophy in its most neutralized form is of a piece with the greatest sophist.[20] The laws of Euthydemus and Dionysodorus are those of the city that in its relentlessly seamless double entendre cannot know how it is made up.

19 And for his *ta paidia*, whom Socrates had wished to use as bait for Euthydemus and Dionysodorus. *Paidia* is the last word of the Euthydemus. It can mean either "children" or "play."
20 *Republic* 492a5–e6.

Plato: Philosopher? Poet? Both? Or Neither?
Catherine H. Zuckert

The questions in the title of this essay arise as a result of the distinctive character of Plato's writings. Unlike his student Aristotle who wrote treatises in which he examines the opinions and arguments of others, but gives his own view of things, Plato wrote dialogues in which he relates the conversations of others. He never speaks in his own name or puts forth a position or argument as his own. There are a few letters attributed to him, but scholars doubt the authenticity of most, if not all; and even in the case of the generally accepted Seventh Letter, these communiqués report events in Plato's life and describe arguments or positions he took rather than presenting his arguments or positions.

How then can we discover what Plato thought? In *Plato's Philosophers* I argued that we see Plato's hand—and thus, so to speak, his thought—in the organization and structure of the dialogues, both as single works and as a whole. He does not speak in his own name, but he did choose to show these particular individuals in conversation with each other, at the places and times suggested, with the results indicated. To get at what Plato thought, we thus have to begin by looking at the way in which he set up each of the dialogues and then move to the question of the way in which they are related. That means we first need to read each of the dialogues as a prose drama—a drama that has characters, a setting, and an action or outcome. Beginning with the characters, we observe that in each dialogue there is one dominant philosophical figure. Sometimes, as in the *Timaeus, Sophist,* and *Statesman,* there is another philosopher present, but Plato does not show his philosophers in dialogue with one another. The dominant philosopher is usually, but not always Plato's teacher, Socrates. Since Socrates is not the only philosopher depicted, however, we cannot and should not assume that Socrates speaks for Plato. But, because Socrates is by far the most common philosophic voice, we cannot take one of the others as Plato's spokesman either. Plato not only presents a variety of philosophers, moreover; he also shows these philosophers adapting their speeches or arguments to a variety of different interlocutors.[1] As Hans Georg Gadamer points out, the arguments in Platonic dialogues cannot and should not be read like scientific treatises, as if they were addressed to a general, anonymous reader or audience.[2] On the contrary, all the arguments need to be read as given by a certain kind of philosopher to a specified person or persons at the time and place indicated. And, if you ask, why did Plato make it all so complicated by putting all these specifics between his thought and the reader's comprehension thereof, I would respond that he did so as a reflection or picture of what is in fact the case: philosophy is an activity engaged in by embodied individual human beings, at certain times and places, in communication with others.

But if we read the dialogues as prose dramas, should we not be troubled by the fact that in the *Republic* Socrates explicitly bans dramatic poetry from his "city in speech" not only in his presentation of the education of the guardians in Books 2 and 3, but also after he has concluded at the end of Book 9 that their "city" may serve merely as the paradigm in terms of which an individual should try to order his or her own soul? If Plato is a dramatic or "literary" artist as well as a philosopher, as most commentators today would admit, isn't he involved in a performative contradiction—arguing that imitative poetry, i.e., works that present the interactions of specific characters dramatically, should be banned, even if his dialogues are written in prose rather than verse?[3]

---

1   Catherine H. Zuckert, *Plato's Philosophers* (Chicago: University of Chicago Press, 2009, 1–7.

2   Hans Georg Gadamer, *Plato's Dialectical Ethics*, trans. Robert M. Wallace (New Haven: Yale University Press, 1991), 2–4.

3   Among the scholars emphasizing the combination of philosophy and literature in the dialogues are Leo Strauss, *The City and Man* (Chicago: Rand McNally, 1964), 50–65; Michael Frede, "Plato's Arguments and the Dialogue Form," in *Methods of Interpreting Plato,* ed. James Klagge and Nicholas D. Smith (Oxford: Clarendon Press, 1992), 202–19; Diskin Clay, *Platonic Questions: Dialogue with the Silent Philosopher* (University Park: Pennsylvania State University Press, 2000); and Charles H. Kahn, *Plato and the Socratic Dialogue: The Philosophical Use of a Literary Form* (Cambridge: Cambridge University Press, 1996).

In a narrow sense, Socrates might appear not to be contradicting his own speeches in deed. In explaining the reasons why they should ban dramatic poetry from the city in Book 3, he explicitly says that he will "speak without meter" (393d), because he is not *poiêtikos*.[4] He also argues that they should ban dramatic poetry and only allow the recitation of narratives, because they do not want future guardians to learn to act or dissemble. And, Plato lets us know, the next day Socrates narrates to an unidentified auditor or auditors the conversation we read in the *Republic*. So, what Socrates does in retelling the conversation is within the bounds of his strictures against poetry.

But Plato does not narrate this or any other conversation he presents in the dialogues. Nor are the characteristics of poetry that Socrates finds troubling restricted to its rhythm or it non-narrative character. He proposes to regulate the content as well as the form of the public presentations of the stories of the deeds of gods and men, because he recognizes that human beings learn so much by imitation. Future guardians should, therefore, only be allowed to "imitate what's appropriate to them from childhood, men [*andras*] who are courageous, moderate, holy, free, and everything of the sort" (395c). And he concludes that "if a man who is able by wisdom to become every sort of thing and to imitate all things should come to our city, wishing to make a display of himself and his poems, we would fall on our knees before him as a man sacred, wonderful, and pleasing; but we would . . . send him to another city . . . while we ourselves would use a more austere and less pleasing poet and teller of tales . . . who would imitate the style of the decent man and would say . . . what we set down as laws at the beginning, when we undertook to educate the soldiers" (398a–b). Although Socrates argues that a just city would regulate both the form and the content of the poetic works disseminated among its citizens, he explicitly recognizes both the greatness of the art of the poet and the possibility that there are forms of poetry and myth-telling that should be admitted, perhaps even fostered, in a just city. He raises that possibility again, moreover, at the end of the dialogue in Book 10. Readers are thus prompted to ask

4   Citations to *Platonis Opera*, ed. John Burnet (Oxford: Clarendon Press, 1900–1907), Vol. IV; translations slightly modified from Allan Bloom, *The Republic of Plato* (New York: Basic Books, 1968).

whether the Platonic dialogues represent that kind of beneficial poetry and myth.

When Socrates returns to the question of poetry in Book 10, it is no longer so much a question of what is needed to educate soldiers or the formation of their character as it is what helps or harms the minds of listeners. Looking back on the city they have constructed in speech as the paradigm for an individual soul, he tells Glaucon that they were especially right to exclude any form of imitative poetry because the works of "the tragic poets and all the other imitators . . . maim the thought (*dianoia*) of those who hear them and do not have knowledge of how [things] really are as a remedy (*pharmakon*)" (595b). The problem that comes to the fore in Book 10 is not so much the tension between the requirements of educating guardians and the stories traditionally told about the gods and heroes by the poets. The question now concerns the respective truth, knowledge and educational effects of poetry, on the one hand, and philosophy, on the other.

The arguments Socrates gives to show that they were right to banish poetry nevertheless appear to be poor ones. At the very least, they seem to contradict (or exclude) Socrates' own behavior in the dialogue and thus to justify readers' concluding not merely that Socrates is not a philosopher of the kind he says ought to rule in a just city, but that he and his examinations of the opinions of others should be banned along with the poets.[5] Socrates first suggests that in presenting images of "images," that is, sensible things, which are themselves shaped or defined by invisible, purely intelligible or "divine" ideas, the works of the poets are three times removed from the truth. But, as all readers of the *Republic* know, Socrates himself employed some very famous images—of the "ship of state," the sun, divided line, and cave—in explaining why philosophers should rule and what they need to learn.

Socrates next faults the poets for describing the works of various artisans, the most important being the art of legislation, but not establishing

5   Seth Benardete, *Socrates' Second Sailing: On Plato's "Republic"* (Chicago: University of Chicago Press, 1989); Mary P. Nichols, *Socrates and the Political Community: An Ancient Debate* (Albany: State University of New York Press, 1987), 29–98; and Rosyln Weiss, *Philosophers in the "Republic": Plato's Two Paradigms* (Ithaca, NY: Cornell University Press, 2012), have all emphasized the difference between Socrates' own mode of philosophizing, as illustrated in Plato's *Republic,* and his descriptions of philosophy in that dialogue.

schools as the sophists do to teach their students how to be virtuous or how to rule. Yet Plato's readers can hardly fail to object: In the *Republic* Plato has shown Socrates telling his brothers what a ruler should do and know without actually teaching them either how to rule or what they need to know. In other words, Socrates himself would appear to be liable to the critique he makes of Homer.[6]

Socrates might not be as subject to the third criticism he makes of the poets—that their works arouse the passions and thus weaken the calculating part of the soul that ought to control human emotions. Socrates' examinations of the opinions of his interlocutors involve the use and exercise of reason and so would appear to strengthen that part of the soul in opposition to mere feelings. It can hardly be said, however, that neither Socrates nor Plato seeks to arouse the passions of his interlocutors or audience. One need think only of the *Symposium* and the *Phaedrus* in which Plato shows that Socrates presents philosophy as an essentially erotic activity and tries to arouse a love of wisdom in his conversational partners.

Unless we wish simply to dismiss Socrates' judgment on the poets as obviously ill-founded or maintain that Plato's depiction of his teacher is inconsistent, if not contradictory, we need to take a second look at Socrates' critique of the poets in Book 10 to discover its actual basis and point. And what we discover through such a re-examination, I shall argue, is that Socrates' concluding critique of the poets does not concern their distinctive mode of writing (in verse) or their use of images. It is aimed rather at the substantive understanding of the world he attributes to all previous poets and philosophers—except Parmenides—in the *Theaetetus*

6   Laurence Lampert, *How Philosophy Became Socratic: A Study of Plato's "Prota-goras," "Charmides," and "Republic"* (Chicago: University of Chicago Press, 2010), argues that in showing Socrates persuade his brothers that "philosopher-kings" ought to rule, in the *Republic* Plato was, in fact, putting forth the same understanding of the world that poets like Homer had expressed before and fabricating a new religion of the "ideas" for non-philosophers. I disagree with this reading for reasons I explain in this essay, and have responded specifically to Lampert in a review essay, "Is There a Straussian Plato?," *The Review of Politics* 74 (2012): 109–26, as well as "Partial Answers to Persistent Problems," *Perspectives on Political Science* 40, 4 (2011): 209–17.

7   In support of the proposition that Socrates does not object to the form so

(152d–e).[7] In his analysis of the poets' use of visible images, Socrates first objects, in effect, that their sense-based understanding of everything as becoming is not complete or accurate, because it does not include unchanging, purely intelligible forms of being like the concepts of equality and similarity on which mathematics is based. Second, Socrates objects, these poets cannot depict the kind of philosophy he practices as the only truly satisfying form of human existence, because no one would ask the question he typically raises about what something is unless that person thought that there were purely intelligible, unchanging forms of being.[8] In the *Theaetetus* Socrates describes Homer as the general of the great army of those who suggest that everything is always becoming and that nothing, therefore, exists in itself. It does not appear to be an accident, then, that Socrates' concluding critique of the poets in the *Republic* is delivered specifically with reference to Homer.

Let me turn now to examine Socrates' arguments in somewhat greater detail. In considering what imitative poetry is, Socrates first asks Glaucon to consider a "handworker able to make not only all implements but also everything that grows naturally from the earth, [including] all animals— himself too . . . and in addition, earth and heaven and gods . . . and everything in Hades" (596c). But, when Glaucon observes that such an artisan would be a "wonderful sophist," Socrates suggests that Glaucon could do something similar merely by taking a mirror and carrying it around; "quickly [he] will make the sun and things in the heaven; the earth; himself and other animals and implements and plants and everything else that was just mentioned" (596d–e)—everything, that is, that is visible.

Like a painter, a man with a mirror makes images of the sensible things.[9] But, Socrates then reminds Glaucon, the sensible things poets and painters copy, especially when these things are products of human art, are themselves copies or images of the things that truly are, which are not

much as the content of previous poetry, it is not irrelevant to note that Parmenides presented his arguments in the form of a poem, written like the *Theogony* of Hesiod, in dactylic hexameter.

8   See Leo Strauss, "The Problem of Socrates," in Thomas L. Pangle, ed., *The Rebirth of Classical Political Rationalism* (Chicago: University of Chicago Press, 1989), 182–83.

9   Cf. Bloom, "Interpretive Essay," *The Republic of Plato*, 428.

visible or sensible.[10] The painted or poetic imitations are, therefore, not merely three times removed from the truth; they also represent only partial and hence distorted views of what truly is.

Can an artist or poet who uses such sensible images present a picture of the whole? Socrates suggests that the medium of sensible imitation precludes it. Thus "when anyone reports to us about someone, saying that he has encountered a human being who knows all the crafts and everything else that single men severally know . . . it would have to be replied to such a one that he is an innocent human being who he seems to have encountered some wizard and imitator and has been deceived. Because he lacked the knowledge of things as they truly are necessary to put the imitation to the test, that man seemed all-wise to him" (598c–d). Socrates had earlier praised the man who is by wisdom able to imitate all things; now he accuses the poets of not possessing this wisdom and so not being able to imitate all things truly or in fact.

Socrates does not merely fault the poets' claim to know the whole; he also denies their claim to know and therefore teach the good and bad of

10   The relation between images and things corresponds to that Socrates had imaged earlier on the lower portion of the divided line (509d–510a). But Socrates' suggestion that the idea of which the couch is made by a carpenter is an image "in nature, made (*ergasathasthai*) by god, as we would say" (597b) is extremely puzzling. Nowhere else in the Platonic corpus does Socrates (or any other Platonic philosopher) suggest that the eternal, unchanging, hence purely intelligible ideas are made and so come into being. By saying that the couch, an example which is obviously a product of art, is made by god, Socrates would seem to be suggesting that anything purely intelligible and thus eternal would necessarily have a divine origin or cause. The products of this "god" or "*phutoourgos*" seem to include everything on the upper or intelligible part of the divided line (510b–511c), the ideas presupposed by the arts as well as the kinds of things to be found in nature—in sum, the models for the "artifacts, statues of men and other animals" that Socrates said earlier (514b–515a) cast the shadows the human beings chained to the floor of the cave see. The *phutoourgos* to which Socrates refers here (597b) is not the same as Timaeus' *demiourgos* who merely copies pre-existing eternal models. (*Timaeus* 28a–19a) The idea of a couch is clearly derivative from that of a human being and what such a being can use. According to Socrates' "hypothetical" logos in the *Phaedo* (101d–e), such "ideas" might, like the objects of the arts of legislation and justice in the *Gorgias*, be subsets of the more general idea of the good.

human life. He observes that it has been said of "tragedy and its leader, Homer . . . that these men know all arts and all things human that have to do with virtue and vice and the divine things too" (598c–e). But, Socrates objects, all these poets know is how to make pleasing images in speech which only persuade those who do not possess the knowledge of the things or activities in question.[11] There is no evidence that Homer or any other poet actually knew an art like medicine or how to be a general and hence could teach another.[12] Nor has any poet actually drawn up laws for any city—or demonstrated his practical wisdom by inventing a useful tool or technique. By presenting images of "kings" like Achilles and Odysseus, who seek glory and wealth rather than knowledge, Socrates charges, poets like Homer merely fabricate images of self-seeking, unjust rulers, which appeal to people who do not know any better.

11 Cf. Socrates' comparison of poetry to rhetoric, *Gorgias* 500e–502e.
12 Socrates' suggestion that people would go to Homer or to any other poet for instruction might appear ridiculous. Who would believe he could learn to be a general or a doctor from Homer? Perhaps in response to that question, in the *Ion* Plato dramatizes a conversation between Socrates and a rhapsode who claims that someone can learn these arts by listening to, or even better, by memorizing and reciting Homer's epics. In that conversation Socrates quickly shows by interrogating Ion that a) the rhapsode has no understanding of what an art or any other kind of knowledge really is, and that b) unlike the practitioners of arts Socrates and Thrasymachus described in Book 1, the rhapsode practices his "art"—or, more properly, trade—for the sake of making money by entertaining others. Unlike Hippias, the sophist who claimed to know and to be able to make everything a human being needs, Ion is satisfied merely with reciting, i.e., copying, Homer's imitation of human activities, arts, and virtues. His recitations are clearly copies of copies, three times—or more— removed from the truth. He gives them primarily to enrich himself, not to instruct, educate, or improve his auditors. In the *Ion* Plato shows that the worst effect poets have on their audience may not be to present them with bad examples or to tempt some to deceive others by acting a role. The worst effect poets have on their listeners is to make them believe that by merely hearing or repeating the words, they share the inspiration and wisdom of the poet, especially concerning the divine. Cf. Allan Bloom, "An Interpretation of Plato's *Ion*," *Interpretation* 1 (1970): 43–62, reprinted in Thomas L. Pangle, *The Roots of Political Philosophy: Ten Forgotten Socratic Dialogues* (Ithaca: Cornell University Press, 1987), 371–95.

Earlier in the dialogue (523a–525a) Socrates had observed that when we are confronted by a difference between a sensible thing and its reflection, we use calculation (*logismos*) to determine what is truly the case. Here he reminds his interlocutors that calculation is neither taught nor can it be imaged by poetry. Instead, Socrates now contends, by sympathetically appealing to the passions and so arousing them, poetry strengthens the parts of the soul that calculation (*logismos*) should control. Poetry does not, therefore, provide the education necessary for the development of a well-ordered soul. It does not have the power of mathematics to re-direct the mind from its attachment to sensible things and toward an investigation of the purely intelligible.[13] Instead of helping spectators bring order to their lives by their attention to that which is true and lasting, poetry encourages listeners to give way to their own transitory feelings of joy and grief. It thus tends to make its audience immoderate rather than self-controlled.

Because the charm of poetry is so great, Socrates nevertheless concedes, he would be delighted to readmit it, *if* poets could show that their works can contribute to the development of just human beings with well-ordered souls. He concludes his conversation with Glaucon and Adeimantus by indicating what the nature of such poetry would be.

First, Socrates suggests, poetry that promotes justice has to inculcate belief in the immortality of the soul. Traditional Greek beliefs about the gods and the afterlife propagated by the poets did not. To illustrate his point, Socrates asks Glaucon whether he has not perceived that our soul is immortal and indestructible, and Glaucon responds, "No, by Zeus!" If he is not to do an injustice, Socrates tells Glaucon, he must maintain that the soul is immortal. However, although Socrates assures Glaucon that it is not difficult to affirm that the soul is immortal, the reasons he gives for thinking so are not persuasive.[14] Since souls are not destroyed by bodily disease or

---

13 Hans-Georg Gadamer, *The Idea of the Good in Platonic-Aristotelian Philosophy*, trans. P. Christopher Smith (New Haven: Yale University Press, 1986), 82–83, emphasizes that the purpose of mathematical education in the *Republic* is turning the soul from the sensible to the intelligible.

14 The fundamental problem is that Socrates never states in the *Republic* what he thinks the soul is. On the contrary, in drawing the parallel between the three parts of the city and the three parts of the soul earlier he explicitly said that "we'll never get a precise grasp of it this way; there is another longer

by their own vices or corruption, he concludes, they cannot be destroyed. And in that case, there will always be the same number of souls. Socrates admits that "it's not easy for a thing to be eternal that is both composed out of many things and whose composition is not of the finest." Indeed, in both the *Phaedrus* and the *Phaedo* Socrates suggests that such a proof of the immortality of a dissoluble combination is impossible.) But, having maintained earlier in the *Republic* that the soul has three parts, Socrates here contends merely that we are not able "to see its true nature—whether it is many-formed or single-formed" so long as it is "maimed by community with body and other evils" (611b–612a). In other words, as Socrates acknowledges in the *Phaedrus* (246a), we mortals will never be able to say or know definitively what the soul is.

Strictly speaking, Socrates does not claim to know what the soul is and thus whether it is the kind of thing that can be immortal. Nor does he claim to know what happens to human beings after they die. Like a poet or teller of tales, he relates a story he claims to have heard from another: that a man named Er had almost died, but then lived to tell the tale of what he had seen in the underworld. Partly because it is not set in verse and is a narrative, this "myth" provides an example of the kind of poetry that Socrates thinks would support justice.[15] That poetry not merely asserts the immortality of the soul; it also makes individuals responsible for the character and course of their own lives. They are not the victims of impersonal fate or fates.

By explicitly setting his "myth of Er" in contrast to the story Odysseus tells King Alkinoos about his own travels, including a trip to the underworld, Socrates also indicates what he finds attractive about Homer's epics and where he fundamentally disagrees with the "general" of the tragic

road" (435c–d). In the *Phaedrus* 245c–246a he argued that the soul is immortal because it is self-moving, but he warned that it would take a discourse longer than any mortal could give to say what its idea is.

15 A computer search of the Platonic corpus on the Thesaurus Linguae Graecae for all the times Socrates explicitly says he is re-telling "myths" or a combination of *mythos* and *logos* (*mythologia*) shows that they concern the soul and the afterlife (in contrast to the "myths" about the origins of the city and not the soul or the afterlife told by Protagoras, the Eleatic Stranger and the Athenian Stranger).

poets.[16] In Hades Homer shows Odysseus talking to *"psychai,"* but these souls are able to speak only after they have drunk blood and so reacquired a connection with the body. In their usual state, souls in Hades do not appear to be able to converse, think, or remember. A few notable individuals are shown to have been punished (like Tantalus and Sisyphus) and one, Heracles, is said to have been rewarded with an immortal life with the gods on Olympus. But most seem to be doomed to persist wordlessly as shades, with no hope of reincarnation or rebirth.

In Socrates' account of what Er saw in Hades, souls are first judged, rewarded or punished, and then brought to a field where they can contemplate the intelligible order and beauty of the cosmos in the orbits of the planets and the resultant harmony of the spheres both in color and music.[17] The souls thus learn that there is an eternal order and that everything is not always in process of becoming or degenerating, before they are reincarnated and reborn. The future embodiments of these souls are not products of some impersonal "fate" or destiny, moreover. Although the three "fates," said to be daughters of necessity, keep the spheres in motion, they merely seal the choices the individual souls make concerning their future lives. According to the "myth of Er," neither the gods nor the intelligible order of nature determine the shape and outcome of human lives. On the contrary, individual souls choose the form of their future life on the basis of what they had learned or failed to learn, cherished or hated, in their previous existence.

16 John Sallis, *Being and Logos,* 2ⁿᵈ ed. (Atlantic Highlands, NJ: Humanities Press International, 1986); Evan Brann, "The Music of the Republic," *St. John's Review* 39 (1989–1990): 1–103; and Jacob Howland, *The "Republic": The Odyssey of Philosophy* (New York: Twayne Publishers, 1993), also emphasize the parallels between the *Republic* and the *Odyssey.*

17 In *Plato's Cosmology: The TIMAEUS of Plato* (London: Routledge & Kegan, 1937), 75, 87–88, Francis MacDonald Cornford points out both the similarity and the difference between the depiction of the revolution of the spheres in the myth of Er and that to be found in the *Timaeus* 36c–d. In contrast to the description in the *Timaeus* there is no allowance for the tilting of the earth in the description of the orbits in the *Republic*. The reason is that the vision described in the Republic is of intelligible motions presented directly to the soul; it is not embodied like the planets whose orbits become visible to the eye of the astronomical observer.

"Having lived in an orderly regime in his former life, participating in virtue by habit, without philosophy," Er reported, the first chose to be a tyrant without "noticing that eating his own children and other evils were fated to be a part of that life." When he saw what it actually entailed, this man lamented his hasty choice, but it was too late. Er also described the selections of future lives made by individuals named in the *Odyssey*. Angry over the loss of Achilles' armor, Ajax decided to become a lion rather than a man; Agamemnon chose to become an eagle. Not wanting to be generated from a woman, Orpheus chose the life of a swan. Other musicians selected other birds; swans and musical animals decided to become human. "By chance," Er concluded, "Odysseus' soul had drawn the last lot and went to choose. From memory of its former labors it had recovered from love of honor, so it looked for a long time for the life of a private man who minds his own business, and with effort found one" (620c). Readers of the *Republic* would remember that Socrates had defined justice earlier as minding one's own business.

The "moral" Socrates draws from Er's story does not concern the rewards and punishments human beings receive after death so much as the responsibility each has for the shape and direction of his own life. And that moral reflects a central fact of human existence that does not depend upon Socrates' problematic assertion of the immortality of the soul. Even if our souls are not immortal, each of us is constrained and shaped by the particular place, family, and regime into which we are born, as well as by our particular natural inclinations or talents and experience. But within these constraints each of us still has the power to choose. The effective "moral" of his story, Socrates thus concludes, is that "each of us must . . . above all . . . seek to learn . . . who will give him the capacity to distinguish the good and the bad life" (618b–c). And that person, Socrates suggests, is a philosopher who seeks to discover what is truly good and beautiful. It is not, as Homer's description of the blind singer in the *Odyssey* suggests, a poet.

But, readers might object: Didn't Er (and hence Socrates) acknowledge that at least one of Homer's heroes had learned how to choose? Shouldn't the *Odyssey*, if not the *Iliad,* then be admitted to provide the necessary education? To understand Socrates' expulsion of the poets, we have to examine the ways in which he seems to agree, and yet disagrees, with Homer a bit further.

According to Er, "from memory of its former labors, . . . Odysseus' soul had recovered from love of honor . . . [and] so looked for the life of a private man who minds his own business" (620c). Because minding one's own business was the definition of justice Socrates gave earlier in the *Republic* (433a), it would appear that Odysseus had learned to be just from his travels and homecoming. The question that first arises, however, is whether Er has correctly stated the moral or teaching of Homer's epic. In the *Odyssey* we hear an account of the hero's trip to Hades where he learns from a variety of shades that the most important and satisfying aspects of human life are to be found in the mutual understanding and sympathy of those closest to us—parents, wives, and children. As members of a family, Homer suggests, human beings not only share the experience of birth and death; we consciously live in the face of it. In both his epics the poet shows that knowing we must die forces human beings to choose who and what is most important to us. (These choices are analogous to the selection of a way of life that Er reports souls make before they are reborn.) If our lives were unending, we would not have to choose or hence to know the good and the bad of human existence. Like the Homeric gods, immortal human beings would be childlike, irresponsible, and immoral; we would, as the sophists urged, willfully seek to maximize our own pleasure. But Homer shows that, when given an opportunity to live forever in apparent bliss with the nymph Calypso, Odysseus chooses, as a result of what he learned in Hades, to return to Penelope. The epic poet thus indicates that love and friendship (as opposed to sexual union, pleasure, or ecstasy) are possible only on the basis of the mutual understanding and consequent trust that develops on the basis of a shared experience of living in the face of death.[18] It is our foreknowledge of our inescapable demise and consequent separation that makes us cherish our love and loved ones. Because everything that comes into being must also fade, however, Homer also lets his audience

---

18 When Odysseus returns to Ithaca and is greeted by Athena, we thus see him accept her claim that she has been with him the whole time, that they are two of a kind, and that she, therefore, loves and helps him without question. A prudent mortal does not challenge the truthfulness of an immortal—even concerning their differences. Cf. *Odyssey* 13.313–423. By way of contrast, at her urging we subsequently see him test the truthfulness and loyalty of all the members of his family and household.

know that Odysseus cannot simply return home to stay. In Hades Tiresias tells the hero that he will have to leave Ithaca again and travel to a place where they know nothing of the sea. When he meets a man who mistakes an oar for a winnowing fan, he must plant the oar as an offering to Poseidon. Odysseus will thus recognize his debt to the god of the sea. It was Poseidon's persecution that forced Odysseus to undertake his ten years of travel, through which he acquired his education about the good and bad of human existence, and finally recovered from his love of honor. Then and only then could Odysseus return home and die in peace and prosperity.[19]

In the Platonic dialogues we see that Socrates agrees with Homer that what is truly good is to be found in and through private friendships. Socrates insists, however, that these friendships have to be based not merely on shared experience of our mortality or—as in the case of both of Homer's heroes—dedicated to an accumulation of wealth and fame to bestow upon our heirs. In arguing that guardians should not be exposed to the description Homer gives of Hades and the lives of the shades, because it would sap their courage, Socrates had objected first and foremost to the shade of Achilles telling Odysseus that "I would rather be on the soil, a serf to another, to a man . . . whose means of life are not great than rule over all the dead who have perished" (*Odyssey* 11.489–91; *Republic* 386c). That very statement might be read to show that Achilles also had "recovered from love of honor" (as would his response to the ambassadors from Agamemnon in Book 9 of the *Iliad*). However, Homer also reports that, in light of the news of the glorious achievements of his son, Achilles walked away from his encounter with Odysseus in Hades happy. And in the *Iliad*, Homer shows that, although Achilles denied that the honor and wealth Agamemnon promised was worth risking his life for, he nevertheless re-entered the battle later. Knowing that he would die, he chose to avenge the death of his beloved friend Patroclus. Nor does Homer show Odysseus returning to Ithaca merely to be re-united with his family, any more than he had showed that Achilles returned to Phthia as he threatened. Odysseus returned to reclaim his kingdom. And in order to regain his position, Homer lets us see at the end of the poem, Odysseus had not merely slaughtered all the suitors who sought to replace him; he would have killed virtually all his fellow

19   *Odyssey* 11.120–37.

citizens, when they attacked him to avenge the deaths of their sons, if the wise Athena had not intervened. As Plato reminds his readers in other Socratic dialogues, most of those who heard the Homeric epics recited did not conclude that the private life was best. On the contrary, Achilles and Odysseus were taken to embody "heroic" virtues, including dedication to the search for honor, political pre-eminence, and wealth.[20]

In his "myth of Er" Socrates points both to a deeper reading of Homer and to a deep disagreement with the epic poet. Socrates agrees with Homer that the desire animating the best human beings is not merely a desire to overcome death by winning fame. Even less is it a desire to avoid pain or to maximize pleasure. It is a desire to be understood both for what we are and what we are not—and yet still to be loved. Human beings do not bond or stay together over time merely out of fear or greed. We do not simply try to avoid the bad; we positively admire the beautiful and seek the good. Insofar as we possess self-knowledge, we recognize that as mortals we will never be perfect. We do not come to understand our imperfections merely in light of the inevitable end of our own existence and yearning to negate, if not to overcome it. We positively long for a qualitatively better, more satisfying way of life and join with others in an attempt to achieve it. We love and are loved not so much for our achievements as for our aspirations. Because we are mortal creatures, the striving to improve our lives is necessarily ongoing and unending. It is, Socrates insists, an effort to improve, not merely to preserve or defend. Improvement requires knowledge not only of our limitations; it also depends upon our having an intimation, if not a full-blown vision, of what is truly good and beautiful. In contrast to the dumb shades Odysseus encountered in Hades, the souls in Socrates' myth of Er are thus given a view of the beautiful, because intelligible, order of the cosmos before they choose the specific form of their future existence and are reborn.[21]

20 Such a reading of Homer is by no means limited to ancient authors. Cf. Arendt, *Human Condition*, 8–9, 19, 24–25, and Alasdair MacIntyre, *After Virtue* (Notre Dame: University of Notre Dame Press, 1984), 2nd ed., 121–30.

21 These reflections on the disagreement between Socrates and Homer concerning the good and bad of human life help explain two of the distinctive features of the dialogue in which Socrates explicitly takes up the question with which he concludes the *Republic*: what is the good life for us? In the *Philebus*

The "myth of Er," I conclude, is a typically Socratic form of poetry or "fiction"—a likely tale concerning two subjects of which no mortal can have first-hand or certain knowledge—the soul and the afterlife. In his dialogues, Plato also shows that other philosophers, Timaeus and the Eleatic Stranger, as well as the self-proclaimed "sophist" Protagoras, relate other kinds of "myths" about the origins of the cosmos and human society—two other subjects about which no human being can have first-hand knowledge or certainty. Plato's dialogues represent a more comprehensive type of "poetry" or imitation than the Homeric epics, however, because they include arguments based on purely intelligible concepts or ideas in addition to "myths" or stories and imitations or images of a variety of different kinds of human beings. The speeches and deeds of these human beings are not presented in verse, because Plato did not want to appeal to the feelings or sensibilities of his readers so much as to provoke them to think. He wrote dialogues rather than treatises in which he presented several different philosophic voices or positions, because he understood that human beings have to seek knowledge of the whole, but he was not sure that anyone had or could achieve such a comprehensive view. In opposition to the poets and philosophers who preceded him, he insisted that there are purely intelligible, unchanging, and thus eternal forms of being. But he never presented an all-inclusive list or entirely consistent lists of these beings or "ideas": nor did he (nor any of his philosophers) explain how the purely intelligible beings are related to one another or how sensible forms of existence "participate" in them. In sum, Plato was a distinctive kind of poet or imitator, because he was a distinctive kind of philosopher. He was a seeker of wisdom who had more than an intimation of the kind of knowledge he sought, but recognized that he had not entirely achieved it and doubted that anyone else could.

the discussion of the question is shown to be ongoing. Socrates and Philebus are first said to have been debating the issue before the dialogue begins. The discussion between Socrates and Protarchus is then said to continue after the dialogue ends. Jacob Klein emphasizes the lack of beginning or end to the conversation in "About Plato's *Philebus*," *Interpretation*, 2/ 3 (Spring 1972): 157–82, as does Seth Benardete, *The Tragedy and Comedy of Life: Plato's PHILEBUS* (Chicago: University of Chicago Press, 1993), 87–88.

Shaftesbury and Plato on How to Write
Abraham Anderson

We tend to think of Plato as an author who is interesting—or not—because of the content of his views; because he proposed and argued for certain doctrines about knowledge, or virtue, or justice.[1] Sometimes we find him objectionable, because he seems to us "metaphysical" and dogmatic, in contrast to the good Socrates with his humble avowal of ignorance. This way of reading Plato has had three effects. First, readers have sought to establish a doctrine for Plato, normally some version of the "theory of Forms." Second, scholars since the early nineteenth century have sought to correct the traditional canon of Plato's writings by excluding, among those that were not attested by Aristotle as Platonic, dialogues whose doctrine seemed to contradict that of those known to be authentic. It is hard not to see in this undertaking a resemblance to the purging of the Biblical Canon by the Protestant Churches in the sixteenth century.[2]

Third, even among the dialogues admitted to be Platonic, a distinction

---

1   The "we" used in the early pages of this essay is not meant to correspond to the readers of the present volume, but to those who hold opinions about Plato, Socrates, Shaftesbury, Xenophon, and philosophy generally standard in modern universities.

2   On the modern revision of the Platonic canon, see Thomas L. Pangle, ed., *The Roots of Political Philosophy: Ten Forgotten Socratic Dialogues* (Ithaca: Cornell University Press, 1987), editor's introduction. In "The Origins of our Present Paradigms," C. C. W. Taylor notes that "One of the earliest [major German Platonic scholars of the nineteenth century], Ast 1816, recognizes only fourteen dialogues as authentic." See *New Perspectives on Plato, Modern and Ancient*, ed. Julia Annas and Christopher Rowe, Center for Hellenic Studies Colloquia 6 (Trustees for Harvard University, Washington, D.C., distributed by Harvard University Press, Cambridge, Mass., and London, England, 2002), 77.

has been made between those—the "early" dialogues—that portrayed Socrates as posing questions about virtue, but not making metaphysical assertions or advancing a "theory of Forms"; those—the "middle" dialogues—in which this theory was elaborated by Plato and put in the mouth of Socrates—and those—the "late" dialogues—which on the view of some seemed to criticize this doctrine, and which in any case moved away from the literary and moral drama of the middle dialogues.[3]

The view that what characterized Plato was his doctrine—his theory of Forms—has a source in Aristotle. Aristotle assigns a doctrine of Forms to Plato, and indeed gives it more definiteness than do Plato's Dialogues. Socrates, on the other hand, Aristotle identifies with the doctrine that knowledge is virtue, but not with a teaching on the Forms. But the nineteenth- and twentieth-century contrast between Plato as dogmatic and mystical metaphysician-theologian and Socrates as humble moral teacher and investigator of virtue has a distinctively modern flavor. When we regard Plato as a metaphysician, we mean something next door to a Christian theologian. And the distinction between Socrates the investigator of virtue and Plato the mystical theologian cannot help reminding one of that between Jesus the moral teacher and Paul the theologian in nineteenth-century Bible criticism.[4]

The contrast between Socrates and Plato has also been thought to receive support from Socrates' supposition in the *Apology* that if the oracle called him the wisest of men, this was only because he was the only one who knew that he did not know; from his declaration in the *Theaetetus* that he is a midwife of the conceptions of others;[5] and from the contrast between

---

3   On these distinctions, see Julia Annas, "What Are Plato's 'Middle' Dialogues in the Middle Of?," esp. 1–4, in Annas and Rowe, *New Perspectives*. She criticizes these distinctions, which are defended in "Comments on Annas," by Dorothea Frede (25–35). Taylor, Inwood, Kahn, and Griswold, authors of other essays in that book, speak directly to these distinctions, objections to them, and responses to those objections, though the other essays in the volume are also relevant, particularly those by Blank, Gill, Penner, and Rowe.

4   On the distinction between Socrates and Plato, see Annas and Rowe, *New Perspectives*, especially the essays by Annas, Frede, Sedley, Blank, Taylor, Inwood, Penner, and Rowe.

5   David Sedley, in "Socratic Irony in the Platonist Commentators," discusses

Socrates' doctrine that no one ever chooses evil willingly and the doctrine of the tripartite soul in the *Republic* and *Phaedrus*, which asserts that one's desires can contradict one's reason.[6]

The view of Plato as a dogmatist has antecedents not just in Aristotle, but in the Cynics, the Epicureans, the Pyrrhonists, and the Middle and Neo-Platonists, but it is by no means universal in the tradition. In the New Academy, for example, Plato's notion of Forms was not thought of as a dogma or doctrine, and was held to be consistent with skepticism.[7] And it faces an important difficulty: if there was such a strong contrast between Socrates and Plato, the first characterized by a skeptical knowledge of ignorance and the latter by a dogmatic theory of Forms, how could Plato have put his teachings into the mouth of Socrates? After all, Plato himself is our chief source for the view of Socrates as characterized by refutation of positive views and the knowledge of ignorance. How can he have portrayed Socrates in this way, and yet still have used him to present the teaching on the Forms, if Socratic ignorance is incompatible with the Platonic treatment of the Forms? How can he have used Socrates as his mouthpiece if the treatment of the Forms is really dogmatic? Those who hold that Plato was not a dogmatist call attention to the dialogue character of his writings, and the fact that he is not himself a character in any of them. These facts, they argue, mean that we cannot assign any view to Plato directly, at least on the basis of the Dialogues. The dialogue character of Plato's writings also, it has been thought, supports the view that he was not a dogmatist, but a

different interpretations of the midwife passage in Cicero, in the anonymous *Theaetetus* commentator, and in Antiochus of Ascalon (Annas and Rowe, *New Perspectives,* 48), none of whom, however, wished to dissociate Socrates from Plato.

6   On the relation between Socrates and Plato and views on this relation in older and newer secondary literature, see Annas and Rowe, *New Perspectives,* esp. Annas, Frede, Penner, Rowe.

7   On the New Academy see Sedley in Annas and Rowe, *New Perspectives,* 48. See also Annas's discussion on 5–6 of the view of Plutarch and the anonymous *Theaetetus* commentator that "'there is only one Academy'—that is, that there was a continuous tradition from Plato encompassing both the skeptical Academics and the later doctrinal Platonists." For a discussion of ancient views of Platonism, see Lloyd P. Gerson, "What Is Platonism?," *Journal of the History of Philosophy,* 43 (2005): 253–76.

skeptic who does not assert any doctrine but simply presents us with a free movement of discussion, the play of contrary views.[8] There is, of course, the evidence of the Letters; but the Second Letter (314c) contradicts the view that the Dialogues teach doctrine. Precisely for this reason, those who regard Plato as a dogmatist often reject the authenticity of the Second Letter.

Reflection on our reading of Plato therefore allows us to test our conception of philosophy itself—that it is primarily doctrine. I propose to read Shaftesbury's account of, and reception of, Plato as a way of testing our views on Plato and philosophy. In order to do this, however, we must begin by forgetting our own views, and allow ourselves to get a sense of Shaftesbury's. Only then will we be able to make a proper comparison.

Because of the time and place in which he lived, we might assume that Shaftesbury read Plato anachronistically; that he read him as a "Platonist," i.e., as a Neo-Platonist, in the manner of the seventeenth-century Cambridge Platonists.[9] We might be tempted to think that Shaftesbury must therefore have missed our careful distinctions between an ironical and non-dogmatic Socrates and a dogmatic and metaphysical Plato, and that Shaftesbury's "idealism" means that he could not help but make this mistake. But in fact his reading of Plato overlaps in interesting ways with our own, though it also differs from it.

The first thing that strikes us about Shaftesbury's treatment of Plato is that it is not unambiguously admiring. On the contrary, Shaftesbury appears to have a certain ambivalence towards Plato. Or rather, his posture actually seems to be more critical than admiring—and in a way much like our own. For he seems to value Socrates for his good-hearted humor, his lack of pretension, while he seems to mistrust Plato for his tragical or "sublime" character. Plato is too high-flown. For this reason, Shaftesbury

---

8   For the classic representation of the New Academy, which understood Plato in this way, see Cicero, *Academica*.

9   On the relation between Shaftesbury and the Cambridge Platonists, see Dirk Grossklaus, *Natürliche Religion und aufgeklärte Gesellschaft: Shaftesburys Verhältnis zu den Cambridge Platonists* (Heidelberg: Universitätsverlag C. Winter, 1998). On the neo-Platonism of the latter, see, e.g., 177, 233.

appears to prefer Xenophon, whom he speaks of as taking "the genteeler part."[10]

Now this response to Plato is both familiar and unfamiliar to us. The criticism of Plato as tragical and sublime reminds us not just of our own mistrust of Plato as a "metaphysician" and dogmatist, but of Nietzsche's

10   Anthony Ashley Cooper, Third Earl of Shaftesbury, *Characteristicks of Men, Manners, Opinions, Times*, Foreword by Douglas den Uyl (Indianapolis: Liberty Fund, 2001); I, 254–55. (See also III, 247–48.) The page numbers used in these footnotes for references to the *Characteristicks* are not those of the Liberty Fund edition, but those used by Shaftesbury himself when making reference to passages from the *Characteristicks* in the notes, and which correspond to the 1714 edition. These were reproduced in the 1732 edition which forms the basis of the Liberty Fund edition, and are given in the margins of the Liberty Fund edition. (Searchable pdfs of each of the three volumes of that edition are available for free download from the Liberty Fund website.) For the association between Plato and tragedy, which is only hinted at, see the notes to I, 252–53.

   Lawrence Klein, reporting on Shaftesbury's notebook on Socrates, the "Design of a Socratick History" (PRO, 30/24/27/14), says that "Shaftesbury criticizes Plato for 'drawing Socrates into Metiphysical and Theological Notions' which Shaftesbury perceived as suiting Plato's philosophical ends but not as representing Socrates historically"; Lawrence E. Klein, *Shaftesbury and the Culture of Politeness* (Cambridge: Cambridge University Press, 1994), 108. Socrates was rather a "civic philosopher" who is more accurately portrayed by Xenophon.

   The manuscript is discussed in more detail by Laurent Jaffro in "Which Platonism for Which Modernity? A Note on Shaftesbury's Socratic Sea-Cards," in *Platonism at the Origins of Modernity*, ed. Douglas Hedley and Sarah Hutton (Springer Netherlands, 2008), 255–67. Jaffro describes in the "Design of a Socratick History" the contrast between the simple style of Xenophon and the sublime and metaphysical style of Plato which Klein speaks of, a contrast which Shaftesbury makes in "Advice to an Author" (Hedley & Hutton, *Platonism*, 256–63). The "Design of a Socratick History" is in the Shaftesbury papers at the Public Records Office, London, under the number PRO, 30/24/27/14. It can be found in *Cooper, Anthony Ashley, Third Earl of Shaftesbury, Standard Edition: Complete Works, Selected Letters and Posthumous Writings, in English with German Translation*, ed. W. Benda, G. Hemmerich, W. Lottes, et al. (Stuttgart: Frommann-Holzboog, II. Moral and Political Philosophy Band 5, Chartae Socraticae: Design of a Socratick History, 2007).

mention, in *Beyond Good and Evil*, of Epicurus' characterization of Plato as a "dionysiokolax," a lick-spittle of Dionysus—that is, of tyrants.[11] Plato had frequented the court of Dionysus, tyrant of Syracuse, and Epicurus is accusing him of being a flatterer of that tyrant. But this characterization, Nietzsche explains, is associated with the view of Plato as an actor; "Dionysiokolakes" was a nickname for actors, since drama was dedicated to the god Dionysus. Epicurus is accusing him of making philosophy theatrical and high-flown in a way that flatters the pretensions of tyrants and their love of the magnificent, and of being a flatterer of the desire for glory. Philosophy should on the contrary be retiring and unpretentious.

Now, while we can tell that Nietzsche's view of Epicurus is not without irony—he speaks of him as "the little garden god," and appears to suggest that Epicurus' criticism of Plato was based partly on envy and resentment of Plato's ability as a poet and at capturing the imagination of his readers— we can also tell that Nietzsche to some extent shares Epicurus' irony towards Plato's inclination towards the dramatic and the high-flown, which he associates with Plato's "moralism," which in turn he associates with Plato's "spirituality," his assertion of "soul" or of a world behind the world of appearance. Nietzsche, on the contrary, denies that there is such a world, and rejects the assertion of it as a piece of dogmatism grounded in a love of moral purity; as he associates the very idea of truth embodied in the notion of Forms as a byproduct of this same moralism.[12]

Now while we can tell that there is a good deal in *Beyond Good and Evil* that we do not agree with—its attacks on democracy, on feminism, on modern scholarship as an expression of the democratic spirit—we also feel that this criticism of Plato is something we can agree with. We too are inclined to think that Plato's doctrine of Forms is an expression of a desire for moral purity, though we reject it on grounds that are more explicitly democratic than Nietzsche's: it implies a priestly elitism, a sharp distinction between those who know the truth and those who do not; it fosters the illusory belief in an immortal soul, which again seems to us both pretentious and moralistic,

11   Friedrich Nietzsche, *Beyond Good and Evil*, in *Basic Writings of Nietzsche*, trans. and edited, with Commentaries, by Walter Kaufmann (New York: Modern Library, 1968) #7, 204.

12   Ibid., Preface, 193.

and tending towards an authoritarian doctrine which claims to secure the good of that soul—tending, that is, towards Christian theology of the more dogmatic sort. We find the notion of "truth" troubling for the same reason, unless it is reduced to the most unpretentious form—say, the principle that "snow is white" is true if and only if snow is white—and stripped of all associations with a transcendent standard of judgment and morals.[13]

But Shaftesbury not only criticizes Plato for his tragical or sublime tone and manner; he contrasts him unfavorably with Xenophon. What, we want to ask, can possibly be meant by that? One way to answer this question would be by taking our clue from the term Shaftesbury uses to praise Xenophon: he is "genteeler" than Plato. We now think we see what he is about: Shaftesbury likes Xenophon because he is "gentlemanly," because he provides a form of Socratism compatible with the beliefs of good military men, sober country gentlemen, etc. But now our interest in Shaftesbury and his reading of Plato suffers a serious decline. We are not ourselves used to taking Xenophon seriously, nor certainly any account of Socrates adjusted to the preconceptions of soldiers and country gentlemen. We are used to thinking of Xenophon as a rough fellow who understood little of Socrates, and took him simply as a sound moral teacher, and who failed to notice that Socrates raised any questions about knowledge or the justification of one's views about morals—i.e., that he philosophized.[14]

And even if we ourselves are attracted to the view that Socrates was more a "moral philosopher" than a "metaphysician"—that he was more concerned to figure out what was right than what was true, and therefore less inclined to authoritarian doctrines about Absolute Truth—we are still concerned to hold on to the notion of philosophy as something that involves argument and demands for justification. And in this respect, Xenophon falls short. Shaftesbury's praise of Xenophon therefore seems to confirm a

13 See Anthony Gottlieb, "The Truth Wars," *New York Times Book Review*, Sunday, July 24, 2005, a review of Simon Blackburn, *Truth: A Guide* (Oxford: Oxford University Press, 2005) and Michael P. Lynch, *True to Life: Why Truth Matters* (Cambridge: Bradford Book/MIT, 2005).

14 On the modern view of Xenophon, see Klein, in *Shaftesbury and the Culture of Politeness*, 44. On Shaftesbury's view of Xenophon in the "Design for a Socratick History," ibid., 107–11; see also Jaffro's "Which Platonism for Which Modernity," 259–61, 264.

standard view of Shaftesbury himself: that he was not a philosopher, but a literary man, or a belle-lettrist; a great lord who dabbled in learning and the "beaux-arts," and whose dilettantish character is clear from the essayistic and scattered character of his writing, so different from the earnest and scrupulous systematic approach of a Hutcheson or, even better, a Richard Price. This view, be it noted, is not a new one; it goes back to Mandeville and, a bit later, to Thomas Brown's *Essays On the Characteristics*, a work of great influence in the eighteenth century, and which Mill in his *Autobiography* mentions as one of the books most important to the formation of his mind.

What, then? Was Shaftesbury just a great lord who dabbled in literature, and who lacked the professional concentration and scrupulousness of the true academic philosopher, who alone has the patience to write soberly and scientifically? Was he just a playful dilettante?

Perhaps. But it should be noted that this does not seem to have been the view of Leibniz and Montesquieu, Hume[15] and Rousseau, Kant and Schiller,[16] Mendelssohn and Herder,[17] all of whom took Shaftesbury rather seriously as a thinker—though the respect of some of these authors will not weigh very heavily with us as evidence of Xenophon's being a philosopher, since we think of them, too, as literary men rather than philosophers. And Kant's attitude is not unambiguously respectful.[18] But at least

---

15 See, e.g., David Hume, *Enquiry Concerning the Principles of Morals*, in Enquiries Concerning the Human Understanding and Concerning the Principles of Morals [1777], ed. Lewis Amherst Selby-Bigge (Oxford: Clarendon Press, 2nd edition, 1963), reproduced in Online Library of Liberty, Section I, 134.

16 See Fabienne Brugère, *Théorie de l'art et philosophie de la sociabilité chez Shaftesbury* (Paris: Honoré Champion, 1999), 359–62.

17 See, e.g., Johann Gottfried Herder, *Einige Gespräche über Spinoza's System nebst Shaftesbury's Naturhymnus* (Gotha: Ettinger, 1787).

18 Kant's most unambiguous praise of Shaftesbury is in the program for his courses for the winter semester of 1765–66, where he speaks of Shaftesbury as one of those who have done most to advance our understanding of the foundations of all morality (Ak. 2:311). In the Inaugural Dissertation, however, Shaftesbury is criticized as an Epicurean (Ak. 2:396). The essay on the use of teleological principles in philosophy, Ak. 8:39–84, which was written while Kant was formulating the project of the *Critique of Judgment*, seems influenced by Shaftesbury. So does the *Dreams of a Spirit Seer* Ak. 2:311–73 and Kant's

Leibniz[19] and Hume should be taken seriously. Oddly enough, or perhaps not surprisingly, a number of the thinkers I have just listed also took Xenophon himself seriously; one has only to think of Rousseau's citation of him in the *Discourse on the Sciences and the Arts*.[20] But that work too will seem to many specialists in philosophy a mere literary exercise.

But what of our distinction between philosophy and literature itself? Is this distinction fully clear and justified? Are we right to assume to know what each is, and what the difference between them is, and what we should look for in each?

Here, perhaps, we arrive at the nub of the matter. It turns out that Shaftesbury himself was perfectly aware of this distinction, or something rather close, in pretty much the form we make it; and that when he wrote as he did this was not the result of mere incapacity for philosophy or a frivolous preference for the prettiness of literature, nor because of an imagination which drew him more than his intellect, but resulted from a conscious philosophical view about how to write. Shaftesbury's interest in and reading of Plato has everything to do with this view, which both informed his reading of Plato and was informed by it. What was that view?

Shaftesbury on How to Write

In "A Letter Concerning Enthusiasm," Shaftesbury begins by wondering about the way ancient poets dedicated their poems to the Muses. Modern

letter to Mendelssohn of 8 April 1766, Ak. 10:69–73. References to Kant's works are to Akademie Textausgabe, Berlin: Walter de Gruyter & Co., and the reference to Kant's correspondence is to the Akademie Edition as reproduced in Kant im Kontext II, Werke, Briefwechsel, u. Nachlass, Komplettausgabe, published by Karsten Worm, 2005. See also Herder's remark in the Viertes Wäldchen of the *Kritische Wälder*, where Kant is spoken of as a German Shaftesbury; cited by Brugère, *Théorie de l'art*, 9. On the relation between Kant and Shaftesbury, see Jean-Pierre Larthomas, *De Shaftesbury à Kant* (Paris: Didier Érudition, 1985). For this and other matters, see also the select bibliography of works by and about Shaftesbury by Laurent Jaffro. http://jaffro.net/Shaftesbury.htm last updated August 19, 2004.

19 On Leibniz's reception of Shaftesbury, see Brugère, *Théorie de l'art.*, 365–66.
20 Jean Jacques Rousseau, *Discours sur les sciences et les arts, Oeuvres complètes* (Paris: Gallimard, 1964), vol. 3, p. 25

poets imitate these dedications, but these imitations are flat and unconvincing. Why is this? What is it about modern writing that makes it implausible to dedicate a poem to a Muse? Shaftesbury suggests that it is this: the ancients thought that poetry was something divine; that it contained truth or wisdom. "We Christians," on the contrary, think that no one could have faith in the Muses or in poetry;[21] faith, we think, can be directed only to the teaching of the Bible. But Plato, it turns out, agreed with the ancient poets to the extent of thinking that all great things, even philosophy, came from "enthusiasm" or the feeling of inspiration, though by "enthusiasm" he meant not literal inspiration but the "sublime in human Passions," as Shaftesbury puts it.[22] This raises interesting questions about the proper character of philosophical writing. It makes one wonder whether such writing should be more like poetry than like a treatise, because it has to evoke and begin from enthusiasm in order to lead the reader to philosophical thought.

But if the "Letter" is concerned with the value of enthusiasm, it is at least equally concerned with the means of moderating it. In the "Letter," Shaftesbury argues that ridicule is an essential test of doctrines—even and particularly of grave doctrines, doctrines about religion and morals.[23] In "Sensus Communis, or, an Essay Concerning the Freedom of Wit and Humour," Shaftesbury addresses objections to this proposal by asking: is it permissible for us to use ridicule about ourselves?[24] That is, are we allowed to use laughter to test the truth of things we ourselves take as sacred? There is a difficulty, he goes on to explain, faced by the moderns that was not faced by the ancients.[25] The moderns, he says, are compelled to wear a mask, because of the prevalence among us of the demand for adherence to a received opinion—he is clearly thinking of Christian orthodoxy. This forces modern authors, when they wish to write freely, to imitate the people of Italy, who in order to release the tension that comes from living under an Inquisition engage in buffoonery.[26] He speaks also of the masks worn at a

---

21 *Characteristicks*, I, 6.
22 I, 53.
23 I, 10–12, cf. 19–20, 22–23, 28.
24 I, 60.
25 I, 83–84; see also I, 73–75
26 I, 71–73.

carnival in Paris or Venice; if an Ethiopian were to laugh at these because of their unnaturalness, he would be right; but if, when the masks came off, he were to laugh at the white skin of the inhabitants as unnatural because he had never seen it before, he would be wrong.[27] From the fact that one is surrounded by unnaturalness, it is wrong to conclude that there is no such thing as nature. Shaftesbury's remark, it soon becomes clear, is about Hobbes: Hobbes has been led by his fear and horror for the artifice with which the spirit of enthusiasm is raised and conducted to conclude that there is no such thing as nature. That is, he has been led by the unnaturalness of the use of religion around him to conclude that religion is never anything but an artifice on the part of rulers or priests.[28]

Hobbes has attacked the effects of Christianity on human politics as unnatural, and rightly; but because Christianity has inherited and made some use of ancient teachings, Hobbes also rejects the latter as unnatural, and denies in fact that there is any standard of "the natural."[29] The modern hostility to the prejudices and distortions imposed on human nature by theological orthodoxy, and the anger and fear these distortions inspire in us when we begin to see them as alien impositions, may lead us to deny that there is such a thing as a natural standard of fitness or the fine. Because he thought this, Hobbes undertook to "new-frame the human Heart," using simpler and more convenient materials—that is, replacing the understanding of human beings as beings inspired by the "divine" (whether understood as something supernatural or as something natural) with an understanding of them as simply selfish, and of all teachings about the divine as simply illusions or cheats.[30] But Hobbes' solution is unsatisfactory, because it does not allow us to understand where these illusions or cheats came from, or how they are grounded in nature.[31] For it cannot be the case that humans

27 I, 82–85.

28 I, 88–90.

29 On the denial that there is such a thing as the morally natural, see I, 84–85. On the rejection of the ancients because of their association with Christianity, see I, 86. That these remarks apply to Hobbes becomes clear on I, 88-89, and particular the last footnote to 88, where Shaftesbury refers to Hobbes by name.

30 I, 115–17; see also 90.

31 Cf. I, 117–19.

are simply selfish: Hobbes' own desire to warn us against the dangerous beliefs in charity or republican virtue seems itself to spring from a philanthropy whose existence contradicts his own account of human nature.[32]

Shaftesbury proposes to treat both Biblical melancholy and fanaticism,[33] and Hobbes' melancholy reaction against it, by cultivating a "sensus communis" or shared sense of public good; this, he holds, can best be cultivated by "the freedom of wit and humour," which allows us to "test" doctrines with the test of ridicule. In his story about the Ethiopian, as well as in the "Letter," Shaftesbury argues that laughter can help free us of the gloomy earnestness associated with an enforced orthodoxy. Might laughter be an indispensable effect of philosophical writing or philosophical thought, indispensable because it alone can free us not just of particular dogmas but of our tendency to dogmatism? Shaftesbury's remarks about Hobbes raise a further question: can philosophy be characterized not just by its ability to produce laughter, but by the kind of laughter it produces—the laughter, for example, arising from Hobbesian satire against religion, or on the other hand the laughter produced by Shaftesbury's "Sensus communis," which, while it seeks to defend Hobbes, seeks also to calm the Hobbesian fear of fanaticism?

The project of treating both Christian enthusiasm and Hobbes' reaction to it brings us to the third treatise, "Soliloquy, or, Advice to an Author," and with it to the question of writing and Plato. Here Shaftesbury begins from the problem of "advice." The difficulty with advice, he tells us, is that usually those who give it, not those who receive it, seem to be the true gainers, since in giving it the former display their own wisdom and authority at the expense of the latter.[34]

After reading "Sensus Communis," one cannot help supposing that the "advice" Shaftesbury has in mind is not just everyday advice but also, and above all, theological "advice," that is, authoritative teaching, such as is delivered in sermons and enforced through burnings at the stake. The enforced passivity of mind resulting from this sort of "advice," which is tied in turn to the existence of an obligatory opinion, results in the contortions

32 I, 89–90.
33 On this fanaticism, see I, 26–30.
34 I, 153–54.

spoken of in "Sensus Communis."[35] It is, in Shaftesbury's view, destructive of reason, political freedom, and naturalness; in particular, it destroys a natural sense of humor and of the ridiculous, and with it a natural sense of the fine or fitting. The Christian attempt to redeem the world, or rather to redeem humanity from the world, is profoundly opposed to the free unfolding of human nature and the human faculties.[36]

The ancient poets, Shaftesbury said, who were reputed wise, had a way of giving advice which had the advantage of not seeming to do so; he cannot say how they lost their pretension to wisdom.[37] Of course, he has already told us; they lost it because of the authority of Christian revelation.[38] Shaftesbury seems to wish to revive the way of the ancient poets over the Christian way of imparting a doctrine "in form." Shaftesbury seeks to defend the claims of poetry as a means of moral instruction.[39]

Shaftesbury disagrees with Christian practice in another way. Against the Christian conception of "advice" as sermon, catechism, or theological doctrine, Shaftesbury favors free give-and-take. "Must I always be a listener only?" he had asked in "Sensus Communis," citing Juvenal.[40] He considers the objection that it cannot be reasonable to mock or contest what has been established by reason,[41] i.e., Christian theology, insofar as it claims to ground itself in philosophy and natural reason. To this he answers that according to his conception of reason, what it consists in above all is freedom of mind, and the greatest danger to it is "formalism" and "gravity." "*Gravity*," he had said in the "Letter," "is of the very Essence of Imposture."[42] The

---

35   I, 71–73, cf. 83–84.
36   See Shaftesbury's ironical discussion of Christian meditation and the "*Task-Reading*" associated with it, "in which a TASTE is not permitted." I, 343.
37   I, 155.
38   See the "Letter," e.g. I, 6–7.
39   See, e.g., I, 193–98 (though here the subject of the moral value of poetry is mingled with the discussion of the relation between poetry and philosophy), 206–09, 250–51, 258–59, 269n, 275–77, 315–17, 328–29, 332–42, 357–58, III, 205–06, 230–33, 285. This defense includes within it a defense of Socratic dialogue, since according to Shaftesbury Socratic dialogue is a form of poetic imitation (I, 193–94).
40   I, 70 and the note.
41   I, 69.
42   I, 11.

assumption of authority associated with solemn proclamations of doctrine, or with piety about articles of belief, is the greatest enemy of reason. It is particularly dangerous to reason, he will later propose, because it claims to appeal to reason; a false philosophy is especially destructive of freedom of mind because it takes the place of such freedom. It distracts us from the essential philosophical task of seeking self-knowledge and happiness by substituting for this something that seems to promise these things, but cannot give them.[43]

Christianity is characterized by what he will later call "the unnatural union of philosophy and religion."[44] It is because Christianity involves theology, and has done so, at the latest, since it incorporated the schools of philosophy of the neo-Platonics and Pythagoreans in late antiquity, that it is far more dangerous to freedom of mind than was ancient paganism. Ancient paganism could tolerate philosophy by its side, since they were not truly rivals. Christianity and philosophy, on the other hand, can easily come into conflict, because Christianity founds its authority on its claim to teach an obligatory doctrine. Christianity must therefore reject the free exercise of reason insofar as the latter threatens the orthodoxy Christianity seeks to enforce. This is at the core of the Christian rejection of nature: the most unnatural thing Christianity does is to impose an obligation on our thoughts, on reason itself.[45] This act of violence leads to the modern view that there is no nature in the ancient sense—no standard of truth or right in the world or the human mind without revelation.[46] It leads to the view,

---

43 See I, 286–90, where Shaftesbury alludes to scholastic theology, and I, 291, 294, 299–303, which has more to do with modern philosophy. On the defectiveness of modern philosophy, and its replacement of self-investigation with abstract doctrine, see I, 116–17, 286–94, 299–303, 333n., II, 185, 188–90, III, 159–61, 193–94, 211–16, 225–26. On the origins of "false philosophy" (in the form of patristic and scholastic theology, which like modern philosophy provides us with a system that takes the place of thought) see III, 79–82.

44 III, 80.

45 I, 83–84.

46 On the Christian denial that virtue is natural, cf. I, 97–98; on the effects of this denial on modern moral philosophy, cf. I, 123. According to Shaftesbury Epicurus differed from the modern teachers of selfishness in not holding that it was natural (I, 116–18). He therefore held that virtue was unnatural (since

held by modern philosophy, that there is nothing rational and intelligible about nature, except insofar as it is reconstructed by modern philosophy to make it easily comprehensible and manipulable.[47]

We now begin to see how Shaftesbury would have responded to our conception of philosophy, which informs our reading of Plato. From his point of view we are mistaken to think that philosophy first of all consists in doctrines, or in the attempt to establish doctrines. Rather, philosophy consists first of all in the free play of minds.[48] Philosophy should not seek to be authoritative—to achieve a doctrine which it can make compulsory for others, or which it can establish by means of a demonstration irresistible by the human mind. Instead, it can and must leave room for doubt and disagreement, even if it thinks that it will ultimately be possible to take account of all objections. For it recognizes that human minds are different, and that they cannot simply be remade in order to force them to accept what we have come to see as the truth.[49]

This view of philosophy goes with an acceptance of the possibility that there might be wisdom which might not be comprehensible to everyone. For example, Socrates may be wise, though he is mysterious to most of us.[50]

----

it required constraining nature). Christianity did not invent religious unnaturalness (cf. I, 48), which is rooted in human nature (I, 48–52), as Epicurus and Lucretius recognized. It did systematize it and dispose it to persecution, by uniting it (unnaturally) with philosophy (III, 79–82).

47 Cf. I, 116, II, 189–90, III, 160. The view that nature is not rational is naturally allied to the view that human reason is not natural, and that it can only be achieved through method and constraint.

48 II, 189.

49 On the dogmatism of modern philosophy, and its desire to remake human nature, see I, 116; II, 190; III, 160. On the diversity of human minds, see, e.g., I, 62–63, 83–84. On "*Moral* Science" as "*Self-converse*" rather than modern method, see I, 287–89.

50 I, 194–96. On Berkeley's criticism of Shaftesbury for accepting a gap between philosophical understanding and what is communicable to common sense, see Brugère, 264–81. On Shaftesbury on the general problem of whether philosophy can be communicated, see Laurent Jaffro, *Éthique de la communication et art d'écrire* (Paris: PUF, 1998), especially Introduction, 7–22. On Shaftesbury's doubts, see 9, 13.

The work of understanding Socrates may be long and arduous, and never fully completed. Further, it may involve a continual process of self-criticism and self-reconstruction. It may be that we have to "gain an eye" before we can see the truth; that it is not accessible to us as we now are, but that we must become different in order to grasp it. It may be that knowledge is virtue, not in the sense that it suffices to memorize a formula supposed to contain the truth in order to become good, but that we cannot actually gain knowledge about things, including ourselves, without undergoing a long and perhaps never-completed process of improvement in our whole souls, including our desires and sense of beauty.[51]

This would be odd if what we meant by "virtue" were simply conscientiousness in the ordinary moral sense. For it is hard to see how being conscientious in this sense—dutiful—can be either a necessary or a sufficient condition for grasping truth. It is also not easy to see how virtue can be a condition of grasping truth as truth is understood by modern science or modern scholarship, since modern science and scholarship conceive of truth precisely as what can be demonstrated, and thus made clear independently of the moral and imaginative dispositions of its auditors, though sober scrupulousness may be required for doing good scientific work.

It is easier to understand how virtue can be required for grasping truth if by truth we mean not simply "scientific" truth—what can be demonstrated to all who pay attention—but above all truth about the human good.[52] It makes sense to suppose that that might require virtue, not in the sense of religious conscientiousness or scientific sobriety but of an openness of mind opposed to the desire for an authoritative doctrine. Such a disposition might in turn require knowledge, particularly a knowledge of oneself[53]—and in particular a knowledge of ignorance, which purges us of dogmatism and opens us to curiosity.[54]

---

51   For discussions of a variety of such processes, in the individual and in societies, see I, 69–70, 156–57, 188–89, 142–45,148–62, 173–87, 205–10, II, 109.
52   I, 145–47, 353–55.
53   I, 170–71, 173–74, 204–05, 294–99, II, 236–38, 426–27, III, 158–59, 201–03, 204–06.
54   II, 189–91.

In Shaftesbury's first work, the "Inquiry Concerning Virtue and Merit," he had considered the question of whether virtue was necessarily dependent on faith—of whether, for example, there could be a virtuous atheist. He had argued that virtue did not depend directly on any opinion,[55] but on the affections as modified by habit and opinion—on "manners." Morals do not depend on true doctrine. This seems to mean that the task of moral philosophy is not primarily to provide us either with a theological grounding of duty, or with a substitute which appeals (like Hobbes' law of nature) to a science of human nature, nor with some more teleological doctrine of cosmic order. Insofar as moral philosophy is concerned with promoting virtue, it will seek to do so by speaking to the affections.[56]

Now we begin to suspect that Shaftesbury might not have failed to write systematically out of incapacity, but that he might have chosen quite deliberately to avoid the treatise-style in the pieces we have been considering. That Shaftesbury was not incapable of writing treatises is shown by the fact that the "Inquiry Concerning Virtue and Merit," which is included in the *Characteristicks,* is itself a treatise. The "Inquiry" is important to Shaftesbury for its arguments that morals are rooted in natural sociability. Shaftesbury describes the manner of the "Inquiry" as "methodic," and it is clear that this manner has its uses, in his view.[57] But Shaftesbury did not regard writing "in form" as fully adequate for treating "*Moral* Science," which in its essence is "*Self-converse*."[58] For this purpose he prefers dialogue,

55 II, 44–45.

56 II, 438–42. The aim of philosophy is not primarily the attainment of a true doctrine, but the cultivation of wisdom and virtue and the achievement of happiness. Philosophy is not a matter of making plans for the future of society, as in Hobbes—plans intended to capture public assent by their rational compellingness (see I, 116 on Hobbes as "projector," i.e., one with a scheme of reform). Nor is it a matter of mere theoria separate from the pursuit of moral virtue, as Aristotle suggests in his description of philosophy as contemplation at *Nicomachean Ethics* X, 7. On the relation of Shaftesbury's teaching that virtue is grounded in the affections rather than in dogma to Bayle's claim that atheists can be virtuous, see Jaffro, *Éthique de la communication*, 181, 207–208.

57 Cf. his discussion of the "methodick or scholastick Manner" (I, 256–57) and his characterization of the manner of the "Inquiry" as methodic (III, 284).

58 I, 287.

which does not subdue the reader to the authority of the author but teaches him to see himself as if in a mirror.[59]

What we really need to do, according to Shaftesbury, is to begin to question ourselves, which we can only do if we begin to become aware of what we think. The activity of doing this he calls "Soliloquy," and seems to model it on the soliloquies of Hamlet and the diary of Marcus Aurelius.[60] But the promotion of this activity is also, he says, the goal of writing philosophy in dialogues. In the Socratic dialogues, he tells us, there are two parts: the part of Socrates, the "perfect character," who is mysterious and veiled; and the "second characters," who all have their faults but also their distinctive characters, and whom we can more easily compare with ourselves. Socrates plays the part of a "better self," which we can try to gain for ourselves by questioning ourselves; the "second characters" show us actual human characters as they are, with all their flaws, and thereby allow us

59 See I, 201–02. In volume three of the *Characteristicks*, the "Miscellaneous Reflections," Shaftesbury adopts the persona of an anonymous critic to comment on his "treatises." Speaking as the critic, he tells us that "The Moralists," because it is a dialogue, is "an Undertaking of more weight" according to Shaftesbury's rules than the methodical "Inquiry" (III, 284–85). Cf. also III, 135–36, 189–91, 205–06 for some ironical comments on the grave manner of the "Inquiry."

60 For Shaftesbury's initial discussion of "Soliloquy," see "Advice to an Author," I, 153–93. On *Hamlet*, see I, 275–76. On the Stoic roots of Shaftesbury's notion of soliloquy, and on his debt to Marcus in particular, see Jaffro, *Éthique de la communication* and *Exercices*. In his account of soliloquy, Shaftesbury is particularly anxious to avoid anything recalling Christian admonition or meditation. "Whatever Manner in Philosophy happens to bear the least resemblance to that of Catechism, cannot, I'm persuaded, of it-self, prove very inviting. Such a smart way of questioning our-selves in our Youth, has made our Manhood more averse to the expostulatory Discipline." I, 306. This applies particularly to the moderns. "I naturally call to mind the extreme Delicacy and Tenderness of modern Appetites, in respect of the *Philosophy* of this kind [self-examination]. What Distaste possibly may have arisen from some medicinal Doses of a like nature, administer'd to raw Stomachs, at a very early age, I will not pretend to examine." (I, 306, just above the passage I quoted first.) Cf. also I, 173–74, 163–64, where he contrasts soliloquy with memoir-writing, and 164–65, where he contrasts it with writings by religious self-examiners; on the reading of religious meditation as "*Task*-Reading," see 343–44.

to begin to study ourselves as real, flawed characters and to free ourselves of our peculiarities.[61]

Shaftesbury characterizes Socratic dialogue as containing within it "both *the heroick* and *the simple, the tragick,* and the *comick Vein*" (I, 121). This characterization of Socratic dialogue as complex and containing both tragedy and comedy seems better to accord with Shaftesbury's characterization of Plato, who "took the Sublime part," than his characterization of Xenophon. Xenophon's genius, he tells us, was "natural and simple". He speaks of Xenophon as "that philosophical MENANDER of earlier Time, whose Works one may wonder to see preserv'd from the same Fate; since in the darker Ages thro' which they pass'd, they might probably be alike neglected, on the account of their like Simplicity of Style and Composition" (I, 159).

Shaftesbury's characterization of Socrates himself, the "philosophical PATRIARCH," as "containing within himself the several Genius's of Philosophy,"[62] corresponds to his description of Socratic dialogue. Shaftesbury's characterization of Socrates as engaging in "a conceal'd sort of Raillery intermix'd with the Sublime," like that of Homer,[63] also seems better to fit the dialogues of Plato, who as he says "took the Sublime part," than those of Xenophon, who avoided it.

Shaftesbury's characterization of Socratic dialogue as containing within it "the tragick" vein, when combined with his characterization of Socrates as engaging in "a conceal'd sort of Raillery intermix'd with the Sublime," suggests that Platonic dialogue includes, beneath its sublimity, the same concealed sort of raillery that Socrates intermixed with that manner.[64] If so, then Plato is not really so "tragical" or "sublime" as he seems,[65] but is actually engaged in a kind of "tragicomedy," like that which Shaftesbury attributes to Homer. He says of this sort of tragicomedy that it is dangerous

---

61 I, 193–96. The account of Shaftesbury's view of Plato I give here and just below, as a poet resembling Homer, is not far from that proposed by Jaffro in "Which Platonism for Which Modernity?" 266–67 (see also 263–65).

62 I, 254.

63 I, 198.

64 See *Symposium* 223d.

65 For his taking of the "Sublime part," see I, 254; see also 253, where Shaftesbury speaks of Plato as "the sublime Philosopher."

although valuable.[66] It is dangerous, apparently, because we can miss or misapprehend the comic elements, and fall too much in love with myths, wonders, and tales of the supernatural.

In other words, it is, on the surface, too "tragic," too "sublime"; it has the histrionic character of which Nietzsche speaks in *Beyond Good and Evil*—the style we associate with "Platonism." If Plato's style is dangerous, in Shaftesbury's view, that is, we may suspect, for the same reason as it was in Nietzsche's—because it is "enthusiastic" or otherworldly, because it tends towards theology and "Platonism for the masses," or the Christian doctrine of the soul and the afterlife.[67]

In saying that Plato's style is not simply "tragical" but a subtle tragicomedy, however, Shaftesbury is indicating that Plato's writing incorporated the comic side of philosophy, which for Shaftesbury is higher than appeals to the sublime, but did so by associating it with the tragical or sublime. This would suggest that Plato's writing better represents the full complexity of Socrates and Socratic dialogue than does that of Xenophon, because like Homeric poetry it includes within itself both the tragic and the comic manner, as well as the concealed sort of raillery that Socrates intermixed with the sublime.

---

66 "Even *Comedy* itself was adjudg'd to this great Master; it being deriv'd from those *Parodys* or Mock-Humours, of which he had given the [*not only in his *Margites*, but even in his *Iliad* and *Odyssey*] Specimen in a conceal'd sort of Raillery intermix'd with the Sublime.—A dangerous Stroke of Art! And which requir'd a masterly Hand, like that of the philosophical Hero, whose Character was represented in the *Dialogue-Writings* above-mention'd." I, 198. Cf. also 246n–247n and 252n–253n). For the discussion of philosophical dialogue, see I, 193–96.

67 For Shaftesbury on the love of wonders (in this case, miracles), see I, 147–48. This is part of his criticism of the Christian belief in revelation. Compare I, 242–43, in Shaftesbury's account of the history of genres. Compare his discussion of the modern love of travelers' tales, I, 344–50, and its relation to the Christian love of wonders. Cf. also II, 202: "'tis not to be imagin'd how serviceable a *Tale* is, to amuse others besides mere Children; and how much easier the Generality of Men are paid in this Paper-coin, than in Sterling Reason." On the heroic, see his remark on Desdemona at I, 347–49. He associates her love for a tale-telling "*Hero* of the black Tribe" (349) with the appetite for supernatural objects.

From hence [the similarity of Socratic and Homeric "conceal'd sort of Raillery intermix'd with the Sublime"] possibly
we may form a Notion of that Resemblance, which on so many
occasions was heretofore remark'd between the Prince of Poets,
and the Divine Philosopher, who was said to rival him, and who
together with his Contemporarys of the same School, writ
wholly in that manner of Dialogue above-describ'd.[68]

But Shaftesbury's characterization of Socrates and of Socratic dialogue
at the same time suggests that Plato and Xenophon are not in fundamental
disagreement about the Socratic teaching. On the contrary, Xenophon's
"genteeler style," if it is more explicitly (though discreetly) comic than the
sublime style of Plato, may actually correspond to Plato's true intentions.
But Shaftesbury at the same time offers an explanation of why philosophy
had to begin with the more "tragic" tone of Plato, which was also used by
Socrates himself, rather than the genteel and simple style of Xenophon.

He does so by means of the parallel he draws between the history of
Greek drama and the history of Socratic dialogue. Greek drama had its
roots in Homer, who contained within himself both comedy and tragedy.
Tragedy simply put Homer on stage. Tragedy preceded comedy, since it is
the easiest manner of the two.[69] But the sublime and bombastic manner of
early tragedy had to be purged by the broad jokes of early parody before
tragedy could attain the naturalness of Euripides. It was not till then that
the Old Comedy was fully formed, and it was not till later that comedy in
turn attained the refinement of Menander.[70]

---

68 I, 198.
69 I, 244. Cf. his prior remark "that amidst the several Styles and Manners of
    Discourse or Writing, the easiest attain'd, and earliest practic'd, was the Mi-
    raculous, the Pompous, or what we generally call the SUBLIME." (I, 242.)
70 For his history of tragedy and comedy, Shaftesbury cites the authority of Aris-
    totle's *Poetics* and *Rhetoric*. See I, 242n, 243–46 including the notes, 250 and
    the note, and III, 140–41 as well as of Plato's *Minos* (I, 247n), Horace's *Art of
    Poetry*, at I, 247–48, 251, and Strabo at I, 252. One might add that modern
    philosophy had to begin with the Old Comedy of Hobbes (symbolized by the
    puppet-show at Bartl'emy Fair, I, 27–28) before it could arrive at the New Co-
    medy to which Shaftesbury aspires, though he is constrained to practice tra-

Something similar happened in the writing of Socratic dialogue, or Socratic imitation.[71] Speaking of Homer, Shaftesbury says:

> There was no more left for *Tragedy* to do after him, than to erect
> a Stage . . . Even *Comedy* itself was adjudg'd to this great Mas-
> ter; it being deriv'd from those *Parodys* or Mock-Humours, of
> which he had given the Specimen in a conceal'd sort of Raillery
> intermix'd with the Sublime.—A dangerous Stroke of Art! and
> which requir'd a masterly Hand, like that of the philosophical
> Hero, whose Character was represented in the *Dialogue-Writings*
> above mention'd.[72]

Here Shaftesbury seems to treat Socrates himself as the author of the Dialogues in which his disciples represented him—at any rate, he suggests that Socratic conversation prefigured those Dialogues. Socrates, like Homer, combined tragedy and comedy by means of his "masterly Hand." He was first succeeded by Plato, who took the sublime part. "He of mean birth" took the "Satirick" or "reproving" part, "which in his better-humour'd and more agreeable successor, turn'd into the Comick kind, and went upon the Model of that antient Comedy which was then prevalent."[73] "Another noble Disciple, whose Genius was towards Action, and who prov'd after-wards the greatest Hero of his time [Xenophon] took the genteeler part, and softer manner."[74]

Why did philosophy have to follow this path, in Shaftesbury's view?

gicomedy instead (see below). For Shaftesbury's view of Hobbes, see I, 88–90. On English success at comedy, see I, 259, where he mentions Butler's *Hudibras* and Buckingham's *Rehearsal* in the notes. On Shaftesbury's natural history of literature, see Klein, *Shaftesbury and the Culture of Politeness*, 205.

71 Itself a form of poetry and in particular of drama, I, 193–94. See also 254, the second footnote, where Shaftesbury says of Plato "His *Dialogues* were real POEMS (as has been shown above, *pag. 193*, &c.),"

72 I, 198.

73 I, 254. The two philosophers in question seem to be Diogenes and Crates, as Shaftesbury indicates through a footnote which refers us back to "the two last Citations, *pag. 252.*"

74 I, 254–55.

We may take our cue from his remarks on tragicomedy in Homer and on the development of tragedy: it was because philosophy, like Homer and tragedy after him, had to capture and recruit the melancholy and tragic emotions associated with ancient piety and the love of wonders before it could temper them to true self-control.[75]

In the history of drama, Marcus Aurelius shows that

> this first-form'd Comedy and Scheme of ludicrous Wit, was in-troduc'd upon the neck of the SUBLIME. The familiar airy Muse was privileg'd as a sort of *Counter-Pedagogue*, against the Pomp and Formality of the more solemn Writers.

But something similar, Marcus indicates, occurred in the history of philosophy:

> And what is highly remarkable, our Author shews us, that in Philosophy it-self there happen'd, almost at the very same time, a like *Succession* of Wit and Humour; when in opposition to the sublime Philosopher, and afterwards to his grave Disciple and Successor in the Academy, there arose *a Comick* Philosophy, in the Person of another Master and other Disciples; who person-ally, as well as in their Writings, were set in direct opposition to the former: not as differing in Opinions or Maxims, but in their Style and Manner; in the Turn of Humour, and method of Instruction."[76]

Xenophon is not mentioned in this passage, but what Shaftesbury says here confirms that, on his view, Xenophon and Plato do not differ in opinions or maxims.

From the preceding discussion, we can see why Shaftesbury prefers the manner of Xenophon to the manner of Plato: Xenophon avoids the

---

75 Re: Homer, see I, 242–43; re: tragedy, see I, 242–44.
76 I, 253. By the "grave Disciple" Marcus means Xenocrátes, and by "another Master" he means Crates, as Shaftesbury lets us see by citation in the notes (252n, 253n).

"dangerous Stroke of Art" which characterizes Socrates' own manner, as well as that of Homer and Plato: the "conceal'd sort of Raillery intermix'd with the Sublime." This manner is dangerous because it encourages the taste for the sublime, and thus a melancholy enthusiasm, even as it satirizes that taste.

At the same time, we can see that the manner of Plato is more fundamental than the manner of Xenophon, because it more directly represents the complexity of Socrates himself, and because it, like the style of Homer, performs the original work of capturing the tragic emotions and the love of the miraculous in order to begin to tame them. At the same time, Shaftesbury's history of philosophical styles indicates that Xenophon and Plato do not differ about the true Socratic teaching, and that Xenophon is in a way superior to Plato because he makes explicit what in Plato is concealed—the true comic character of that teaching—and because he avoids stirring up the tragic emotions.

But this suggests two things: first, that we can only fully understand Xenophon in relation to Plato, as bringing out the true comic teaching of Plato and Socrates, which in Plato and Socrates was intermingled with the tragic and sublime. And second, that we can best understand Plato with the help of Xenophon, who (along with the "Comick Philosophy" of the Cynics, referred to by Marcus) brings out the comic vein concealed in Plato and in Socrates.[77] He does so, moreover, with no loss of what is truly "divine" and elevating in Socrates and Plato. In Xenophon we find "an original System of Works, the politest, wisest, usefullest, and (to those who can understand the *Divineness* of a just *Simplicity*) the most amiable, and even the most elevating and exalting of all un-inspir'd and merely human Authors."[78] But we must note the qualification: "to those who can understand the *Divineness* of a just *Simplicity*." Xenophon's simplicity means that he is accessible only to the few.

One reason for his inaccessibility may be that he can only be understood by those who combine "the *Scholar*-part with that of the real

---

77   See Jaffro, "Which Platonism for Which Modernity?" 262n25, on Shaftesbury's remark that Xenophon's *Apology* "rectifyes" while at the same time "owning (as may be perceiv'd) the truth of Plato's Apology."

78   III, 248.

Gentleman and *Man of Breeding*." Philosophy, like learning generally, when exiled from the world to "Cloisters" and "*unpractis'd* Cells," becomes "dronish, insipid, pedantick, useless, and directly opposite to the real Knowledg and Practice of the World and Mankind."[79] Learning without good breeding and experience of the world and action is illiberal and incapable of understanding true refinement. Compare Shaftesbury's remark that "without a *Capacity* for Action, and a Knowledg of the World and Mankind, there can be no Author naturally qualify'd to write with Dignity, or execute any noble or great Design"; this characterization of the qualities of an author who can "write with Dignity," Shaftesbury indicates, applies both to Plato and to Xenophon.[80]

Shaftesbury's account of Plato as writing with a "conceal'd Raillery" which combines sublimity with comedy suggests a way of reconceiving the tension between Plato's aporetic[81] and his speculative manner.[82] This tension is not an inconsistency, which can only be resolved by assigning the two manners to different periods in Plato's intellectual development. Rather, there is no Plato without both. The knowledge of ignorance is impossible

79 I, 333n.

80 III, 247; compare III, 159–62, and cf. II, 293–94. On philosophy's need for gentlemanly largeness of soul as opposed to the illiberality of the mere scholar, see *Republic*, 490c–496e. On the distinction between intelligence and largeness of soul, see 518e–519b.

81 The dialogues ending in aporia are often assigned to the early period of Plato's writing. The *Theaetetus*, however, which is also aporetic, does not have the stylistic characteristic of "early" but of "middle" dialogues, according to the measures of technical stylometry which divide Plato's dialogues into three manners understood as corresponding to three periods; see Kahn, "On Platonic Chronology," in *New Perspectives*, 104–05. In order to sustain the notion of a "middle" period characterized by dogmatic assertions, however, the *Theaetetus* has commonly been assigned to the "late" dialogues.

82 The dialogues which seem more assertive about the existence of Forms, and which talk about recollection, have often been assigned to Plato's "middle" period, when he is thought to have turned from reporting on Socratic questioning to the making of dogmatic assertions. As Kahn points out, many of the dialogues usually assigned, on this basis, to the "middle" period belong, according to stylistic criteria, to the "early" dialogues, and some to the "late." See Kahn, "On Platonic Chronology," 94, 103–05. Cf. also C. C. W. Taylor, "The Origins of our Present Paradigms," in the same volume, at 79.

without the eros for the intelligible. Plato's Socrates is always both comical and sublime. He always retains (though he sometimes conceals) his irony towards bombast, even and especially his own. The fact that he also appeals to the love of the mysterious in no sense conflicts with his comic side, since his comedy depends on and is meant to correct his sublimity.[83] On Shaftesbury's view, this was also true of Socrates himself.

Shaftesbury's Imitation of Platonic Tragicomedy in "The Moralists"

In Volume Three of the *Characteristicks*, Shaftesbury comments on the earlier treatises in the person of an anonymous critic. This commentary is called "Miscellaneous Reflections." Commenting on Shaftesbury's own dialogue, "The Moralists," the anonymous critic tells us that it combines "the *simple, comick, rhetorical,* and even the *poetick* or *sublime.*"[84] Shaftesbury's style resembles Plato's mixed style more than it does the divine simplicity of Xenophon.

The motto of "The Moralists"[85] is "let us seek truth in the groves of the Academy."[86] This motto, together with Shaftesbury's description of the style of the work, suggests that in "The Moralists" Shaftesbury imitates the tragi-comic doubleness of Plato's Socrates. How does he do so? Near the beginning of "The Moralists," the narrator, Philocles, begins by rehearsing to Palemon a dialogue that had occurred between them.[87] Palemon has been complaining of the wickedness of mankind and human nature. Philocles starts by teasing him, supposing that his complaints arise from a disappointment in love.[88] Subsequently, Palemon reproaches Philocles for a lack of seriousness or sincerity, asking whether he is as little sincere in

---

83 Compare David Blank, "Comments on Sedley," *New Perspectives*, 65. See also Charles L. Griswold, Jr., "Comments on Kahn," 136–37. See also Christopher Gill, "Dialectic and the Dialogue Form," especially his remarks on 164; both in *New Perspectives*.

84 III, 285. Cf. 285n–286–87 and 287n.

85 From Horace. See the title page to "The Moralists," II, following 177.

86 That is, the Platonic Academy.

87 II, 181–83, and again II, 192–221. The dialogue is presented in a letter from Philocles to Palemon.

88 II, 192–99.

actions as in words—i.e., whether he lacks moral virtue as well as moral seriousness in speech.[89] Philocles then changes his tone and, using as he says
the skeptical privilege, begins to argue the other side. He begins to defend
Providence by praising the beauties of nature. He moves, as we might put
it, from comedy to the sublime.[90]

Palemon is surprised at his change of character, as he puts it. Philocles
then says that Palemon would have been even more surprised if he had met
him a few days ago, when he had just got back from the country where he
had been visiting his friend Theocles, whom he describes as his "Aegeria."[91]
Egeria was the nymph to whom the Roman king Numa claimed to speak
when he went off into solitude, and from whom he claimed to have received
the laws and religion of Rome. Machiavelli was not the first to suggest that
Egeria was Numa's invention. Philocles' characterization of Theocles as his
"Aegeria" may therefore be a hint that Theocles is Philocles' invention (perhaps a device, like Egeria, for giving sanction to a new religion and a new
set of laws). In that case, it will also make sense to suspect[92] that the account
of the dialogue between Philocles and Theocles is a dramatization of a "soliloquy" that Philocles has had with himself.[93]

Philocles then narrates his conversations with Theocles. What is most
striking for us is the distribution of roles between Philocles and Theocles.
While Theocles speaks of Philocles as a "Proselyte to Pyrrhonism,"[94] i.e.,
a skeptic who refuses either to assert or deny. Theocles, on the other hand,

89 II, 208.
90 II, 208–18.
91 II, 222.
92 In the light of Shaftesbury's account of the function of dialogue as a means of
    promoting soliloquy, see I, 195–96.
93 Though Shaftesbury will indicate that the dialogue which follows, and which
    involves two other characters besides Philocles and Theocles, is meant to be
    as natural as possible—that is, it is meant really to imitate the characters of
    Shaftesbury's contemporaries. III, 285n.
94 II, 351; cf. II, 355: "Let PYRRHO, by the help of such another, contradict me,
    if he pleases", II, 355. He is spoken of or speaks of himself as a skeptic at II,
    206, 268, 306, 323, 332, 351–52, 354, and by allusion at 374 ("your scrupulous
    Philosophy") and 437 (in saying that he will turn philosopher, Philocles means
    that he will abandon Pyrrhonism). See also, e.g., "Miscellaneous Reflections"
    III, 287, 294, 295, 342.

is spoken of, and speaks of himself as, devoted to "ENTHUSIASM";[95]—though he also urges Philocles to "pull me by the sleeve" if he gets too carried away.[96] What are we to make of this distribution of roles? How does it fit the motto of "The Moralists"—"let us seek truth in the groves of the Academy"? Where is "the Academy," or Plato, in "The Moralists"? Theocles, when making his speeches, seems, it is true, like a "Platonist," if by this we mean someone like Diotima, or Socrates when he gives his speech about love in the *Phaedrus*.[97] But what about the "Pyrrhonist" Philocles? What is he doing in "The Moralists" if "The Moralists" is Platonic?

To answer this question, I would recall that "the Academy" is associated not merely with Platonism in this sense—the "enthusiastic" or sublime[98]—but with skepticism—the skepticism of the New Academy, which was the rival to the skepticism of the Pyrrhonists. Even before his rehearsal of his conversation with Palemon, Philocles offers a description of this teaching:

> You know too, that in this *Academick* Philosophy I am to present you with, there is a certain way of Questioning and Doubting, which no-way sutes the Genius of our Age . . . .Of all Philosophy, how absolutely the most disagreeable must that appear, which goes upon no establish'd Hypothesis, nor presents us with any flattering Scheme, talks only of Probabilitys, Suspence of Judgment, Inquiry, Search, and Caution not to be impos'd on, or deceiv'd? This is that *Academick* Discipline in which formerly the Youth were train'd . . . . Hence that way of DIALOGUE, and Patience of Debate and Reasoning, of which we have scarce a Resemblance left in any of our Conversations, at this season of the World."[99]

---

95 400–01.

96 II, 375; cf. II, 380.

97 For Diotima, see *Symposium* 201c–212c; for Socrates in the *Phaedrus*, see 242e–257b.

98 In the "Miscellaneous Reflections" Shaftesbury says that Theocles assumes the role of a "feign'd Preacher." III, 287.

99 II, 189, 191.

Philocles' description of the "*Academick* Philosophy" suggests the following hypothesis: that "The Moralists" "seeks truth in the groves of the Academy" not merely by presenting us with the "Platonist" Theocles, but precisely by combining the "enthusiast" Theocles with the "Pyrrhonist" Philocles. Together, the Pyrrhonian skepticism or suspense of judgment of Philocles and the enthusiasm of Theocles make Academic or Platonic philosophy, which combines skepticism as knowledge of ignorance with an openness to "the divine." That openness is regulated by the knowledge of ignorance, or by irony towards claims of inspiration. It is the Platonic combination of "inspired" poetry with skepticism that provides Shaftesbury's model of philosophy.[100]

But enthusiasm and skepticism by themselves are not enough: the combination is meant to issue in "soliloquy" and self-knowledge. As we saw in discussing the relation of dialogue to soliloquy, the best way of practicing soliloquy is through the study of "characters." First and foremost we must understand our own; but we can only come to understand our own character by studying others', and not just those of our contemporaries but, since our contemporaries are so unnatural, those of other times and places. And the understanding of characters is to be achieved by the study of "styles"—of literary styles, but also of moral styles, or varieties of "manners."[101] We can only come to know characters by becoming

100 My discussion of Philocles and Theocles, and indeed this essay as a whole, was completed in 2009, and does not take account of a dissertation in Political Science defended at Loyola University, Chicago, in 2010 by Travis Sean Cook, "Sea-Cards for the Impetuous Muse: A Reading of Shaftesbury's *Characteristicks*," available on eCommons. I have become aware of this dissertation only in doing final corrections of this essay in late July of 2016, and have not had time to study it. I would not be surprised if some of my conclusions have been anticipated by Cook; as my discussion shows, I think there is something right about his suggestion in the Preface, p. 15, "that Philocles rather than Theocles is the true hero of the dialogue," insofar as he means that Shaftesbury is more skeptical, and less enthusiastic, than has commonly been thought—though as III, 225 indicates, we should not dismiss the "formal and grave Sentiments" of "our *Author*" in the "Inquiry," which correspond to the teachings of Theocles, as merely feigned.

101 Whence the title "Characteristicks of Men, Manners, Opinions and Times." Men, opinions, and times can only be understood together, and in relation to

"critics" of taste, including both moral and literary taste, the true windows into characters.

We now begin to see why Shaftesbury assumed the aspect of a "literary man," despite his attraction to the asceticism of Marcus Aurelius.[102] He does so because it is only through the study of the beautiful and of tastes in the beautiful, he thinks, that we can come to know human souls or characters. This is precisely a Platonic teaching, made most explicit in the *Phaedrus*, *Symposium*, and early books of the *Republic*.

Let us come back then to the difference between Shaftesbury's conception of philosophy and our own. We tend to think of philosophy as an attempt to demonstrate a thesis or doctrine. As I mentioned earlier, Shaftesbury has reservations about the practice of writing philosophy in "treatises," or following the "methodic" way.[103] Shaftesbury's says of this style that

> 'Tis from this Genius that firm Conclusions and steddy Maxims are best form'd: which, if solidly built, and on sure ground, are the shortest and best Guides towards Wisdom and Ability, in every kind;

He goes on, however,

> but if defective, or unsound, in the least part, must of necessity

manners or habits of action and feeling. On manners see I, 194, on manners and taste see I, 338–39 (cf. I, 283 on "Taste in Morals," I, 316–17 on the Muses and "Numbers," and I, 333–43 on taste, manners, and morals), III, 154 on taste and morals, III, 163 on manners and morals, I, 165–66 on Soliloquy as a reflection on manners, I, 172–74 on moral self-knowledge (though Shaftesbury does not here speak explicitly of taste), I, 256–60 on the moral significance of different literary styles, I, 277–78 on manners, morals, and the proper judgment of authors.

102 On the importance of Stoicism for Shaftesbury, see Jaffro's *Éthique de la communication*. See also his edition of Shaftesbury's Askemata, notebooks in service of Stoic self-discipline: *Shaftesbury, Exercices* (Paris: Aubier, 1993).
103 I, 256–57.

lead us to the grossest Absurditys, and stiffest Pedantry and Conceit."[104]

In other words, it can lend itself to the dogmatism of false philosophy, and to the dogmatic giving of "advice."[105] Philosophy is indeed a giving of "advice," but Shaftesbury prefers to do this in the manner of Homer or the Socratics: that is, to give advice without seeming to do so. Philosophy can give us advice by means of a "poem" or "imitation of characters." In so doing, it leads us to see and reflect on "men, manners, opinions, and times"—i.e., on ourselves, and on the effect on us of our "manners, opinions, and times," or rather on the ways in which these penetrate and constitute us.

Only in this way can we begin truly to question our opinions; not by having them refuted systematically, but by seeing how local they are, how much they are tied to the peculiarities of our passions, characters, and times; by becoming "critics" of our own taste and our own style, that is, of our own sense of the beautiful or the fitting, and from there advancing to reflect on what the standards are by which we judge ourselves, that is, on our opinions about what is really true and good.[106] Nor is this enough: for when we engage in such reflection, we must keep an eye on the possibility that our tastes are in need of improvement;[107] that we have failed to go far enough in the Socratic activity of self-questioning.

104 I, 256–57. On the dogmatism of modern philosophy, see I, 88–90, I, 116–17, I, 286–303, II, 189–91, III, 160, 193–94, III, 211 on "*Moon-blind* WITS" ; on the dangers of meditation see III, 225–26. On the theological origins of modern dogmatism see III, 79–82.

105 I, 256–57; on the modern abandonment of dialogue style in favor of treatise style, see II, 187–88. See also Shaftesbury's remark, at III, 285, that "The Moralists," because it is a dialogue, is "an Undertaking of greater weight" according to Shaftesbury's rules, than the methodical "Inquiry." Cf. also III, 135–36, III, 191, III, 205 for some ironical comments on the grave manner of the "Inquiry."

106 To examine myself in this way is not a matter of modeling my taste on anyone else's, taken as an authoritative standard. "Were a Man to form himself by one single Pattern or Original, however perfect; he wou'd himself be a mere *Copy*." III, 260n, towards the end of the long note which continues onto the following two pages.

107 I, 341–44, II, 401–02, III, 172–73.

The surest sign that we have failed to stay open to the possibility that we have failed at this is the self-satisfaction that goes with "gravity," and which tends to issue in the claim to authority over others, and the expectation that they will do what we say because we tell them to. The beginning of wisdom, on the other hand, is to learn that nobody can be "made" to think something; that one can learn only, as Theocles points out at the end of "The Moralists," through midwifery, by being brought to give birth to one's own conceptions, and then learning to test these. Our standards are "innate" not in the sense that they were in us from birth, but in the sense that they come from us, inhabit us, and govern our passions;[108] the doctrine of recollection of the *Meno* must be qualified in the light of the doctrine of midwifery of the *Theaetetus*.[109]

In the "Miscellaneous Reflections," we have seen, Shaftesbury assumes the role of an anonymous critic who discusses the first two volumes of the *Characteristicks*. Speaking in the voice of the anonymous critic, Shaftesbury raises an objection to the design of "The Moralists." He criticizes Shaftesbury for violating the unities of action and time by "making his first Part, *in order*, to be last *in time*." He could easily have avoided this. "He need only to have brought his first Speakers immediately into Action, and sav'd the narrative or recitative part of PHILOCLES to PALEMON, by producing them as speaking Personages upon his Stage."[110] Shaftesbury's criticism of the design of "The Moralists" is not meant seriously, of course; rather, it is to

108 On the dependency of our passions on our opinions, see I, 185, 294–97, 302–03, 320–23, II, 33–34, 45–46, III, 196–206. Jaffro suggests that Shaftesbury's doctrine of moral sense, in the *Inquiry*, was a tactical simplification of his real views, intended to support Bayle's thesis that atheists can be virtuous. It does this by separating virtue from opinion. In fact, Shaftesbury does not really think that virtue is detachable from opinion (see *Éthique de la communication et art d'écrire*, 180–81). At II, 45, where Shaftesbury says that "that natural Affection and anticipating Fancy, which makes the sense of Right and Wrong," is not easily manipulated, he qualifies this by saying "Neither *Theism* therefore, nor *Atheism* . . . being able to operate immediately or directly in this Case, but indirectly, by the intervention of opposite or favourable Affections casually excited by any such Belief . . ." In other words, beliefs can affect the standard of right and wrong by changing our affections.
109 On innateness and midwifery, see "Moralists," II, 410–11.
110 III, 285n.

be understood in the light of his declaration that he wants to make his readers into critics, to teach them the art of reading and the freedom to challenge the author. His remark challenges us to ask why the dialogue between
Philocles and Palemon precedes rather than following the sublime speeches
of Theocles, and is narrated in a letter rather than placed upon Shaftesbury's "Stage."

As we saw earlier, Philocles speaks of Theocles as "my Aegeria," and
this sounds like a hint, we proposed, that the conversation with Theocles is
an invention.[111] Whether or not we draw this inference, it seems clear that
the conversation between Philocles and Theocles can only be understood
against the background of the conversation between Philocles and Palemon.
In placing the conversation of Philocles and Theocles after that between
Philocles and Palemon, Shaftesbury is doing several things. First, he is
hinting to us that the conversation with Theocles is an invention by Philocles for the sake of Palemon. Second, he is allowing us to become intoxicated with Theocles, and to forget the details of the initial conversation
which provides the framework and occasion for the conversation with Theocles. Third, he is asking us to notice that Philocles, even after his supposed
conversation with Theocles, has not become an enthusiast, although he can
play the part of one, and to consider why. We may not notice or make much
of the initial hint that Theocles is an invention ("my Aegeria"), or that

---

111 See Philocles' remarks about the difficulty of furnishing an account of his
conversation with Theocles: "I was now *alone*; confin'd to my Closet; oblig'd
to meditate by my-self; and reduc'd to the hard Circumstances of *an Author*,
and *Historian*, in the most difficult Subject. But here, methought, propitious
Heaven, in some manner, assisted me. For if *Dreams* were, as Homer teaches
us, sent from the Throne of JOVE; I might conclude I had a favourable one, of
the *true* sort, towards the Morning-light; which, as I recollected myself, gave
me a clear and perfect Idea of what I desir'd so earnestly to bring back to my
Memory. I found my-self transported to a distant Country . . . No sooner had
I consider'd the Place, than I discern'd it to be the very same where I had talk'd
with THEOCLES the second Day I was with him in the Country. I look'd about
to see if I cou'd find my Friend; and calling THEOCLES! I awak'd. But so powerful was the Impression of my Dream, and so perfect the Idea rais'd in me,
of the Person, Words, and Manner of my Friend, that I cou'd now fansy myself philosophically inspir'd, as that ROMAN *Sage* by his AEGERIA, and invited,
on this occasion, to try my Historical MUSE." II, 221–222.

Philocles has not been converted, till we read the criticism in the "Miscel-laneous Reflections"; but when we do, we are meant to go back and inves-tigate our own enthusiasm in the light of Philocles' hint and his initial conversation with Palemon.[112]

Despite Theocles' adjuration to Philocles that he must "pull me by the Sleeve when I grow extravagant,"[113] Shaftesbury does not mind first-time readers being swept away by Theocles. But we are not meant, if we are care-ful readers, to be simply captivated by Theocles or to suppose that he simply speaks for Shaftesbury. On the contrary, his effusions, and above all his air of enthusiasm or rapture itself, must be qualified in the light of the fact that they have not fully persuaded Philocles, or that their effect has not been lasting.[114]

One might object, of course, that this is not Theocles' fault, but that of Philocles' frivolity, his preference for "freedom" or free thinking. But we must remember that Theocles is Philocles' Egeria; that Theocles in fact is Philocles, or an aspect of Philocles. The skeptic himself harbors the en-thusiast. The full teaching of "The Moralists" is Theocles' enthusiasm in the light of Philocles' playful reserve towards it; elevation of soul together with comic open-mindedness and questioning. In other words, we must read it in the light of the history of philosophy Shaftesbury provides us with in "Advice to an Author" and recapitulates in the "Miscellaneous Re-flections," according to which the high or sublime tone of Plato had to be corrected by the cynicism and the comic tone of his immediate successors[115] and by the "genteeler" tone of Xenophon.[116]

---

112 As well perhaps as of the conversation with the older and younger gentlemen that takes place at Theocles' country house.

113 II, 375.

114 One might compare the relation between the criticism of "The Moralists" in the "Miscellaneous Reflections" on the speeches of Theocles to the relation between the discussion of writing in the *Phaedrus* and Socrates' praise of love as a divine madness, which precedes that discussion.

115 II, 253, 254 in the notes, which suggest that Shaftesbury is speaking of Dio-genes and Crates, the founders of the Cynic school. (Klein proposes that Shaf-tesbury means Antisthenes and Diogenes. See Klein, *Shaftesbury and the Culture of Politeness*, 43 and 43n.)

116 I, 254–55; cf. III, 248.

Later, Shaftesbury says "MORE REASONS are given by our Author himself, for his avoiding the direct way of DIALOGUE . . ."[117] His note refers us to Philocles' discussion of the difficulty of writing dialogues among the moderns.[118] Philocles, Shaftesbury thus indicates, is Shaftesbury himself.

Just before his criticism of the design of "The Moralists," Shaftesbury suggests that the difficulty faced by the moderns in writing dialogues has to do with the fact that philosophy and morals are

> so wide of common Conversation, and, by long Custom, so appropriated to the *School*, the *University-Chair*, the *Pulpit*, that he thinks it hardly safe or practicable to treat of them elsewhere, or in a different Tone. He is forc'd therefore to raise particular Machines, and constrain his principal Characters, in order to carry a better Face,[119] and bear himself out, against the appearance of *Pedantry*. Thus his *Gentleman*-Philosopher THEOCLES, before he enters into his real Character, becomes a feign'd *Preacher*. And even when his real Character comes on, he hardly dares stand it out; but to deal the better with his *Sceptick*-Friend, he falls again to personating, and takes up the Humour of the *Poet* and *Enthusiast*.[120]

The philosopher cannot be represented as a philosopher in a modern piece of writing, because the consideration of moral and philosophical topics have been reserved for preachers. Shaftesbury's "Moralists" must therefore attempt to inflect the mode of speaking of preachers in the direction of philosophy, rather than representing philosophical conversation directly.[121]

---

117 III, 290.
118 II, 187.
119 Here we should perhaps think of the discussion of masks and the compulsion exercised by Christianity over faces in "Sensus Communis," I, 82–85.
120 III, 287–88.
121 Shaftesbury's indication that Theocles' true character is disguised, first behind the mask of a preacher, later behind the aspect of a poet and enthusiast, does not mean that there is no truth, from Shaftesbury's point of view, in Theocles' evocations of cosmic order, and his appeals to the beauty and intelligibility of

What Did Shaftesbury Learn from Plato? A Hypothesis about the Development of Shaftesbury's Views on Socrates, Plato, and Philosophical Writing

In "Which Platonism for Which Modernity? A Note on Shaftesbury's Socratic Sea-Cards," Laurent Jaffro has proposed that Shaftesbury saw himself not as a Platonist but as a disciple of Socrates and a Stoic. He founds this claim on a careful study of Shaftesbury's manuscript, the "Design of a Socratic History."[122] This manuscript is the project and preparatory notes for a book on Socrates which Shaftesbury intended to write in the "simple style," whose great exemplar is Xenophon.[123] The book was to treat first of the historical Socrates and then of the fabulous Socrates.[124] It involved a systematic examination of evidence from Plato, Xenophon, Aristophanes, Athenaeus, and elsewhere.[125] "Xenophon was regarded as the true historian of Socrates, while Plato was responsible for the fabrication of a legend."[126]

In his notes, Shaftesbury tells himself

> Remember to make a kind of Comparison between Plato and Xenoph [sic]. Plato . . . so taken up with Sublime & Mystical things & in his Poetick raptures perpetually looses himself as to wt regards the Character of Socrates not only putting things in his Mouth utterly far from him: but making him sometimes an absolute Sceptick (whence the Claim of Sextus Empericus and ye Academicks . . . . Sometimes a Sophist & Caviller. Sometimes a Poet & *Vates* in divine fury doing things wholly out of his Character.[127]

nature. For a declaration that the corresponding doctrine of the *Inquiry* does represent Shaftesbury's real views, and is not "feign'd Seriousness carry'd on . . . in such a manner as to leave no Insight into the Fiction or intended Raillery," see III, 225.

122 See Jaffro, "Which Platonism," 256.
123 Jaffro, ibid., 259.
124 Jaffro, ibid., 257.
125 Jaffro, ibid., 256–57 and 256 n4.
126 Jaffro, ibid., 257.
127 Jaffro, ibid., 261. Jaffro cites p. 35 in the ms.

Jaffro, speaking of Shaftesbury's account of Plato, indicates that, "even though Plato's interpretation of Socrates is distorted by Platonic doctrines, this should be carefully qualified."[128] He shows how it should be qualified, on Shaftesbury's view, by discussing Plato's treatment of the Socratic daimon. Though Plato "gives a character of divinity to Socrates's demon and to Socrates himself . . . Plato," Jaffro says, "does not completely yield to a mystical interpretation of the demon." Rather, Plato's reference to the oracle at Delphi may be understood, Shaftesbury suggests, on the one hand as praise of Socrates' moral character, second, as a way of avoiding "ye Character of irreligion so universally at ye time imputed to ye Philosophers." Socrates' references to his daimon in Plato's Dialogues, according to Shaftesbury, do not imply belief in "a particular Daemon distinct from the Great God of ye World."[129] Though Xenophon's *Apology* "rectifyes other Apologies," according to Shaftesbury, it must nevertheless be seen as "owning . . . the truth of Plato's Apology."[130]

But there is another sense, Jaffro says, in which Shaftesbury is quite simply a disciple of Plato: with regard to Plato's achievement "*as a poet*," and with respect to the art of writing.[131] As evidence for Shaftesbury's high valuation of Plato as a poet, Jaffro cites Shaftesbury's treatment in "Advice to an Author" of Horace's praise of "Socratic pages," in which Horace says that "wisdom is the origin and source of good writing."[132]

However, Jaffro suggests, Shaftesbury regarded this model of writing as obsolete, because while "Platonic dialogues were a picture of simplicity," modern manners are too formal to permit moderns to imitate Platonic dialogue in a modern setting. When writing his "Design of a Socratic History," Shaftesbury thought it was possible to "adapt the ancient 'Socratic pages' to fit the needs of modern readers . . . But he did not complete the project; and then in place of it he put the ancient model as worthy of being

128 Jaffro, ibid., 261.
129 Jaffro, ibid., 262–63; 66–67 in the ms.
130 Jaffro, ibid., 262 n25; 8 in the ms.
131 Jaffro, ibid., 263.
132 Jaffro, ibid., 264–65; see *Characteristicks*, I, 192 and 192n, 193–94. The "Sea-Cards" of Jaffro's title are, as he says, a pun of Shaftesbury's on Horace's Socraticae Chartae. Compare I, 192n with I, 205–06; see Jaffro, "Which Platonism," 264–65.

imitated and at the same time *de facto* inimitable, as he makes clear in his *Soliloquy* ["Advice to an Author"].[133] "That is why," Jaffro proposes, "in *Soliloquy* Shaftesbury puts aside the question of the true history of Socrates . . . He focuses on the poetics of the dialogue . . . and he presents Plato as a poet." He cites a passage from the manuscript which pointed towards this new direction:

> What Idea to have of Plato, with what preparation come to read him. Dramatick pieces [sic] a Tragedy in the lofty Poetick Style & Fiction. How far regard to Truth in a Tragedy? the same in Plato, main Circumstances preserv'd in these pieces—in others that were no way historicall but merely metaphisicall [sic] philosophicall Faults of Chronology.
> Plato ye Poet of Philosophers as Homer ye Philosopher of Poets . . . .
> Favourable significance of ye word Enthousiasme as to Deity. & in this Sense Plato a Noble Enthousiast.[134]

Jaffro sums up as follows:

> "To summarize my argument, the reappraisal of Plato as a poet is a consequence of the depreciation of Plato as a philosopher."[135]

While the "Design of a Socratic History" has long been known to students of Shaftesbury, it has never before received the sort of examination Jaffro has given it, and his investigation of it marks a fundamental advance in our understanding of Shaftesbury's views on Socrates, Plato, and Xenophon, and in our understanding of Shaftesbury's development.[136] Nevertheless, I should like to propose an alternative account of that development, though one based entirely on the evidence Jaffro has presented and in part on his own discussion of it.

133 Jaffro, ibid., 265. The passage which Jaffro cites from Shaftesbury is found on I, 203–04.
134 Jaffro, ibid., 266; 36 in the ms.
135 Jaffro, ibid., 267.
136 On the "Design of a Socratick History," see also his "Le Socrate de Shaftesbury: Comment raconter aux Modernes l'histoire de Socrate?" *Socrate in Occidente*, ed. Ettore Lojacono (Florence: Le Monnier Università, 2004), 66–90.

Jaffro himself points out in discussing the passage just quoted from the manuscript that "This last remark on the positive meaning of the word 'enthusiasm' (which at that time usually signifies 'fanaticism') is very important" because it anticipates the *Letter Concerning Enthusiasm* which was to appear in 1708. And this observation points to an alternative to Jaffro's conclusion. The Shaftesbury of the *Characteristicks*, I would like to propose, has abandoned his earlier depreciation of Plato as a philosopher, in part because he has decided that Plato's tragic and sublime tone is fundamental for the Socratic project of taming enthusiasm.[137]

In support of this claim, I would like to cite another passage in defense of Plato that Jaffro quotes from the manuscript:

> Those that would decry Plato, will object that he is . . . .[sic] & Enthousiastick, Fabulouse . . . .All this in some degree true. But then on the other side, wt Majesty! what Decorum! what Graces!. . . Homer I call all this, truly poeticall and Pindarick . . . .Thus also ye Objecters may say that He is puerile trifling, full of Sophistry, of Circumlocution, not concise in his Dialect & use of Logick . . . .But then on ye other side, what Politeness what demonstration of Humanity in Conversation, what Antidote to heat & Animosity wt Good Humour & Decent Mirth

137 See also Jaffro himself, in "Le Socrate de Shaftesbury," 79: "L'affirmation de la superiorité de Xénophon sur Platon est entièrement relative au projet des *Socraticks*. Elle tient à la nécessité de receuillir un témoignage historique plutôt qu'une doctrine spéculative et, en même temps, à la décision d'adopter le style simple plutôt que le style sublime." See also "L'admiration de Shaftesbury à l'égard de Platon ne faiblit jamais," 78). The decision to abandon the project of the *Socraticks* in favor of the *Characteristicks* was itself, according to Jaffro, the product of a philosophical decision, to the effect that the simplicity of ancient style is no longer possible (see 90). The result of this decision, according to Jaffro in "Le Socrate," is that Shaftesbury turned from Socratic irony to ridicule—the style of the "Letter Concerning Enthusiasm"—in the manner of Lucian and Swift. The comparison of the style of the "Letter" to that of Lucian is extremely illuminating. But I do not think that Shaftesbury's adoption of this manner means that he has simply abandoned Socratic irony; I shall argue that the *Characteristicks*, both as philosophy and as writing, are strongly influenced by Plato.

& Pleasantry throughout (opposite to Moroseness) what Pattern of Conversation? (as it were a Charm to soften rough Dispositions).[138]

Furthermore, I cannot agree with Jaffro that Shaftesbury thought it was impossible to imitate Socratic dialogue in modern Europe. Shaftesbury certainly says that dialogue style is difficult to achieve in modern Europe,[139] and that the masks of preacher and poet he is compelled to make Theocles wear, and other devices in "The Moralists," are responses to this difficulty.[140] But consider Shaftesbury's good-humored declaration that "The Moralists" "must, according to his own Rules, be reckon'd as an Undertaking of greater Weight" than the "Inquiry" because

> It aspires to *Dialogue*, and carrys with it not only those poetick Features of the Pieces antiently call'd MIMES; but it attempts to unite the several Personages and Characters in ONE *Action*, or *Story*, within a determinate Compass of *Time*, regularly divided, and drawn into different and proportion'd *Scenes*: And this, too, with variety of STYLE; the *simple, comick, rhetorical,* and even the *poetick* or *sublime*; such as is the aptest to run into Enthusiasm and Extravagance. So much is our Author, by virtue of this Piece, a POET *in due form*, and by a more apparent claim, than if he had writ a PLAY, or *dramatick Piece*, in as regular a manner, at least, as any known at present on our Stage.[141]

In the note to this passage, Shaftesbury says

> That he is conscious of this, we may gather from that Line or two of Advertisement, which stands at the beginning of his first Edition. "As for the Characters, and Incidents, they are neither

---

138 Jaffro, "Which Platonism," 267. I have omitted part of Jaffro's quotation; 72–73 in the ms.
139 Besides I, 203–04, cited earlier, see II, 187–92 and III, 290–91.
140 III, 286–91.
141 III, 285–86.

wholly feign'd *(says he)* nor wholly true: but according to the Liberty allow'd in the way of DIALOGUE, the principal Matters are founded upon Truth; and the rest as near resembling as may be. 'Tis *a Sceptick* recites: and the Hero of the Piece passes for an *Enthusiast*. If a perfect Character be wanting; 'tis the same Case here, as with the Poets in some of their best Pieces. And this surely is a sufficient Warrant for the Author of a PHILOSOPHICAL ROMANCE."—Thus our Author himself; who to conceal, however, his strict Imitation of the antient poetick DIALOGUE, has prefix'd an auxiliary Title to his Work, and given it the Sirname of RHAPSODY . . . .But whatever our Author may have affected in his *Title-Page*, 'twas so little his Intention to write after that Model of incoherent Workmanship, that it appears to be sorely against his Will, if this *Dialogue-Piece* of his has not the just Character, and correct Form of those *antient Poems* describ'd.[142]

Jaffro suggests that the presentation of "The Moralists" as a letter, which on Shaftesbury's view is, he says, a characteristically modern form, deprives it of the simplicity of a true Platonic dialogue.[143] But according to the anonymous critic of the "Miscellaneous Reflections," Shaftesbury could easily have avoided this feature:

He needed only to have brought his first Speakers immediately into Action . . . . Nor had our Author been necessitated to commit that Anachronism, of making his first Part, in order, to be last in time.[144]

Thus according to the anonymous critic, the use of the letter form was not a necessary result of the modern setting, but a simple error on Shaftesbury's

142 III, 285n–286n.
143 "But this dialogue between Philocles and Theocles is related by Philocles within a letter, which creates a sort of alienation effect"; "Which Platonism," 265n33. On the contrast between letters, treatise, essays, and the simplicity of Platonic dialogue, see Jaffro, ibid., 266.
144 III, 285n–286n (at the end of the long note).

part. We have argued, however, that the anachronism produced by the letter form is not an error, and that the anonymous critic's objection to it was a hint to the reader to consider the significance of that order—i.e., a hint that we should temper our enthusiasm for Theocles in the light of Philocles' irony at the beginning, which is chronologically later than his supposed conversations with Theocles.

Jaffro says that Shaftesbury abandoned the book on Socrates because he concluded that the simplicity of Platonic dialogue was impossible in modern Europe. But on Jaffro's own account Shaftesbury does not regard Plato's style as simple.[145] And indeed Jaffro himself suggests that the abandonment of the project for a book on Socrates was accompanied by a new appreciation for the complexity of Plato's style as an appropriate style in philosophy.[146] The complex design of "The Moralists," I have argued, is actually necessary in order first to awaken our enthusiasm, and then to make us see, if we are careful, that it needs to be subjected to skeptical scrutiny. The fact that the dialogue is contained within a letter does not establish a contrast with the simplicity of Platonic dialogues, since many of these involve equally complicated framing devices. As for Theocles' wearing the mask of preacher and poet, Plato's Socrates wears both masks at different times.[147]

I would propose, accordingly, that Shaftesbury abandoned the book on Socrates because he had come to appreciate the complex, tragi-comic style of Platonic dialogue as intrinsically valuable, and ceased, therefore, simply to devalue it by comparison with the simplicity of Xenophon. He did so, I would propose, because he came to see that it was necessary for the eliciting and taming of enthusiasm. The Platonic movement between enthusiasm and skepticism, about which Shaftesbury had complained in the "Design of a Socratic History," is essential to the design of "The Moralists," as the

---

145 "Which Platonism," 259, 261, 267.

146 Jaffro, ibid., 266–67.

147 For his wearing of the mask of the poet, see notably his speech in praise of eros in the *Phaedrus*. For a "priestly" speech, see his rendition of Diotima in the *Symposium*. Shaftesbury was certainly interested in the complexities of the *Phaedrus*. To support the claim that philosophers were "eminent in the *critical* Practice," Shaftesbury cites the *Phaedrus* "where an entire Piece of the Orator Lysias is criticiz'd in form," at III, 280n.

combination of the sublime and the comic is essential to the virtues of the Socratic dialogue as described in "Advice to an Author."[148]

What then did Shaftesbury learn from Plato? To understand this, it will be useful to consider Shaftesbury's favorable use of the term "enthusiasm," a use which, as Shaftesbury tells us, he draws from Plato. The remark Jaffro cites from the "Design" about "Favourable significance of ye word Enthousiasme as to Diety. & in this Sense Plato a Noble Enthousiast" points forward, as he says, to the "Letter Concerning Enthusiasm." Shaftesbury there cites Plato as the source for his own use of "enthusiasm" to mean "whatever was sublime in human Passions."[149] This observation, I would propose, may supply a clue to Shaftesbury's development.

Shaftesbury's first published writing was the first version of the "Inquiry Concerning Virtue and Merit," in which he argued that virtue is founded in nature rather than in theological doctrine, and that atheists can be virtuous. He next wrote "The Sociable Enthusiast," the first version of "The Moralists." In the "Miscellaneous Reflections," he speaks of "The Moralists" as

> a kind of *Apology* for this reviv'd Treatise concerning *Virtue* and *Religion*. As for his APOLOGY (particularly in what relates to *reveal'd Religion*, and *a World to come*), I commit the Reader to the disputant Divines, and Gentlemen, whom our Author has introduc'd in that concluding Piece of Dialogue-Writing . . . .[150]

Why did Shaftesbury write "The Sociable Enthusiast"? He may have been moved to do so in part, the passage just quoted suggests, by the desire to provide an "apology" in "what relates to revealed religion, and the world

---

148 As Jaffro says, "Shaftesbury's interpretation of dialogue form as a means of concealment for the author rectifies his former reading of Plato on Socrates. Indeed Plato's Socrates is not the historical Socrates, nor can he be reduced to Plato's double: he is a fictional character." "Which Platonism," 267.

149 I, 53. In the note, 53n, Shaftesbury cites *Phaedrus*, 241e, *Meno*, 99d, and *Apology*, 22b, along with Plutarch, *Cato Major* 22.

150 III, 191.

to come," for the doctrine of the "Inquiry." The "Inquiry" had argued that virtue was grounded in nature, that atheists could be virtuous,[151] that superstition could corrupt the moral sense.[152] All of this tended to expose Shaftesbury, and philosophy as he understood it, to the charge of atheism or at the very least of contempt for revealed religion.

Shaftesbury may therefore have turned to Plato for an "Antidote to heat & Animosity . . . as it were a Charm to soften rough Dispositions,"[153] such as Plato's way of writing provides along with its "Enthousiastick" and "Fabulouse" character, according to the "Design of a Socratic History."

Shaftesbury's concern to defend himself against the charge of atheism may have led him to reflect on the value of an "apology" which, like Plato's, speaks continually of the divine. Shaftesbury had remarked on the value of such invocation of the divine in lines Jaffro quotes from the "Design of a Socratick History":

> Remember as to ye Oracle of Delphos the Commendation of ye Oracle & Priests (upon the Hypothesis of Human Policy & nothing supernaturall) the assistance given to all the Wise men & Founders of Republicks . . . Now the oracle pronounc'd in Socrates favour may (upon this Hypothesis) have a double reason. First yt Socrates was really so good and wise & as such they had correspondence with him as with Lycurgus &c. & in ye next place that He being all along carefull to avoid ye Character of irreligion so universally at yt time imputed to ye Philosophers (as particularly Anaxagoras a little before Protagoras at that very time & in reality to all ye Naturall Philos. & Sophists) to prevent this he was ever carefull of outward religion & therefore advic'd consulting the Oracle Sacrafize &c. (on wch account he might have favour) & constantly taught this to his Disciples whence that constant Character of Piety

---

151 II, 4446.
152 II, 46–47.
153 Jaffro, "Which Platonism," 267; 72–73 in the ms. I have omitted part of Jaffro's quotation.

yt runs through the Life & writings of Xenoph. That of Plato's going farther by what he drew from Chaldea Egypt Pythagoras &c.[154]

The *Apology* is one of the sources Shaftesbury cites for Plato's use of "enthusiasm."[155] He cites *Apology*, 22b, where Socrates is speaking of the inspiration of poets, seers, and prophets, "who deliver all their sublime messages without knowing in the least what they mean."[156] The assimilation of poetry to prophecy, and vice versa, will be central to Shaftesbury's understanding of enthusiasm in the *Characteristicks*, from the "Letter Concerning Enthusiasm" through "The Moralists."

Shaftesbury may, however, have had another, more purely philosophical motive for writing "The Sociable Enthusiast": the desire to reflect on the roots in human nature of bigotry and superstition, and of religious emotion generally, along with their relation to the sociability and love of the whole which he had argued was natural to human beings. This desire might also have led him to reflect on the treatment of "enthusiasm" in Plato—in the *Apology*, but also in the *Phaedrus* and *Meno*, the other sources Shaftesbury cites.[157]

154 Jaffro, ibid., 262–63; 66–67 in the ms. Shaftesbury's interest in an "Antidote to heat & Animosity" and in an "apology" for the "Inquiry" may have been stimulated by his conversations with Bayle, who was much concerned with such antidotes and apologies.

155 At I, 53n, as noted above.

156 Plato, *Apology*, translated by Hugh Tredennick, in *Plato: The Collected Dialogues including the Letters*, ed. Edith Hamilton and Huntington Cairns (Princeton: Princeton University Press, 1985) 8. The passage runs into 22c.

157 I, 53n. At *Meno*, 99d, Socrates says of the virtue of eminent statesmen that "when by their speeches they get great things done yet know nothing of what they are saying, are to be considered as acting no less under divine influence, inspired and possessed by the divinity." Plato, *Meno*, translated by W.K.C. Guthrie, Hamilton Cairns edn., 383. Socrates, after saying "haven't you noticed that I've got beyond dithyramb, and am breaking out into epic verse, despite my faultfinding? What do you suppose I shall do if I start extolling the other type? Don't you see that I shall be possessed by those nymphs into whose clutches you deliberately threw me?" Plato, *Phaedrus*, 241e, translated by R. Hackforth, Hamilton-Cairns edition, 489.

At any rate, he borrows his favorable use of the term "enthusiasm" from Plato, along with Plato's use of it to mean "the sublime in human passions." It seems plausible, therefore, that the conception of "The Sociable Enthusiast" is the effect of Shaftesbury's revaluation of Plato. This seems plausible for another reason: the resemblance between the complex design of "The Moralists" and Plato's way of writing dialogue, and in particular the combination of sublimity and raillery, enthusiasm and skepticism, which characterizes both Shaftesbury's dialogue and Plato's, and which Shaftesbury at least seems to criticize on several occasions in the "Design of a Socratic History."

It was also this turn towards Plato, I would propose, which led Shaftesbury to the writing of his reflection on enthusiasm in the "Letter Concerning Enthusiasm." We may perhaps think of the "Letter" as a philosophical "apology" before the fact for the publication of the "Moralists"—an "apology" for its apparent enthusiasm, and an explanation of why that apparent enthusiasm was necessary; in the spirit of Xenophon's "Apology," which Shaftesbury, as Jaffro reports, characterizes as an apology for the "Magnificent speaking . . . of Socrates so set out by Plato & others."[158] Xenophon's "apology" for Socrates' "Magnificent speaking" is a defense of Socrates against the charge of folly, for speaking in such a way as to get himself condemned—that is to say, for speaking boastfully ("magnificently"). Xenophon "apologizes" for this by explaining that Socrates knew perfectly well what he was doing, since he wished to get himself condemned to death. Shaftesbury's anticipatory "apology" for the "Magnificent speaking" of "The Moralists" in the "Letter Concerning Enthusiasm" has another character: he is showing that he is not himself a preacher or poet-enthusiast, as one might conclude from the speeches of Theocles, but has other reasons for speaking as if he were. A similar "apology" is offered within the body of "The Moralists" by the introductory conversation reported by Philocles, and another is offered within the "joint-Edition,"[159] i.e., the *Characteristicks*, by Shaftesbury's comments on "The Moralists" in the "Miscellaneous Reflections."[160]

158 "Which Platonism," 262 n25; 8 in the ms.
159 III, 190–91.
160 III, 284–290.

The *Characteristicks* as a Piece of Writing

Shaftesbury claims that the first version of the "Inquiry" was published without his permission:

> His *Amanuensis* and he, were not, it seems, heretofore upon such good Terms of Correspondence. Otherwise such an unshapen *Foetus*, or false Birth, as that of which our Author in his Title-page complains, had not formerly appear'd abroad. Nor had it ever risen again in its more decent Form, but for the accidental Publication of our Author's First Letter, which, by a necessary train of Consequences, occasion'd the revival of this abortive Piece, and gave usherance to its Companions.[161]

Shaftesbury's reference to his "Amanuensis" alludes to his reply, in "Advice to an Author," to the question "Why a Writer for *Self-entertainment* shou'd not keep his Writings to himself, without appearing in *Publick*, or before the *World*."[162] He there claims that

> For my own part, 'tis of no concern to me, what regard the Publick bestows on my Amusements; or after what manner it comes acquainted with what I write for my private Entertainment, or by way of *Advice* to such of my Acquaintance as are thus desperately embark'd.
>
> 'Tis requisite, that my Friends, who peruse these *Advices*, shou'd read 'em in better Characters than those of my own Hand-writing. And by good luck I have a very fair Hand offer'd, which may save me the trouble of re-copying . . . . I have not, indeed, forbid my *Amanuensis* the making as many as he pleases for his own benefit. . . . 'Tis a Traffick I have no share in, tho I accidentally furnish the Subject-matter.[163]

161 III, 190.
162 I, 303–304.
163 I, 304.

Shaftesbury's claim that he has no concern with the publication of his works is in some tension with his declaration in the "Miscellaneous Reflections" that the accidental publication of the "Letter . . . by a necessary train of Consequences" occasioned the revival of the "Inquiry" and the publication of "its Companions," since that "necessary train of Consequences" clearly involved a careful plan of sequential publication. The first three of those companions in "this *Joint*-Edition of our Author's *Five Treatises*," he tells us, "are preparatory to the Fourth"—the "Inquiry," as "The Moralists" is an "apology" for it.[164]

Shaftesbury's air of casualness about his writings is clearly a deliberate affectation, as he himself indicates when he says that he gave "The Moralists" the surname "A Rhapsody" in order to conceal "his strict Imitation of the antient *poetick* DIALOGUE . . . As if it were merely of that *Essay* or *mix'd* kind of Works, which come abroad with an affected Air of Negligence . . . ."[165] His claim about the accidental origins of the *Characteristicks* is also qualified by the remark of the commentator, earlier in the "Miscellaneous Reflections," that

> Notwithstanding the high Airs of SCEPTICISM which our Author assumes in his first Piece; I cannot, after all, but imagine that even there he proves himself, at bottom, *a real* DOGMATIST . . . [who] holds a certain *Plan* or *System* peculiar to him-self, or such, at least, in which he has at present but few Companions or Followers.
>
> On this account I look upon his Management to have been much after the rate of some *ambitious* ARCHITECT; who being call'd perhaps to prop a Roof, redress a leaning Wall, or add to some particular Apartment, is not contented with this small Specimen of his Mastership: but pretending to demonstrate the Unserviceableness and Inconvenience of the *old* Fabrick, forms the design of a *new* Building, and longs to show his Skill in the principal Parts of Architecture and Mechanicks.[166]

164 III, 190–91.
165 III, 285n.
166 III, 133.

What is this "new Building" which, according to the anonymous critic, Shaftesbury is trying to construct in writing the *Characteristicks*? Shaftesbury cannot simply mean the *Characteristicks* itself, since Shaftesbury says that the "new Building" is intended to replace an "old Fabrick," and a new book does not normally replace an older book in the way that a new building can replace another building on the same site. To answer the question of what the "new Building" is which Shaftesbury is seeking to construct, we must therefore ask what is that "old Fabrick" whose "Unserviceableness and Inconvenience" he claims to have demonstrated, and which the "new Building" is intended to replace. Shaftesbury may give us a clue when, in the "Miscellaneous Reflections," he says

> Had I been a *Spanish* Cervantes, and with success equal to that comick Author, had destroy'd the reigning Taste of *Gothick* or *Moorish* Chivalry, I cou'd afterwards contentedly have seen my *Burlesque*-Work it-self despis'd, and set aside; when it had wrought its intended effect, and destroy'd those *Giants* and *Monsters* of the Brain, against which it was originally design'd. Without regard, therefore, to the prevailing *Relish* or *Taste* which, in my own Person, I may unhappily experience, when these my Miscellaneous Works are leisurely examin'd; I shall proceed still in my Endeavour to refine my *Reader's* Palate . . . in the lower Subjects: that by this Exercise it may acquire the greater Keenness, and be of so much the better effect in Subjects of a higher kind, which relate to his chief Happiness, his *Liberty* and *Manhood*.[167]

Shaftesbury, then, does not mind if future readers despise the *Characteristicks* for its style, so long as it destroys "those *Giants* and *Monsters* of the Brain, against which it was originally design'd." What are those "giants and monsters"? They cannot be the objects of a bad literary taste alone, for Shaftesbury hopes that his refining of his reader's palate will not merely refine his literary taste, but his taste "in Subjects of a higher kind, which relate to his chief Happiness, his *Liberty* and *Manhood*."

167 III, 253–54.

The building which Shaftesbury wishes to construct, I would propose, is a new system of morals, founded in a new moral taste. Immediately after speaking of the "new Building" which "my Author" wishes to construct, the anonymous commentator had said:

> 'Tis certain that in matters of Learning and Philosophy, the Practice of *pulling down* is far pleasanter, and affords more Entertainment, than that of *building* and *setting up* . . . .
>
> Our Author, we suppose, might have done well to consider this. We have fairly conducted him thro' his *first* and *second* LETTER, and have brought him, as we see here, into his *third* Piece. He has hitherto, methinks, kept up his *sapping* Method, and *unravelling* Humour, with tolerable good Grace. He has given only some few, and very slender Hints of going further . . . . 'Tis in his following Treatise that he discovers himself openly, as a plain *Dogmatist* . . . .[168]

The "building," apparently, is primarily to be achieved by "The Inquiry" and "The Moralists," but it must be preceded by the "pulling down" carried out in the first three pieces. And these first three pieces certainly do offer a demonstration of "the Unserviceableness and Inconvenience" of an *"old Fabrick,"* that fabric being, quite simply, Christianity and the monarchical order of modern Europe. Shaftesbury is not simply a philosopher or a poet, but a legislator, as Philocles' reference to Theocles as "my AEGERIA"[169] and the anonymous commentator's implicit identification of Philocles with Shaftesbury[170] suggests. For if Theocles is Philocles' Egeria, and if Shaftesbury is Philocles, then Shaftesbury is Numa, the lawgiver of ancient Rome.[171]

168 III, 134–35; on "our Author's" dogmatism, see also 133.
169 II, 222.
170 He does so by attributing Philocles' comments on the difficulties of writing dialogues among the moderns to "Our Author." See my comments on III, 290, above.
171 For a discussion of Shaftesbury's political and cultural "building" project, see Klein, *Shaftesbury and the Culture of Politeness*, Part II. In suggesting that Shaftesbury wishes to replace the "old Fabrick" consisting in Christianity and the

How is Shaftesbury's construction of this "building" tied to his study of Plato? It was, I would propose, his reflection on Plato's apology for Socrates that inspired "The Sociable Enthusiast." That led in turn to the writing of the "Letter Concerning Enthusiasm," in which Shaftesbury "apologized" in advance, in the spirit of Xenophon's *Apology*, for the "Magnificent speech" of the not-yet-published "Moralists."[172] The publication of the "Letter" led to its defense in "Sensus Communis," which in turn led to the elaboration of Shaftesbury's reflections on writing, advice, and soliloquy in "Advice to an Author."

Shaftesbury was thus led to a work which mimics in the large the construction of "The Moralists": raillery, followed by solemnity. But the "sublimity" of the "Inquiry" and "The Moralists" should not cause us to overlook the raillery of the first three pieces, which qualify and correct that sublimity just as the "conceal'd raillery" used by Socrates and Plato qualify and correct their sublimity, and issue in a tragi-comic complexity of manner. Shaftesbury, we might say, was led by Plato to discover the necessity of "a conceal'd sort of Raillery intermix'd with the Sublime.—A dangerous Stroke of Art! and which requir'd a masterly Hand, like that of the philosophical Hero, whose Character was represented in the *Dialogue-Writings* above-mentioned."[173]

monarchical order in Europe, I do not mean that he wishes to make a frontal attack either on the Church of England or the British monarchy. On the contrary, Shaftesbury is more interested in reconstructing these institutions than in making a frontal assault on them. He agrees with Harrington that "a People shou'd have a *Publick Leading* in Religion" (I, 17), and implies that this is a better way of restraining enthusiasm and favoring sociability than the separation of Church and State. See Klein, *Shaftesbury and the Culture of Politeness*, 155. Klein associates Shaftesbury's writing of the *Characteristicks* with a turn from the "Country Whig" valuation of simplicity and military virtue to a concern with "politeness" suitable to legitimating a Whig establishment (ibid., 143–50) and a new readiness to appreciate the need for compromise in politics (ibid., 143). It is tempting to associate this change with Shaftesbury's increased appreciation for the complexities of Plato, and perhaps with a new reading of the simplicity of Xenophon which made it complementary with, rather than simply a competitor to, the style of Plato.

172 See "Which Platonism," 262 n25, and my earlier remarks on it.
173 I, 198.

Shaftesbury's way of writing such a mixed style may not appeal to many readers nowadays. If it is less graceful than Plato's, this is in part for a reason to which Shaftesbury himself drew our attention: the fact that modern manners made it harder to present philosophical dialogue as arising naturally from everyday life, a fact which compelled him, among other devices, to have Theocles "before he enters into his real Character, [become] a feign'd *Preacher*" before, "to deal the better with his *Sceptick*-Friend, he falls again to personating, and takes up the Humour of the *Poet* and *Enthusiast*."[174]

Our manners are less formal than those of Shaftesbury's contemporaries, but it is not altogether clear that it would be easier to write a dialogue of the kind Shaftesbury has in mind today than it was when he wrote. The manners which make it difficult to set a dialogue in modern times, in other words, are not just the formal manners of monarchies but the inclination to preaching characteristic of monotheism; this is a feature of modern manners which, it can be argued, has survived not merely the passing of monarchy but the weakening of monotheism itself. This would not have surprised Shaftesbury, who implied that the dogmatism of modern philosophy and political theory is an heir to that of monotheism even when it opposes that monotheism.[175]

In any case, the very complexity of Shaftesbury's imitation of Plato may help us better to appreciate the complexity of Plato himself, as Shaftesbury presents him to us. And the study of what Shaftesbury did with Plato, or what Plato taught him to seek to do, may help us better to understand what Plato himself aimed at, and how his complexities, and in particular his mingling of raillery with the sublime, were as necessary to Plato's ends as Shaftesbury's imitation of that mingling was to his own.

This brings me to a final point on which I must differ from Jaffro's discussion in "Which Platonism." Jaffro says: "To summarize my argument, the reappraisal of Plato as a poet is a consequence of the depreciation of Plato as a philosopher."[176] But can Plato's lessons in the art of writing really be

---

174 III, 287–88.

175 I, 88–90, 116–17, 286–303, III, 225–26; cf. also III 80–81 on the roots of philosophical enthusiasm, though here Shaftesbury speaks explicitly only of theology and not of the modern critique of theology.

176 Jaffro, "Which Platonism," 267.

separated from his philosophy? The passages from which Jaffro draws his title would suggest that they cannot. For by the *"Philosophical Sea-Cards"* which guide the poet,[177] Shaftesbury, as I mentioned earlier, means simply the "Socratic pages" referred to by Horace in *The Art of Poetry* as the teachers of good writing.[178] Shaftesbury leads up to his citation of Horace by saying

> Now such as these *Masters* and their Lessons are to *a fine Gentleman* [Shaftesbury seems to mean masters at arms, dancing-masters, and teachers of riding and wrestling[179]], such are *Philosophers*, and Philosophy, to *an Author*.[180]
>
> The Philosophical Writings, to which our Poet in his *Art of Poetry* refers, were in themselves a kind of *Poetry*, like the *Mimes*, or personated Pieces of early times. . . . 'Twas not enough that these Pieces treated fundamentally of *Morals*, and in consequence pointed out *real Characters* and *Manners*: They exhibited 'em *alive*. . . . And by this means they not only taught Us to know *Others*; but, what was principal and of highest virtue in 'em, they taught us to know *Our-selves*.[181]

In other words, philosophy teaches authors to write by teaching them self-knowledge, i.e., by teaching them philosophy, as Shaftesbury understands it. In teaching Shaftesbury the art of poetry, therefore—i.e., the art of philosophical writing—Plato was also teaching him philosophy.

As we have seen, Shaftesbury did not think that the Platonic art of writing was outmoded. Nor, it seems clear, did he think that philosophy, as Horace and Plato, on Shaftesbury's view, understood it—the knowledge of self, achieved through soliloquy, learned from the study of dialogue—was outmoded or inaccessible.[182] Can we accept, or learn from, Shaftesbury's view that philosophy is identical with the art of writing, because the art of

177 I, 205.
178 See I, 192n, and "Which Platonism," 264–65.
179 See I, 190–91.
180 I, 191.
181 I, 193–94.
182 Jaffro himself demonstrates the inseparability of self-knowledge from the art of writing for Shaftesbury in his *Éthique de la communication et art d'écrire*, his

writing is identical with self-knowledge? Can we take seriously the notion that philosophy is self-knowledge? Can we learn from Shaftesbury's view that the aim of philosophy is (in part at least) the taming and redirection of enthusiasm—a view which he seems to have learned from Plato? And can we use this view of philosophy to help us understand Plato?

We will surely not be able to take these views seriously if we understand them as excluding the view of philosophy as a pursuit of knowledge. And we will not be able to avoid opposing the view of philosophy as pursuit of knowledge to the view of philosophy as self-knowledge unless we can take seriously Shaftesbury's view that there is really something to be learned about ourselves, of a sort that will help us live. Nor will we be able to reconcile the view of philosophy as pursuit of knowledge with the view of philosophy as the art of writing unless we can take seriously Shaftesbury's view that the way both to know ourselves and to learn how to write is by studying ourselves in a mirror of *"real Characters* and *Manners"* which can teach us to know both *"Others"* and *"Our-selves."* We might be prepared to accept that we can learn these sorts of things by reading novels[183]— though that view, too, is rather out of fashion—but it is hard for us to think of it as the task of philosophy. Perhaps this view of philosophy is too unfamiliar for us to know how to respond to it; perhaps it requires further discussion before it can be properly understood.

I would like to thank Michael Davis and Laurent Jaffro for reading and commenting on this paper in draft. I would also like to express my gratitude

---

ground-breaking study of Shaftesbury's *Askemata* or exercises in relation to his views on writing. Not only does the alternative I am proposing to Jaffro's argument in "Which Platonism" depend almost entirely on the evidence he presents there, it also draws inspiration from *Éthique de la communication*.
183 As we have seen, Shaftesbury compares his aims in writing to those of Cervantes. He is not without influence on the art of the novel. On Shaftesbury as a teacher of writing, see Lorrie Clark, "Shaftesbury's Art of 'Soliloquy' in *Mansfield Park,*" *Persuasions* (Jane Austen Society of North America, No. 24, 2002). I thank David Sidorsky for making me aware of this valuable article. Fielding, too, was strongly influenced by Shaftesbury, as were many other writers (both of explicitly philosophical works and of novels, essays, and poetry) in Britain, Germany and France.

for the very helpful comments offered by the anonymous referee for the *Journal for Eighteenth-Century Studies*. I am also grateful to John Bussanich for consultation and advice about secondary literature, and to Martha K. Zebrowski for inviting me to present this paper in a panel on Plato in eighteenth-century Britain at the British Society for Eighteenth-Century Studies, January 2006.

Rousseau on the Theory and Practice
of Poetic Imitation

Denise Schaeffer

Rousseau initially intended his essay "On Theatrical Imitation" to be part of the *Letter to D'Alembert*, but explains in his prefatory notice that he chose not to include it in the longer work because it did not "fit" into that work "comfortably."[1] Although the two works address similar themes, "On Theatrical Imitation" has distinctive features that make it worthy of consideration on its own terms. The essay not only treats the question of poetic imitation as its subject matter, but is itself an example of imitation, as it reproduces the critique of poetry in Plato's *Republic*—with some subtle but significant disparities.[2] On the surface, Rousseau presents a straightforward critique of poetic imitation that tracks, more or less faithfully, Socrates' critique in Book X, while also incorporating references to Books II and III of the *Republic* and Book II of the *Laws*. Rousseau weaves together these various Platonic references into a new whole that performs a type of poetic imitation even as it criticizes the practice in general. By attending to the form as well as the content of the essay, we might better appreciate the complexity of Rousseau's position.

---

1   Jean-Jacques Rousseau, "On Theatrical Imitation," in *Essay on the Origin of Languages and Writings on Music*, ed. and trans. John T. Scott (Hanover, N.H.: University Press of New England, 1998), hereafter cited parenthetically in the text, followed by volume and page number of *Œuvres complètes de Jean-Jacques Rousseau*, ed. Bernard Gagnebin and Marcel Raymond, 5 vols. (Paris: Gallimard, 1959–1995).

2   For a reading of "On Theatrical Imitation" that emphasizes the similarities to Plato, see David Lay Williams, *Rousseau's Platonic Enlightenment* (University Park: Penn State University Press, 2007), 155–62.

{383}

The argument of "On Theatrical Imitation" consists of two major claims: first, that poetic imitation is third-rate (an imitation of an imitation, twice removed from what is truly real), and that it is morally deleterious because it makes us admire what is bad and scorn what is good, especially in the theater. In other words, poetic imitation corrupts judgment. At times, Rousseau's account of the effect on morals can seem quite formulaic: imitation can be good when we are imitating good, virtuous examples, but is bad for us when the substance of the examples is bad. However, while this apparently tidy formulation may capture many of the explicit claims Rousseau makes in this essay and elsewhere, it does not do justice to the essay as a whole. Rousseau does more here than to build a case against poetic imitation; he also elucidates the question of what it would mean to produce *good imitators*, not simply imitators of good things.

Rousseau begins by specifying what he means by imitation. He draws a sharp contrast between the "abstract, unique and independent" idea of a thing and "the number of examples of this thing which may exist in nature" (337; V:1196). The original idea exists "in the understanding of the Architect, in nature, or at the very least in its Author along with the all the possible ideas of which he is the source" (338; V:1197). He then turns to the Architect's palace (the physical palace that the architect brings into being) which he calls an "image" of the original idea. Finally, he introduces the painter whose painting of a palace is based on the physical palace (the "image") rather than on the original idea and is thus a mere "imitation." The authors of the three palaces, according to Rousseau, are: God, the architect, and the painter. Imitation is twice removed from the original, and only the original is truly real.

Although Rousseau insists that the architect does not make the original model, which exists in the mind "in advance," he subtly introduces the fact that the architect will likely produce some sort of blueprint or design in advance of constructing the physical palace, if only to guide the work of construction. In the *Republic*, Socrates speaks of a carpenter, not an architect, and distinguishes between the idea of a bed, the artifact of a bed, and the painting of a bed. While reproducing the logic of Socrates' argument, Rousseau's substitution of the architect for the carpenter, and the complexity and scale of a palace instead of a simple bed, implies the necessity of an intermediate level between the purely abstract model and the physical fabrication. This is reinforced later in the essay, where Rousseau (without mentioning the architect specifically) refers to a kind of design or representation distinct from poetic representation or imitation. It is an art of representing objects in which one "draws up a plan and takes exact dimensions" (339; V:1198).

The architect reappears toward the end of the essay, becoming an analogue for the philosopher. In explaining this affinity, Rousseau emphasizes precisely this "design" aspect of the architect's art: "The Poet is the Painter who makes the image; the Philosopher is the Architect who draws up the plan." The philosopher "measures before drawing" (344; V:1204). Insofar as the architect engages in planning and measuring to draw up a plan, the fact that it is a not only a representation of the idea but also a "plan" suggests that it functions as a model as well as an image. This model is one step removed from the abstract, divine model, and at the same time distinct from the physical palace. The architect's plan thus occupies a middle ground between the purely abstract and the particular. It is *both* a model to be followed *and* an image of the purely abstract model that exists only in idea or in nature.

We see a similar complexity in the relationship between original and copy arise in another brief but significant alteration that Rousseau makes to the Platonic account. He introduces an example that does not appear in Plato's text by posing a question to the reader: if someone were faced with a choice between a portrait of one's mistress and the original, which do you think he would choose? (341: V:1200). He adds that one would certainly choose an actual house over a painting of a house. By referring to the particular mistress and the particular house as "originals," Rousseau seems to depart from his (and Socrates') larger argument in which the actual house is presented as already a step removed from the original. Moreover, while it is most likely that one would prefer an actual house to a painting of a house, the matter is less clear when it comes to a beloved. Rousseau is well known for narratives in which the idea of the beloved looms larger than the actual person. In *Emile* he states explicitly that romantic love is actually love of the image that one has of the beloved. Moreover, in *Les Solitaires*, the sequel to *Emile*, Emile chooses to hold on to the idea of Sophie in all of its purity, and abandons his actual, imperfect beloved. Rousseau's claim in "On Theatrical Imitation" ignores these possibilities, insofar as he implies that one would *always* prefer the living individual. Furthermore, in identifying the living particular with the "original," he contradicts his own argument earlier in the essay that the true original is the idea that exists in the divine mind or at least in the architect's mind—in either case, an abstraction, not a tangible particular. According to his earlier argument, neither the portrait nor the mistress herself is the original, but rather something like the Platonic idea of the beloved, in light of which both the portrait and the actual person should be judged. But by eliding two senses of what it means to be an original, Rousseau indirectly raises the question of whether it is possible, and what it would mean, for a pure abstraction to guide judgment, and whether there is an intermediate level of representation that functions to make the abstraction accessible and visible and, not least importantly, *beautiful*— without reducing it to a misleading image or to mere imitation. In other words, what does it mean to particularize it, without making it just another particular? This is what is at stake in his discussion of the model the architect creates (like a blueprint), as distinguished from both the model in nature and the particulars derived from it.

Rousseau's concern for the possibility of an intermediate level that functions somewhere between philosophical abstraction and poetic representation stems from his sense that poetic representations are absolutely necessary to judging well, even if they more often contribute to the disabling or corruption of judgment. In other words, the antidote to the unhealthy seductive effect of poetry is not simply the sober counterweight of calculation. Insofar as the philosopher's activity is analogous to that of the architect, the philosopher, too, must create a "plan." But in translating the abstract model into a second-order model, he strives to make something visible. His activity thus has something in common with that of the painter.[3]

However, Rousseau draws a sharp distinction between the two, arguing that the painter cannot possibly have any idea of what is real, because if he knew it, he would act on it rather than painting it. "The compass of his art is founded only on ignorance" and he is "not in a position to give a rational account" of that which he depicts (340; V:1199). Turning from painting to

---

3   There is a similar parallel in the *Republic* in that the genuine philosopher imitates the forms.

consideration of the dramatic poets, Rousseau concludes that they, too, lack knowledge of what they represent. Even when they produce images of virtue, talent, or other positive qualities, these are qualities "that they do not themselves have" (342; V:1202). Rousseau goes on to suggest the possibility that the painters and poets are deliberately duplicitous and knowingly misrepresent the real in order to establish their own authority. In short, they claim that their representations conform to the truth, either because they doesn't know any better or because they deceive. Either way, they present their judgment as truth, which misleads the spectator in turn. Whether in painted images or on the stage, beautiful representations create "an illusion for those who, sensitive to rhythm and harmony, allow themselves to be charmed by the enchanting art of the Poet and yield to seduction by the attraction of pleasure" (343; V:1203). Rousseau criticizes *how* the poet presents "truth" as well as *what* is presented.

Although he strongly emphasizes the poet's ignorance, Rousseau interjects the following consideration, drawn from the *Laws* rather than the *Republic*, to raise a possible objection to his own argument: "You will object to me that the Philosopher himself does not know all the arts about which he speaks either, and that he often extends his ideas as far as the Poet extends his images" (344; V:1204). In response to this objection, Rousseau points out that unlike the poet, the philosopher "does not present himself as knowing the truth; he seeks it, and in the course of his seeking, he proposes his doubts as doubts and his conjectures as conjectures" (344; V:1204). Thus the distinction between them does not ultimately depend on what knowledge they do or do not possess, but rather on what it is that they *seek*, and what it is that they *show* to their audience. Both of their representations are imperfect, but the crucial issue is whether these are presented to the audience in a misleading way, as the highest model of that which is, or whether their imperfect, partial status is made apparent. The revelation of incompleteness is ultimately what distinguishes the philosopher's design from the poet's.

Returning to the argument found in *Republic* X, Rousseau continues to make the case that poetic representation corrupts judgment. First, it does so by presenting what is base in a positive light. This "spoils and changes our judgments about the laudable things" (347; V:1207). It not only reverses our judgments but also corrupts judgment at a deeper level by arousing and strengthening the lowest part of the soul. "Painting, and the art of imitation generally, practices its operations far from the truth of things by combining with a part of the soul deprived of prudence and reason . . . ." (345; V:1205). Just as the poet's "compass" in creating is nothing other than ignorance, the spectator's compass in judging the poetic creation is similarly problematic. "It is not at all the most noble of our faculties, namely reason, but a different and inferior faculty that judges by appearance and yields to the charm of the imitation" (345; V:1205). The habit of being moved by the travails of pitiable characters on stage weakens the rule of reason while arousing and nourishing the passions. Reason, "thus losing power and empire over itself, grows accustomed to be under the passions" (348; V:1209). The inversion in our judgments of conduct as admirable or detestable is accompanied by, and intensified by, an inversion in the proper ordering of reason and passion in the soul.

To strengthen his case against poetic representation, especially with regard to the issue of control over the passions, Rousseau (following Socrates) contrasts the pitiable characters one sees on stage with the example of a moderate man who resists the temptation to abandon himself to grief. Whereas the theatrical characters cry and moan and wallow in their misery, the wise and virtuous man, Rousseau tells us, "will not be seen to abandon himself to an excessive and unreasonable grief; and if human weakness does not permit him to overcome his affliction completely, he will temper it by constancy. A just shame will make him close up within himself a part of his pains; he will 'blush' to say and do in the presence of others that which he does in private (such as to cry and moan)." In short, "not being able to be in himself such as he wishes, he at least tries to offer himself to others such as he should be" (346; V:1206).

This moderate individual is thus engaging in a kind of representation of himself to others. Anyone who only witnesses his placid exterior cannot see that this exterior is a response to pain and suffering. If it is not seen in response, then it is not instructive. It is a false representation that seems to offer "the whole at once." However, if it is presented in response—if the internal struggle is revealed—then the moderate man will "represent" a type of self-contradiction. And yet it is precisely the quality of self-contradiction that Rousseau sees as so problematic about the characters typically seen on stage. Instead of offering to the audience a "sublime image of a heart that is master of itself, that hears only the voice of wisdom," the dramatic poet "charms the spectators by characters who are always in contradiction, who want and do not want . . ." (346; V:1206). This parallels the painter's tendency to portray "colors without consistency" (340; V:1200). Variability delights. Because poets appeal to pleasure, they portray characters who are themselves driven by pleasure, who judge their courses of action according to the resultant pain or sensual pleasure. And "it is impossible for the man, thus presented, ever to be in accord with himself" (345; V:1206). This lack of self-accord is a presented as a point of contrast with the moderate man. But the moderate man, too, is in contradiction, although of a different type. He does not *only* hear the voice of wisdom; he experiences internal struggle in striving to gain control over his passions. To be sure, this tension is resolved in favor of reason, but the resolution is described by both Socrates and Rousseau as a function of suppressing the tension in public. The internal contradiction is superseded by a contradiction between what is shown and what is felt, the exterior and the interior. This public face of constancy is what makes this individual a good example for others. Yet this is precisely why he is rarely depicted by the dramatic poets. Variability is charming; constancy is boring.

In criticizing the stage for representing "all men, even those presented as models, as otherwise affected than they should be . . ." (345; V:1206), Rousseau presumably seeks to offer a corrective model of how one *ought* to respond to life's travails, and the moderate man seems to fit the bill. Yet what makes him a good model limits his effectiveness as a model. The visible mark of his self-control is the achievement of a public face of constancy. But this achievement, by definition, hides the contradiction between the internal and external. So what makes the virtue of moderation visible makes its operation invisible. To depict such a noble individual with accuracy would be to make the internal contradiction part of the representation, along with the contradiction between what is shown publicly and what is kept private. What, then, is the difference between the tension in this virtuous soul, and the tension in the weaker soul that Rousseau criticizes? The answer may seem obvious, in that it all depends on which way the tension is resolved—that is, it depends on which part of the soul prevails. But Rousseau does not focus on the resolution. Instead, his rendition of Socrates' argument *lingers* on the point about the moderate man's internal struggle, dwelling on it at greater length than does Socrates. Furthermore, Rousseau adds a statement to the effect that even when the character depicted by the poet achieves the correct response to misfortune, the very exposure to contradiction is itself problematic for the spectators: "even when they [the characters on stage] do their duty," these characters make spectators think that "virtue is a sad thing since it makes its friends so miserable" (347; V:1207). On the one hand, he claims that portraying moderation without struggle will fail to move the audience; on the other, he claims that preserving the internal struggle in a portrayal of moderation runs the risk of having a deleterious effect on morals.

Thus whereas Socrates argues (and Rousseau agrees) that most dramatic depictions are problematic because they cause an *inversion* in our standards of judgment, conditioning the audience to admire what is weak and scornful and to look down upon what is truly noble and good, Rousseau not only reiterates this point but also takes another step. This additional step muddies the waters, and he seems to leave us with a no-win situation by suggesting that *any* representation of internal contradiction, whether in an example of weakness or in an example of eventual overcoming, risks producing a negative effect on the spectator. Yet if the poet does *not* represent the internal contradiction on the way to showing the constancy, the image is not only unmoving but also misleading in that it fails to capture the essential feature of the overcoming of internal struggle in the achievement of constancy. It represents "the whole at once." There is a double difficulty in depicting the greatness of the great-souled man who hides his pain: "hiding" his pain and struggle is the key to his virtue, but to *show* this hiddenness one must expose the warring passions, which risks having an unhealthy effect on opinions.

This calls to mind the distinction Rousseau draws earlier in the essay between the art of representing objects and the art of making them understood. "The first pleases without instruction; the second instructs without pleasure" (339; V:1199). Rousseau associates the first with measurement, and thus with the philosopher, by association with the architect. The philosopher "measures before drawing" (344; V:1204). Here, Rousseau associates the activity of measuring with the absence of pleasure; drawing up a plan and taking exact dimensions "does nothing very pleasant for the sight." At the same time, Rousseau affirms the value of this approach. Measurement, "giving successively one dimension and then the other, instructs us slowly about the truth of things, whereas the appearance offers the whole at once, and, under the presumption of a greater capacity of mind, flatters the senses by seducing amour-propre" (339; V:1199). While the philosopher may refrain from seducing the audience with an illusory "whole at once" that flatters their pride by appealing to their prejudices, it is also the case that his approach as described here "instructs without pleasure." Consequently, this instruction "is sought out only by people in the art." In this framework, what makes the philosopher a better source of instruction than the poet is precisely what limits his effectiveness as an instructor.

What would it mean to portray the moderate man in a way that instructs slowly by presenting "one dimension and then the other," to use Rousseau's language? The moderate, constant, self-possessed character is neither easily imitated nor easily understood. Rousseau echoes this point in *Emile* when he advises educators to avoid striving to appear flawlessly virtuous in the eyes of their pupil, for this will make their example *less* effective rather than more effective. "All those perfect people are neither touching nor persuasive."[4] It also resonates with remarks he makes about the limitations of using Emile as an instructive example. In Book IV, when preparing to discuss the cultivation of good taste, Rousseau leaves his imaginary pupil to the side and positions himself as the main character in an imaginative thought experiment about the pleasures he would pursue if he were rich. "Permit me for a moment, in order to develop my idea better, to leave aside Emile, whose pure and healthy heart can no longer serve as a rule for anyone, and to seek in myself an example that is more evident . . . ."[5] This substitution does not resolve the difficulty, which persists in the anecdote that follows. Although Rousseau is well known for praising the "simplicity of taste that speaks straight to the heart"[6] and disapproving of the decadent tastes of urbane elites, his defense of such simplicity is hardly simple. He begins by arguing that even if he were rich, he would

---

4   Jean-Jacques Rousseau, *Emile, or On Education*, ed. and trans. Allan Bloom (New York: Basic Books, 1979), 334.
5   *Emile*, 344.
6   *Emile*, 342.

prefer the simple pleasures in life. In making the case for this preference, however, he presents it as a conscious choice made in full recognition of a complex field of possibilities. In order to prove to his reader even as a rich man he would choose simple pleasures, he must exhibit some visible quality of wealth, and so he gives to his imagined self the primary marker of a wealthy man in the countryside: the hunt. Participating in this exclusive activity leads to a miserable downward spiral as he must acquire additional material possessions to support this lifestyle, until finally he renounces exclusive pleasures and returns to simplicity. In this narrative, Rousseau presents himself as an example of someone moving *toward* the goal, rather than occupying the desired state effortlessly and flawlessly.[7]

Similarly, in "On Theatrical Imitation," Rousseau's straightforward critique of theatrical imitation is that it leads to a reversal of standards, but the underlying issue to which he draws attention is that contradiction is necessarily inherent in *both* positive and negative imitative examples, and that the spectator must be capable of bringing critical judgment to bear on *both* types. In other words, the proper stance is not simply to follow or identify with the architect, but to see the poet's images for what they are, and also to see the architect's drawn-up model for what *it* is, which is superior to the poet's images but is still not the real (or original) itself.[8] This is also the basis for the essay's indirect defense of poetry, which not only imitates Socrates' speech at the end of Book X reinstating honor to the poets, but also enhances it. Specifically, Rousseau's presentation and commentary on the moderate man ultimately points to how poetic representation might itself play a role in countering the tendency toward "the whole at once." For in fact it is the poet who can simultaneously reveal and conceal the moderate person's internal struggle. That interiority can be hidden from the other characters

---

7   For a lengthier discussion of this episode in *Emile*, and other instances in which Rousseau cultivates the reader's critical distance from Emile with a view to educating judgment, see my *Rousseau on Freedom, Education and Judgment* (University Park: Penn State University Press, 2014).

8   For a discussion of music as providing "a model through which Rousseau could conceive of a form of representation that was not politically or morally detrimental" (345), see C. N. Dugan and Tracy B. Strong, "Music, Politics, Theater, and Representation in Rousseau," in *The Cambridge Companion to Rousseau* (Cambridge: Cambridge University Press, 2001), 329–64.

on stage, but made apparent to the audience. What the poet's character hides, the poet reveals. The art of representation, as Rousseau understands and performs it, has the potential to capture both constancy and contradiction by offering both successive dimensions and a "whole."

Although constancy and moderation are admirable qualities worthy of imitation, Rousseau's corrective is not a simple inversion of the poet's tendency to portray them as scornful or painful. One may endeavor to portray a virtue in a positive rather than negative light, but if this endeavor presents it as a "whole at once" it will be an overly simplistic and thus insufficient corrective to the poet's tendency to depict variability and moral weakness. Yet the philosopher who is too perfectly modeled on the architect—who measures carefully in order to show "first one dimension and then the other"—runs the risk of "instructing without pleasure" and thus failing to instruct at all.

Rousseau's own activity in "On Theatrical Imitation" is a combination of these two styles. He describes his own essay as the activity of extracting Plato's disparate comments on theatrical imitation and assembling them into a whole. One might say that by dispensing with the dialogue form, he presents a "whole at once." At the same time, even in creating this whole, he manages to present one dimension and then another—for example, by presenting Homer in one light and then another. He echoes the Platonic text by noting that Homer was neglected in his own time, and uses this as "evidence" or reasoning to prove that Homer and other poets do not know what they write about, or else their knowledge would have been recognized. He chides Homer for failing to produce any disciples.[9] Yet he then goes on to underscore the admiration that Homer received in later times as he came to be considered the model for all tragic authors. Either this simply reflects an arbitrary change in public opinion, or it indirectly tells us something about what it means to be a good model. Producing disciples is analogous to producing exact copies or unreflective

---

9   For an in-depth discussion of the significance of the discussion of Homer in "On Theatrical Imitation," see Pamela K. Jensen, "The Quarrel Between Philosophy and Poetry Reconsidered: Rousseau's 'On Theatrical Imitation,'" in *Rousseau and Criticism*, ed. Lorraine Clark and Guy Lafrance (Ottawa: North American Association for the Study of Jean-Jacques Rousseau, 1995), 183–94.

imitators who engage in servile imitation.[10] But the subsequent praise of Homer suggests that the poet can be a model in the sense that the essay ultimately endorses: a model that inspires imitations that do *not* take the model to be the "whole at once." To be a good imitator one must be to some degree a bad imitator, that is to say, one must imitate with strategic inexactness. This is precisely what Rousseau demonstrates in his own creatively inexact imitation of Plato.

10 See Leonard R. Sorenson's distinction between "correct" imitation and "corrective" imitation in "Rousseau's Socratism: On the Political Bearing of 'On Theatrical Imitation,'" *Interpretation* 20:2 (1993): 135–55. Sorenson's argument is that because "On Theatrical Imitation" is a "corrective" imitation of Plato, the essay presents Rousseau's own views.

Publications by Michael Davis

BOOKS

Ancient Tragedy and the Origins of Modern Science (Carbondale, IL: Southern Illinois University Press, 1988).

Aristotle's Poetics: *The Poetry of Philosophy* (Lanham, MD: Rowman and Littlefield, 1992); reprinted as *The Poetry of Philosophy: On Aristotle's* Poetics (South Bend, IN: St. Augustine's Press, 1999).

The Politics of Philosophy: A Commentary on Aristotle's Politics (Lanham, MD: Rowman and Littlefield, 1996).

The Autobiography of Philosophy: Rousseau's The Reveries of the Solitary Walker (Lanham, MD: Rowman and Littlefield, 1999).

Aristotle – On Poetics, co-translator and co-editor (with Seth Benardete) and author of the Introduction (South Bend, IN: St. Augustine's Press, 2002).

Encounters and Reflections: Conversations with Seth Benardete, participant (with Robert Berman and Ronna Burger); (Chicago: University of Chicago Press, 2003).

Wonderlust: Ruminations on Liberal Education (South Bend, IN: St. Augustine's Press, 2006).

The Soul of the Greeks: An Inquiry (Chicago: University of Chicago Press, 2011).

The Music of Reason: Plato, Rousseau, and Nietzsche (Philadelphia: University of Pennsylvania Press, 2019).

EDITED COLLECTIONS

Essays in Honor of Richard Kennington, a special Festschrift issue of the *Graduate Faculty Philosophy Journal* 11, 2 (1986).

The Argument of the Action: Essays on Greek Poetry and Philosophy by Seth Benardete, ed. and introduction, with Ronna Burger (Chicago: University of Chicago Press, 2000).

The Archaeology of the Soul: Essays in Greek and Roman Philosophy and Poetry by Seth Benardete, ed. and introduction, with Ronna Burger (South Bend, IN: St. Augustine's Press, 2012).

SELECTED ARTICLES AND CHAPTERS

"Courage and Impotence in Shakespeare's *Macbeth*," *Essays from Sarah Lawrence College*, 4, 2 (1979); reprinted in revised form in *Shakespeare's Political Pageant*, ed. Joseph Alulis and Vickie Sullivan (Lanham, MD: Rowman and Littlefield, 1996): 219–36.

"Review of Plato's *Apology of Socrates* by Thomas West," *Independent Journal of Philosophy* 3 (1979): 151–52.

"Socrates' Pre-Socratism: Some Remarks on the Structure of Plato's *Phaedo*," *The Review of Metaphysics* 33 (1980): 559–77.

"Review of *The Dialectic of Action: A Philosophical Interpretation of History and the Humanities* by Frederick Olafson," *The Review of Metaphysics* 34 (1980): 153–55.

"Plato and Nietzsche on Death: An Introduction to Plato's *Phaedo*," *Ancient Philosophy* 1 (1980): 69–80.

"Philosophy and the Perfect Tense: On the Beginning of Plato's *Lovers*," *Graduate Faculty Philosophy Journal* 10, 2 (1985): 75–97.

"Aristotle's Reflections on Revolution," in *Essays in Honor of Richard Kennington*, *Graduate Faculty Philosophy Journal* 11, 2 (1986): 49–63.

"Politics and Madness," in *Greek Tragedy and Political Theory*, ed. J. Peter Euben (Berkeley: University of California Press, 1987), 142–61.

"On the Being of *The Being of the Beautiful*," review article for *Ancient Philosophy* 7 (1987): 191–200.

"Cannibalism and Nature," *Metis: Revue d'Anthropologie du Monde Grec Ancien* 4 (1989): 33–50.

"Politics and Poetry: Aristotle's *Politics* Books VII and VIII," *Interpretation* 19, 2 (1991–1992): 157–68.

"Das Ziel der Zweckursache: Aristoteles' *Metaphysik* A," Roland Dollinger trans., in *Philosophia Naturalis: Beiträge zu einer zeitgemässen Naturphilosophie* (Arzt, Dollinger und Dürckheim Hrsg., Königshausen & Neumann, 1996), 323–39.

"Euripides among the Athenians," *The St. John's Review* 44, 2 (1998): 61–81.

"The Tragedy of Law: Gyges in Herodotus and Plato," *The Review of Metaphysics* 53 (2000): 635–55.

"On the Intention of Plato's *Cleitophon*," *Metis: Revue d'anthropologie du monde grec ancien* (2002 [1998]).

"Unraveling *Ravelstein*: Saul Bellow's Comic Tragedy," *Perspectives in Political Science* 32 (2003): 26–31.

"Father of the Logos: The Question of the Soul in Aristotle's *De Anima* and *Nicomachean Ethics*," *Epoché* 7, 2, (2003): 169–87.

"Seth Benardete's Second Sailing: On the Spirit of Ideas," *The Political Science Reviewer* 32 (2003): 8-35.

"Tragedy in the Philosophical Age of the Greeks: Aristotle's Reply to Nietzsche," in *The Impact of Aristotelianism on Modern Philosophy* (*Studies in Philosophy and the History of Philosophy,* 39), ed. Riccardo Pozzo (Washington, DC: Catholic University Press, 2004), 210–30.

"Preface" to Seth Benardete's *Achilles and Hector: the Homeric Hero* (South Bend, IN: St. Augustine's Press, 2005).

"The Riddle of the Middle: A review of A Democracy of Distinction: Aristotle and the Work of Politics *by Jill Frank,"* The Claremont Review Website, May 5, 2006

"Making Something from Nothing: On Plato's *Hipparchus,"* *The Review of Politics* 68 (2006): 547–63.

"The Grammar of the Soul: On Plato's *Euthyphro,"* in *Logos and Eros: Essays Honoring Stanley Rosen*, ed. Nalin Ranasinghe (South Bend, IN: St. Augustine's Press, 2006), 57–71.

"Aristotle's Dialogue with Socrates, by Ronna Burger," Review Article, *Polis: The Journal for Ancient Greek Political Thought* 26 (2009): 133–39.

"Euripides' *Helen*: the Fake that Launched a Thousand Ships," in *Logos and Muthos*, ed. William Wians (Albany: SUNY Press, 2009), 255–71.

"The Essence of Babel: Rousseau on the Origin of Languages," in *The Companionship of Books: Essays in Honor of Laurence Berns* (Lanham, MD: Lexington Books, 2012), 229–50.

"The Music of Reason in Rousseau's *Essay on the Origin of Languages,"* *The Review of Politics* 74 (2012): 389–402.

"'The Soul of Achilles,' excerpted from *The Soul of the Greeks*," *The Montreal Review*, June 2012.

"Philosophy in the Perfect Tense: On Plato's *Lovers*," in *Socratic Philosophy and its Others,* ed. Christopher Dustin and Denise Schaeffer (Lanham, MD: Lexington Press, 2013), 265–86.

With Gwenda-lin Kaur Grewal, "The Daimonic Soul: On Plato's *Theages*," in *Socratic Philosophy and its Others,* ed. Christopher Dustin and Denise Schaeffer (Lanham, MD: Lexington Press, 2013), 35-50.

"'What's Wrong with This Picture?': on *The Coast of Utopia*," in *Natural Right and Political Philosophy: Essays in Honor of Catherine Zuckert and Michael Zuckert*, ed. Ann Ward and Lee Ward (South Bend, IN: Notre Dame University Press, 2013).

"Plato's *Minos*: The Soul of the Law," *The Review of Politics* 78 (2016): 343–63.

"This and That: On Plato's *Laches*," *The Review of Metaphysics* 70 (2016): 253–77.

"On the Coherence of *Plato's Philosophers*," *The Review of Politics* 80 (2018): 241-46.

DISSERTATION

The Duality of Soul in Plato's Philebus, Doctoral Dissertation, The Pennsylvania State University (1974).

Contributors

Abraham Anderson is Professor of Philosophy at Sarah Lawrence College.

Jonathan N. Badger is Tutor at St. John's College, Annapolis.

Robert Berman is Professor of Philosophy at Xavier University of Louisiana.

Ronna Burger is Professor of Philosophy, Catherine & Henry J. Gaisman Chair and Director of Judeo-Christian Studies, and Sizeler Professor of Jewish Studies at Tulane University.

Kenneth DeLuca is Senior Lecturer in Government & Foreign Affairs at Hampden-Sydney College.

Gwenda-lin Grewal is the Blegen Research Fellow in Greek & Roman Studies at Vassar College.

Scott R. Hemmenway is Professor Emeritus of Philosophy at Eureka College.

Paul Kirkland is Associate Professor of Political Science and Great Ideas at Carthage College.

Mary P. Nichols is Professor Emerita of Political Science at Baylor University.

Denise Schaeffer is Professor of Political Science at College of the Holy Cross.

Contributors

Paul Stern is Professor of Politics at Ursinus College.

Richard Velkley is Celia Scott Weatherhead Distinguished Professor of Philosophy at Tulane University.

Lisa Pace Vetter is Associate Professor of Political Science at University of Maryland, Baltimore County.

Ann Ward is Professor of Political Science at Baylor University.

Lee Ward is Professor of Political Science at Baylor University.

Catherine H. Zuckert is Nancy Reeves Dreux Professor of Political Science Emeritus at the University of Notre Dame.

Michael Zuckert is Nancy Reeves Dreux Professor of Political Science Emeritus at the University of Notre Dame.